Exhibitions and Symposia

Kulturstiftung Sibirien

Sustaining Indigenous Knowledge

Learning Tools and Community Initiatives for Preserving Endangered Languages and Local Cultural Heritage

Edited by Erich Kasten and Tjeerd de Graaf

Verlag der Kulturstiftung Sibirien
SEC Publications

Bibliografische Informationen der Deutschen Nationalbibliothek:
Die Deutsche Nationalbibliothek verzeichnet diese Publikation in der Deutschen Nationalbibliografie: detaillierte bibliografische Daten sind im Internet über <http://dnb.d-nb.de> abrufbar.

ISBN: 978-3-942883-12-2
Herstellung: Books on Demand GmbH, Norderstedt

CONTENTS

1 Introduction 7
Erich Kasten and Tjeerd de Graaf

Programmes to Preserve Endangered Languages

2 Multilingualism and Language Teaching in Europe: The Case of Frisian and the Work of the Mercator European Research Centre 17
Tjeerd de Graaf and Cor van der Meer

3 The Use of Sound Archives for the Investigation, Teaching and Safeguarding of Some Endangered Uralic Languages 35
Victor Denisov and Tjeerd de Graaf

4 Documentation and Revitalisation of Two Endangered Languages in Eastern Asia: Nivkh and Ainu 49
Tjeerd de Graaf and Hidetoshi Shiraishi

Community Experiences and Alternative Pedagogical Concepts in the Russian North

5 Learning Tools for Preserving Languages and Traditional Knowledge in Kamchatka 65
Erich Kasten

6 Learning your Endangered Native Language in a Small Multilingual Community: The Case of Tundra Yukagir in Andriushkino 89
Cecilia Odé

7 Anthropology and Applied Anthropology in Siberia: Questions and Solutions concerning a Nomadic School among Evenki Reindeer Herders 105
Alexandra Lavrillier

8 Challenging the State Educational System in Western Siberia: Taiga School by the Tiuitiakha River 129
Stephan Dudeck

9 Boarding School on Yamal: History of Development and Current Situation 159
Elena Liarskaya

10 Model for the Tundra School in Yamal: a New Education System for Children from Nomadic and Semi-nomadic Nenets Families 181
Roza Laptander

11 Towards a Digital Infrastructure for Kildin Saami 195
Michael Rießler

Experiences in Preserving Indigenous Languages and Knowledge from other Parts of the World

12 Building Yi (M)other Tongue: Virtual Platforms, Language Maintenance and Cultural Awareness in a Chinese Minority Context 219
Olivia Kraef

13 Bilingual Intercultural Education in the Andes 249
Teresa Valiente Catter and Michael Dürr

14 Epilogue 259
Nikolai Vakhtin

Appendix

Illustrations 269
Notes on the contributors 270
Index 275

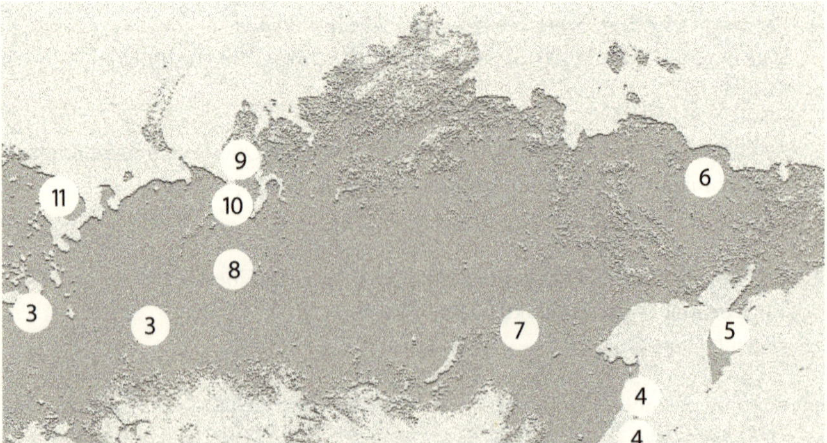

1 INTRODUCTION

Erich Kasten and Tjeerd de Graaf

General remarks

Much has been said and written about the endangered languages and cultures of native minority peoples in the recent past. Maps and extensive lists with shrinking numbers of speakers have continuously been compiled and numerous conferences have been held, where these issues have been discussed by well-informed international scientists, most often with participation of representatives of the *intelligentsia* of the given native peoples. These organisations and scholars must be credited for having directed attention to this issue within the academic community and among the general public. But at the same time the loss of cultural and linguistic diversity and the underlying processes that are the subject of critical debate here have sped up on a global scale, and as it is documented by the authors of this volume, this has also taken place in Russia during the last 20 years. Even more worrying is the fact that solutions are not in sight to stop or to divert such problematic trends.

Perhaps it is time that we, scholars and representatives of the academic community and of relevant international organisations who have been promoting these issues with honest and best intentions, ask ourselves why the proclaimed goals are far from being accomplished. At first sight it seems that most individual programmes and activities are appropriate and certainly quite useful as such. What might be missing is a coordinated strategy that takes some very basic considerations for future orientations and relevant efforts into account. In other words: it will be useful to consider certain important parameters which might have been missing and compare these parameters for several different cases.

But 'coordinated strategy' should not be misunderstood as it can in fact be misleading (see Vakhtin, p. 262, *this volume)*, because it immediately reminds us of the top-down language preservation policies and programmes during the later Soviet period, with the introduction of standardised teaching materials for the languages of the peoples of the Russian North (cf. Kasten 78, *this volume*). There is no doubt, that community driven diverse grassroots movements that carefully listen and pay attention to particular local needs, are the most appropriate strategy here. Although, these might draw upon the broad experience of previous developments that we aim to discuss and to coordinate here for this volume and for future initiatives.

In this book we present a series of papers which are related to the way in which indigenous knowledge in minority communities is sustained and how attempts are made to safeguard endangered languages. In October 2011 and January 2012 we organised two seminars where a limited number of scholars – most of them authors who contribute to this book – discussed the drafts of their contributions. These seminars were devoted to the preparation of learning tools for preserving endangered languages and traditional knowledge in Siberia, with comparative examples from other parts of the world. They were attended by scholars with backgrounds in social anthropology, ethnolinguistics and related fields who study the documentation of endangered languages and traditional knowledge and the use of new media for the implementation of learning tools for native communities, in particular in Siberia.

The main part of the book consists of articles on community experiences and alternative pedagogical concepts in the Russian North, but we have added some contributions from colleagues who consider similar problems in other parts of the world (Europe, China, Japan). During the seminars, a collegial and lively intellectual exchange took place which resulted in detailed reports. This process has made it possible for the authors to improve and refine their papers. In the following sections we shall specify some general critical questions which resulted from our discussions and briefly summarise the contents of the various papers.

The question of motivation

Most vital for the success of any activity to sustain linguistic and cultural diversity is the motivation of the local people to share these concerns, and accordingly to take up relevant measures that we – as foreign scientists – can only help to design and encourage, but which we are usually not able or supposed to implement. Closely linked to the indispensable proper motivation is the credibility of such initiatives that is further discussed by Kasten (p. 83, see also Kraef, p. 234, Lavrillier p. 116, *this volume*). If local communities perceive these programmes as serving mostly the individual or academic needs of the researcher or funding organisation, it becomes difficult to communicate to them the real meaning of the entire endeavour.

But also for other reasons than those mentioned above the necessary motivation among the local population can sometimes be low or even lacking. One reason might be that the particular cultural heritage of one's people or ethnic group often no longer has sufficient status in the given native community as opposed to other expressions of mainstream culture, against which it is not always easy to compete. In Soviet times, native culture, as representing a lower stage of society's development towards communism, was declared inferior by the state propaganda (see Lavrillier, p. 114, *this volume*), while some ethnic features had been demonstrated often more as 'folkloristic' elements that even today can sometimes serve as 'ethnic ornamentation' (see Dudeck, p. 150, *this volume*). The former role of state propaganda is now assumed more subtly and even more efficiently by commercial mass media, in which 'global' lifestyles and values are incessantly transmitted and presented as – often questionable – role models for one's own behaviour. However, this is a more general problem that certainly does not apply to native communities alone.

But what does it mean to members of a native community to preserve their own cultural heritage, and what can induce them to do so? First of all, a particular language has local variants which have often developed over time and distinguish each given group from others. In this way language serves as one (of many) important constituents of a person's multiple or layered identity (Kasten 2005a: 246 ff.; see also Dudeck, p. 149, Lavrillier p. 120, *this volume*). At the same time, a certain language is usually intimately connected to other kinds of traditional knowledge, especially the particular ecological knowledge of the group, as well as to its oral traditions such as stories and legends through which important worldviews and values are transmitted to the young from an early age. Such worldviews and values have developed over generations and have proven to be useful or even indispensable to securing and enhancing social life and appropriate behaviour towards nature with regard to the sustainable use of their natural resources – under often extreme conditions. To be in command of this knowledge connects a person back to his or her distant past, to one's ancestors and to the history of the entire group – this usually provides an essential sense of security and self-esteem. For most of us such identifications are self-evident, but one usually only becomes aware of them when one is about to lose them.

Many native people, especially youth, are facing this situation, and not only in Russia, but also in many other parts of the world, with all the well-known consequences resulting in psychological and behavioural problems of various kinds. In contrast, examples have shown that useful discourses with new ideas from the outside – and in future mostly via internet (see Michael Rießler, Olivia Kraef, *this volume*) – and consequently the needed adaptations to the modern world are much better accomplished when such natural steps are taken from the basis of pride and self-esteem with regard to one's own culture. Therefore, preserving and strengthening one's own cultural heritage makes it easier especially for native youth to integrate successfully into mainstream society. Here the use of modern facilities provided by information technology (Facebook, YouTube, Twitter, etc.) can play a crucial role.

Some essays in this volume stress this important fact: how ethnic pride and self-esteem can be built up in various ways (see Kasten, p. 73, *this volume*). Presenting native culture to foreign audiences can also lead to other and sometimes misleading motivations, if it is seen that way more (or exclusively) as a commodity (Kasten 2004: 25 ff.). Therefore, community members should be convinced that it is in their own interest to see the maintenance of their cultural heritage not exclusively with a view to immediate – financial – return. However, this is not always easy to explain or to justify under the given pressing economic conditions that many of them are facing and have to master these days.

This relates to the complicated and probably controversial issue of whether or in which ways the efforts of community members should be remunerated in this collaborative process. One problem is that paid information is usually biased and of a different quality (cf. Margaret Mead's correspondence with Ruth Benedict that vividly illustrates such shortcomings, Mead 1979: 97) if it is not connected to the informant's more far-reaching own interests such as the preservation of the cultural heritage of one's ethnic group. Furthermore, it can turn out to be counter-productive even in other ways, if the native expert is too generously compensated for his or her contribution. Usually this creates envy and anger within the community, if certain persons become privileged and singled out that way. This consequently would only distance or even isolate them from others. Thus, often well-meant attitudes on the part of the researcher can cause the opposite of what is desperately needed: the strong motivation of the whole community to work together for the given common goal without internal tensions or jealousies. Kasten (p. 81f., *this volume*) discusses some options of how to deal with this sensitive issue; Odé and Lavrillier also address how jealousies can counteract or raise negative consequences within a project (*this volume*).

In sum, it is important for the credibility of the given joint effort that everybody lives up to the same standards that are proclaimed and set for the proper motivational foundation in such projects. As an indispensable precondition for any successful work, it seems that this has to be made clear to all who are involved in this process. The entire native community should be convinced that it, in the first place, would benefit most in the long run from the expected outcome. But it should be a prime concern as well for foreign researchers to contribute to such projects which will preserve the linguistic and cultural diversity of humankind in general. They should pursue such activities even if they are not adequately acknowledged and academically and financially supported by governments and other authorities.

Further topics of general importance in the contributions to this volume

In most papers the common use of the unqualified term 'speaker' is problematic unless the actual language competence is further explained. In most cases the numbers appear more or less random and are often misleading. In most case studies of this volume the important difference is pointed out between a person who still masters the language fluently or has only auditory competence (the so-called 'passive user'), while in many cases he or she might still be able to respond in more or less fragmentary speech in that language. Furthermore, a distinction should be drawn between those who still have learnt the native language from their parents at home and those to whom it had been taught as a second language at school – as those in the latter case have often acquired different characteristics during this process. (More on the typology of speakers, see: Tsunoda 2005: 117–133.)

A central issue in the book is how to specify the position of the endangered languages which are considered: how many dialects, how many speakers (according to their degree of speech competence), how it is used in various situations, etc. Some of these languages have very few or no speakers left and one could ask the question how these last active speakers use the language. This will also determine how a literary standard can be developed for the written language. Is this standard based on one of the dialects and is it accepted by speakers or passive users of the other dialects? In most of the cases presented here (such as for Nenets, Nivkh, Itelmen, Evenk, Even and Koryak), this creates problems and people refuse to learn the standard or do not accept it from their children when they get lessons at school (Kasten, p. 78, Lavrillier, p. 109, *this volume*).

Stephan Dudeck remembers a comment by Eugen Helimski that some elders deliberately decided to break the transmission of their Nganasan language, as they saw the inability of the younger generation to learn the language in a complete way with all its folklorist richness and different registers, and with all poetic forms and expressions. Thus, instead of spoiling the language they opted for a language shift. The protagonist of the film *Itelmen stories* had shared similar concerns with Erich Kasten in the mid-1990s, such as those given here for the Nganasan, especially that the dialectical varieties of his (and other) villages were not sufficiently reflected in the standardised Soviet teaching materials since the 1980s (Kasten, p. 68, *this volume*). A blog on our seminar that refered to this elder's comment (http://arcticanthropology.org/2012/01/11/sec-seminar/) could not grasp this broader background of his isolated quote from the film.

The use of prescriptive dictionaries and grammars presents specific problems: most of these are not written for the teaching of children and often they use a variety of the language different from the language which the children speak at home or hear from their (grand)parents. Therefore, the use of sound material of various dialects might be useful. It can be shown in combination with one written standard while the teacher can use the spoken variety which is appropriate.

An important aspect is the use of information technology for e-learning, which in several articles (see Kraef, Lavrillier and Rießler, *this volume*) has been mentioned as an important way to teach and learn the endangered languages. In particular the new social networks can play a role when stimulating the use of these languages among young representatives of communities, where a minority language is less used.

The use of special alphabet conventions, such as additional diacritics in the writing system, requires special attention in the educational process. It will be very difficult for children (who often do not speak the language) to master a system of new graphemes in addition to the existing letters of the main language (see Rießler, *this volume*). This is in particular the case when the required phonemic differences do not exist in the main language and have very low functionality or are practically no longer in use.

Most of the papers show that much can be done for the benefit of minority communities and their language and culture. The following sections of this introduction summarize the contents of these papers which describe some programmes to preserve endangered languages, community experiences and alternative pedagogical concepts in the Russian North and experiences in preserving indigenous languages and knowledge from other parts of the world.

Programmes to preserve endangered languages

The first part of the book presents a number of programmes that contributed successfully to the preservation of endangered languages. Tjeerd de Graaf and Cor van der Meer inform us in their article on *Multilingualism and Language Teaching in Europe* on the case of Frisian and the important work of the Mercator European Research Centre, whose programme is also devoted to the study of other minority languages in Europe. The primary involvement of the Fryske Akademy lies in the domain of the history, literature and culture related to the West-Frisian language. The users of its nearest relatives, the East- and North-Frisian languages in Germany, are less numerous and these languages are included in the list of the most endangered languages of Europe. This report describes the present-day position of the Frisian language as one of the minority and regional languages of Europe. A survey is given of the available resources on Frisian and on the work of the Mercator Centre in the field of minority language learning. This may be useful for the study of minority language situations elsewhere in the world.

In another article Tjeerd de Graaf and Victor Denisov underline *The Use of Sound Archives for the Investigation, Teaching and Safeguarding of Some Endangered Uralic Languages*. In Russia many old sound recordings still remain hidden in archives and in private possession where the quality of preservation is not guaranteed. This review article presents the results of the project on 'Safeguarding and Preservation of Sound Materials of Endangered Languages for Sound Archives in Russia' (2006–2008) and describes some earlier projects related to these historical recordings, such as the project 'Voices from Tundra and Taiga' (2002–2005). The authors have made part of these sound materials available and added them to the acoustic database developed with colleagues in the sound archive of the Russian Academy of Sciences in St. Petersburg. The aim of these projects is to re-record the material and safeguard it in storage facilities, which will modernise the possible archiving activities in the Russian Federation and bring them up to date with the present day world standards of the International Association of Sound Archives (IASA 2005). The authors concentrate on a selection of recordings of some endangered languages in the Russian Federation, for which documentation is very important. As specific case studies, they consider the recovered sound material for a few Uralic languages, in particular Khanty and Udmurt, for which historical sound recordings are presented in sound archives in the Russian Federation and abroad. The authors consider these materials' potential for the development of modern learning tools and teaching methods and evaluate the present day situation for the teaching of Udmurt and other minority and regional languages in the Russian Federation.

The final chapter of this first part of the book deals with the *Documentation and Revitalisation of Two Endangered Languages in Eastern Asia: Nivkh and Ainu.* Tjeerd de Graaf and Hidetoshi Shiraishi draw a comparison between two adjacent ethnic groups, namely the Ainu of Hokkaido and the Nivkh of Sakhalin. They follow the historical development of the border areas between Japan and Russia and describe the prevailing situation of these aboriginal peoples on both sides of the border. The legal measures taken by the Japanese government for the promotion of Ainu culture and the development of learning tools have consequences for the Ainu community and the possible revitalisation of the Ainu language. The Nivkh community within the Russian Federation is a typical example of the multitude of ethnic minority groups spread across this vast territory. The Ainu case can be compared and used as a model for possible (legal) measures to be taken regarding minority languages and cultures such as Nivkh with an outlook for future improvement. The authors consider the use of new media for these native communities and pay attention to the development of adequate modern learning tools and culturally related teaching methods. Various options are provided, starting with such basic ones as organising language courses and arranging other language-related activities.

Community experiences and alternative pedagogical concepts in the Russian North

In the second part of this volume, the authors discuss community experiences and alternative pedagogical concepts in the Russian North that aim to sustain endangered languages and local knowledge and that they have followed and closely monitored during many years, in some cases since the early 1990s. In his article *Learning Tools for Preserving Languages and Indigenous Knowledge in Kamchatka,* Erich Kasten gives first an overview of various projects on these issues that he and his team have carried out in Kamchatka with the Itelmen, Even and Koryak peoples. A particular emphasis of these projects was on producing together with native experts new learning tools in which modern technologies have been applied and continuously adapted to rapidly developing newly available formats. He tries to capture the intense community discourse over these programmes that include besides initiatives to preserve endangered languages even more aspects of endangered cultural traditions such as ecological knowledge. Furthermore, he analyses the role that performing arts can play, in particular for the youth, to preserve and to further develop important traditions in order to maintain and enhance new cultural diversities.

Cecilia Odé addresses similar issues in her article *Learning your Endangered Native Language in a Small Multilingual Community* in which she presents a case study of Tundra Yukagir in Andriushkino. In her analysis she points out the quite unique multilingual environment that is created by various native peoples living in this village, and with them it is not easy for the Tundra Yukagir language to compete. Cecilia Odé first describes the curriculum and the learning tools and clearly identifies their shortcomings and offers prospects for future improvements. For this, she gives much room to children and to teachers to express themselves about what learning their native language can mean to them.

In her article on *Anthropology and Applied Anthropology in Siberia*, Alexandra Lavrillier focuses on questions and solutions around a nomadic school among the Evenk reindeer herders. She first gives an overview of the history and the actual debate on applied anthropology within the theory of anthropology. Besides this, the demand of the indigenous people gave her the main impetus for her direct involvement in designing and implementing alternative pedagogical concepts in the form of a nomadic school, as such a model relates more closely to traditional lifestyles of reindeer herding communities. This paper also gives an overview of the attempts at the creation and the experiences of nomadic schools in eastern Siberia in the early 1990s. On the basis of her many years of experience with the creation of a nomadic school in 2005 which is still functioning, Alexandra Lavrillier discusses the particular ethical, political, social and educational issues that such a school may raise, and explains the solutions adopted by this applied anthropology project.

Similar experiences with alternative educational models that are connected to the cultural past and actual traditional lifestyles of the given native people are presented and discussed by Stephan Dudeck with regard to Forest Nenets reindeer herders. In his article *Challenging the State Educational System in Western Siberia: Taiga-School at the Tiuitiakha River* he emphasises that it was not as much the content of the school curriculum, which was almost the same as that of the boarding school in the village, but the organisation of the educational process and the context of the work of the small taiga school that differed so much from the conventional system of education. He analyses the difficulties that arose after the thirteen years of existence of that school, which might lead to a discontinuation of this initially promising initiative. In his conclusion, Stephan Dudeck places the school project and its educational ideas in the broader context of attempts to reform the educational system for indigenous groups in Siberia after the breakdown of the Soviet Union.

In her article *Boarding School on Yamal* Elena Liarskaya analyses the changes in the relationship between school, state and Siberian indigenous peoples, based on the archival, printed and field materials connected with the school at the Yamal cultural centre in Yar-Sale. The author shows that there was no integral Soviet school policy in the North. She gives a short description of the main stages of the interrelations between the school and local people in Siberia and demonstrates how tasks and functions are fulfilled by the school at different stages. The author discusses in detail certain features of the school in the 1930s (the period of initial mass education in that region), and the specifics of relations between boarding schools and nomadic schools at that time. Then she compares the aims and functions of the school on Yamal at present, and, consequently, shows the fundamental changes that have taken place over time.

Roza Laptander's article *Model for the Tundra School in Yamal* refers to another Nenets group, the Tundra Nenets who live in Western Siberia. She investigates a project that represents a new educational system for children from nomadic and semi-nomadic Nenets families. The first nomadic schools started to work earlier than boarding schools in the 1930s but they were not successful. Recently this type of education was introduced again by the Nenets writer Anna Nerkagi and aims to overcome the harmful consequences of earlier boarding schools during the later Soviet period. Roza Laptander presents and discusses the pedagogical outline of this new experimental nomadic school. The trailblazer, Anna Nerkagi, wants the children to be aware of the harmful effects of civilisation. The children are taught life and love through dedicated labour and they speak just Nenets language.

The language situation of the Kildin Saami, living further west on the Kola peninsula in Northwestern Russia, is at the centre of Michael Rießler's article *Towards a Digital Infrastructure for Kildin Saami*. Its focus is on language planning and the creation of a digital infrastructure in the minority context. Methodologies of applied linguistic research at the interface between language planning, language documentation and language technology are discussed on the basis of ongoing research being undertaken in cooperation between local research centres and from the perspective of a critically endangered language of Northern Russia. Outcomes of this project have good potential to be used for similar learning tools with other peoples of the Russian north.

Experiences in preserving indigenous languages and knowledge from other parts of the world

In another part of this book, comparative experiences are given on similar initiatives to preserve linguistic and cultural diversities for other native or minority peoples living beyond Russia in other parts of the world. In her article *Building Yi (M)other Tongue* Olivia Kraef addresses virtual platforms, language and culture in a Chinese minority context, while using the example of the Yi. Based on a content analysis of the main and most popular websites and online forums relevant in this context, this article examines and analyses the function these virtual platforms play in regard to Yi (Nuosu) language proliferation among groups of young Yi. The author specifically attempts to assess through what means (and potentially with what aims) these virtual platforms promote, or perhaps even reverse, the meanings of Yi language preservation among young Yi communities in China. Furthermore, Olivia Kraef gives an outlook on whether or not Yi language as promoted through these platforms can in the long run become a 'true' alternative means to current language and culture preservation in academic and educational institutions.

Finally, an even more distant perspective on the issues that have been discussed here mainly for indigenous peoples in the Russian context is given by Teresa Valiente Catter and Michael Dürr. Their article *Bilingual Intercultural Education in the Andes* presents the practice of intercultural bilingual education in Latin America, focussing on the Quechuan languages. It raises questions of curriculum development and the factors relevant for preparing teaching materials related to the intercultural approach and the aptness of the national language as a medium for the education of indigenous communities. On the other hand, the practical linguistic factors to be taken into account in defining a written variety of an indigenous language and the social factors favouring or obstructing language loyalty are discussed.

In the *Epilogue*, Nikolai Vakhtin discusses previous and present trends and possible future ways for preserving endangered languages and indigenous knowledge among the peoples of the Russian North. The editors thank him for having directed our attention to problematic academic attitudes and approaches in this regard in the past that have been discussed at length and frankly in many of the articles of this volume, with the aim and the hope of providing possible answers and showing new directions.

The editors and all authors would also like to sincerely thank Beverley Stewart for her insightful – and certainly often not easy – copy editing of the texts that were written by authors from various foreign linguistic backgrounds. The Foundation for Siberian Cultures is thanked for having hosted the seminars and provided the inspiring and warm atmosphere which led to the outcome of this productive discourse.

References

Kasten, Erich 2004. Ways of Owning and Sharing Cultural Property. In *Properties of Culture – Culture as Property. Pathways to Reform in Post-Soviet Siberia*, E. Kasten (ed.), 9–32. Berlin: Dietrich Reimer Verlag. http://www.siberian-studies.org/publications/PDF/cpkasten2.pdf

— 2005. The Dynamics of Identity Management. In *Rebuilding Identities. Pathways to Reform in Post-Soviet Siberia*, E. Kasten (ed.), 237–260. Berlin: Dietrich Reimer Verlag. http://www.siberian-studies.org/publications/PDF/rikasten2.pdf

Mead, Margaret 1979. *Letters from the Field, 1925–1975*. R.N. Anshen (ed.). New York: Harper & Row.

Tsunoda, Tasaku 2005. *Language Endangerment and Language Revitalization. An Introduction*. Berlin / New York: Mouton de Gruyter.

2 MULTILINGUALISM AND LANGUAGE TEACHING IN EUROPE: THE CASE OF FRISIAN AND THE WORK OF THE MERCATOR EUROPEAN RESEARCH CENTRE

Tjeerd de Graaf and Cor van der Meer

Introduction

The work of the Fryske Akademy (Frisian Academy) and the Mercator European Research Centre on Multilingualism and Language Learning is devoted to the study of minority languages in Europe. The primary involvement of the Fryske Akademy lies in the domain of history, literature and culture, as they are related to the West-Frisian language. The users of its nearest relatives, the East- and North-Frisian languages in Germany, are less numerous and these languages are included in the list of the most endangered languages of Europe. This report presents the present-day position of the Frisian language as one of the minority and regional languages of Europe. After sections on the characteristics of the language, its speakers, language use, multilingualism and language policy, we consider the organisations which are involved in the documentation and safeguarding of the language, in particular the Mercator European Research Centre on Multilingualism and Language Learning. A survey of the available resources on Frisian and on the work of the Mercator Centre will be presented, which can be useful for the study and safeguarding of minority language situations elsewhere in the world, such as in Siberia.

General remarks on the Frisian Language

Frisian is spoken in the north-western part of Europe, and has its most important branch in the province of Friesland in the Netherlands. When the distinction with the smaller branches in Germany (North-Frisian and East-Frisian) has to be made, it is also called West-Frisian (not to be confused with the geographic name West-Friesland for the Northern part of the province Noord-Holland). The three languages West-Frisian, East-Frisian and North-Frisian are not mutually comprehensible. In the following we shall limit ourselves to the most important member of the language group, West-Frisian in the Netherlands, which henceforth will be referred to as 'Frisian'.

The Frisian language belongs to the Germanic family of languages. In this family the coastal West-Germanic subgroup is represented by English and Frisian, whereas the continental subgroup consists of (High- and Low-)German and Dutch. Historically (in the time before the Anglo-Saxons went to the British Isles), Old-Frisian and

Old-English were very similar. As late as the 8th century, the Germanic languages Old Saxon, Old Franconian, Old Frisian, etc. were still close to each other. During the whole of the Middle Ages, Friesland was monolingual and largely autonomous under the leadership of frequently changing tribal chiefs. Old Frisian was not only the spoken language but also the official language of government and judicial power. Old Frisian laws and legal documents have survived from the 13th century.

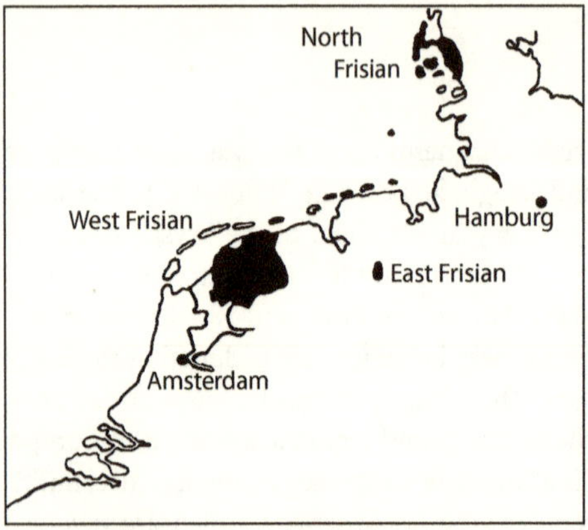

|1| Areas in Europe where Frisian is spoken

Modern Frisian still shares certain features with English, but the influence of Dutch and the similarity with this language has become very strong. This is due to the fact that after the sixteenth century, Dutch was used as the official language of the Netherlands in the local government, the judiciary, in schools and churches. Frisian virtually ceased to be used in written form until a revival occurred at the end of the 19th century. Since then Frisian has gradually regained access to more areas of life and developed into Modern Frisian. In recent decades it has acquired a modest place (alongside Dutch) in government, the judiciary and education.

Language characteristics

The modern Frisian language has an official standard writing system. There was a revision of the spelling in the second half of the 20th century, but at the moment no additional changes are underway. The prescriptive norm for the Frisian language is described in *Frisian Reference Grammar* by Pieter Meijes Tiersma (1985, 1999). This norm of standard Frisian is officially promoted in schools and administration, but the overall dominance of the Dutch language makes the promotion difficult. For details about the grammar of modern Frisian we refer to this book, which is the only grammar of Frisian currently available in English and which describes the correspondences and contrasts with English. Together with the Frisian-English dictionary, which the Frisian Academy published in 2000, the book provides a useful source of information for those interested in the Frisian language.

Although there are many contrasts with English, Frisian is genetically the closest related language to English. The tremendous influence of French on English and of Dutch on Frisian, along with natural changes over time, has obscured this, but even today certain features common to Frisian and English (as opposed to Dutch and German) document this relationship.

The use of Frisian and multilingualism

Frisian is spoken in the province of Friesland and in a few border villages in the neighbouring province of Groningen. The provincial government and several municipalities have started a language policy that gives Frisian equal rights to Dutch. In the last decades the name of the province (Fryslân) and many local place names have officially been converted to Frisian. In this review we shall use Friesland, which is the current English name for the province.

Frisian and Dutch are both spoken in the province of Friesland, where Dutch as the official national language has the highest prestige. Frisian presently has official status in the Netherlands as the second language of the state. Its spelling has been standardised and Frisian is used in several domains of Frisian society, thereby breaking through the dominance of Dutch. Apart from domains such as the judiciary, public administration, radio and television, the Frisian language can also be used within the province for education.

Nevertheless, it can be stated that the Frisian language is mainly spoken in the homes of Frisian people, in the countryside and in informal situations. In more formal surroundings, such as shops in town and government offices, many people shift to Dutch, even if Frisian is their first language. In larger groups of people, the presence of one Dutch speaking-person may suffice to trigger language shift of the whole group from Frisian to Dutch. Because of the fact that most Frisians (in particular the older ones) got their school education only in Dutch, many of them are not able to use the Frisian language in writing and prefer reading in Dutch. This is the main reason that the newspapers contain very little written Frisian.

The provincial government of Friesland and a number of municipalities make frequent use of both written and spoken Frisian. The regional broadcasting company Omrop Fryslân does radio and television broadcasts where standard Frisian is well-represented and accepted by speakers of the dialects. In the interviews on radio and television, one can hear the dialects spoken in bilingual conversations, and Dutch also plays an important role. There are Frisian church services (the bible was translated into Frisian only in 1943), and every year Frisian language books are published and theatre plays performed.

The province of Friesland has about 600,000 inhabitants and about half of these can be considered first-language speakers of Frisian. A sociolinguistic study in 1994 revealed that 94 % of the population of Friesland can understand the language, 74 % can speak it, 65 % are able to read Frisian (however, most of them read Dutch more easily) and 17 % write Frisian. Frisian is spoken in 55 % of the homes. Speakers of Frisian form a (great) majority in most rural areas, and a (small) minority in the towns and cities, on the Frisian Isles and in the Stellingwerven (two Low-Saxon municipalities in the south-eastern part of the province). Practically all Frisian speakers are bilingual in Dutch. Most mother-tongue speakers of Dutch in Friesland can understand Frisian, but are not able or not willing to speak it.

In the past, language use in Friesland could be characterised as a stable diglossic situation (Frisian for the country and informal domains, Dutch for the town and formal domains). In the last century, Dutch has also invaded the old Frisian domains (rural community matters and the family), primarily as a result of migration and mixed marriages. In this way, language use changed into a sort of informal (and receptive) polylingualism. General attitudes to Frisian have become more positive, and it has become acceptable to use it in more and more domains (radio, newspapers, etc.).

As stated before, Dutch is still dominant in economic, political and religious spheres. Therefore Frisian is strongly influenced by it, particularly at the lexical level. More and more people say, for example, *sleutel* ['key'] rather than *kaai*, and *boven* ['above'] instead of *boppe*. On the other hand, the influences of Frisian on Standard Dutch are meagre – some of the only words to have found entry into Dutch are those from typical Frisian sport terminology such as *skûtsjesilen* (competitive sailing with traditional sailing boats).

The third language in Friesland is English, which has growing importance in all parts of the Netherlands. As the European Union countries are becoming more united, English is increasingly being used as a means of general communication, in particular in international firms, commercial contacts, science, pop culture, higher education, etc. In many advanced courses in Dutch universities and similar educational institutions, English is used as the medium for teaching, in particular with a growing group of students from abroad. This also holds for Friesland.

Language policy

Until recently, a national language policy for Frisian was not formally expressed by law, but finally in 2011, such a law was prepared by the government. Official Dutch policy started with the Van Ommen Committee (1970), which produced a report that recognised the responsibility of the national government with regard to Frisian. An important principle of the report was recognition of Friesland as a bilingual province. The use of the Frisian language in specified domains is clearly restricted to the province of Friesland. The committee stated that the central government should focus on safeguarding the identity of the Frisian language and culture, in collaboration with provincial and municipal authorities. According to the report, this means that the national government has the function of resolving specific problems caused by bilingualism in the Frisian culture. An immediate result of the report was that a small sum of money in the national budget was directed to organisations with key roles in maintaining the Frisian language and culture.

In general, Frisian speakers can use their own language in contacts with public authorities, as the provincial administration and a number of other bodies have made this a matter of policy. Documents issued by public authorities are generally only in Dutch; Frisian or bilingual ones are very exceptional. In courts of justice, all parties, including the defendant and witnesses, are allowed to speak Frisian. If need be, the court can employ the services of an interpreter. Courts of justice in Friesland accept civil actions brought in Frisian, but this can cause problems in case of an appeal to a higher court. Documents published in Frisian only are not legally binding. Public signs can be in Frisian, in Dutch, or bilingual, depending on the choice of the municipality concerned.

|2| Bilingual Frisian-Dutch signposts of placenames

Current language policy regarding the Frisian language is based on the Frisian Language and Culture Covenant, an agreement between the provincial and the central government. This was drawn up in 1989, renewed in 1993, and redrafted in 2001 on the basis of the European Charter for Regional or Minority Languages (BFTK-Bestjoersôfspraak Fryske Taal en Kultuer 2001–2010, Staatscourant 125, 3 July 2001). This Council of Europe document was signed in 1992 and ratified by the Dutch government in 1996. With respect to Frisian, it contains 48 concrete measures (part III), and other regional languages in the Netherlands obtained merely symbolic recognition from the national government (part II). In the covenant of the BFTK, it is declared that it is desirable to make it possible for citizens, local authorities, organisations and institutions to express themselves in Frisian. The covenant also states that both provincial and central governments are responsible for preserving and reinforcing the Frisian language and culture. Lastly, it states that resources must be provided to create suitable conditions for this purpose.

This means that:

- the national government determines general education, culture and media policies in Friesland, although, as far as Frisian is concerned, it has to respect the European Charter;
- the province of Friesland determines policy regarding the Frisian language and ensures the execution of this policy;

- the national government provides the province with the means to execute its policy as regards Frisian;
- provincial policy concerning Frisian and national policy concerning general education, culture and media have to reinforce each other where possible.

On several occasions, Friesland and its government have insisted on the necessity of a comprehensive language law, and at present (March 2011) such a law has been presented to the national government.

Frisian in education

The role of Frisian in primary education dates back to 1907, when the local government offered a grant to support Frisian lessons after regular school hours. Frisian was then taught as an extra-curricular subject. Legislative provisions for Frisian only began in 1937 with amendments to the Education Act of 1920. Although Frisian was not specifically mentioned, the changes to the act made it possible to teach Frisian as a regional language in higher grades during Dutch lessons.

However, nothing was arranged for the use of Frisian as a medium of instruction. In 1950, nine primary schools began to experiment with bilingual education and in 1955, bilingual schools obtained legal basis. Frisian became an optional subject throughout primary school, and the use of Frisian as a medium of instruction was allowed in the lower grades. By 1959, the number of bilingual schools had risen to 47. Starting in 1959, the Dutch state financed the Paedagogysk Advysburo of the Fryske Akademy (Frisian Academy), which merged into the organisation CEDIN for the northern provinces.

The Paedagogysk Advysburo (Pedagogical Advisory Bureau) is an institution that has offered educational advice and guidance to bilingual schools. Around 1970, these had risen to 84 schools, which was 25 per cent of all primary schools in the province. In 1974, the Primary Education Act was modified. Frisian became an approved teaching medium in all grades and an obligatory school subject throughout primary education as of 1980. Preparations for the implementation of this new policy included the following extensive activities: the training of 3,000 teachers; special parents' evenings at all schools; the development of new learning material; the re-working of television and radio for schools and, finally, the introduction of Frisian as a subject at teacher training colleges.

In 1985, the Primary Education Act was replaced by a completely new Act for Primary Education in the Netherlands. In 1998, the Education Act was changed again. Except for some textual changes, the legal arrangements for Frisian in primary education remained the same.

Since 1980, Frisian has been taught in all primary schools, both public and private. In many of these schools, Frisian is also used to varying degrees as a teaching medium, alongside Dutch. There is no provision for primary education entirely through Frisian, although some preschool groups are conducted exclusively in Frisian. At secondary level it is also possible to use Frisian as a teaching medium for some subjects, but this is infrequently done. There is no secondary schooling entirely in Frisian, but in some schools Frisian can be used as language of instruction, and Frisian can be taken as an exam subject. In the early 1980s, the subject was offered by 25 % of all secondary schools on an optional basis, and about 5 % of all students availed themselves of this opportunity. Since 1993, Frisian has been an obligatory subject in the first three years of secondary education. The two teacher-training centres in Friesland are required to offer Frisian to their students. They have a policy which stipulates that all students must attend Frisian classes. This qualifies them to teach Frisian in primary schools. Secondary school teachers of Frisian are trained at the part-time higher vocational education college in Ljouwert/Leeuwarden and at the University of Groningen, after having studied the language as a main subject at either of the universities in Groningen or Amsterdam. At the University of Leiden, Frisian is a subsidiary subject. There is an extensive network of adult language courses in Frisian.

The current Primary Education Act (Wet op het Primair Onderwijs – WPO, 1998) lists a number of subjects that all primary schools have to teach without prescribing the number of hours or how schools should teach those subjects. In 1993, the Minister of Education defined attainment targets (*kerndoelen*) for these subjects. These targets were modified to some extent in 1998. In the Netherlands it is the minister of education in The Hague who determines these attainment targets. The minister may be corrected by the national parliament, but not by the Frisian parliament. According to recent studies, only 30 % of the primary schools in Friesland meet these targets for Frisian. On March 14, 2005, the Frisian executive for education signed a covenant on the implementation of language policy with the Dutch state, and subsequently discussed the covenant in the regional parliament. The covenant mentions lower attainment targets for Frisian than for Dutch. Various political parties were angry because this was completely contradictory to their decision that Frisian targets should be equal to those for Dutch.

Together with other regions with lesser-used languages within the European Union, special projects have been initiated in the field of trilingual education. In seven schools in Friesland, three languages are used as a medium of instruction: Frisian, Dutch and English. The Frisian Academy is involved in the coordination of these projects and the evaluation of their results.

Afûk and EduFrysk

The Algemiene Fryske Ûnderrjocht Kommisje (Afûk, a foundation to promote the knowledge and use of the Frisian language) is a cultural institution in Leeuwarden

|3| Trilingual school in Friesland

with special tasks in the field of education (see www.afuk.nl). Firstly, it has a bookshop in the centre of town where books related to the Frisian language and culture are sold. It also is an editing house producing numerous books and other publications, in particular educational material and the Frisian monthly journal De Moanne (www.demoanne.nl).

The Afûk organises courses on Friesland and its language and culture, which for instance take place on the island of Terschelling. It also houses a special translation service, *stipepunt Frysk*, where texts are translated from and into Frisian. Special educational methods are developed for language classes and in particular for children who grow up and go to school in a bilingual Frisian-Dutch situation, or even in trilingual schools, where Frisian, Dutch and English are used. Very successful programmes are provided by the so-called Tomke-books for small children, and the online learning facility *EduFrysk*. Tomke is a Frisian speaking cartoon figure for young children (aged 0–6 years) with the objective of promoting multilingualism. To celebrate its 10th anniversary, there were musical theatre performances in the province of Friesland.

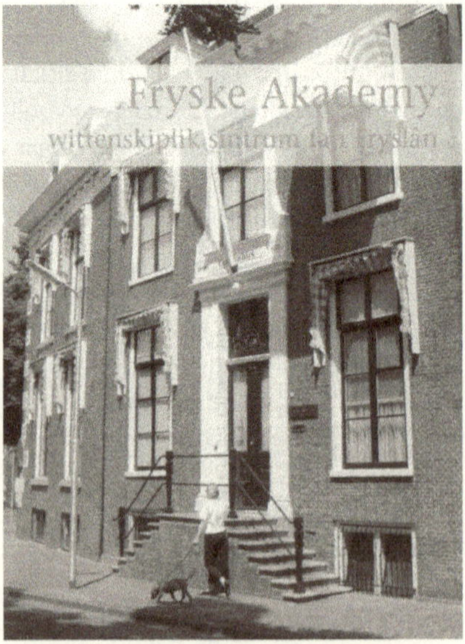

|4| Building of the Fryske Academy

Anyone with questions about Frisian grammar and the use of the language can receive aid from the Language Desk. The Desk answers questions about spelling, phrasing or terminology, and can give advice concerning the composition of Frisian texts. The Language Desk is specialised in translating texts containing technical terms into Frisian (e.g. notarial acts, official and technical documents). Information can be obtained about place names in Friesland, foreign geographic names, computer terminology, terminology in special areas, such as for inland shipping, creation of new words, etc.

The Afûk is (mainly) funded by the regional government. It has several commercial counterparts, for instance, the language agencies Taalburo Popkema, specialised in translation and linguistic research (www.taalburopopkema.nl) and DAT Tekstbureau, specialized in literary translation, editing and the production of Frisian audiobooks (www.dattekstbureau.nl).

EduFrysk (www.edufrysk.com/) presents an innovative multimedia online learning facility, which allows people to learn the Frisian language in their own time and at their own speed. It contains a multitude of texts, poetry, musical performances, videos, dictations and several kinds of exercises. The programme keeps a record of the student's progress, and by placing the mouse over a word one can discover the meaning of Frisian words, consult a dictionary and listen to the pronunciation. EduFrysk is one of the most complete language learning facilities on the internet, which is financially supported by the Frisian provincial government and has modules on several levels of ability. Target groups are students, teachers and interested learners, who not only live in Friesland, but in principle anywhere in the world with access to the internet. The language of instruction is Dutch but an English version is in preparation. For this one can for instance think of 'root seekers' in America, where many descendants of Frisian emigrants live.

New features in the programme are the possibility for users to create their own profile, work in virtual communities and with expert groups, use podcasts and language games. The programme is permanently extended with new issues and it also has large educational potential for application for other minority languages in the world. In this way, the internet can play a very important role in the education and safeguarding of minority languages in the world and stimulate the revitalisation of endangered languages.

The Fryske Akademy and other authoritative sources on the language

The main authoritative source on the Frisian language is the Fryske Akademy (Frisian Academy) with its Departments of Linguistics, History and Social Sciences.

The Department of Linguistics is focussed on linguistic research into all phases of Frisian: Modern Frisian (with its dialectical variants), Middle Frisian and Old Frisian. There are special projects on the phonology and grammar of Frisian and on the research into Frisian dialects, such as Town-Frisian and non-Frisian dialects connected with Frisian. Several language corpora have been developed by the Frisian Academy, such as the New Frisian language corpus, which is a digital collection of Frisian books, scientific magazines and newspaper articles, which can be used to investigate various aspects of Frisian culture, including language and literature. The corpus contains more than 25 million words. The texts in the New Frisian language corpus provide a tool for keeping scientific research on Frisian culture up to date, since language and culture change over time. The New Frisian language corpus is of vital importance to several ongoing projects. The New Frisian language corpus is accessible via the internet to everybody who wants to make use of it. Potential users include:

- (Foreign) researchers who conduct research into minority languages like Frisian.
- Translators and writers who want to know in which contexts a given word is used; they can find several instances of sentences in which the relevant word occurs.
- Somebody who remembers a line from a song or a poem can try to find the bibliographical reference in the corpus.
- Frisian emigrants can refresh their knowledge of Frisian language and culture.

The *Dictionary of the Frisian Language/Wurdboek fan de Fryske taal/Woordenboek der Friese taal* (WFT) is the product of the WFT-project which collects the vocabulary of Modern Frisian (Frisian since 1800), described in the period 1800 to 1975. The dictionary is bilingual, the definitions and so on are in Dutch. A volume of 400 pages comes out every year, the first volume came out in 1984. The editorial phase has been finished in 2010, the final editing and publication phase at the end of 2011. Other results of the lexicographic work of the Fryske Akademy are a Frisian-English and a Frisian-Frisian dictionary and dictionaries with special terminologies, such as one for legal matters.

The Department of Social Science of the Fryske Akademy studies the distinguishing features of Frisian society. The central theme of 'multilingualism' is the point of departure for projects about Frisian-Dutch language relationships. Some of the projects are:

Multilingualism and minority languages:

- A regular survey of language use in Friesland;
- The Frisian language abroad: language use of emigrants.

Educational research:

Interest in good education is growing, thanks to increasing and changing demands from our society. Research enables schools and government institutions to gain insight into the current state of affairs, and it also supports and evaluates education policy-making. The following topics are considered:

- Evaluation of the provincial education policy 2007 to 2014 (Boppeslach project);
- Language acquisition and development in young children;
- Trilingual schools.

Social cultural developments:

- Life and worldview of the Frisians;
- Policy research;
- Regional economic research;
- Rural change: farm building conversion.

Some of these activities take place in the framework of the Mercator European Research Centre on Multilingualism and Language Learning.

Publications, media and conferences

There is a relatively large literary production in Frisian. About 100 Frisian books of various kinds are published each year. Friesland has one professional Frisian-language theatre which is very popular. Most towns and villages also have a Frisian amateur drama group. There are a number of museums, libraries and cultural centres. In addition, approximately 20 CDs consisting of popular Frisian music are released every year.

A total of about 30 hours annually of Frisian television is broadcast on Sundays all over the Netherlands. In the rest of the week the provincial television of Omrop Fryslân broadcasts an hour and a half per day in Friesland. There is one provincial radio service, which broadcasts more than 80 hours per week in Frisian. There are also 20 minutes a week for both school radio and school television. There are no daily or weekly newspapers at all in Frisian. Frisian is used in some newspaper articles, however. Just a few (literary) periodicals (like the monthly *De Moanne*) are published in Frisian, but they have limited circulation.

Every three years the Frisian Academy organises the Frisian Philologist Congress, which provides a platform for scholarly discussion concerning Frisian studies in the broadest sense. In 2012, this congress took place in June. In July 2010, the Fryske Akademy hosted the congress of the European Association for Lexicography (Euralex). One of the special features of this successful conference was its focus on the lexicography of lesser-used non-state languages.

Conferences are also regularly organised by the Mercator European Research Centre on Multilingualism and Language Learning, which is located within the Social Science Department of the Fryske Akademy. The work of this centre will be described separately in the following section.

The Mercator European Research Centre

The Mercator European Research Centre on Multilingualism and Language Learning (Mercator or Mercator Centre in short) addresses the growing interest in multilingualism and the increasing need of language communities to exchange experiences and to cooperate in a European context. This centre is the successor of Mercator Education, which was founded in 1987 by an initiative of the European Commission. Since 2007, Mercator is funded by the provincial government of Friesland and the municipality of Leeuwarden. Thanks to this funding, the centre was able to increase its activities and focus on research. Besides, its working area was extended from the member states of the European Union to the member states of the Council of Europe and beyond. In that same period the centre's name was changed to Mercator European Research Centre on Multilingualism and Language Learning. It is based in Ljouwert/Leeuwarden, the capital of Friesland, is part of the Fryske Akademy, and gathers and mobilises expertise in the field of language learning at school, at home and through cultural participation in favor of linguistic diversity in Europe.

The centre aims to be a platform in Europe and an independent and recognised organisation for researchers, policymakers and professionals in the field of education and language learning, and it endeavours to favor linguistic diversity within Europe. The starting point lies in the field of regional and minority languages. Yet, immigrant languages and smaller state languages of Europe are also a topic of study.

Successful ongoing activities of the Mercator European Research Centre are: research, the series of Regional Dossiers, the Network of Schools and the organisation of international conferences and expert seminars.

The Mercator European Research Centre develops its research programme in line with its experience and on the basis of the data collections available.
Scientific research is being conducted at the following three levels of aggregation:

- the way in which language and multilingualism take place within individuals in a cognitive-psychological sense (intra-individual and individual; psycho-linguistics);
- the way in which language and multilingualism between individuals are realised, acquired (transfer, teaching, training, and testing) and experienced in mutual contact with the language itself and by the individuals who use the language (inter-individual and socio-linguistics). This implies the linguistic study of language contact, language mergers, creolisation, code switching, language surveys, new teaching methods and the issue of inter-cultural and bilingual didactics;
- the way in which language and multilingualism are practised in a society in terms of policy, institutes, legal structures and strategy (governance and organisation), language strategy and planning.

Recent research activities focussed on:

- Language learning and acquisition; various aspects of bilingual and trilingual education, such as interaction in multilingual classrooms, language proficiency in different languages, teachers' qualifications for the multilingual classroom, and the development of standards.
- Stimulating and improving multilingualism; the study of role models, language attitude, language vitality, immersion programmes, the position of (new) media, relations between Regional and Minority Languages (RML) and immigrant languages.
- Added value of multilingualism; international comparison of the social status of languages, socio-economical value of languages.

The recent published inventory of *Trilingual Primary Education in Europe* (Bangma, Van der Meer and Riemersma 2011) presents a number of case studies (e.g. Friesland, the Basque Country and Finland) as well as a number of small scale initiatives in trilingual education. The results of trilingual primary schooling in Friesland are encouraging: pupils have mastered Dutch equally well as other pupils, but Frisian better, and they speak English more easily (see Ytsma 2007). The model of trilingual schooling will be expanded to other schools and extended to a trilingual stream in secondary education. Research on trilingual education will focus on the actual results in terms of language command, but also on the longitudinal approach, the use of both Frisian and English as media of instruction, and on the implications for teacher training.

Whenever possible, research will be carried out in a comparative European perspective. On behalf of the Congress of Local and Regional Authorities (CLRAE) of the Council of Europe, Mercator carried out the study *The Development of Minimum Standards on Language Education in Regional and Minority Languages* (De Jager and Van der Meer 2007). With reference to the European Charter on Regional or Minority Languages, the present situation of ten languages in eight countries has been evaluated. The outcomes show a great variety in terms of time investment, teaching materials, teacher qualifications and the curriculum. This report will be used for the setting of minimum standards by the Council of Europe. Research results are disseminated through publications (on the website, on paper) and through conferences in collaboration with European partners.

The series of Regional Dossiers meets the growing need for basic information on education in minority language settings. The dossiers present an up-to-date description of the position of a minority language at all levels in the educational system of a state. The Regional Dossiers are written by experts according to a fixed structure. Each dossier is updated once every five to eight years. In this way the dossiers can also be used for comparative research. So far, some 40 languages of EU member states have been covered. In the years to come, the series will be extended with the coverage of other languages: smaller EU state languages, minority languages of Council of Europe member states outside the EU and beyond. The whole series of regional dossiers is available online at the website of the Mercator European Research Centre.

The Network of Schools consists of around 100 schools in 20 European regions where a regional or minority language is taught. The goal of the Network of Schools is to create a platform for bilingual and multilingual schools in minority regions in Europe in order to facilitate the exchange of information and experiences. The Network of Schools is intended for schools at the pre-primary, primary and secondary level. These schools actively teach and use the minority or regional language, aside from the state language, in the curriculum, and they often teach English as a third language.

Recently Mercator started to create a European Network of Teacher Training Institutes. These institutes are training future teachers for bilingual and multilingual education. This Network will not only create a platform for the exchange of information and experiences, but will also function as the instrument to further development of common projects in terms of language transmission, adequate levels of language command, didactics and testing.

The Mercator European Research Centre organises conferences and expert seminars on a regular basis. Important themes for the conferences are: measurement and good practice, educational models, language vitality, development of minimum standards, teacher training, and the application of the Common European Framework of Reference. The main target groups for the Mercator European Research Centre are professionals, researchers, and policymakers from all member states of the Council of Europe and beyond. In June 2012, the Mercator Centre hosted the 13th International Conference on Language and Social Psychology (ICLASP).

During the first years of its existence, Mercator Education has cooperated with two partners in a network structure: Mercator Media hosted at the University of Wales in Aberystwyth and Mercator Legislation hosted at the Ciemen Foundation in Barcelona. The Mercator European Research Centre has expanded its network in close cooperation with a number of partner organisations working in the same field: the Research Institute for Linguistics of the Academy of Sciences in Budapest, Hungary, and the Mälardalen University in Eskilstuna, Sweden. The network created in this way is introduced in the following section.

The Mercator European Network of Language Diversity Centres

This network connects multilingual communities across Europe, promoting knowledge sharing and facilitating structured exchange of best practice and cutting edge initiatives through its programme of activities. Focus lies on multilingual regions dealing with regional or minority languages, but also immigrant languages and smaller state languages, with emphasis on language needs arising from migration and globalisation.

This network builds on the achievements of the former Mercator Network, which was founded in 1987. The specific topics chosen are: the use of media and information technology, legal provisions with respect to minority language learning, and developments in language teaching and learning. The Mercator Network aims to contribute to improving language vitality by analysing language visibility as well as cultural, economic and social opportunities for language use. The envisaged function of the Network is to be a platform for the exchange of research results, information, experience and good practice in the field of language learning and linguistic diversity. Communication among policy-makers, language planning professionals and those involved in language transfer and teaching will take place in face-to-face meetings at annual conferences and workshops as well as through publications and in online activities. In addition, the Mercator Network aims to be a reference point for these target groups as well as for academics and students by providing accurate and reliable information, which can inform policy development at all levels of government and administration.

The Mercator Network is a member of the European Civil Society Platform on Multilingualism. The platform was created as an initiative of the European Commission in 2009. Almost 30 different networks working in the field of multilingualism are members of this platform. Out of this platform a project called 'Poliglotti4'.eu was initiated. 'Poliglotti4.eu' is a project promoting multilingualism in Europe. Its website reports on best practice in language policy and language learning, and provides policymakers, teachers, learners and civil society organisations with a powerful toolkit for benchmarking and enhancing their activities in non-formal and informal education and learning sectors. The project is funded through the European Commission's Lifelong Learning Programme.

As successful policies need public support, it is also important to inform the public at large of the benefits of linguistic diversity and multilingualism. The Mercator Network's activities can contribute to embracing positive attitudes towards multilingualism within minority and majority language communities. This includes disseminating information on the language-related policies of the European Commission. But above all, it means raising public awareness of language-related issues among speakers and non-speakers of minority and smaller state languages. The focal point is the role of language as an influential factor within social cohesion, economic prosperity and the specificity of regional identity. The Mercator Network's approach is inclusive of immigrant minorities and deaf communities as well as regional and smaller state languages, and mutual understanding and cooperation are key elements in all aspects of the work. Though the emphasis is on academic research, the wider work of institutions responsible for language learning and language use, and the implementation of new teaching and policy models play an important part in the Mercator Network's activities.

Concluding remarks

In Europe there is a growing awareness of the value of linguistic diversity and the need to learn languages. The objective of the Council of Europe and the European Union is that all Europeans learn to speak at least two other languages in addition to their mother tongue. This not only refers to some of the major languages of Europe, such as English, French, German, or Spanish, but also to smaller state languages, immigrant languages, and regional and minority languages. All these languages together create the linguistic diversity of Europe. This characteristic diversity, however, needs to be protected and promoted at all levels. For example, the Province of Friesland, the

Dutch government, and the European commissioner for multilingualism all emphasise the relevance and importance of multilingualism. The Council of Europe stimulates language teaching and learning by means of conferences, projects and comparative studies, whereas the European Union has its own Integrated Lifelong Learning Programme (2007–2013) that explicitly wants to promote language learning and supports linguistic diversity. This creates a clear need for up-to-date information and research.

The Mercator European Research Centre tries to meet this need by participating in developing a multitude of activities ranging from carrying out research projects and making inventories of existing research to conducting comparative studies and providing language dossiers, search engines and articles on regional and minority languages, immigrant and smaller state languages, as well as sign languages. At present the activities of the Mercator Centre take place on a European scale, but there is a growing interest from other parts of the world (Canada, China, Siberia) from where information is requested about possibilities to handle the problems of multilingualism and the safeguarding of minority languages. For this purpose, the Frisian case and the work of the Mercator Centre may present an illustration and a source of inspiration.

References

Beetsma, Danny 2002. *Trilingual Primary Education in Europe. Inventory of the provisions for trilingual primary education in minority language communities of the European Union*. Ljouwert/Leeuwarden: Fryske Akademy.

Bangma, Idske, Cor van der Meer and Alex Riemersma 2011. *Trilingual Primary Education in Europe; Some Developments with Regard to the Provisions of Trilingual Primary Education in Minority Language Communities of the European Union*. Ljouwert/Leeuwarden: Fryske Akademy.

Cenoz, Jasone and Durk Gorter 2005. Trilingualism and Minority Languages in Europe. *International Journal of the Sociology of Language* 171: 1–5.

De Graaf, Tjeerd and Pieter Tiersma 1980. Some Phonetic Aspects of Breaking in West-Frisian. *Phonetica* 37: 109–120.

De Jager, Bernadette and Cor van der Meer 2007. *The Development of Minimum Standards on Language Education in Regional and Minority Languages*. Ljouwert/Leeuwarden: Fryske Akademy.

European Charter for Regional or Minority Languages 1998. *Explanatory Report*. (ETS no. 148). Strasbourg: Council of Europe.

Extra, Guus and Durk Gorter 2008. The Constellation of Languages in Europe: an Inclusive Approach. In *Multilingual Europe: Facts and Policies*, G. Extra and D. Gorter (eds.), 3–60. Berlin: Mouton de Gruyter.

Gorter, Durk 2005. Three Languages of Instruction in Fryslân. *International Journal of the Sociology of Language* 171 (2005): 57–73.

Riemersma, Alex and Sikko de Jong 2007. *Frisian: The Frisian Language in Education in the Netherlands*. Ljouwert: Mercator Education [Regional Dossiers Series]. Online at www.mercator-research.eu.

Tiersma, Pieter M. 1985, 1999. *Frisian Reference Grammar*. Dordrecht: Foris Publications.

Ytsma, Jehannes 2007. Language Use and Language Attitudes in Friesland. In *Multilingualism in European Bilingual Contexts (Language use and attitudes)*, D. Lasagabaster and A. Huguet (eds.), 144–163. Clevedon: Multilingual Matters.

Further information can be found on the following websites about Frisian and other minority languages. Part of this report is based on texts from these websites:

http://www.fryske-akademy.nl
Website of the Frisian Academy

http://www.languages-on-the-web.com/links/link-frisian.htm
General information about Frisian and its relation to other languages

http://www.languageandlaw.org/FRISIAN/FRISIAN.HTM
Web site by the Frisian-American author Pieter Tiersma

http://www.afuk.nl
Cultural institution for education in Frisian

http://www.berneboek.nl
On the first interactive book for children

http://www.mercator-research.eu
Homepage of the Mercator Research Centre. The site contains the series of regional dossiers, the network of schools, a database with organisations and bibliography and many rated links to minority languages

http://www.mercator-network.eu/
The Mercator European Network of Language Diversity Centres and portal for the partners of the network

http://www.networkofschools.org
Website of the Network of Schools, a network of around 100 schools in Europe dealing with regional or minority languages in the curriculum. This network is maintained by the Mercator Research Centre

http://www.eurydice.org
Eurydice is the information network on education in Europe. The site provides information on all European education systems and education policies.

http://www.ethnologue.com
Encyclopedic reference work cataloguing the world's known living languages

http://europa.eu.int/comm/education/langmin.html
At the website of the European Union an explanation is given of its support for regional or minority languages.

http://www.conventions.coe.int/
European Charter for Regional or Minority Languages (1992) and Framework Convention for the Protection of National Minorities (1995) European Treaty Series/Série des traités européens ETS 148 and 157, Strasbourg.
http://www.ogmios.org
Foundation for Endangered Languages

3 THE USE OF SOUND ARCHIVES FOR THE INVESTIGATION, TEACHING AND SAFEGUARDING OF SOME ENDANGERED URALIC LANGUAGES

Victor Denisov and Tjeerd de Graaf

Introduction

In Russia many old sound recordings still remain hidden in archives and in private possession where the quality of preservation is not guaranteed. This review article presents the results of projects on the safeguarding and preservation of sound materials of endangered languages for sound archives in Russia and describes some projects related to these historical recordings, such as the project 'Voices from Tundra and Taiga' (2002–2005). We have made part of these sound materials available and added them to the acoustic database developed with colleagues in the sound archive of the Russian Academy of Sciences in St. Petersburg. The aim of these projects is to re-record the material and safeguard it in storage facilities which will modernize the possible archiving activities in the Russian Federation and bring them up-to-date with the present day world standards of the International Association of Sound Archives (Schüller 2005). In these projects we are concentrating on a selection of recordings of some endangered languages in the Russian Federation, for which documentation is very important. As specific case studies we consider the recovered sound material for a few Uralic languages, in particular Khanty and Udmurt for which historical sound recordings can be found in sound archives in the Russian Federation and abroad. We consider the possibilities how to use these materials for the development of modern learning tools and teaching methods and evaluate the present day situation for the teaching of Udmurt and other languages in the Russian Federation.

Historical data in sound archives and the first related research projects

There is a pressing need to document endangered languages, as many of them can disappear within the next few decades. Language loss leads to the irrevocable loss of the human cultural heritage and it is important to safeguard the world's cultural diversity expressed in the use of many languages. In order to make this possible languages should be well documented and the documentation of linguistic fieldwork from earlier times, which often is hidden in endangered archives, should be saved.

At the time when the first sound recordings of language and folklore were made in Europe, it became obvious that a central facility was needed for the preservation of the valuable data which had been collected. Around the beginning of the 20th century this led to the establishment of sound archives, the earliest and the most important of which was founded in Vienna (1899), soon followed by the foundation of similar institutions in Berlin (1900) and St. Petersburg (1908). In the beginning of the 20th century the phonogram archives of three important European empires (Austria, Germany and Russia) were in regular contact with each other. Due to the political developments in Europe after the Russian revolution these contacts have been interrupted and only at the end of the 20th century new possibilities for joint projects have become possible.

One of the examples for this has been the participation of the Vienna Phonogrammarchiv in various joint European projects, which the second author initiated together with Russian colleagues in the University and the Russian Academy of Sciences in St. Petersburg.

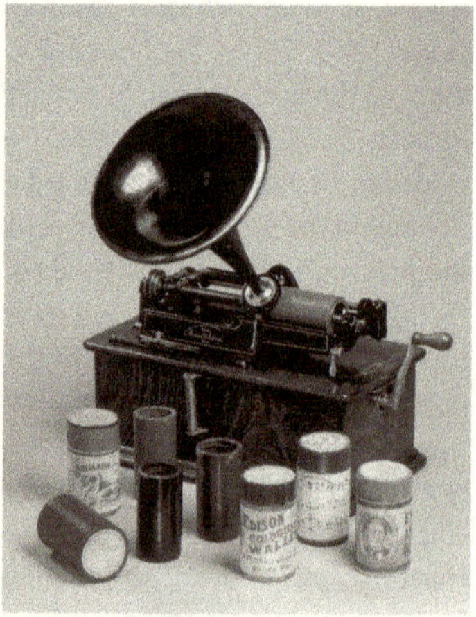

|5| The collection of wax cylinders in the Pushkinsky Dom.
|6| Edison-Home-Phonograph (about 1905) with a collection of wax cylinders from the Berliner Phonogramm-Archiv.

The sound archive of the Russian Academy of Sciences, located nowadays in the Institute of Russian Literature (the Pushkinsky Dom) in St. Petersburg contains more than 6,000 wax cylinders of the Edison phonograph (see *Figure 6*) and 350 old wax discs. In addition, an extensive fund of gramophone records exists and one of the largest collections of tape-recordings of Russian folklore. These represent the history of Russian ethnography and contain a wide range of materials (De Graaf 2001, 2002). Many of these recordings form one of the basic collections used in joint projects with the Pushkinsky Dom in which the authors participated. The first of these projects on 'The Use of Acoustic Data Bases in the Study of Language Change' (1995–1998) has been financially supported by the organisation INTAS of the European Union in Brussels. In a second INTAS project, 'St. Petersburg Sound Archives on the World

Wide Web' (1998–2001) part of the sound recordings have been placed on the internet and are now available for further study (De Graaf 2004). For both projects, the Phonogrammarchiv of the Austrian Academy of Sciences was partner and responsible for the technical aspects. In this way the Russian archive obtained the newest reconstruction technique and could use the experience of the Austrian colleagues, who have a leading position in this field.

For our third INTAS project on 'The Construction of a Full-text Database on Balto-Finnic languages and Russian dialects in Northwest-Russia' (2000–2003) we prepared an inventory of the Finno-Ugric minority languages in the vicinity of St. Petersburg and the southern and middle parts of Karelia. The phonogram archive in St. Petersburg also contains important sound material on Yiddish, the language of the Jews in Eastern Europe, which at the beginning of the 20th century was used by millions of speakers in the Russian empire. Together with specialists in St. Petersburg, we further explored the related acoustic data in the sound archive. This took place in the framework of a project with the title 'Voices from the Shtetl, the Past and Present of the Yiddish Language in Russia' (1998–2001), for which we have obtained financial support from the Netherlands Foundation for Scientific Research NWO (De Graaf, Kleiner and Svetozarova 2004). We also completed a study on the language of the Siberian Mennonites and other colonial Germanic dialects in the Russian empire (De Graaf 2008).

In the following sections we describe in more detail some projects, which can be considered as a continuation of the earlier reconstruction work of historical sound recordings.

|7| The Pushkinsky Dom

Voices from Tundra and Taiga

Important activities related to linguistic databases in St. Petersburg concern the recordings of Russian dialects and minority languages in Northern regions of the Russian Federation (De Graaf 2004). Within the framework of the research program 'Voices from Tundra and Taiga' the Netherlands Foundation for Scientific Research (NWO) financially supported our joint work in the period 2002–2005. We combined the data from old sound recordings with the results of modern fieldwork, in order to give a description of the languages and cultures of ethnic groups in Russia. We studied endangered Arctic languages and cultures of the Russian Federation, which must be described rapidly before they become extinct (De Graaf 2004). One of the results of these projects is a catalogue of the sound recordings related to the Peoples of the North in Russia, which can be found in the Phonogram Archive of the Pushkinsky Dom (Burykin et al. 2005)

|8| Catalogue of the sound collections for the project 'Voices from Tundra and Taiga'

In these projects the reconstruction techniques of the earlier projects are applied to the historical sound recordings of some of the disappearing minority languages of Russia, such as Nivkh (Gilyak) and Uilta (Orok) on Sakhalin and Yukagir and Tungusic languages in Yakutia. Our goal is to set up an audio- and video-library of recorded stories, and of the folklore, singing and oral traditions of the peoples of Sakhalin and Yakutia. Thus the existing sound recordings in the archives of Sakhalin and Yakutia will be complemented by the results of new fieldwork expeditions. The copies of data obtained are added to the existing archive material in local centres and in St. Petersburg and part of it is made available on the internet and on CD-ROM.

This research project and the related documentation is carried out in close co-operation with scholars in local administrative centres such as Yuzhno-Sakhalinsk who participate in the archiving of the sound recordings and in fieldwork expeditions. These scholars were trained at St. Petersburg State University, and specialists from St. Petersburg and the Netherlands also visit them in order to start new centres for the study and teaching of local languages and related subjects. For this purpose we organised a special seminar for Nivkh teachers in Yuzhno-Sakhalinsk in October 2003 (De Graaf and Shiraishi 2004).

The results of modern fieldwork and the reconstructed data from sound archives as far as they are of satisfactory quality provide important information for the preparation of language descriptions, grammars, dictionaries and edited collections of oral and written literature. A particular aspect of further work will be the phonetic analysis of speech sounds in these recordings and the possible diachronic research on language change. The recordings can also be used to develop teaching methods, in particular for the younger members of certain ethnic groups, who do not have sufficient knowledge of their native language and who want to learn about their culture. Details about the data obtained will become available on the internet and provide a possibility for the exchange of information with other institutions all over the world. This global collaboration will make it possible to learn more about the cultures and languages of the peoples of Russia and it can also provide new methods of teaching these topics. In this way our projects contribute to the documentation and to the preservation of Russia's cultural heritage.

In the following sections we consider special case studies for two other languages, which resulted from our projects, namely about Khanty and Udmurt.

The historical sound recordings of Khanty by Wolfgang Steinitz

In 1935 the German researcher Wolfgang Steinitz – who at that time was working at the Institute for the Peoples of the North in Leningrad – was able to make a fieldwork trip to Siberia in order to investigate the language and folklore of the Khanty people, whose language belongs to the Ugric branch of the Finno-Ugric language family and is related to Hungarian. The scientific results of this study trip have been published by Steinitz in his *Bericht an das Institut für Nordvölker (INS) über eine Studienreise in den Kreis der Ostjaken und Wogulen im Jahre 1935* and in the diary about this expedition (Steinitz 1980). In these documents Wolfgang Steinitz describes the use of a phonograph and the material he has recorded, indicating the number on the wax cylinders, the place of the recordings and their contents (Swetosarowa 2006).

In 1937, during the time of repression Steinitz was forced to leave the Soviet Union and he went to Sweden. He was allowed to take most of his fieldwork data and other scientific material with him, except the phonographic cylinders. Until recently it has been assumed that these early sound recordings of the Khanty language had been lost and were possibly destroyed in Leningrad during the war. However, during our joint project work in the phonogram archive of the Institute of Russian Literature (Pushkinsky Dom) in St. Petersburg we learnt that the sound material of Khanty made by Steinitz is kept as a separate collection in the archive.

In this collection one can find 30 wax cylinders, whereas Steinitz mentions 31 items in his written account of the expedition. These recordings have been documented and copied on analogue tapes, but somehow his collection of recordings passed into oblivion. This can be explained by the fact that since its establishment very little information about the rich collection of the St. Petersburg Phonogram Archive could be found in the open literature and only recently this has become available as a result of the research project 'Voices from Tundra and Taiga' (Burykin et al. 2005, Swetosarowa 2006). The only published complete inventory of the phonogram archive has been prepared by Sophia Magid in 1936 (Magid 1936) and there the Steinitz collection is not yet represented. Initially this collection was taken to the Institute for the Peoples of the North and from there later to the Folklore Section of the Institute for Anthropology and Ethnography.

In 2005, within the framework of the international project 'Voices from Tundra und Taiga' the earlier mentioned catalogue of the recorded materials from the Peoples of the North in the Russian Federation has been published (Burykin et al. 2005). Here the Steinitz recordings are described under number 127 as phonographic cylinders with sound material from the Khanty (Ostyaks) in Siberia, which were made in 1935 by Wolfgang Steinitz (1905–1967) and obtained from the Institute of the Peoples of the North in Leningrad. These 30 wax cylinders contain all together 44 sound recordings, mostly songs such as bear songs, two fairy tales, four shaman performances, etc.

To the Steinitz sound material corresponds a document from the collection of manuscripts in the phonogram archive which provides a preliminary description of the material from the expedition. This list, which is probably produced by Steinitz himself, allows a more precise specification of the sound recordings and their contents. It has been one of the tasks of the project 'Voices from Tundra und Taiga' to add many important details to the separate sound documents. In this way the book which has been published as a result of this project (Burykin et al. 2005) could be completed with a database on CD-ROM which contains copies of the original recordings together with all relevant data (title, kind of recording, place and time, informant, tone quality, duration). Together with the Steinitz recordings other important data have been described in this publication and specimens of texts and sound examples have also been provided on CD-ROM for the work of other important scholars like Shternberg, Shirokogoroff, Bogoraz and Magid.

From the available data some interesting historical facts could be reconstructed about the adventures of Steinitz during his stay in the Soviet Union and his fieldwork experience. He started the recordings with his informants on the day after his arrival in the Khanty village Lokhtotkurt in July 1935. About this fact he makes the following note in his diary:

> "Abends kommt Matvej Kitvurov, Musikant .... Er bringt sein Instrument ... Spielt 'Programmusik' ... ich will Aufnahme machen: Wir schicken die Kinder raus, ich stelle den Phonographen genau ein (100 Drehungen) ...
> [In the evening arrives Matvej Kitvurov, musician ... He brings his instrument and ... Plays 'program music' ... I want to make recordings: We send the children outside, I switch on the phonograph exactly (100 rotations) ...]."

In collection 127 this recording of 31 July 1935 has the cylinder number 4080. The expedition to the Khanty people was originally planned for a period of six months, but probably due to the political situation in the Soviet Union it was shortened to less than three months and at the end of his stay Steinitz had to hurry to the last boat. In his diary (Steinitz 1980) one can read:

> "Kann leider Arbeit nicht beenden ... Bis ¾ 8 Uhr gearbeitet, dann alles liegen lassen, zu einer Sitzung im Pedtechnikum gelaufen ... Los, über den Berg nach Samarov, zum letzten Dampfer.
> [Unfortunately I cannot finish the job ... Until 7:45 I have been working, then I left everything behind, hurried to a session of the pedagogical technical college ... Then in a hurry, across the mountain to Samarov, to the last steamboat]."

The result of the project 'Voices from Tundra and Taiga' will allow a further comparison of the acoustic database with texts of this diary and provide the possibility to learn about the way Steinitz has been working with Khanty informants in a difficult period of Soviet history and has been able to contribute to the field of Finno-Ugric studies in a very important way (for more details see Swetosarowa 2006).

Sources of Finno-Ugric language and folklore

During the realization of the project 'Safeguarding and Preservation of Sound Materials of Endangered Languages in the Russian Federation for Sound Archives in St. Petersburg' in the years 2006–2008 we became familiar with a number of historical linguistic and folklore collections in the Phonogram Archive of the Institute of Russian Literature (Pushkinsky Dom) belonging to the cultural heritage of the Finno-Ugric peoples (Denisov 2008, De Graaf and Denisov 2008). It is known that the total number of the population speaking Finno-Ugric languages (a branch of the Uralic language family) is approximately 25 million and most of these languages beside Hungarian, Finnish and Estonian are located in the Russian Federation.

We managed to consult the catalogues of the Phonogram Archive of the Pushkinsky Dom in order to determine a number of recordings belonging to the above mentioned Finno-Ugric peoples (Burykin et al. 2005):

Estonian – 3 collections;
Karelian, Vepsian and Finnish (Ingrian) – 8 collections;
Khanty – 5 collections;
Komi – 9 collections;
Mansi – 5 collections;
Mordvinian – 5 collections;
Mari – 5 collections;
Udmurt – 5 collections.

The Udmurt collections which in 1929–1940 had been collected during linguistic and ethnological expeditions to the territory of Udmurtia by well-known collectors and researchers such as Kuzebai Gerd, J. A. Eshpai, M. P. Petrov, V. A. Pchelnikov and

Z. V. Evald have attracted our special attention. These collections include 320 phonograph recordings, which in the 1980s were rerecorded onto analogue magnetic tapes. With the help of sound engineers of the Pushkinsky Dom these Udmurt collections were digitized, whereas also the corresponding written archival materials were scanned. Udmurt sound recordings jointly with the hand-written documents are still of a great interest for experts in the field of Finno-Ugric folklore and linguistics in Udmurtia and abroad.

In Izhevsk, the capital of the Republic of Udmurtia, there are quite a few other important Udmurt linguistic and folklore collections which after the 1950s were recorded onto analogue magnetic tapes and cassette tapes. These collections are mainly located in the two leading scientific and educational institutions: in the Udmurt State University and in the Udmurt Institute of History, Language and Literature of the Russian Academy of Sciences (Ural Branch). For example, in the Udmurt Institute of History, Language and Literature the estimated size of these sound collections is given as about 600 hours which is stored on about 1,000 cassette tapes and open reel tapes. The contents of these tapes is related to linguistic and folklore data of Udmurt, Mari and other regional languages. Taking into consideration the deteriorating analogue sound carriers (open reel and cassette tapes) and the poor conservation conditions we suggest that these sound recordings should be collected and digitized according to the demands and regulations of the International Association of Sound Archives (IASA) (Schüller 2005).

In 2008 we completed the research project 'Safeguarding and Preservation of Sound Materials of Endangered Languages in the Russian Federation for Sound Archives in St. Petersburg', which has been financially supported by a grant from the Endangered Archives Programme at the British Library in London, sponsored by Arcadia, with reference number EAP 089. As a follow-up we received a new grant in 2010 for the project EAP 347 on 'Vanishing Voices from the Uralic World: Sound recordings for archives in Russia (in particular Udmurtia), Estonia, Finland and Hungary'. One of the project partners in this project is the Tartu Folklore Archive (Estonian Literary Museum) in Estonia. Its members play a role as advisors and have a good experience with the organisation of storage facilities, technical equipment and standards of digitization in accordance with the IASA principles (Schüller 2005).

In 2012 we shall finish the reconstruction of the Udmurt material in the Udmurt Institute for History, Language and Literature of the Ural Branch of the Russian Academy of Sciences in Izhevsk (Udmurtia). After the EAP 347 project period (2010–12) the sound recordings in the Udmurt archives will become available for research and for other purposes, such as in teaching facilities. In this project it is our aim to make a selection of a large part of this collection, digitize the selected tapes and store the items on digital hard discs which will be kept in the archive and also sent to other archives where colleagues are interested in this material. Specimens on CD will be on request provided to scholars who do research in a particular field of the Uralic languages and cultures. According to the rules of the British Library the material will be available in open access, not only in St. Petersburg, but also in one of the peripheral institutions, where the conservation conditions will be updated. It is very important that in this way the data will become available for general use. This will provide an example for the policy of sound archives in all parts of the Russian Federation and contribute to the safeguarding of the cultural heritage of this country.

The Udmurt language in the Russian Federation and education in Udmurt

At present national education in the Udmurt Republic functions within the framework of two international legal documents, the Universal Declaration of Human Rights and the Convention of Children's Rights as well as on the basis of the 1992 Educational Law of the Russian Federation. Chapter 2 of this law considers the unification principle for the culture and education, and the protection and development of national cultures and regional traditions in the multinational state. Chapter 6 of the same law determines that the citizens of the Russian Federation have the right to use their native language in the sphere of education.

All these above mentioned documents facilitate the principle ability of citizens of the Russian Federation who belong to ethnic and language minorities or indigenous populations to use their mother tongue, to learn about their culture and to obtain education related to this culture. Nevertheless, in many national regions of the Russian Federation, including the Finno-Ugric Republics the situation is quite complicated with respect to the preservation of national culture, traditions, language and folklore as well as to the education in the native languages. This situation is also determined by economical and political factors, by the demographic situation in the republics and by the so-called 'optimization of schools', the decreasing number of primary and secondary schools in small rural settlements. But just in these rural areas the native languages are more extensively used, because there still exist a good environment for the language and its use in local communication. Even in schools in the countryside the teaching of the native languages is limited to 2–4 hours per week and at the same time there are insufficient contemporary teaching and teacher training methods available for its maintenance.

In the Finno-Ugric Republics of the Russian Federation a great deal of the native children has no possibility to get school education in the language of their nationality. This happens in spite of the existence of numerous acts of legislation devoted to the development of the minority language and culture as well as the existence of officially adopted declarations about state national politics on the federal and regional level. Unfortunately the majority of these acts of legislation have only a declarative character and the reality is not in accordance with these declarations. As a demonstration of the real situation the following facts and figures can be given: between the years 1989 and

2003 the percentage of Udmurt people in the population of Udmurtia has diminished from 30,9% to 29,3 % (in absolute figures: from 714,800 to 636,900). Within the same period of time the total number of Udmurt people who still actively use their mother tongue has diminished from 460,580 to 330,800 (which is a decrease to 71,2 %). This means that the process of language loss takes place much faster than the diminution of the Udmurt population in general. At the same time the number of pupils with education of the Udmurt language is also decreasing from 31,240 in 1990 to 22,100 in 2006.

During this period an unfavourable situation also occurred with respect to the printing of books and newspapers. For this one can compare the following figures: in 1990 Udmurt newspaper circulation amounted to 100,000 copies, but in 2007 it amounted to only 20,000. During the same period of time the number of book publications per year reduced to only 11 books with less than 50,000 copies. The last years have also seen a decrease in time for the broadcast of TV and radio programs in the Udmurt language.

In the Udmurt Republic the 'Legislation Act on Popular Education' was accepted on December 19, 1995. Since then this Act started to stimulate innovation processes on all levels of the national education. New educational institutions were created (gymnasiums, lyceums, colleges), which accepted modern innovative principles like a variety of different subjects, a specific approach to the pedagogical activity, a new content of the educational process, etc. Teachers started to create their own specific programs for separate subjects with the use of information technology. For example, in one of the districts of the Udmurt Republic – in the Malopurginky district, about 40 national and regional programs of this kind have been developed. Unfortunately all these programs could not be coordinated by a single educational institution or municipality, which might improve their low level and limited quality. Until 1996 it was not possible to bring these programs up-to-date with modern ideas within a special central scientific research institution.

It is important to point out that since then the authorities of the Udmurt Republic have started to realize the necessity of changes in the national schools with unification efforts for the teaching and development of special manuals and other educational facilities. In December 1996, a special Institution, the Scientific Research Institute of National Education for the Udmurt Republic was opened in Izhevsk. This institute got the task to provide scientific and methodological support of the educational process in the schools of present-day Udmurtia. First of all the Institute organised several solid investigations into the problems and needs of ethnocultural education in the Udmurt Republic. Within the following 10 years four investigations have been organised among the Udmurt population.

These investigations revealed that the majority of informants support the idea that the national language should be a basic element for the unification of the Udmurt people. Beside that, the feeling of a common origin is also considered to be a uniting factor for the Udmurt population. Nevertheless the results of the investigations show that at the present time there is a serious crisis in relation to the national self-identification of the Udmurt people. It is in particular important to indicate the resulting answers to the question: "What is your attitude to your nationality and to the problem of preservation of your mother tongue and culture?" Practically all representatives from the older generation showed their positive attitude towards their Udmurt nationality. Beside this another tendency can be found: the younger the respondents, the higher the percentage of Udmurt people with an indifferent attitude towards their own nationality. This fact reveals a serious tendency of 'ethno-nihilism', where people become indifferent towards the Udmurt culture in Udmurtia. This tendency is not only typical in the Udmurt Republic. Such a kind of 'language nihilism (indifference)' of a certain – mainly young – part of the indigenous population is quite characteristic for other small nations of the Russian Federation. According to the census data in the Russian Federation obtained in 1989 about 50 % of the Karelians, 40 % of the Bashkir, Komi, Mordva and Udmurt and 20–25 % of the Tatar, Mari, Chuvash and Yakut do not regard the language of their nationality as their own language, most of the time they use the Russian language. During the period from 1970 until 1989 the number of such representatives among small nations who don't have command of their national language doubled (*Sociolinguistic Encyclopedia* 2000). This tendency is still an active process going on in spite of some increasing interest towards the national language and culture.

At present the language situation in the Udmurt Republic causes a certain anxiety among the experts. The point is that 35 % of the Udmurt pupils regard Russian as their native language, whereas the same tendency is typical for their parents as well. When using the Russian language in everyday life, the Udmurt nevertheless still consider themselves as having Udmurt identity according to their origin, family ties and culture. But this situation can last for at most one or two generations, after which people will be more and more assimilated into the Russian nationality. With the loss of the mother tongue the Udmurt people cease to think in their native language and in the future there will be an inevitable loss of Udmurt consciousness and mentality. Only the preservation and revitalisation of the native language can stabilize the current language situation in the Udmurt Republic as well as in other areas with national minorities of the Russian Federation.

For the preservation and revitalisation of native languages it is necessary to use a set of measures including the improvement of educational methods and teacher training courses. The policy of the state should be realistic and rational towards the native language and create positive conditions for the improvement of national self-consciousness of the Udmurt people. The introduction and use of multimedia will play an important role in this process.

As it was mentioned before, one of the most important conditions for the preservation and revitalisation of the Udmurt language is the attitude of Udmurt people towards their native culture. From our experience we are aware of the fact that the availability of numerous publications and wide public presentation of historical recordings with the native language and folklore from different sound archives provokes great interest and even a certain pride among the native people of Udmurtia. Such archival recordings could be used for educational purposes and constitute an integral part of study books for Udmurt on DV-discs or other means of modern information and communication technologies. All these measures can make the representatives of the indigenous people (including local politicians and *intelligentsia*) understand the importance of the preservation of minority languages and cultures in the Russian Federation and its role in the world's cultural heritage.

Final remarks

The earlier research project EAP089 on 'Reconstruction of Sound Materials of Endangered Languages in the Russian Federation for Sound Archives in St. Petersburg', which was financially supported by the Endangered Archives Programme of the British Library, has been the first project in the Russian Federation where the recommendations of the International Association of Sound Archives in the reports IASA-TC 03 and IASA-TC 04 have been taken into account. The new digital copies from private collections have enriched the phonogram archive of the Pushkinsky Dom, whereas other copies were also provided to the British Library, the St. Petersburg Institute for Linguistic Studies, the Vienna Phonogrammarchiv and to the scholars, who produced the original recordings and who will now be able to do further research with digital techniques.

At present the main problems for most Russian sound archives are related to the lack of financial support and technical specialists for the preservation and description of the collections. Moreover, there are no good local standards for this work and there is not sufficient exchange between the archives and support from outside Russia. The access of interested persons to the collections should be improved and a national program for the support of these archives should be developed. In the future we hope to further convince the authorities in other Russian institutions with important sound archives (such as the one in Izhevsk) that work in this field should be in agreement with the IASA requirements and the recommendations of UNESCO and that sufficient financial support for this purpose should become available. In order to attract the attention of Russian technicians and scientists to the IASA principles staff members of the EAP089 project have prepared a Russian translation of the IASA report *The Safeguarding of the Audio Heritage: Ethics, Principles and Preservation Strategy*, which has been published on the IASA website (see: www.iasa-web.org/downloads/publications/TC03_Russian.pdf).

It is important that sound archives in the Russian Federation join the International Association of Sound Archives. When in Russia up-to-date sound archives will be available with experienced technical personal and sufficient financial support, they can also play a useful role in the IASA and arrange their policy according to the accepted world standards, such as for the general access to the archived material and the ways to obtain copies of it. The availability in Russia of sound archives with the most up-to-date technical facilities will be of utmost importance, providing a source of historical linguistic material for linguists specializing in the languages spoken by minorities in the Russian Federation.

On the basis of this material it will be possible to develop special techniques and educational methods for the minority languages of Russia. Many of these languages are endangered and it is important to obtain all existing sound materials and to make new recordings of speakers of these languages. In this way joint international projects will further contribute to the documentation and the preservation of the world's important cultural heritage. This holds in particular for the safeguarding and documentation of endangered minority languages in the Russian Federation.

References

Burykin, Aleksei, Albina Girfanova, Aleksandr Kastrov, Yuri Marchenko and Natalia Svetozarova 2005. *Kollektsii Narodov Severa v Fonogrammarkhive Pushkinskogo Doma.* [Collections on the Peoples of the North in the Phonogram Archive of the Pushkinskii Dom]. Faculty of Philology, University of St. Petersburg.

Denisov, Victor 2008. Zapisi Udmurtskogo Yazyka i Folklora v Fonogrammarkhive Instituta Russkoi Literatury (Pushkinskii Dom). In *Rossiia i Udmurtiia: Istoriia i Sovremennost'* [Recordings of the Udmurt Language and Folklore in the Phonogram Archive of the Institute of the Russian literature (Pushkinskii Dom). Russia and Udmurtia: History and Present], 879–884. Izhevsk.

De Graaf, Tjeerd 2001. Data on the Languages of Russia from Historical Documents, Sound Archives and Fieldwork Expeditions. In *Recording and Restoration of Minority Languages, Sakhalin Ainu and Nivkh,* Murasaki, K. (ed.), 13–37. ELPR report. Suita, Osaka.

— 2002. The Use of Sound Archives in the Study of Endangered Languages. In *Music Archiving in the World, Papers Presented at the Conference on the Occasion of the 100th Anniversary of the Berlin Phonogramm Archiv,* 101–107. Berlin.

— 2004. Voices from Tundra and Taiga: Endangered Languages of Russia on the Internet. In *Lectures on Endangered Languages: 5 - Endangered Languages of the Pacific Rim C005,* Sakiyama, Osamu and Fubito Endo (eds.), 143–169. Suita, Osaka.

— 2008. Dutch in the Steppe? The Plautdietsch Language of the Siberian Mennonites and their Relation with the Netherlands, Germany and Russia. In *Proceedings of the IXth International Conference of the Foundation for Endangered Languages,* 23–31. Stellenbosch, South Africa.

De Graaf, Tjeerd, Yuri Kleiner and Natalia Svetozarova 2004. Yiddish in St. Petersburg: The Last Sounds of a Language. In *Proceedings of the Conference "Klezmer, Klassik, jiddisches Lied. Jüdische Musik-Kultur in Osteuropa"*, 205–221. Wiesbaden: Harrassowitz Verlag.

De Graaf, Tjeerd and Hidetoshi Shiraishi 2004. Capacity Building for some Endangered Languages of Russia: Voices from Tundra and Taiga. In *Language Documentation and Description, Vol. 2, The Hans Rausing Endangered Languages Project*, 15–26. London: School of Oriental and African Studies.

De Graaf, Tjeerd and Victor Denisov 2008. Sokhranenie Zvukovogo Naslediia Narodov Udmurtskoi Respubliki: Opyt Vedushchikh Zvukovykh Arkhivov Mira. [Preservation of the Sound Heritage of the Peoples of the Udmurt Republic: Experience of the World's leading Archives]. In *Rossiia i Udmurtiia: istoriia i sovremennost'.* [Russia and Udmurtia: History and Present], 866–878. Izhevsk.

Magid, Sofia 1936. Spisok Sobranii Fonogramarkhiva Folklornoi Sektsii IAE Akademii Nauk SSSR [List of the Collections in the Phonogram Archive of the Folklore Section of the Institute for Anthropology and Ethnographics, Academy of Sciences of the USSR]. *Sovetskii Folklor* 4–5: 415–428.

Schüller, Dietrich (ed.) 2005. *The Safeguarding of the Audio Heritage: Ethics, Principles and Preservation Strategy, IASA Technical Committee - Standards, Recommended Practices and Strategies, IASA-TC 03.* (Russian Translation by Victor Denisov and Natalia Svetozarova)

Sociolinguistic Encyclopedia 2000. *The Written Languages of the World: The Russian Federation. The Sociolinguistic Encyclopedia*. Moscow.

Steinitz, Wolfgang 1980. *Ostjakologische Arbeiten*. Band 4: Beiträge zur Sprachwissenschaft und Ethnographie, 433–435 and 397–432. Den Haag.

Swetosarowa, Natalia 2006. Verschollen geglaubte Feldforschungsaufnahmen. Zur Sammlung Wolfgang Steinitz im Phonogrammarchiv St. Petersburg. In *Die Entdeckung des Sozialkritischen Liedes. Zum 100. Geburtstag von Wolfgang Steinitz.* J. Eckhard (Hrsg.), 49–60. Münster: Waxmann Verlag.

4 DOCUMENTATION AND REVITALISATION OF TWO ENDANGERED LANGUAGES IN EASTERN ASIA: NIVKH AND AINU

Tjeerd de Graaf and Hidetoshi Shiraishi

Introduction

This article draws a comparison between two adjacent ethnic groups, namely the Ainu of Hokkaido and the Nivkh of Sakhalin. We shall follow the historical development of the border areas between Japan and Russia and describe the prevailing situation of these aboriginal peoples on both sides of the border. The legal measures taken by the Japanese government for the promotion of Ainu culture and the development of learning tools have consequences for the Ainu community and the possible revitalisation of the Ainu language.

The Nivkh community within the Russian Federation is a typical example of the multitude of ethnic minority groups spread across this vast territory. The Ainu case can be compared and used as a model for possible (legal) measures to be taken regarding minority languages and cultures such as Nivkh with an outlook for future improvement. We shall consider the use of new media for these native communities and pay attention to the development of adequate modern learning tools and culturally related teaching methods. Various options are considered, starting with such basic ones as organising language courses and arranging other language-related activities.

Historical Background

In the 17th and 18th centuries, the homelands of the Ainu and the Nivkh northeast of Japan were little known and stories about this northern border area were so contradictory that European cartographers were unable to record its position correctly. Some portrayed Hokkaido (then called *Ezo* or *Matsumae*) linked to Sakhalin as a huge separate island, others as a continuation of the Japanese mainland. Some joined it to Asia, others even to the North American continent. Before the arrival of the Japanese, the Russians and other people from Europe, little information was available about the original inhabitants.

After having settled on the island of Deshima at the beginning of the 17th century, the Dutch began to play an important role in Japan. The Japanese enabled them to introduce European culture and science, and they became active in establishing contacts between the Japanese and the outside world. This was also the case in the relations of Japan with Russia and in the exploration of the territories north of Japan (De Graaf 1993, De Graaf and Naarden 2007). One of the Europeans who contributed to the discovery of these territories was the Frisian sailor Maerten Gerritszoon de Vries (Robert 1975, Witsen 1705). He was the first European to explore Hokkaido, the Kurile Islands and Sakhalin, and to draw a map of this region during his voyage in 1643. During his trip, De Vries came into contact with the local Ainu population. Another Dutchman, Nicolaas Witsen, described in his book (Witsen 1705) the voyage of De Vries together with abundant information about the peoples of Northeast Asia, their history, natural environment, culture, language and way of life. An interdisciplinary team of specialists prepared a Russian translation of this book and considered its various aspects: history, ethnology, linguistics, geography, etc. (De Graaf and Naarden 2007). This publication was launched in St. Petersburg in October 2010.

After further discoveries and expeditions to this part of the world, its geographic situation became better known and it was found in the beginning of the 19th century that the Ainu people lived on Hokkaido, the Kurile Islands and the southern half of Sakhalin, whereas the Nivkh were their northern neighbours on Sakhalin and the nearby continent. These peoples occupied an area rich in natural resources with abundant deer and salmon. Their culture was based on hunting, fishing and gathering edible plants, and a spiritual relationship with phenomena of the natural world, for the Ainu personified as *kamuy*, deities. The Ainu and Nivkh people originally did not have a written language but they had a very rich orally transmitted literature which included tales and legends, which expressed the experiences and morals of everyday life from generation to generation. We shall first elaborate on the situation of the Ainu.

The Ainu in Japan

Originally the northern part of the Japanese main island Honshu was inhabited by Ainu people, whereas there are indications that they also lived on the southern tip of Kamchatka. Traces of the Ainu on Honshu are found in geographic names, but as a result of historical developments they also disappeared from Sakhalin and the Kurile Islands (De Graaf 2004b).

In the sixteenth century many Japanese immigrants began to settle on Hokkaido and to engage in large scale fishing and trading. The Japanese area (*Wajinchi*) was located in the southern part of the island (Matsumae), while the Ainu people lived in the areas called *Ezochi*: the rest of Hokkaido (the name of the island since 1868), *Karafuto* (Sakhalin) and *Chishima* (Kurile Islands). The southern Kuril islands of Etorofu and Kunashiri are at the moment disputed territories between Japan and Russia. Their original inhabitants were also the Ainu and the first map of these islands was made by Maarten Gerritsz de Vries and published by Witsen in his book *Noord en Oost Tartarye* (De Graaf and Naarden 2007; Witsen 1705).

The growing influence of the Japanese immigrants and the fact that the Ainu were forced to work for them gave rise to a number of wars, which the Ainu lost. After the battle of *Kunashiri-Menashi* in 1789, the Tokugawa Shogunate (Japanese government) gained direct control over the southern half of Ezo, and in 1807 it extended this control to the northern areas. On Hokkaido the Ainu fell completely under the control of the Japanese, who claimed these territories as part of Japan, in this way resisting the growing influence of Russia from the north. In 1854, at the signing of the border treaty of *Shimoda* between Russia and Japan, it was decided that the boundary would be set between the islands of Etorofu and Uruppu (on Russian maps the *Proliv Friza* = Strait of De Vries) and that Sakhalin would be made into an ethnically mixed territory. The text of the treaty was written in Dutch (which at that time was the European language most used in Japan) with translations into Japanese and Russian. In 1875, a new border treaty was concluded in St. Petersburg, where Sakhalin became Russian territory and the Kurile Islands part of Japan. Afterwards a large number of Ainu from Sakhalin had to relocate to Hokkaido. They suffered from the abrupt change in lifestyle and the prevalence of diseases, and many of them died. In later times various other forced resettlements of the Ainu would follow and the result is that their number has decreased and that at present they can only be found in Japan, mainly on Hokkaido.

During the Meiji era (1868–1912), under a government policy of assimilation, the Ainu were oppressed and exploited by the Japanese. The modernisation of Japan caused the central government to pay serious attention to the exploration and economic development of Hokkaido. For this purpose the Hokkaido Settlement Mission (*Kaitakushi*) was established as an administrative organisation to rule the region, and a large number of former samurai and farmers emigrated from the Japanese mainland to Hokkaido. *Ainu mosir* ('the people's land'), where the Ainu had freely hunted and gathered food, became part of the territory of Japan and was given to Japanese immigrants.

The Meiji government forced the Ainu to assimilate, whereas the *Kaitakushi* prohibited the traditional way of hunting and fishing, and confiscated their lands. Under state-sponsored assimilation policies, discrimination and poverty relegated the Ainu to the lowest ranks of Japanese society. With the introduction of the Japanese way of life and special compulsory education, the traditional system of learning from one's elders was broken down and the original social and cultural patterns of the Ainu population were destroyed. As a consequence, the Ainu language, together with the traditional lifestyle almost completely disappeared within a couple of generations (Siddle 1996).

According to a survey conducted in 2006 by the Hokkaido government, the Ainu population of Hokkaido then numbered 23,782 people (Hokkaido 2006). Many Ainu and people of mixed origin were eager to forget about their Ainu origin and until the present there are many of them who fear discrimination and prefer to hide this origin. Therefore it is rather difficult to estimate the right number of people having the Ainu ethnic background. At present, the number of Ainu living mainly in Hokkaido is estimated at between 24,000 and 50,000, but only very few of them still speak the language.

Laws and linguistic rights for the Ainu

The Ainu have lived in Hokkaido, Sakhalin, the Kurile Islands and Honshu since ancient times, and have built their own history, language and culture. When the Meiji government enforced its law in Hokkaido, it incorporated the land of the Ainu, basically confiscating their land, forcing assimilation policies, and denying the Ainu people their traditional culture. In this process, discrimination and prejudice toward the Ainu were strengthened. In 1899, the 'Hokkaido Aborigine Protection Act' was passed. This act primarily aimed to provide relief for the Ainu and help them become engaged in agriculture. However, it referred to the Ainu as 'former aborigines', which gave rise to further discrimination.

In 1946, at the Hokkaido Ainu Convention in Shizunai, Hokkaido, the Hokkaido Ainu Association was established with the aim to provide better education for the Ainu and to create social welfare facilities. In 1961, the association changed its name to the Hokkaido *Utari Kyookai* (Association). In April 2009, the association changed its name to The Ainu Association of Hokkaido (*Hokkaido Ainu Kyookai*). This association is actively engaged in solving various problems experienced by the Ainu. (see www.ainu-assn.or.jp). In 1984, the Hokkaido *Utari Kyookai* (Association) proposed that the government should introduce a new law which would replace the Hokkaido Aborigine Protection Act. Since then, the association has conducted an active campaign to demand that the national government enact this law as soon as possible. Furthermore, various activities have been promoted to revive the Ainu language and to preserve and maintain Ainu culture, such as traditional dancing and various ceremonies.

During the preparation of this new legislation many controversial problems had to be solved. The original draft, submitted by the Hokkaido prefectural government and the Ainu Association, has been changed by the Japanese government in such a way that, to the regret of several Ainu representatives, it does not mention the rights of the Ainu as an indigenous people anymore, which would allow for the provisions related to the United Nations' Declaration for the Rights of Indigenous Peoples (Dietz 1999). However, in this 'Law on the Promotion of Ainu Culture and Facilitation of Popular Understanding of Ainu Tradition' the Japanese government acknowledges for the first time the existence of a separate ethnic group inside the country and calls for respect of its culture and traditions. This is a change in attitude compared to the year 1986, when Prime Minister Nakasone stated that "Japan is a racially homogeneous nation and there is no discrimination against ethnic minorities with Japanese citizenship".

The Ainu then have become an internationally recognised indigenous population. In July 1997 the Japanese government finally introduced the *Ainu Shinpo* (New Ainu Law) and abolished the 1899 Hokkaido Aborigine Protection Act (Tsunemoto 1999). The purpose of this new law is "to realise a society in which the ethnic pride of the Ainu people is respected and to contribute to the development of diverse cultures in the country, by the implementation of measures for the promotion of Ainu culture, the spread of knowledge related to Ainu traditions, and the education of the nation, referring to the situation of Ainu traditions and culture from which the Ainu people find their ethnic pride". According to article 3 of this *Ainu Shinpo*, the national government should make efforts "to promote measures for the nurturing of those who will inherit Ainu culture, the fruitfulness of educational activities concerning Ainu traditions, and the promotion of the study of the Ainu culture".

In 1997, after the preparations for the Ainu Shinpo were made by the Hokkaido government, the Hokkaido Development Agency approved the establishment of the Foundation for Research and Promotion of Ainu Culture (FRPAC) as a public service corporation (www.frpac.or.jp). This Foundation has offices in Sapporo (Hokkaido) and at the Ainu Culture Centre in Tokyo. Its mission is in accordance with the Law on the Promotion of the Ainu Culture. It is the sole corporation in Japan with the authority to carry out the services provided in the law. One of the tasks of the Foundation is to preserve and promote the Ainu language and traditional culture and to disseminate knowledge on Ainu traditions to the nation. In the year 2003, the Foundation's projects were implemented based on the following four policies: (1) Promotion of comprehensive and practical research on the Ainu, (2) Promotion of the Ainu language, (3) Promotion of Ainu material culture, and (4) Dissemination of knowledge on Ainu traditions.

Teaching of the Ainu Language and Culture

The language is unique to the Ainu and forms the core of their ethnic identity. Because the number of people who use the language has been decreasing yearly due to the aging of native Ainu speakers, Ainu language education is in a very difficult state. For the improvement of Ainu language education, the FRPAC provides learning opportunities to train Ainu language instructors through intensive courses on effective instruction methods based on the grammar and linguistics of the Ainu language, in cooperation with Ainu language researchers. Various descriptions of the Ainu language have been produced, such as the grammar by Tamura (2000).

Ainu language classes are offered in various community centres on Hokkaido and in the Ainu Culture Centre in Tokyo. These centres are very well equipped with modern facilities and often offer interesting expositions related to the Ainu culture. In order to disseminate the Ainu language to the general public, the FRPAC provides opportunities for many people to have contact with and to learn the Ainu language. Language textbooks are provided free of charge and special books on the Ainu history and culture are edited for primary and secondary schools. People who want to practise the language can take part in special speech contests and storytellers of traditional oral Ainu literature, such as *yukar* (epics of heroes), *kamuy-yukar* (stories of deities) and *uwepeker* (old tales), give direct instruction to train their successors. Special attention is paid to the remnants of the Ainu language in the local culture, in particular the interpretation of geographic place names.

Since the 1980s the Ainu cultural and ethnic movements have created a public awareness of Ainu heritage, and popularised Ainu culture. The purpose of teaching Ainu history and culture is to promote understanding of the Ainu and their culture, and to refute the Japanese stereotype of the Ainu as uncivilised people. The Hokkaido Board of Education and the Hokkaido University of Education have taken the lead in funding Ainu studies and education. The Hokkaido Board of Education prepared teaching materials for Ainu history and culture in 1984, and in 1992 it produced a handbook, *Guidelines for the Teaching of Ainu History and Culture*, for every high school in Hokkaido. In 1987, the Utari Association requested that the Hokkaido University of Education teach a course in Ainu history and culture, and in 1991 the five campuses of the University offered seventeen courses wholly or partially devoted to Ainu history, culture, and language. The Ainu themselves, as well as several scholars, are actively researching and writing about Ainu history, language and culture. The 1997 New Ainu Law provides public funds to museums, performance theaters, research centres, and community cultural centres.

Japanese students learn about Ainu history and culture as part of the social science curriculum in elementary, middle and high schools. Ainu issues first appeared in the social studies textbooks in 1961. In addition to textbook-centred instruction, elementary school students and preschoolers become familiar with Ainu culture by making handicrafts, reading folktales, and performing music and dance. Watching a documentary on the lifestyle of the Ainu can also give students a sense of Ainu culture. Since 1978, middle school textbooks have included chapters on Ainu history and cultures. A popular history textbook portrays the Ainu as the victims of Japanese exploitation and prejudice. It refers to Ainu revolts as justifiable resistance against exploitation by Japanese settlers and merchants prior to the 1868 Meiji Restoration. Shakushain, one of the leaders of the resistance, is portrayed as a hero.

More recently, in 2007, Hokkaido University opened the Centre for Ainu and Indigenous Studies (CAIS) with the aim of promoting comprehensive and interdisciplinary research activities concerning indigenous peoples with a special emphasis on Ainu (see www.cais.hokudai.ac.jp). It also strives to establish networks connecting various organisations at home and abroad with the aim of promoting research programmes on Ainu and indigenous peoples. Currently, the academic staff of this

Centre consists of six full-time researchers, twelve part-time researchers and three Ph.D. students from various fields, such as anthropology, linguistics, history, archaeology and laws. The primary characteristic of the Centre lies in its interdisciplinary and international nature.

The CAIS collaborates with the Ainu people and Ainu organisations such as the Ainu Association of Hokkaido and the Foundation for Research and Promotion of Ainu Culture. Together with these organisations research activities and administrative matters are planned and this will serve as a bridge that connects the university with the Ainu. These activities result in symposia, public lectures, social surveys, museum exhibitions, lecture tours, ecotourism and overseas fieldwork. This will encourage widespread understanding and support among members of different ethnic groups.

An important aspect of the Centre is its emphasis on education. Currently, at Hokkaido University, the Centre offers courses that help students develop interest in and gain an accurate understanding of the Ainu people and other indigenous groups throughout the world. Furthermore, an ambitious project for developing teaching programmes and materials for junior and senior high school students in collaboration with local school teachers is being realised. Through such educational efforts, social justice will prevail in Japan, which increasingly is becoming a multiethnic and multicultural country.

Education for the Ainu about the Ainu is as important as education for young Japanese people. The Centre has a positive role to play in this regard. As many senior Ainu people recollect, for a long time the Ainu did not have opportunities to study their own language, culture, history, and rights, and were therefore unable to firmly develop their ethnic identity. Given this unfortunate situation, the Centre takes as its responsibility the creation of a space in which the Ainu people are able to learn about themselves in both academically and socially useful ways.

The Centre regularly organises seminars and workshops on various issues concerning the Ainu and other indigenous ethnic groups. In November 2011, the CAIS organised an international symposium on indigenous people and education, together with the Finnish institute in Japan (Hokkaido Office). This symposium aimed to allow Saami and Ainu to exchange experiences on the use of multimedia in cultural education programmes. The participants introduced various ways of incorporating multimedia material into the education programmes and evaluated their programmes in the discussions. In this way, the CAIS stimulates local language maintenance and international programmes.

The Languages of Sakhalin

The island of Sakhalin belongs to the Sakhalin area (*Sakhalinskaia oblast'*), one of the most eastern territorial units of the Russian Federation, with a size of 87,100 km^2 and a distance from north to south of 980 km. The Kurile Islands are also part of this territory and consist of a chain of 36 islands, 1,200 km in length. A long-time dispute exists between Japan and the Russian Federation over the ownership of the most southern of these islands. From 1905 to 1945, after the Russian-Japanese war, the southern part of Sakhalin (*Karafuto*) was a Japanese colony and during this period many Japanese immigrants (about half a million) settled there (Stephan 1971). The indigenous population of Sakhalin consisted of users of the language isolate Nivkh (formerly called *Gilyak*) and the Tungusic Uilta (formerly called *Orok*) (Gilyak and Orok are pejoratives in Russian) in the North and Centre, and the Ainu in the South. Their numbers were rather small and during the colonisation process by the Russians from the North and by the Japanese from the South, they soon became numerically dominated by these stronger nationalities. Due to their isolated life far from the political centre, they were able to keep their native language and culture for a long time, but since the beginning of the 20th century the assimilation process has gradually become stronger.

In the summer of 1990, Tjeerd de Graaf took part in the first international field work expedition to Sakhalin, with the aim to investigate the linguistic and ethnographic situation of the smaller nationalities on the island. The idea was to look for the remnants of the Ainu population and for the other small ethnic minority groups, in particular Nivkh and Uilta. Unfortunately, during this expedition no more Ainu people could be found and one of the only persons representing the Sakhalin Ainu language and culture was Mrs. Asai Take, who lived in Hokkaido (De Graaf 1992; Murasaki 2001).

The dramatic events of 1945, after the Soviet occupation of the whole island, had enormous consequences for the ethnographic and linguistic situation: practically all Japanese inhabitants left Sakhalin for Japan and together with them many of the Sakhalin Ainu. From all parts of the Soviet Union new immigrants arrived. These were not only Russian people, but also many members of other ethnic groups. Some of them still speak their native language, the others have shifted to Russian. Due to these developments the Sakhalin Ainu population disappeared from Sakhalin, according to the census data. There are probably still Ainu people on the island, but they are registered as another ethnicity and do not speak the language anymore. Officially, Ainu people are now only living in Japan. As we have seen before, the Ainu culture in Japan is stimulated in many ways, but there is only a very small number of speakers left after the earlier repression. This makes it very difficult to obtain a real revival of the Ainu language and culture. Ainu is one of the few small indigenous languages of Japan (together with Ryukuyan, which also is more and more being acknowledged as a minority language). Nivkh is representative of the many minor languages of Russia. In a study by Shibatani (1990), a survey is given of the two indigenous languages of Japan: Ainu and Japanese, whereas in his book on the languages of the Soviet Union, Comrie describes the complicated language situation with more than 120 languages in that country (Comrie 1981).

In Russian demographic data a distinction is made between those representatives of a nationality who still speak their native language as first language and those who speak Russian or another language. The last census of the USSR took place in 1989 and the statistic results for the Sakhalin area (Sakhalin and the Kurile Islands) can be found in De Graaf (1992). From these data we were able to conclude, that in 1989 the aboriginal peoples of the North formed a very small minority within the total population of Sakhalin: for the Nivkh ethnic group, which has the largest number of members, the percentage was only 0.3 %.

Among the small nationalities in the Russian Federation, the minority peoples of the North play a special role. There are nearly thirty different groups, all living in the northern parts of the country bordering the Arctic Ocean from Scandinavia to the Bering Sea and the Pacific Ocean. These peoples of the North were the last ones to be put under effective Soviet rule. In the early 1920s the Soviet regime tried to extend its grip on these peoples and to encourage Russian culture and literacy among them. With this aim a Committee for the Assistance and Protection of the Small Peoples of the North was founded in 1923. The schools in the northern regions brought education to the native population. For this purpose, the native language was used in many cases for the first time in written form, initially with a Latin alphabet and, from the late 1930s, with a Cyrillic alphabet. Many subjects were taught to these peoples in Russian and therefore the schools became media of russification. The northern nationalities are so small, that even a very moderate introduction of (mainly Russian) manpower from outside into their territories could adversely affect their national survival. In the case of Sakhalin, we saw earlier that the number of people belonging to the original population has become much smaller than the number of immigrants. This is also a factor which leads to further russification: Russian civilisation is pushing forward into the remote corners of the Russian Federation and more and more non-Russian natives have been forced to adopt the Russian language and culture.

The Nivkh language

The Nivkh language is a language isolate and is spoken by tribes inhabiting the lower reaches of the Amur River and the northern and central parts of Sakhalin Island in the Far East (Gruzdeva 1998). The language has two main dialects: the Amur dialect and the Sakhalin dialect. Both groups are rather small: altogether about 5,000 people consider themselves Nivkh, and less than 5 % of them are speakers of the Nivkh language. For many dialects, it is extremely difficult to find speakers, such as for the Poronaisk dialect and the Shmid (Northern) dialect. After the Second World War, several Nivkh families from southern Sakhalin moved to Hokkaido (Japan), where Japanese and other non-Soviet linguists studied their language (Austerlitz 1956; Hattori 2000).

The first all-Russian census was organised during the czarist regime in 1897. In that year, the total number of people belonging to the Nivkh ethnic group on Sakhalin was presented as 1,969. They all gave Nivkh as their mother tongue and probably most of them were monolingual. In the second census mentioned, the one of 1926, which was the first organised in the Soviet Union, the total number of Nivkh people was lower, due to the fact that the inhabitants of the Japanese southern part of Sakhalin were not counted. Practically all of them still had Nivkh as their mother tongue. Since that year, however, a decrease in the percentage of Nivkh speakers has set in, whereas the total number of Nivkh on Sakhalin remained more or less stable (about 2,000). In 1989, most Nivkh people (more than 80 %) who were not speaking Nivkh anymore, named Russian as their first language (De Graaf 1992).

The transition from the Sakhalin Nivkh to the Russian language can be explained in a number of ways. One of the most important factors was the growing contact of the Nivkh population with the other inhabitants on the island. Many of them were Russian-speaking people from the continent who came to the island to exploit the many natural resources (oil, coal, wood, fish, caviar). Before that time, the Nivkh people were living as fishermen and hunters in their small-sized villages, but they increasingly came into contact with the immigrants, who also started an active policy of educating and influencing the aboriginal inhabitants of the eastern parts of the Russian Federation.

From the early 1960s, the Nivkh on Sakhalin, like other small minority people, were (in many cases compulsorily) resettled from their small villages to larger settlements such as Chir-Unvd and Nekrasovka, and to small towns (Poronaisk, Nogliki). In his book Bruce Grant gives a comprehensive overview of the socio-economic state of the Nivkh people in this period (Grant 1995). These developments intensified the contact between the minorities and the Russian-speaking population. Important changes took place in the life of the Nivkh: they had to give up many of their national customs and adapt themselves to Russian habits and lifestyle. In particular, the arrival of Russian radio and television in their homes had a great influence. The traditional professions of the Nivkh (fisherman or hunter) were also more and more replaced by other occupations, where the possibility to keep the native language and culture was very limited.

After the Russian revolution, the abolishment of the illiteracy of the native peoples took place with the introduction of writing systems. For the Nivkh language, this was initially based on the Latin alphabet, which was created in 1932 and which, according to some linguists, might have been most suited to the sound structure of the language. In 1953, however, a Cyrillic alphabet replaced this system and since that time the writing system also gave rise to an increasing influence of Russian. Further, the creation of boarding schools for the peoples of the North played a special role. In the 1950s, their children were taken to schools in places far away from their home village. This meant that they could rarely see their family with the result that they lost contact with their language background. In most cases, instruction in these schools was only provided in Russian.

In recent times a development is taking place in favour of the native languages and cultures of the small minorities in the Russian Federation, in particular the Nivkh (De Graaf and Shiraishi 2004). Attempts are being made to revive the Nivkh language, for example by introducing language classes in Nivkh in several schools. In 1980, the Ministry of Education of the Russian Federation initiated a programme for primary and secondary schools, for which text books and dictionaries were edited (Sangi and Otaina 1981; 1984). Special instruction was given to teachers of Nivkh descent about the education of Nivkh children in their own language. This teaching programme was introduced in the special boarding schools for children from the ethnic minorities in Nogliki, Chir-Unvd and in Nekrasovka. We were able to visit these schools and to learn about the teaching methods for Nivkh used in primary education.

During our fieldwork expeditions on Sakhalin, important linguistic material was collected on the languages of the minority groups. Most of the Nivkh consultants for our research project were elderly people with strong motivation to use their language, for example as members of a folkloristic group. Practically all young people we met had no active knowledge of the language, and they only communicated with their parents in Russian. During the interviews we undertook with Nivkh informants, they were very positive about the value of keeping and cultivating their own culture in this way and they want to combine this with a future life as members of the group of nations in the Russian Federation. They agree that the Russian language and culture play a very important role in their lives, but they would like to see the survival of their native language and culture stimulated by all possible means. The edition of a Nivkh-Russian bilingual newspaper *Nivkh Dif* ('Nivkh language'), the writing of more books and journals in Nivkh, and the organisation of special language courses will make it possible to reach that goal.

Voices from Tundra and Taiga

In the foregoing it has been shown that in recent years much important work has been done for the Ainu in Japan and that this is actively stimulated by resources from the Japanese government. The Ainu situation on Hokkaido can be considered as an example of how in Russia and elsewhere one could further proceed with projects on language revitalisation in cooperation with the local language communities. This can be realised by the promotion of the language and culture and by setting up language courses, broadcasting in the language, organising speech contests, training of story-tellers, etc. The main problem in the Russian Federation is the lack of sufficient linguistic rights, financial support for these activities and special programmes necessary to protect the indigenous endangered languages.

Important activities related to linguistic databases in St. Petersburg concern the recordings of Russian dialects and minority languages in the Russian Federation, such as Nivkh, Tungus, Yakut and others (De Graaf 2004a). One of our aims is to use these recordings for the construction of a phonetic database of the languages of Russia, which will have many scientific, cultural and technical applications. Within the framework of the research programme 'Voices from Tundra and Taiga', which started in 2002, we combined the data from old sound recordings with the results of modern fieldwork in order to give a full description of the languages and cultures of ethnic groups in Russia. The endangered Arctic languages and cultures of the Russian Federation must be described rapidly before they become extinct. Our earlier work on the reconstruction technology for old sound recordings found in archives in St. Petersburg has made it possible to compare languages still spoken in the proposed research area with the same languages as they were spoken more than half a century ago, which provided a fortunate start to these projects. The sound recordings in the St. Petersburg archives consist of spoken language, folk songs, fairy tales etc., among others in Siberian languages (Burykin et al. 2005; De Graaf 2004a). One of the languages represented in the collection is Nivkh.

In these projects the techniques developed earlier have been applied to some of the disappearing minority languages and cultures of Russia, such as Nivkh and Uilta on Sakhalin, Itelmen and Koryak in Kamchatka and Yukagir and Tungusic languages in Yakutia. Our goal is to set up a phono- and video-library of recorded stories, folklore, singing and oral traditions of the peoples of Sakhalin, Kamchatka and Yakutia. For the work on Yukagir in Yakutia see the contribution by Cecilia Odé in this volume, whereas the work on Kamchatka is reported by Erich Kasten. The existing sound recordings in the archives of Sakhalin, Kamchatka and Yakutia will be complemented by new fieldwork results. The data obtained are added to the existing archive material partly available on the internet and CD-ROM.

This research project and the related documentation are carried out in close cooperation with scholars in local centres such as the Sakhalin Regional Museum in Yuzhno-Sakhalinsk, who participate in the archiving of sound recordings and fieldwork expeditions. Specialists from St. Petersburg and the Netherlands visit them, setting up new centres for the study and teaching of local languages and related subjects. For this purpose we organised a special seminar for Nivkh teachers in Yuzhno-Sakhalinsk in October 2003.

Spontaneous speech and the reading of prepared texts is collected for ethno-linguistic as well as for anthropological, folkloristic and ethno-musicological analysis. These data are video-recorded and analysed and they will thus illustrate the art of story telling and language use. The above-described texts will be published in scientific journals and books with audio-visual illustrations on CD-ROM and/or on the internet. The materials will thus become available for further analysis to scholars working in the field of phonetics, linguistics, anthropology, history, ethno-musicology and folklore.

|9| Nivkh seminar in Nekrasovka (Sakhalin)

Using a phrase book for school children of Nivkh (Taksami et al. 1982) we recorded a native speaker during our fieldwork trip in 1990. The texts with the illustrations in the book are shown on the internet together with the acoustic data. The separate phonemes are also supplied on a special table and by selecting one of them the student can listen to various speech sounds. This has as the advantage that students will be able to learn the distinction between various separate phonemes, e. g. four plosive sounds of Nivkh, which are variants (allophones) of one phoneme /k/ in Russian.

The second author of this article and his Nivkh colleague Galina Lok published a series of books with Nivkh stories, songs and conversations in which for the first time the corresponding audio-recordings are made available on CD and on the internet. The series, *Sound Materials of the Nivkh Language I-VII* (Shiraishi and Lok 2002 -2010), appeared as a result of the Japanese programme on Endangered Languages of the Pacific Rim (ELPR), supported by the Japanese Ministry of Education and the Sapporo Gakuin University, and the research programme 'Voices from Tundra and Taiga' supported by the Netherlands Organisation NWO. This unique material is not only used by linguists, but also by the language community itself, where it can be applied to teaching purposes. Using data from this series, the second author wrote a dissertation with the title *Topics in Nivkh Phonology*, which he defended at Groningen University in 2006 (Shiraishi 2010).

On the initiative of local organisations, language maintenance activities are undertaken in various locations on Sakhalin. One such organisation is *Kykhkykh* ('swan'), a local organisation based in the village of Nekrasovka in north Sakhalin. This organisation strives to record and propagate the language and culture of Nivkh by making video-recordings of the last speakers of their language, and by publishing booklets and teaching materials. These materials are partly available on the internet. (see www.simdp.ru). One of the latest publications is the Nivkh-Russian dictionary, originally compiled by the late Svetlana Pol'eteva (2011), a former Nivkh schoolteacher of the elementary school in Nekrasovka. In addition, this organisation regularly organises a language course in Nivkh, where the Nivkh people of the younger generation learn Nivkh from a teacher who acquired Nivkh as her first language (see *photo,* p. 61).

Final remarks

In programmes for language safeguarding the various groups involved are the language communities, the linguists and other scholars, the national government and international organisations like UNESCO. The steps taken by the Japanese government in relation to the Ainu Shinpo are an example of what should be done: establishing local research and training centres, providing financial support for training members of the language community and for linguistic research in the field, designing language programmes that train passive and semi-speakers to regain their language ability, creating training programmes for teachers of the non-dominant language, etc.

In June 2011 an International Expert Meeting on the UNESCO Programme 'Safeguarding of Endangered Languages' was held in Paris. During this conference the participants accepted the revision of a report on 'Recommendations on Documentation, Revitalisation and Fortification of Endangered Languages'. In these recommendations for UNESCO the tasks of linguists and other scholars are related to language documentation, analysis, description and archiving. They should work together with the language community members and help them with the archiving of language material, the preparation of special courses and other ways to revitalise the language. The joint project 'Voices from Tundra and Taiga' with colleagues in Russia, Japan and the Nivkh language community on Sakhalin is an example of the way these recommendations for UNESCO could be implemented.

References

Austerlitz, Robert 1956. Gilyak Nursery Words. *Word* 12: 260–279.

Burykin, Aleksei, Albina Girfanova, Aleksandr Kastrov Yuri Marchenko and Natalia Svetozarova 2005. *Kollektsii narodov Severa v fonogrammarkhive Pushkinskogo doma*. [Collections on the peoples of the North in the phonogram archive of the Pushkinskii Dom]. Faculty of Philology, University of St. Petersburg.

Comrie, Bernard 1981. *The Languages of the Soviet Union*. Cambridge: Cambridge University Press.

Dietz, Kelly 1999. Ainu in the International Arena. In *Ainu. Spirit of a Northern People*, W.W. Fitzhugh and Ch.O. Dubreuil (eds.), 359–365. Washington: University of Washington Press.

De Graaf, Tjeerd 1992. The Languages of Sakhalin. *International Journal on the Sociology of Languages*, 94: 185–200.

— 1993. The Dutch Role in the Border Areas of Japan and Russia. *Circumpolar Journal*, 3: 1–12.

— 1997. The Reconstruction of Acoustic Data and the Study of Language Minorities in Russia. In *Language Minorities and Minority Languages*, B. Synak and T. Wicherkiewicz (eds.), 131–143. Gdansk: Wydawnicstwo Uniwersytetu Gdanskiego.

— 2001. Data on the Languages of Russia from Historical Documents, Sound Archives and Fieldwork Expeditions. In *Recording and Restoration of Minority Languages, Sakhalin Ainu and Nivkh*, K. Murasaki (red.), 13–37. ELPR report. Suita, Osaka.

— 2002a. The Use of Acoustic Databases and Fieldwork for the Study of the Endangered Languages of Russia. In *Conference Handbook on Endangered Languages, Proceedings of the Kyoto ELPR Conference*, 57–79. Kyoto.

— 2002b. The Use of Sound Archives in the Study of Endangered Languages. In *Music Archiving in the World, Papers Presented at the Conference on the Occasion of the 100th Anniversary of the Berlin Phonogramm-Archiv*, 101–107. Berlin.

— 2004a. Voices from Tundra and Taiga: Endangered Languages of Russia on the Internet. In *Lectures on Endangered Languages: 5 - Endangered Languages of the Pacific Rim C005*, Sakiyama, Osamu and Fubito Endo (eds.), 143–169. Suita, Osaka.

— 2004b. The Status of Endangered Languages in the Border Areas of Japan and Russia. In *On the Margins of Nations: Endangered Languages and Linguistic Rights. Proceedings of the Eighth Conference of the Foundation for Endangered Languages*, J. Argenter and M. Brown (eds.), 153–159. Barcelona.

— 2009. The Use of Historical Documents and Sound Recordings for the Study and Safeguarding of Endangered Languages. In *Proceedings of the XIIIth Conference of the Foundation for Endangered Languages*. H. Elnazarov and N. Ostler (eds.), 27–33. Khorog, Tajikistan: The Institute of Humanities.

De Graaf, Tjeerd and Hidetoshi Shiraishi 2004. Capacity Building for some Endangered Languages of Russia: Voices from Tundra and Taiga. In *Language Documentation and Description, Volume 2, The Hans Rausing Endangered Languages Project*, P. Austin (ed.), 59–71. London: School of Oriental and African Studies.

De Graaf, Tjeerd and Bruno Naarden 2007. Description of the Border Areas of Russia with Japan and Their Inhabitants in Witsen's North and East Tartary. *Acta Slavica Iaponica, Tomus 24*, 205–220. Sapporo.

Grant, Bruce 1995. *In the Soviet House of Culture*. Princeton: Princeton University Press.

Gruzdeva, Ekaterina 1998. *Nivkh*. München: Lincom Europa.

Hattori, Takeshi 2000. *Hattori Takeshi chosakushuu* [Selected writings of Takeshi Hattori]. Sapporo: Hokkaido shuppan kikaku center.

Hokkaido. 2006. *Hokkaido Ainu seikatsu jittai choosa hookokusho*. [A survey on the socio-economic situation of the Ainu people] Department of Environment and Lifestyle, the Government of Hokkaido. Available from:
http://www.pref.hokkaido.lg.jp/ks/ass/grp/H18houkokusyo.pdf

Murasaki, Kyoko 2001. *Tuytah: Asai Take kojutsu, Karafuto Ainu no mukashi banashi* [Old stories of the Sakhalin Ainu]. Tokyo: Sofukan.

Polet'eva, Svetlana 2011. *Nivghgu-lotighu dif pitghy* [Nivkh-Russian dictionary]. A. Khuriun (ed.). Yuzhno-Sakhalinsk: Sakhalinskaia oblastnaia tipografiia.

Robert, Willem C.H. 1975. *Voyage to Cathay, Tartary and the Gold- and Silver-rich Islands East of Japan, 1643*. Amsterdam: Philo Press.

Sangi, Vladimir and Galina Otaina 1981. *Bukvar' dlia podgotovitel'nogo klassa Nivkhskikh shkol*. Leningrad.

Sangi, Vladimir; Galina Otaina 1984. *Nivkhskii Yazyk, uchebnik i kniga dlia chiteniia dlia I-go klassa*. Leningrad.

Shibatani, Masayoshi 1990. *The Languages of Japan*. Cambridge: Cambridge University Press.

Shiraishi, Hidetoshi and Galina Lok 2002–2003. Sound Materials of the Nivkh Language, I and II. In *Endangered Languages of the Pacific Rim*. ELPR Publications A2-015 and A2-036. Osaka: Gakuin University.

— 2004. *Sound Materials of the Nivkh Language III*. Publication of the International NWO project *Voices from Tundra and Taiga*.Groningen: University of Groningen.

— 2006–2010. *Sound Materials of the Nivkh Language IV-VII*. Sapporo: Gakuin University.
Available on Internet: http://ext-web.edu.sgu.ac.jp/hidetos/

Shiraishi, Hidetoshi 2010. *Topics in Nivkh Phonology*. Dissertation at Groningen University. Saarbrücken: VDM Publishing.

Siddle, Richard 1996. *Race, Resistance and the Ainu of Japan*. London: Routledge.

Stephan, John 1971. *Sakhalin, a History*. Oxford: Clarendon Press.

Taksami, Chuner, Pukhta, M.N.,Vingun, A.M. 1982. *Nivkhgu bukvar'*. Leningrad: Prosveshchenie.

Tamura, Suzuko 2000. *The Ainu Language*. Tokyo: Sanseido.

Tsunemoto, Teruki 1999. The Ainu Shinpo: A New Beginning. In *Ainu: Spirit of a Northern People*, W.W. Fitzhugh and Ch.O. Dubreuil (eds.), 366–368. Washington: University of Washington Press.

Witsen, Nicolaas 1705. *Noord en Oost Tartarye, ofte bondig ontwerp van eenige dier landen en volken, welke voormaels bekent zijn geweest*. Amsterdam: Halma.

5 LEARNING TOOLS FOR PRESERVING LANGUAGES AND TRADITIONAL KNOWLEDGE IN KAMCHATKA

Erich Kasten

Introduction

When the author first came to Kamchatka in 1993, he was able to build upon fieldwork experience that he had acquired while working in the mid-1980s with First Nations groups on the west coast of Canada.[1] At that time, his anthropological methodology was already entrenched in principles of collaborative community-oriented research – not only for ethical reasons (see Lavrillier, *this volume*), but also for the sake of obtaining fieldwork data that should turn out in the years to come to be of particular quality and more significant value.

First, a chronology of various projects is given here that shows how the focus has continuously shifted and expanded depending on new situations and on the different ethnic groups the team was working with – the Itelmens, Evens and Koryaks of Kamchatka. In a final chapter the lessons that have been learnt from these projects are summarised and discussed, in particular against the background of the most inspiring comments that the author received on these issues during the preceding seminars for this publication project,[2] for which all participants are warmly thanked.[3]

Itelmen language and culture

The first project in Kamchatka was on 'Ethnicity processes among the Itelmen', and was funded by the Deutsche Forschungsgemeinschaft (1993–1996).[4] Immediately upon his arrival the author was confronted with the pressing situation of Itelmen language loss and the strong concern of the residents of the main Itelmen village of Kovran on the west coast of the peninsula to maintain or revitalise their language.[5]

At a local community meeting in Kovran in 1993, Erich Kasten and his team assistant and local artist Sergei Longinov were urged by local Itelmen language expert and teacher Klavdiia Nikolaevna Khaloimova and others to implement special measures for the preservation of the Itelmen language, although such an initiative was not part of the original research programme. The prime concern of community members was to preserve local speech variants of the Itelmen language and the corresponding specific local knowledge. For native speakers, these elements were not sufficiently reflected in the standardised teaching materials that had been launched in the 1980s and were used to teach Itelmen in the schools. In most parts of the Soviet Union, similar school materials had been produced since the 1980s to preserve native languages.

One of the problems identified right from the beginning was that Itelmen language education (like native language education in other parts of Kamchatka and presumably in the rest of Russia) was mostly geared towards (and restricted to) the regular school curriculum in terms of topics, content, and methodology. Another problem identified was that the existing teaching materials employed certain standards for the Itelmen language that did not always reflect local language variants still spoken by the older generation. Therefore, many of the elders were critical of these school books. Consequently, the main goal of the project was to preserve the Itelmen language in connection with local culture, i.e. specific natural environments and traditional worldviews, while spatial boundaries among communities were

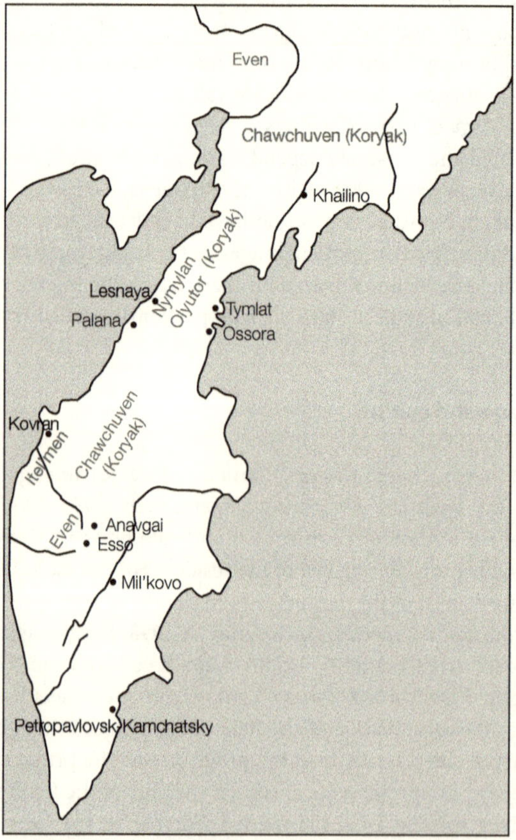

|10| Distribution of indigenous groups in Kamchatka.

expressed by specific local variants of the Itelmen language. This corresponds to the project team's philosophy that presenting language data in connection with local culture can most effectively stimulate interest and contribute to the preservation of endangered languages.

Project priorities were determined as a result of extensive consultation with local residents. Thus, the project team learned that the preservation (if not full revitalisation) of the Itelmen language or even parts of it would help many people to maintain their particular and local identities, and provide them with broader access to other forms of traditional – e.g. ecological – knowledge. The main strategy of the project has been to produce new language learning tools in addition to complementing existing ones, in which Michael Dürr, an anthropological linguist from Berlin, most actively collaborated. Importantly, these new materials now pick up local contents, i.e. themes and environments that local people can more easily identify with, in order to tie language and cultural learning together, to make language learning more meaningful and thus to increase the learners' personal motivation and investment.

The first product resulting from the project was an Itelmen language-learning textbook with Russian translations (Khaloimova et al. 1997). The book addresses relevant Itelmen cultural themes and refers to local social and natural environments, thus stimulating native language maintenance in combination with preserving the cultural heritage and traditional knowledge and practices of the Itelmen people. The book is set up according to thematic modules taken from daily life in the local communities (e.g. fishing techniques, hunting tools, crafts, traditional song). The thematic sections focus mostly on vocabulary and its use in simple expressions, whereas there are no grammar lessons in this book.

The project team recognised that for the Itelmen language to be passed on to younger generations, language learning would have to start at the youngest possible age. We immediately became aware of the problem that most severely endangered languages usually face – the fact that the native language was no longer the mother tongue or first language of the children. Almost all parents had already lost active native speech competence,[6] and young children could only listen to some fragments of Itelmen language that some elders occasionally still switched to when they came together. Thus, the new materials produced are particularly geared towards facilitating learning situations where elders (grandparents) can explain their local environment and culture to very young children (even at pre-kindergarten age), with the help of the illustrations and by using Itelmen words contained in the new textbook. Such language learning situations have proved most effective and rewarding for both 'teacher' and 'learner'.

In this way the very young can be provided at least occasionally with a native language environment at this crucial age for language acquisition at home, where otherwise the Itelmen language is no longer being used. The illustrations of local scenes in the book serve furthermore to trigger memories on the part of the elders who explain these situations to the young. Identification with local content was also seen as a key towards providing incentives and motivation for learning the language and thus for using the book. The illustrations of the textbook relate directly to local culture and traditions; the scenery shown depicts real surrounding locations so that the children become immediately engaged in remembering and identifying them ('... on this street I walk to school every morning ... here I go fishing with my father ...'). This constitutes a significant difference from previous native language textbooks dating from the Soviet era whose illustrations portray such items as astronauts or Red Square.

Local language variation is an important challenge for the production of any language teaching materials. As mentioned above, the existing materials employed certain standards for the Itelmen language that did not always reflect local variants still spoken by the older generation. The new textbook therefore includes several variants of Itelmen language instead of just one 'standardised' version: in addition to the established or 'standardised' variant originally spoken in Sopochnoe (and by project partner K.N. Khaloimova), a second variant is the one spoken in the north in Moroshechnoe, place of origin of one of the most competent remaining native speakers, Georgii 'Gosha' Zaporotskii. Additionally, certain expressions from the particular Kamchadal vernacular were included, reflecting in part words from previous Itelmen varieties.

The textbook was presented to the public in a special ceremony during the *Alkhalalalai* festival in Kovran in 1997, in the presence of educators from nearby villages and district centres. Most of the one thousand copies of the textbook were distributed directly from the publisher to school and village administrations within the Kamchatsky *oblast'* and the Tigil'sky *rayon*.

Such methodological approaches and experiences, as well as the need to explore new technological possibilities (Dürr 1998), had been discussed comparatively at a workshop with international scholars and teachers on native languages from various parts of Russia at the Franckesche Stiftungen in Halle in 1997 (Kasten, ed. 1998).

A multimedia CD-ROM followed the textbook publication (Dürr et al. 2001). The project team recognised that in the eyes of the youth electronic learning tools add prestige to the project materials. The youth were particularly targeted in the preservation effort, so these tools made it more attractive for young people to devote energy to the endeavour. It was also recognised that identification with local and well-known Itelmen customs, personalities and traditional activities could be enhanced by enabling students to listen to actual speakers and to watch the activities in video clips.

The CD-ROM is based on the textbook, but in addition it is also aimed at adult user groups, providing information such as scientific terms of local plant and animal species. The CD follows the same thematic structure as the textbook and can be used together with it. On the CD, all vocabulary and sentences in the book can be heard in the form of sound files, and many of them by various speakers. As a new feature, the listener can now choose from up to eight different variants of the Itelmen language, such as that once spoken in his/her particular ancestral home village, a feature that has become very popular. To provide such a great number of variants of local pronunciations of a certain expression would have been quite confusing in the printed textbook, whereas in the electronic edition of the CD this was easily accomplished. For such reasons, the project team decided to focus mainly on the production of electronic learning tools in the future.

The CD also contains recordings and texts of some Itelmen stories and songs and children's art works, collected for an exhibition project in Germany. This further illustrates the language data in its given contexts; and it provides short video clips on relevant local activities such as dancing and staged ceremonies at the *Alkhalalalai* festival, setting up a fish weir, digging roots in the tundra with a special tool, etc. Besides Russian translations, an English version was added to the CD, as some of the content was considered of interest to other native peoples of the circumpolar North outside Russia and for linguists and other scholars who are not in full command of the Russian language. In particular, this concerns the natural environments and related harvesting/procurement activities, which are very similar all across the circumpolar North.

The official presentation of the CD *Itelmen Language and Culture* took place in 2002 at the Institute for Advanced Teachers' Training in Palana. More than two hundred copies were distributed via the UNESCO Moscow office in Kamchatka, which sponsored the CD's production. A printed version of the CD content is available on the web.[7]

In addition to the above-mentioned jointly produced publications, the project team supported the publication of *Methodical recommendations (materials) for teachers of the Itelmen language* (Khaloimova 1999). This book is directed mainly at future Itelmen teachers and is considered a particularly useful teaching tool at the Institute for Advanced Teachers' Training in Palana. The book is a guide for teachers on how to systematically explain the rather intricate Itelmen grammar to school children of different levels with the help of short examples. This had also been neglected in the textbooks of the 1980s.

Overall, in the data compilation process for the Itelmen project, extensive consultations with local people were carried out to identify and utilise such local content, which they considered important from their own point of view. For example, the topic of toponyms (place names) was given considerable attention, as it was obviously an important issue for local residents to keep memories alive of those places from which they had been relocated against their will into central settlements in the 1960s (it would probably not have been 'politically correct' to include such an issue in school books during the Soviet period).

Furthermore, in the course of the project, Itelmen people (and those who felt their roots to lie in Itelmen culture) who live in the central parts of the Kamchatka peninsula (Mil'kovo district, see *map*, p. 66) – they are also known as Kamchadals – and some Itelmen residing in the main capital Petropavlovsk-Kamchatsky, also started to actively take part in the effort. This led, among other things, to the inclusion of the particular Kamchadal vernacular and vocabulary in the teaching materials produced. The CD eventually also became quite popular in the urban Itelmen community in Petropavlovsk-Kamchatsky, where it has helped Itelmens to restore and substantiate their revitalised identity by strengthening their native language competence.

Many local residents have voiced their satisfaction to the project team, indicating that the project materials have made a substantial contribution to their lives by increasing interest and helping to preserve the Itelmen language at all levels. This was most evident with the CD, which gave Itelmen activists of the younger or middle generation (those between twenty and fifty years old) the chance to revitalise (parts) of their language. For them it would have been more difficult and outright boring to learn from already existing school books whose methodologies had been designed for school classes and for children between the ages of seven and twelve.

Ten years after its first publication, due to changes in the multimedia link administration of Adobe software, some functions of the *Itelmen language and culture* CD no longer operate as they should and as they did before (unless the original software delivered with the CD is installed). A planned updated new edition that will contain even more video material and in better quality is planned in the DVD series of the Foundation for Siberian Cultures. Some additional material for this edition can be viewed already in the Foundation's 'Show on the web', July 2011.[8]

Since 2010, our team has been continuing its work on Itelmen language and culture as part of the programme of the Foundation for Siberian Cultures. According to an initiative of Tjan Zaotschnaja, it's currently focussing on and supporting Itelmen language classes in Petropavlovsk-Kamchatsky and in the Elizova district in Kamchatka.[9]

A number of useful lessons have been learned from our work with Itelmen people and materials since the mid-1990s that could be applied on an even larger scale in subsequent additional projects on Even and Koryak language and culture (see *below*). First, the important use of audio-visual data, as addressed above, in connection with printed learning tools requires continuous adaptation to new and more advanced technical solutions in presenting the material. In the late 1990s we first developed interactive CD editions and eventually switched, in addition to it, to DVD format, which provided us new possibilities at that time. More recently we started to develop additional online versions for at least some of the (video-) materials, that one would not even have thought of 10 years ago, and this probably will be the main trend now in the future (see Kraef, Rießler, *this volume*; although from other seminar participants we learnt that, as in Kamchatka, many communities in the Russian North still lack reliable internet access).

Second, we experienced the particular challenges relating to how to deal with local linguistic variation. This involves the degree to which standards introduced during the Soviet period concerning transcription methods and grammar presentation, to which the younger generation has in the meantime become accustomed, should be revised or modified. Creating new teaching tools that on the one hand contain local or situation-specific language variants and on the other hand remain compatible with standards for grammar and orthography that have been in use for over 20 years (despite differences in original speech patterns of the elder generation), was one of the main challenges faced in the Itelmen project. Later, discrepancies between standardised 'school book' language and 'originally spoken' language became even more evident in later projects for the preservation of Even and Koryak, where direct transcriptions of the recorded texts reflected how people actually spoke.

This leads to the fundamental question of whether the issue of language preservation might be better served if, in contrast to conventional school books, new learning tools and methodologies could place stronger emphasis on actually performed original oral traditions and their local variants. New audio-visual teaching materials based on recorded texts and local contents are nowadays well-suited to addressing this issue.

Third, experiences of this project made us rethink native language pedagogy. Previous Itelmen language programmes and learning tools pretended that it was the children's mother tongue or first language, although this was and is no longer the case. If Itelmen is taught at school, realistically, as a second or foreign language (such as English), the question of motivation: 'what for?' – requires particular justification, especially when other options such as English classes provide young Itelmen with the prospect of better professional career opportunities. Unless a specific native language pedagogy along with a philosophy and viable approach that indicates the importance of preserving the language is used, the motivation of students is usually low. The insufficient outcomes such as those in the Soviet native language programmes in the 1980s using the school books introduced at that time are a clear example of this. In the Itelmen context, the coupling of cultural knowledge with language acquisition in textbooks was one way in which the project team attempted to counter this effect. To encourage Itelmen language training beyond the regular school curriculum, learning tools have also to be conceptualised in such a way that they address even adults who are concerned about revitalising their Itelmen language competence and identity.

Ideally, culturally oriented teaching materials, in particular those with ecological content, should be used in combination with summer school ecological tours at nature sites outside the village (for example, fishing camps), where people practice traditional harvesting activities and where these can be demonstrated by elders. For Itelmen, a pilot project consisting of ecological tours under the guidance of elders has been designed for the purpose of strengthening knowledge of their contextual terminology. This was organised by Itelmen educator Nina Tolman in 2000 with the support of the Franckesche Stiftungen in Halle, Germany. Unfortunately, this programme had to be discontinued due to lack of ongoing funding. This approach has been taken up again, however, in later field projects on Koryak language and culture (see *below*).

This initiative also reflects and is much in line with one of Stephan Dudeck's most important findings from projects that he describes for the Khanty in this volume (see p. 142) – that native language and traditional knowledge should rather be transmitted outside the school curriculum, where it falls under the primary socialisation that only parents and other family members can successfully accomplish.

Finally we concluded that video format provides better teaching methodologies and learning tools, as they come closer to the traditional ways of transmitting knowledge and language competence (see *below*). This allows for better and more natural individual identification with the material by the learner.

Because of its positive results, the Itelmen language and culture project was listed in 2008 in the UNESCO 'Register of Good Practices in Language Preservation' (Kasten 2009b).

Even language and culture

In 1999 and 2000, two seminars were held in Esso in Central-Kamchatka where most native residents are Even, a Tungus-speaking people who immigrated at the beginning of the 19th century from their homelands west of the Okhotsk sea over northern Kamchatka into this area (see *map*, p. 66). From these workshops originated additional initiatives to preserve the cultural heritage of that particular Even group. The first of these seminars, held in 1999 and funded by the Haus der Kulturen der Welt (Berlin), was on the theme 'Traditional worldviews of the peoples of Kamchatka'. Its aim was to prepare for the dance theatre 'The travels of the shaman into worlds beyond' by the Even ensemble *Nulgur* and its tour in Germany the same fall.[10] During this field project many ensemble members conducted their own research with community elders to learn more about these traditions of their ancestors. Seeking artistic expressions of their cultural heritage in songs and dances encouraged many of them to study traditional Even world views, and also attracted attention to their own language. At the same time, the author began to make video recordings of Even texts on life histories and various themes of traditional Even culture with the aim to produce later DVD learning tools from them.

More Even language data was collected the following year, in 2000, at another seminar in Esso and during subsequent fieldwork in the Bystrinsky *rayon*. This seminar was on the theme 'Children of the North – lessons of culture', which was funded by the Franckesche Stiftungen in Halle. For this, scholars from Petropavlovsk-

Kamchatsky, native teachers and culture workers from various villages, artists and children's ensembles from Esso, Anavgai and Palana came together for a lively exchange of educational experiences and cultural practices (Kasten, ed. 2002). Through this process, our methodology in preserving endangered cultural heritage, as it was already drafted and envisaged from earlier experiences during the Itelmen project, was further refined. In a joyful atmosphere especially the youths could live up to their particular Even, Koryak and Itelmen traditions with great pride that obviously enhanced their motivation to further pursue their studies and artistic work on these themes. Such initiatives in preserving and enhancing endangered Even culture in that area provided a favourable starting point for the consequent preparation of learning tools for the forthcoming DVD series *Even language and culture*. It yielded good results because of its integrated approach combining the documentation and study of language data with cultural content or, in this case, with cultural expressions in the arts.

Language data that was collected during this seminar and later in other settlements, reindeer camps and at various fishing sites of this area (Dul'chenko 2010) were first transcribed and translated with the help of the Even language school teacher Marina Tarasova in Anavgai. Later on, Raisa Avak, the director and Even language teacher at the Institute for Advanced Teachers' Training in Palana joined our team and carried on this task. Together with her and Michael Dürr we started in 2007 to produce the first volumes of the DVD series *Even language and culture*, while David Koester from the University of Alaska in Fairbanks assisted us to edit the English translations for this and subsequent editions of the series on *Koryak language and culture*.[11]

During our transcriptions of the Even language material we were confronted again with the same problem and difficult decisions that we already had experienced during our work on Itelmen language. While in school standardised Even textbooks according to the Magadan dialect, that is spoken west of the Okhotsk sea, were used, Even elders still spoke at home their particular speech variant of the Bystrinsky *rayon* – and often did not understand what their grandchildren had learnt at school.[12] As community members urged us to preserve their particular dialect, we decided to design our DVD learning tools accordingly, which then were used in classes in addition to conventional Even language school books.

For this, the new DVD learning tools provide a number of obvious methodological advantages. First, the elaboration of such new approaches made us even more aware of the problem of 'spoken' language versus 'standardised' language. Obviously, a certain standardisation can never completely be avoided, as also with this type of learning tools transliterations and translations must be given. Furthermore, even in audio-visual documentation – that can offer only a 'static' snapshot of a situation at a certain time – the continuous fluidity and variations, i. e. the particular dynamics of a language, cannot be fully captured.[13] That means it is more a matter of searching for the best possible compromise, rather than solving this obvious dilemma, but we will get back to this again later.

Second, the primary focus of the DVD learning tools is on strengthening auditory competence, whereas training grammar and active speech should be accomplished in another step, as far as possible. Most important, it seems to us that native children's first acquaintance with their own native language should be made in a most natural way – by listening and in the proper familiar and cultural environment that can at least be simulated through audio-visual recordings of such situations – viewing older (sometimes already no longer alive) family members during traditional activities and commenting on them. More research and testing has to be done on this important issue. This is why we appreciate the valuable collaboration with local teachers such as Marina Tarasova and Raisa Avak – whereas this important grassroots pedagogical perspective and experience is often neglected in most scientific programmes on preserving endangered languages. Consequently, Raisa Avak also emphasised the need to preserve – together with the Even language spoken in Kamchatka – the particular cultural traditions of this people (Avak 2010: 142). The series on Even language and culture is structured according to the following themes:

- The remembered past;
- Traditional ecological knowledge;
- Clothing and decorative arts;
- Ritual practice and world view;
- Human-environment relations as expressed in tales, songs and dance;
- Conferences, workshops and festivals.

For each of these themes, two to five volumes of about one hour each are in preparation. The DVDs are first of all aimed at the school curriculum and at cultural programmes in Kamchatka, although they can be used as well in international research and in university courses. The DVDs have English and Russian subtitles. Booklets contain the transcribed original texts with either Russian or English translations.[14] It is hoped that this series can be completed within the next three years.

Koryak language and culture

At the seminars in Esso in 1999 and 2000, the author also met with native artists and experts on Koryak culture from Palana (see *map*, p. 66). During the following years, a successful collaboration on Koryak culture developed, in particular with Aleksandra Urkachan, the head of the Department of Folklore at the State Koryak Centre for Arts and Crafts in Palana, that resulted in the elaboration of innovative methodological approaches in order to produce various kinds of learning tools. In 1999, Aleksandra Urkachan joined the ensemble *Nulgur* on its tour of Germany to perform traditional Koryak family songs. In 2000, she invited Erich Kasten to the Nymylan (Coastal Koryak) village of Lesnaya in northwestern Kamchatka, where he attended a seminar on the preservation of Koryak traditions (Kasten, ed. 2004), and where he was for the first time guest at the ritual festival *Ololo*. Immediately both drafted a programme on preserving Koryak cultural heritage that they have carried out since then up until now. In summer 2001, Erich Kasten invited Aleksandra Urkachan to the Max Planck Institute for Social Anthropology in Halle, where he was then working as the coordinator of the Siberian group and where they prepared her book *Veemlen* (Urkachan 2002) for publication. This monograph is extensively used as a highly regarded and useful teaching tool in Kamchatka and has recently been reprinted there as a second edition.

Since the fall of 2001, Aleksandra Urkachan and Erich Kasten have carried out field projects almost every year at various times of the year in northern Kamchatka, in remote villages, at fishing sites, and reindeer camps up to the Khailino area, where they have recorded Koryak texts and documented traditional activities. The focus has been on ritual feasts, the particularly rich tradition of family songs and oral traditions – especially *Kutkiniaku* (Raven) stories – and traditional resource use. On the latter theme they organised in 2002, for example, a series of field seminars in and around Lesnaya, during which elders demonstrated and discussed harvesting and processing activities in their own language Nymylan (coastal Koryak). Preparing for various exhibitions in Germany[15] they documented in detail traditional crafts and techniques of material culture, with commentaries of craftsmen and -women in their local dialects of the Koryak language (Kasten 2003; Kasten and Dürr 2005).

At a workshop in Ossora in 2008, another new methodology was successfully employed. Elders and young artists from various villages came together and discussed and practised innovative ways of transmitting endangered cultural knowledge from older generations to the young. The striking experience from these days of mutual exchange and learning was strong motivation and enthusiasm on all sides. Therefore, it is a priority in our agenda for the years to come to conduct more workshops of this kind in other parts of northern Kamchatka as well. From the extensive cultural information and language data that has been and will be documented during such activities, electronic learning tools and print media are in preparation, and some of them are already published (Kasten, ed. 2010).

In 2012 another project has started in collaboration with the University of Fairbanks, Alaska, that investigates the potential contribution of indigenous knowledge to teaching and learning mathematics.[16] For the Koryak part of this cross-cultural research, one particular focus is on decorative arts, i.e. the documentation and analysis of making patterns that adorn clothing. The results will not only lead us to understand the embedded mathematical processes used in constructing and making everyday tools and artifacts, but will also have the potential to establish an alternative learning trajectory based on indigenous knowledge systems for the teaching of mathematics in indigenous and non-indigenous contexts. For this, a number of special editions are planned on this theme within the DVD series *Koryak language and culture*, together with more publications that are foreseen on other kinds of traditional knowledge.[17]

Additional learning tools and prospects for the future

Edited volumes from contributions to seminars and workshops in Kamchatka and the monographs of native project partners (see above) serve as teaching aids in schools and other cultural curricula in Kamchatka. In addition to these materials, since 2011, the quarterly periodical *Ėchgan* has been edited by Erich Kasten und Aleksandra Urkachan and published by the Foundation for Siberian Cultures in collaboration with one of its partner institutions in Kamchatka, the State Koryak Centre for Arts and Crafts in Palana. It serves as a teaching tool in schools and other institutions of culture in Kamchatka. It is aimed at assisting in teaching native themes, such as traditional ecological knowledge and arts and crafts in conjunction with Koryak language. Texts assembled according to various themes are given in the Koryak language with Russian translations and are presented here more in the tradition of print media and conventional teaching materials, whereas all volumes of this periodical can also be viewed and downloaded for free from the internet.[18]

Another initiative that is currently under preparation aims to integrate our own recently recorded field data with historical information that was collected by scientists during the 18th and 19th centuries in Kamchatka on native knowledge, in particular traditional resource use. This will be pursued through a comprehensive database project starting from the extensive registers that are compiled from the edited volumes of the Bibliotheca Kamtschatica series, edited by Erich Kasten and Michael Dürr and published by the Foundation of Siberian Cultures.[19] This project is carried out in collaboration with the Kamchatka Branch of the Pacific Institute of Geography, Far-Eastern Department of Russian Academy of Sciences (KBPIG, FED RAS), as its foremost focus is on traditional sustainable resource use. Often these historical accounts also contain information about former native plant and animal names. Although the scientists of that time used their own transliterations, as far as they could understand these words in the respective native languages (Dürr, in Kasten et al. n.d.), some of these accounts can be useful to learn more about parts of the vernacular that were used at that time, and that have often got lost or have gone through some variations since then.

To identify former layers in – natural – continuous variations and changes in these native languages will also be a challenge in another project that focusses on oral traditions, in particular the huge stock of raven (*Kutkiniaku*) stories. Even here we aim to compile relevant texts that were recorded by Jochelson and Bogoras – some already as sound files on wax cylinders – at the beginning of the 20th century, in order to compare and to integrate them with the great number of texts on *Kutkiniaku* that have been recorded by us a hundred years later. To show and to study such variation in the Itelmen and Koryak languages is not only interesting from a linguistic or scientific point of view. Also for local native people it helps to connect them back to a more distant past that adds to even greater esteem of their cultural heritage, and that motivates them to preserve and to further develop such valuable traditions. For this aim, the Jochelson Itelmen ('Kamchadal') texts are published in a new edition in contemporary Itelmen orthography with Russian translations (Khaloimova et al. 2013).

This forthcoming work on *Kutkiniaku* traditions reveals another issue that we had already been confronted with during the Itelmen and the Even project, and that now provides us with the opportunity to follow this up more closely. It relates to the fundamental question of to what degree printed versions of oral traditions can adequately reflect some of the significant features and messages conveyed by them. In particular, the ongoing variations and reinterpretations by individual storytellers cannot be caught and identified appropriately if oral traditions are presented in a kind of 'frozen' state in printed editions only. The other point is the important body language that is missing there, whereas it can be captured well in video presentations. Above all, printed oral traditions lose many of the languages' most crucial and valuable qualities, rendering them not only less interesting for the audience, but also prevent them from being further developed and elaborated.[20] Here our foreseen DVD editions on this particular theme will have clear advantages and will open up new possibilities. Certainly, they will stir up more interest on this important theme of the cultural heritage of Koryak culture, as did our previous DVD publications on traditional family songs.[21] This is another significant genre in Koryak culture, whose basic feature and fundamental meaning is, similar to *Kutkiniaku*- and other oral traditions, its continuous variation, which is shown in the performance by different family members (and other speakers).

Our next focus on *Kutkiniaku* oral traditions will direct our attention to even more fundamental themes of Koryak culture, as it will provide access to particular Koryak world views and rules of proper social and ecological conduct and behaviour that are transmitted through these stories in an ironic way to the very young, and at the same time get reinforced among adults and elders. Connected to these and other oral traditions are important values and social and environmental ethics that provided the foundations for these peoples to survive and to create their impressive cultures under harsh conditions over many centuries. To present these materials in an appealing way, particularly to the youth, will be one of the greatest challenges for our team in the years to come.

Lessons learnt from the activities discussed above

At present, the Koryak and Even language is spoken in Kamchatka only occasionally by a shrinking number of elders. Their children sometimes still understand their language, but they are usually no longer able to speak it. While they do not use their language at home, it is no longer transmitted by the current parents' generation to their children as their 'mother tongue' (*rodnoi yazyk*). Such language shift could probably still have been prevented in the 1990s, at least for Koryak and Even, if adequate methodologies had been applied and sufficient state support had been provided to reverse that trend.

From closely monitoring and analysing the methodology of existing learning tools and their use in the school curriculum over the last 20 years, it became obvious that most of them were not able to meet the given challenge. The methodology would have to be fundamentally revised so that the native language were taught again as one's 'mother tongue', and not in the same way as a second language in school. The standardised native language school books, conceptualised and introduced by Soviet state programmes in the 1980s, and still in use, have probably contributed more to the rapid language shift than prevented it. For example, Itelmen school books (*bukvari*) are still written (and printed) in this style in various editions even for advanced classes, although this language is no longer taught in Itelmen communities due to the lack of teachers. Moreover, the complex texts in these books are given without any translations so that these might be understood in this form only by the author herself, and probably by a half dozen of the remaining elder Itelmen speakers. Another methodology, launched in the mid-1990s (Khaloimova et al. 1997) could have been more appropriate here, as these books are designed to be used even beyond the school curriculum (cf. Dudeck, *this volume*). Furthermore, they start with everyday phrases of Itelmen speech that can easily be understood, and on which the revitalisation of that language could be built upon, if community members wish to do so. Since then, more Itelmen learning tools have been designed this way (Degai and Koto 2011, Ryzhkov 2012).

A recent documentation of the use of standardised school books in Koryak classes in Lesnaya illustrates the obvious shortcomings of the previous methodology (Kasten and Dürr 2013). A particular noun is given in Russian that is then looked up by students in the Chawchuven Koryak dictionary (see *cover photo*), written down in the exercise book and then on the blackboard, and eventually pronounced accordingly – whereas it differs considerably from that word in the Nymylan Koryak dialect, still spoken by many elders in that village. The teachers are well aware of this problem and are eager to integrate the new DVD learning tools into their curriculum, not only in their Koryak language classes, but even into other subjects such as local history, ecology and so on (Kasten and Dürr 2013).[22] This has the advantage that it connects

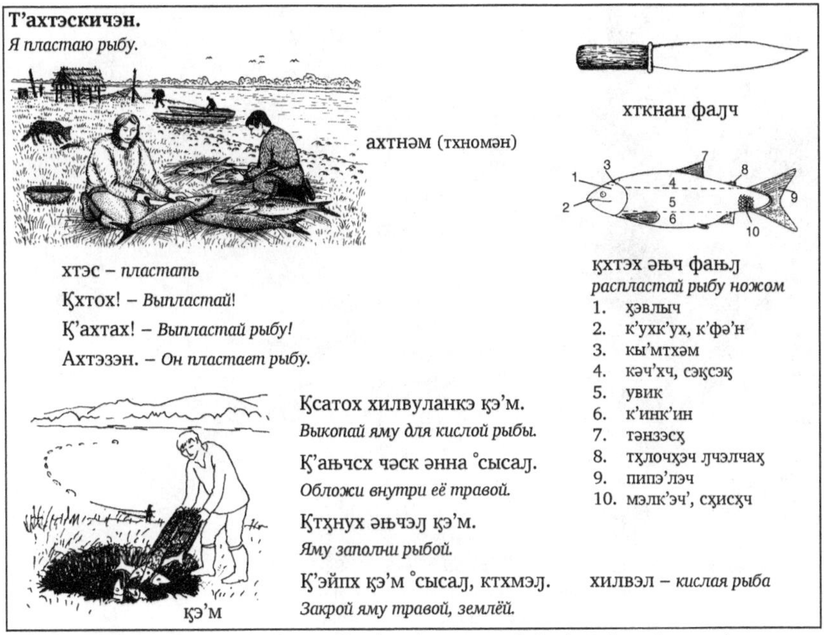

Т’ахтэскичэн.
Я пластаю рыбу.

ахтнәм (тхномән)

хтэс – *пластать*
Ӄхтох! – *Выпластай!*
Ӄ’ахтах! – *Выпластай рыбу!*
Ахтэзэн. – *Он пластает рыбу.*

хткнан фаЈч

ӄхтэх әњч фањЈ
распластай рыбу ножом
1. ӽэвлыч
2. к’ухк’ух, к’фә’н
3. кы’мтхәм
4. кәч’хч, сэӄсэӄ
5. увик
6. к’инк’ин
7. тәнзэсӽ
8. тӽлочӽэч Јчэлчаӽ
9. пипэ’лэч
10. мэлк’эч’, сӽисӽч

Ӄсатох хилвуланкэ ӄэ’м.
Выкопай яму для кислой рыбы.
Ӄ’ањчсх чәск әнна °сысаЈ.
Обложи внутри её травой.
Ӄтӽнух әњчэЈ ӄэ’м.
Яму заполни рыбой.
Ӄ’эйпх ӄэ’м °сысаЈ, ктхмэЈ.
Закрой яму травой, землёй.

ӄэ’м

хилвэл – *кислая рыба*

|11| From ‘Historical-ethnographical teaching materials for the Itelmen language’, Khaloimova et al. (1997), new edition 2012, p. 101.

and presents language and indigenous knowledge in an integrated way, as it has been transmitted in their natural environment before (see illustrations, *next page)*.

From those experiences we are even more confirmed in our approach to integrate programmes on endangered indigenous knowledge into other relevant community activities that raise the peoples’ own high regard for their cultural heritage. This contributes to stimulating the crucial and indispensable motivation, in particular among the youth, to maintain and to further enhance their cultures, for example, through artistic expressions. Therefore, the Foundation for Siberian Cultures supports native artists in performing at museum exhibitions, in addition to its strong emphasis on and contribution to the preservation of endangered languages (Kasten 1998, 2005b, 2009c). It also supports tours by youth dance ensembles[23] in Germany and other parts of Europe. The experiences that they usually have during their visits abroad and the appreciation that they receive there for the artistic expressions of their highly valued cultural heritage are reflected back to their communities where these create favourable results (Kravchenko 2010). In order to direct additional attention to such native performances among an international audience these are also frequent themes in the special internet format of the Foundation for Siberian Cultures, ‘Shows on the Web’.[24] A strong focus of our work should, therefore, be directed towards supporting or creating favourable socio-economic environments

|12| Sharing traditional knowledge with the grandson in Even language at a fishing camp near Anavgai.

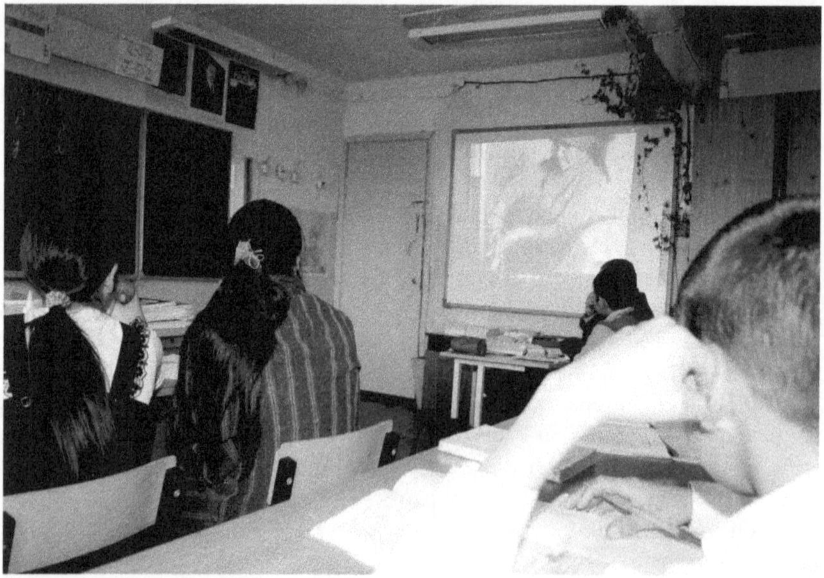

|13| Integrated school class on Koryak language and local history with DVD learning tools in Lesnaya.

in the given communities where it could be made easier for native world views and relevant values and expressions of their own cultures to thrive.

When presenting outward expressions of one's own culture, there is the risk that the performers may come to view their culture as a commodity (see Kasten and De Graaf, p. 9, *this volume*), if they expect immediate (financial) returns from it. This is in line with increasingly commercialised social relations even within native communities, where, fortunately, traditional behaviour and values such as mutual help and sharing are still strong (Kasten 2012: 80 f.). Certainly, artists depend on remuneration for their work in order to make their living and to concentrate on further developing their creative talents. However, for example, selling secret rituals or world views to tourists as kinds of souvenirs can be questionable, as this may remove inherent meanings from these ideas. Many of the important values and orientations that are communicated through such rituals would consequently no longer be transmitted or be properly understood by young people (Kasten 2009a: 29). Therefore, short-term material gain has to be viewed and balanced against possible long-term detrimental effects while presenting and offering one's cultural heritage to others.

On the other hand, new models for creating feedback, even from the artists to support the preservation of endangered cultures in their communities, have been tested and successfully employed. Through a special agreement, their commitment and responsibility to participate in this process was called in and could be demonstrated at home, for example, by the youth ensemble *Shkolnye gody*: A certain part of the financial contribution from German sources for its tour in Germany in 2004 was transferred to them in the form of the edited (Russian) conference volume entitled *Preservation and Revitalisation of Traditional Ritual Feasts of Coastal Koryaks (Nymylans)* (Kasten, ed. 2004) which also serves as a learning tool. Copies of that book were then distributed for free by ensemble members in their home communities in Kamchatka. This made the young artists – another time – proud of their performance upon their return, when they were acknowledged for supporting the culture of their people even at home. Psychologically it is important and stimulating especially for younger people to feel rewarded for such initiatives that do not serve exclusively their own individual gains, but also express their responsibility for the needs of the community as a whole. There might be other creative models of this kind to think of in order to install or support proper (communal) motivation among the young to preserve their native cultures – according to the tradition of these peoples and in contrast to modern more individualistic ways of thinking.

As soon as sufficient project-funding or donations may be made available for the above-mentioned applied programmes in the future, native communities should be compensated in the first place for their valuable contribution in sharing their indigenous knowledge and cultural expertise with us, and with the interested general public. These funds should not be handed over in the form of individual cash payments, in order to avoid detrimental side-effects within the community (see Kasten and De Graaf, p. 9, *this volume*), but should rather be used for certain projects such as community-driven workshops, learning tools and so on.[25] In order to create the appropriate sense of motivation among community members it seems to be important that they become involved in the process, not for the purpose of individual material gain, as this would blur and divert attention from the more significant over-arching aims and from their obligation to take upon themselves their own responsibilities to preserve their endangered cultures.

The latter also concerns Russian state authorities, as these should not get used to the trend of these programmes being mostly sponsored by international organisations and from abroad. Russia has become a prosperous country as a whole, although barely balanced in a fair way among its entire population. It would be up to those who have gained a lot from the economic transformations of the last number of years to assume responsibility towards their country and its people to whom they owe their fortunes. Furthermore, it would be the duty of Russian state authorities to call in these obligations, and direct sufficient funds into these programmes.

Regarding remuneration for the international scientists who direct or participate in the projects that have been presented here, it should be mentioned that they work voluntarily beside their permanent jobs in academic positions or they derive their incomes from other scientific project work. Admittedly, this kind of volunteer work is not always properly understood in Russia, where it has occasionally even been discredited, as already in the 1990s (Alexandra Lavrillier, *personal communication*, 4 October 2011);[26] and especially for young international scientists this cannot offer an attractive perspective – whereas it seems to be the only way to bridge the gap until such projects are adequately funded.

Against this background and according to relevant international standards that also have developed in recent years from similar experiences even in other parts of the world, most programmes of the Foundation for Siberian Cultures are carried out now only on a co-funding basis. In the beginning, in 2002, we sent 100 copies of Aleksandra Urkachan's book *Veemlen* to Kamchatka for free distribution in the communities. However, we later found out that these were sold there and also in other places such as in Khabarovsk by members of a Kamchatkan cultural institution, on their own account. Since then we do not deliver ready-printed and fully financed teaching materials to Siberia any more, as long as our philosophy is not adequately shared by relevant partners there. In order to expect cooperation and co-funding from local authorities we provide – according to recent agreements – only the setting copy of these materials, from which a sufficient number of copies is printed (and financed) in Kamchatka. Only a limited number of copies are given for free to local co-authors and main cultural institutions, libraries and schools in the area to which the traditions that are presented in the materials pertain. Thus, it is up to international organisations and to the Russian authorities to contribute their share to this collaborative and meaningful process.

Conclusions

Many scientific programmes aimed at documenting endangered languages are bound by their guidelines to address community-oriented activities, although these goals often come across as mere tokens of political correctness. In most cases they have not had significant effects in preserving these languages within the communities. On the other hand, such approaches to documenting and analysing endangered languages sometimes give the impression that these languages are being treated more as 'curious specimens' such as items in ancient ethnographic collections. Meanwhile, the pressing need to maintain linguistic and cultural diversity for the future of humankind is often ignored. Apparently, applied anthropological initiatives (see Lavrillier, *this volume*) achieve lower status in scientific research programmes, where they obviously do not attract adequate attention and funding. However more recently one can identify changing trends, such as in current programmes of the National Science Foundation. But so far, scientists pursuing academic careers could expect more credit for keen analysis and elaborate theories than for undertaking struggles at a grassroots level in the communities.

For international organisations it is often the easiest and politically correct option to hand over relevant funds to major native organisations, generally based in the city, and trust that they will carry out the programmes as expected. However, the native urban community is often fragmented and factionalised, especially with regards to securing such funds and deciding how these will be used. Moreover, there is often a great distance[27] – and not only physically – from the city to the regional centres and from there to even more isolated settlements, fishing sites and reindeer camps, where this kind of support is most urgently needed, but only seldom received.

Even international organisations that are active themselves in the region could in many cases attain their proclaimed goals more effectively. Often their focus is more on well-financed fact-finding missions and on series of international conferences on these issues. These activities are not sufficiently matched by consistent and probably more urgently needed concrete initiatives in the communities themselves in order to put into effect relevant programmes there (see Kasten, *above*, Lavrillier, Odé, *this volume*). Therefore, many native people perceive such international organisations more as self-serving groups that are concerned, first and foremost, with meeting their own needs.

Ethnic festivals (*prazdniki*) in urban or regional centres provide Russian government officials and culture workers with auspicious opportunities to celebrate themselves. This is a well-known phenomenon in the tradition of former Soviet practise and is carrying on the political function of its 'Houses of Culture'. Although many residents consider these events a welcome distraction, considerable amounts from the culture budget are consumed this way to demonstrate – well-covered by the media – the government's endeavours in the interests of native cultures. At the same time funds for concrete programmes and relevant learning tools to preserve endangered cultural traditions in more remote settlements far away from these centres are cut back or do not even exist. But it is just in those places where these means could be used most effectively to counteract the afore-mentioned trends of loss of linguistic and cultural diversity. There such diverse and unique traditions in some cases are still alive.

Finally, it is certainly appreciated that scientists and international organisations are concerned about maintaining cultural and linguistic diversity and that they see its endangerment as a serious problem for the future of humankind. The problem is, however, the obviously missing or inadequate balance between fact-finding missions, conference discussions and scientific research on the one hand, and matching programmes and sufficient funding for implementing appropriate measures on the other. First and foremost, the latter may be in the position to stop the ongoing trends of language endangerment and loss of cultural diversities that should have been sufficiently researched and clearly identified by now.

Notes

1 I am grateful to my friends among the Dzawada'enuxw of Kincome Inlet who first taught me the basics of true collaborative projects. For providing me access to conduct a scientific research project on the 'Potlatch' with them I first had to consider what I could give the respective native community in return. Thus we drafted an exhibition project that I brought to fruition at the Ethnological Museum in Berlin in 1989, through which Dzawada'enuxw artists were promoted to a wider foreign public and from which the given Native community benefitted as a whole (Kasten 1990).

2 http://www.kulturstiftung-sibirien.de/pro_1271.html

3 Interim results from these projects were discussed in my seminars at the Free University of Berlin in the 1990s with students who started their own Siberian field projects at that time, and I am particulary grateful to the valuable and inspiring exchanges with Stephan Dudeck during that time.

4 I am grateful to the Deutsche Forschungsgemeinschaft and to the Max Planck Gesellschaft that funded a number of scientific research projects in Kamchatka. However, they did not share the concern for the applied anthropology modules within such projects that are presented in this article and for which no funding was provided, so that these had to be carried out by me and the team aside from my scientific projects on a voluntary basis.

5 For more information on the state of the Itelmen language at the beginning of the project see: Kasten 2009b.

6 The particular native language situation in Kamchatka differs obviously from what we learn in this volume, for example on relevant Evenk and Forest Nenets cases by Alexandra Lavrillier and Stephan Dudeck, whereas the situation in Kamchatka seems to be quite similar to what Hidetoshi Shiraishi and Tjeerd de Graaf have found with the Ainu and Nivkh (*this volume*). As for the Itelmen, also among the Even and Koryak the present parents' generation is not in full command of its native language anymore and is not prepared to use it in primary education. Consequently, the model of nomad schools that seems to be promising for other regions in the Russian North would probably not apply to Kamchatka, where native culturally-related peda-

gogies and learning tools have to be designed differently. Here we should recall and be aware of the shortcomings of any generalised solutions such as those that were promoted in later Soviet times, without taking into consideration that these should fit particular local situations within the country.

7 http://www.siberian-studies.org/publications/PDF/ILC2additions_E.pdf
http://www.siberian-studies.org/publications/PDF/ILC3texts_songs_E.pdf

8 http://www.kulturstiftung-sibirien.de/vir_26_E.html

9 http://www.kulturstiftung-sibirien.de/pro_123_E.html

10 http://www.kulturstiftung-sibirien.de/ver_422_E.html

11 http://www.kulturstiftung-sibirien.de/mat_32_E.html

12 Regarding the Evenk case, Alexandra Lavrillier shared similar concerns, as to her it is not comprehensible that a particular standard for language education at school and for printed learning materials was chosen from Evenk spoken in the Krasnoiarsk area. The particular dialect of the 3,000 Evenk who live there is not representative of the rest of the 30,000 Evenks, where especially among their southern groups much more common features can be found (personal communication, 4 October 2011).

13 Continuous fluidity and variation is obviously an inherent feature of oral traditions. Those texts that we recorded at different times were never the same, but in the meantime were extensively further elaborated. Another striking fact is that it has proven almost impossible to let the given speaker make the transcription of his or her own spoken text, as the person usually insisted on modifying it considerably.

14 Tables of contents and sample clips of the so far published DVDs can be viewed in the internet: http://www.kulturstiftung-sibirien.de/mat_32_E.html

15 Ethnographic items were first collected for an exhibition at the Westfälisches Museum für Naturkunde in Münster in 2003 (and later in Windhoek/Namibia 2005–2007): http://www.kulturstiftung-sibirien.de/ver_415_E.html. Other items were shown at exhibitions at the Zentral- und Landesbibliothek in Berlin in 2005: http://www.kulturstiftung-sibirien.de/ver_416_E.html; and at the *Linden-Museum* in Stuttgart in 2009: http://www.kulturstiftung-sibirien.de/ver_417_E.html

16 http://www.kulturstiftung-sibirien.de/pro_1274_E.html

17 Tables of contents and sample clips of the DVDs that have been published so far can be viewed under: http://www.kulturstiftung-sibirien.de/mat_33_E.html

18 http://www.siberian-studies.org/publications/echgan_E.html

19 http://www.siberian-studies.org/publications/bika_E.html

20 During our seminar, a lively discussion arose on this issue. Tesesa Valiente questioned if oral traditions should be transcribed anyway or if one shouldn't rather leave them as they are. Michael Dürr added that scripting is a highly complicated process of transformation, and the written result is never the same as the oral original. But on the other hand, he continued, you need to write it down for some aspects of teaching, because somebody who is not fluent in the language has otherwise no access to the rich oral tradition without written texts. (personal communication, October 4, 2011)

21 http://www.kulturstiftung-sibirien.de/mat_332_E.html

22 http://www.kulturstiftung-sibirien.de/mat_33.html. Samples from a televison documentary show the integrated use of the new DVD learning tools in the school curriculum in Kamchatka: http://www.kulturstiftung-sibirien.de/vir_31_E.html.

23 http://www.kulturstiftung-sibirien.de/ver_42_E.html
http://www.kulturstiftung-sibirien.de/vir_29_E.html

24 http://www.kulturstiftung-sibirien.de/virtuell_E.html

25 Even here one should be aware of keeping the right balance, as not well thought out (material)

support from the outside could be mistaken as 'missionising' or as 'persuading' the indigenous communities in a paternalistic way to 'imitate' certain moves (cf. Vakhtin, p. 262, *this volume*).

26 See also the latest editions of 'KO-RUS Kurier, Freiwilligkeit als Voraussetzung und Katalysator für zivilgesellschaftliches Engagement', *Newsletter des Auswärtigen Amts der Bundesrepublik Deutschland*, 8. und 9. Ausgabe, 2012, also in Russian.

27 In Kamchatka, similar trends of 'superscribing' native culture and 'top-down concepts propagated by ethnic elites' can be identified such as in the case of the urban Yi community in China described by Kraef (p. 240f., *this volume*).

References

Avak, Raisa 2010. Evenskii yazyk i kul'tura [Even language and culture]. In *Kul'tury i landshafty Severo-Vostoka Azii: 250 let russko-nemetskikh issledovanii po ekologii i kul'ture korennykh narodov Kamchatki* [Cultures and landscapes of northeastern Asia: 250 years of Russian-German research on the ecology and the culture of the native peoples of Kamchatka], E. Kasten (ed.), 141–144. Fürstenberg/Havel: Kulturstiftung Sibirien. http://www.siberian-studies.org/publications/PDF/klavak.pdf

Degai, Tatiana and Rolando Koto 2011. *Kamchatka – mezvin semt* [Kamchatka – my home]. Petropavlovsk-Kamchatskii: Kamchatpress.

Dürr, Michael 1998. Multimedia Materials for Native Language Programs. In *Bicultural Education in the North: Ways of Preserving and Enhancing Indigenous Peoples' Languages and Traditional Knowledge*, E. Kasten (ed.), 269–274. Münster: Waxmann Verlag. http://home.snafu.de/duerr/multimedia.html

Dürr, Michael, Erich Kasten and Klavdiia Khaloimova 2001. *Itelmen Language and Culture*. CD. Münster: Waxmann Verlag.

Dul'chenko, Elena 2010: Izuchenie traditsionnykh znanii korennogo i mestnogo naseleniia Kamchatki [Research on traditional knowledge of native and local people of Kamchatka]. In *Kul'tury i landshafty Severo-Vostoka Azii: 250 let russko-nemetskikh issledovanii po ekologii i kul'ture korennykh narodov Kamchatki* [Cultures and landscapes of northeastern Asia: 250 years of Russian-German research on the ecology and the culture of the native peoples of Kamchatka], E. Kasten (ed.), 125–131. Fürstenberg/Havel: Kulturstiftung Sibirien. http://www.siberian-studies.org/publications/PDF/kldulchenko.pdf

Kasten, Erich 1990. *Maskentänze der Kwakiutl. Tradition und Wandel in einem indianischen Dorf.* Berlin: Dietrich Reimer Verlag.

— 1998. *Kinder malen ihre Welt. Kinderzeichnungen aus Sibirien und von der Nordpazifikküste* (deutscher Text / russkii tekst). Münster: Waxmann Verlag. http://www.siberian-studies.org/publications/PDF/kasten1998b.pdf

— 2003. Zwischen Tundra und Meeresküste: Korjaken und Evenen im Fernen Osten Russlands. In *Unterwegs – Nomaden früher und heute*, A. Hendricks (Hg.), 83–112. Gütersloh: Siegbert Linnemann Verlag. http://www.siberian-studies.org/publications/PDF/kasten2003b.pdf

— 2005b. *Rentierhorn und Erlenholz: Schnitzkunst aus Kamtschatka* (deutscher Text / russkii tekst). Berlin: Zentral- und Landesbibliothek. http://www.siberian-studies.org/publications/PDF/kasten2005a.pdf

— 2009a. Schamanen – sibirische Weltbilder, westliche Gegenwelten. In *Schamanen Sibiriens: Magier, Mittler, Heiler*, E. Kasten (ed.), 24–31. Berlin: Dietrich Reimer Verlag.

— 2009b. *Itelmen Language and Culture*. UNESCO Register of Good Practices of Language Preservation. http://www.siberian-studies.org/publications/PDF/kasten2009.pdf

— 2009c. Schamanische Motive in indigener Kunst. In *Schamanen Sibiriens: Magier, Mittler, Heiler*, E. Kasten (ed.), 204–211. Berlin: Dietrich Reimer Verlag.

— 2012. Koryak Salmon Fisheries: Remembrances of the Past, Perspectives for the Future. In *Keystone Nations: Indigenous Peoples and Salmon across the North Pacific*, B. J. Colombi and J. F. Brooks (eds.), 65–88. Santa Fe: SAR Press.

Kasten, Erich (ed.) 1998. *Bicultural Education in the North: Ways of Preserving and Enhancing Indigenous Peoples' Languages and Traditional Knowledge*. Münster: Waxmann Verlag. http://www.siberian-studies.org/publications/bicult_E.html

— (ed.) 2002. *Deti Severa – Uroki kul'tury. Kul'turnoe nasledie Kamchatki – budushchim pokoleniiam* [Children of the North: Lessons of culture. The cultural heritage for future generations]. G. M. Rassokhina (red.). Petropavlovsk-Kamchatskii: Kamchatskii pechatnyi dvor. http://www.siberian-studies.org/publications/detsev_E.html

— (ed.) 2004. *Sokhranenie i voszrozhdenie traditsionnykh obriadovikh prazdnikov u beregovikh koriakov (nymylanov)* [Preservation and revitalisation of traditional ritual feasts of coastal Koryaks (Nymylans)]. Urkachan A. T., Kosygina F. N., Zaochnaia, T. (red.). Krasnodar: Izdadel'stvo Kamshat. http://www.siberian-studies.org/publications/praznym_E.html

— (ed.) 2010. *Fol'klor i khudozhstvennoe tvorchestvo narodov Severa Kamchatki* [Folklore and arts of the peoples of northern Kamchatka]. Urkachan A. T., Zaochnaja T. (red.). Fürstenberg/Havel: Kulturstiftung Sibirien / Norderstedt: BoD. http://www.siberian-studies.org/publications/folklor_E.html

Kasten, Erich and Michael Dürr 2005. *Feasting with the Seals: Koryaks and Evens in the Russian Far East*. DVD. (German / English / Russian subtitles). Berlin: Zentral- und Landesbibliothek.

— (eds.) 2013. *Sustaining Endangered Languages and Indigenous Knowledge*. Video DVD with a booklet in English/Russian/Chinese/Spanish languages. Supplement to this edited volume. Fürstenberg/Havel: Kulturstiftung Sibirien.

Kasten, Erich, Michael Dürr, Marie-Theres Federhofer, Erki Tammiksaar und Diana Ordubadi (n.d.). Der Beitrag deutschsprachiger Gelehrter zur frühen Nordostsibirienforschung. In *Reisen an den Rand des Russischen Reiches: Die wissenschaftliche Erschließung der nordpazifischen Küstengebiete im 18. und 19. Jahrhundert*, E. Kasten (ed.). Fürstenberg/Havel: Kulturstiftung Sibirien.

Khaloimova, Klavdiia 1999. *Metodicheskie rekommendatsii (materialy) uchiteliu itel'menskogo yazyka* [Methodical recommendations (materials) for the teacher of Itel'men language]. Petropavlovsk-Kamchatskii: Izdadel'stvo Kamshat. (New edition: 2013, Fürstenberg/Havel: Kulturstiftung Sibirien.) http://www.siberian-studies.org/publications/PDF/khaloimova1999.pdf

Khaloimova, Klavdiia, Michael Dürr, Erich Kasten and Sergei Longinov 1997. *Istoriko-etnograficheskoe uchebnoe posobie po itel'menskomu yazyku* [Historical-ethnographical teaching materials for the Itelmen language]. Petropavlovsk-Kamchatskii: Kamshat. (New revised edition: 2012, Fürstenberg/Havel: Kulturstiftung Sibirien.) http://www.siberian-studies.org/publications/itelmenuchebnik_E.html

Khaloimova, Klavdiia, Michael Dürr and Erich Kasten (eds.) 2013. *Itel'menskie teksty* [Itelmen texts]. Collected and compiled by V.I. Jochelson, in contemporary Itelmen orthography and with Russian translations. Fürstenberg/Havel: Kulturstiftung Sibirien.

Kravchenko, Valerii 2010. Krasota zashchishchaet nash mir [The beauty defends our world]. In *Kul'tury i landshafty Severo-Vostoka Azii. 250 let russko-nemetskikh issledovanii po ekologii i kul'ture korennykh narodov Kamchatki* [Cultures and landscapes of northeastern Asia: 250 years of Russian-German research on the ecology and the culture of the native peoples of Kamchatka], E. Kasten (ed.), 153–170. Fürstenberg/Havel: Kulturstiftung Sibirien. http://www.siberian-studies.org/publications/PDF/klkravchenko.pdf

Ryzhkov, Viktor V. 2012. *Kivvechkh (Rucheëk)* [stream]. Razgovornik na itel'menskom i russkom yazykakh, Skazki narodov Severa. [Conversation manual for the Itelmen and the Russian languages, tales of the peoples of the North]. Petropavlovsk-Kamchatskii: Kamchatpress.

Urkachan, Aleksandra 2002. *Veemlen (Lesnaya) – zemlia moikh predkov.* [Lesnaya – the land of my ancestors]. Petropavlovsk-Kamchatskii: Izdadel'stvo Kamshat. http://www.siberian-studies.org/publications/PDF/urkachan.pdf

6 LEARNING YOUR ENDANGERED NATIVE LANGUAGE IN A SMALL MULTILINGUAL COMMUNITY: THE CASE OF TUNDRA YUKAGIR IN ANDRIUSHKINO [1]

Cecilia Odé

In admiring memory
of Anna Gavrilovna Vyrdylina

Introduction

This paper discusses the language situation of the Tundra Yukagir in the multilingual community of the village of Andriushkino. According to the data for 2005 on the website of the Sakha Information Agency (www.ysia.ru/nkol.php), the taiga and tundra of the Nizhnekolymsky *ulus* (Nizhnekolymsky district), where the village of Andriushkino is situated, has a surface area of nearly 88,000 km^2 with less than one person per 10 km^2.

During fieldwork in Andriushkino in the winter of 2009, I collected some statistics at the administrative office of the village and at the school. In 2009, the population of Andriushkino was 895 people, 607 belonging to the minority peoples Yukagir (223), Even (349), Chukchi (21), Evenki (4), and a few Dolgan (6) and Nenets (4). The other 288 people are mostly Yakut, and only 30 Russians inhabit the village. These numbers include the nomads living on the tundra. This small and exceptional multilingual community with eight peoples poses an especially complicated picture for the schools in the village, where teachers have to deal with different ethnic groups speaking completely unrelated languages. There is a strong hierarchy though in the use of these languages. Russian is the dominant language in school, whereas Yakut is the dominant language in daily life, also among the minority peoples. This will be further discussed where appropriate in this article.

The people are fishermen, hunters, herders, and in the village they work in the school, in the polyclinic, in the administrative office, the meteorological station, the heating installation, shops and the like. But many people are unemployed and more or less self-supporting in their daily life. Sometimes they move to other villages hoping to find work, or move to the capital Yakutsk if they can afford the expensive trip. Others may fall into a state of depression and start drinking. As in many Siberian villages, drinking by both men and women, even at an early age, is a very serious problem. The village has a cultural centre where almost every Saturday concerts and other cultural events are held, often followed by a discotheque. For these events villagers sew costumes and make accessoires themselves and it is amazing how good and inventive they are at designing these. Music and songs are usually accompanied by a disco-beat at an unbearable pitch, also the traditional music that they are so proud of. The commonly heard reason is that otherwise young people would not come to the concerts. Yet songs and storytelling performed in the traditional way by elders are silently listened to by all generations with respectful attention. The cultural centre is also used for bigger national and regional feasts. There is a small polyclinic with one doctor, some nurses, a cook and a pharmacy. For serious diseases patients go by helicopter to Chersky, some 300 km east of Andriushkino (over land 450 km), which has a hospital. If patients cannot be helped there either, they fly to the capital Yakutsk at a distance of 1800 km (over land more than 3000 km) to the southwest of Chersky, a flight that takes four to five hours.

Shops are mostly located in a room in a private house where articles and food are sold at ridiculous prices because of transport costs and the monopoly owners have on the products. Fresh food is not available, at best there are some deep frozen products. As many villagers are fishermen and hunters, there is no lack of fresh fish and meat. In summertime berries are gathered and preserved or deep frozen for the long winter. These berries are extremely rich in vitamins. Though the summer is short, villagers manage to make greenhouses of wooden poles covered with thick plastic and within a few months vegetables such as tomatoes, cucumbers and cabbage can be harvested and are then preserved or bottled. Note that preserving products is no problem in the permafrost area, where it suffices to dig a cellar in the ground to keep your fresh stock deep frozen. During the three month summer holiday villagers are busy preparing for winter.

The Tundra Yukagir people, their villages and their language [2]

Tundra Yukagir is, together with Kolyma Yukagir and other isolated Siberian languages like Nivkh, a Paleo-Siberian or Paleo-Asian language. To this group of languages belong, for example, also the Chukotko-Kamchatkan and Eskimo-Aleut languages (*Yazyki mira, Paleo-aziatskie Yazyki*, 1997).

Tundra Yukagir is a seriously endangered language in Arctic Russia that together with Kolyma Yukagir forms one language family. Tundra Yukagir (henceforth: TY) is spoken by the people with the same name in the northeast of the Russian Federation in the Republic of Sakha (also: Yakutia) between the lower Indigirka and the lower Kolyma. The exact size of the population is unknown, but is probably about 700. The number of good speakers of the language is dramatically lower than this. For a discussion of the term 'speaker' the reader is referred to Kasten and De Graaf (p. 10, *this volume*). In this article, a speaker is someone who is fluent in his native language in speaking and understanding, though not necessarily in reading and writing. In the literature, approximately 50 people still having a reasonable knowledge of their native language is usually mentioned. During fieldwork in 2010, however, I registered the names of 62 speakers: 28 in Andriushkino, 13 in Chersky, 6 in Kolymskoe, 15 in Yakutsk. Their age varies from 4 to 80 years, but most speakers are over 50 years old. The older generation was mainly born on the tundra. Nowadays it is hard to tell how many members of the TY people living on the tundra master their native language, so the number may be even higher. Most TY speakers are fluent in Yakut and Russian, and often in other indigenous languages of the area, such as Even and Chukchi. Most TY speakers live in the village of Andriushkino on the Alazeia River and on the tundra, mostly north of the village. They also live in Chersky and Kolymskoe, on the lower Kolyma River.

As a Yukagir settlement, Andriushkino has a special official status: *Administratsiia natsional'nogo yukagirskogo obrazovaniia 'Olërinsky suktul'* [Administration of the National Yukagir Education Settlement 'Olëra tribe'] in the Lower Kolyma District of the Republic of Sakha. The Olërinsky *suktul* is named after the river and lakes Olër and the TY word *suktuul* 'tribe'. Andriushkino is the only village in the Russian Federation where the TY language is taught in all classes of the school from kindergarten to the highest, eleventh, class of the secondary school. Note that all other subjects are taught in Russian and courseware and learning materials are also in Russian.

Traditionally, the Tundra Yukagir are nomadic reindeer herders. They adopted herding from the neighbouring Chukchi, as originally they were hunters. Since their origin is beyond the scope of this article, for a more detailed description the reader is referred to Forsyth (1992: 74–80), Kurilov (2006: 3ff.), Maslova (2003: 1–2) and Pakendorf (2007: 18). In these sources reasons why the TY people decreased from about 5500 in the beginning of the seventeenth century to about 2500 at the end of the seventeenth century, and to some 700 today, are also discussed. To give an impression: war, oppression by other peoples, natural disasters and epidemic diseases (smallpox), but also mixed marriages especially with Evens are the main causes of this decrease. Some Even and Yukagir don't even know exactly who they are, because they switched their nationality administratively more than once, if this was beneficial for them.

Tundra Yukagir language consultants

Since 2004, the following TY speakers have been or still are my main native language consultants (the approximate ages indicated between brackets are from the year 2010):

- in Chersky: Akulina Innokent'evna Struchkova (74), Vasilii Nikolaevich Tret'iakov (57), Liubov' Vasil'evna Kurilova (62), and the late Varvara Khristoforovna Neustroeva († 2008) and Anna Nikolaevna Kurilova (†2008);
- in Andriushkino: Fedora Ivanovna Borisova (50), Matriona Nikolaevna Tokhtosova (69), Svetlana Alekseevna Atlasova (65), Maria Nikolaevna Kurilova (65), Anasta-

sia Semënovna Tataeva (50), Proskop'ia Ivanovna Pavlova (46), Dora Nikolaevna Tataeva (48), Anna Egorovna Tret'iakova (78), Il'ia Ivanovich Kurilov (55), Vasilii Ivanovich Kurilov (50), Fedosiia Il'inichna Kurilova (20) and her daughter Alayii (4) who is named after the TY tribe Alayii, Il'ia Ivanovich Kurilov, the singer (50), Dar'ia Nikolaevna Kurilova (67), Anastasiia Semënovna Kurilova (47), Akulina Ivanovna Malysheva (55) and the late Anna Gavrilovna Vyrdylina († 2010);
- in Yakutsk: Gavril Nikolaevich Kurilov (72), Nikolai Nikolaevich Kurilov (61), Polina Ivanovna Sintiakova (55) and the late Ekaterina Ivanovna Tymkyl' († 2005).

All consultants master speaking and understanding, but not all are good at reading and writing, if at all, which is not surprising, as there is no special need to write the language and hardly any written literature exists.

Our native consultants were almost all born on the tundra in a reindeer herder family and lived a nomadic life until the age of seven, when they had to go to school. Not all of them went to school at the obligatory age. Those who did had great communication problems as TY was usually the only language they knew, since until 1958 all subjects were taught in Yakut and learning materials were also in Yakut (Struchkov 2008: 91).

From 1958 until the present day, all subjects and learning materials at schools except native languages are in Russian. For the older generation (in 2010 fifty years old or older) going to school was a drama, as TY and all other minority languages were practically forbidden until 1980, though not officially or by law. School children were punished for speaking their native language and indoctrinated with the idea that they should be ashamed of their native language as being an inferior language, and using it would isolate them from other peoples, as I was told by a 48 year-old TY teacher at a primary school, recounting to me her personal experience. The school children rapidly started to learn Yakut and later Russian and became bi- or trilingual. This is long since the case, also in other regions. However, at home they were also discouraged from speaking their native language. Children did and do not always live together with their parents, but stay with other non-TY families, so depending on the frequency of contact with their parents, they may gradually start to forget their native language.

The school in Andriushkino

The first school in the area Nizhnekolymsky *ulus* was founded in 1930 in the settlement Khara-Tale, some 3 km from the village. In 1941, the village was built under the name *Ondoriuskė* 'Andriushka', hence the name Andriushkino. In 1947, the primary school was moved to the village and in 1961 the school was extended to eight classes. It was in 1993 that the school obtained the special status of National Secondary School (Vyrdylina 2006: 57–58).

Andriushkino has a kindergarten with two classes and a primary and secondary school with eleven classes. In 2010 in the kindergarten there were altogether 76 children, and 175 in primary and secondary school. Not all of the approximately 80 TY children go to TY language classes, as Yakut is considered more useful for the children's future and their career (see also p. 100 ff.). Sometimes non-TY children join the TY classes. Russian is obligatory for all. Until recently there were four teachers of Tundra Yukagir. In February 2010, the TY population lost its most experienced teacher and linguist, Anna Vyrdylina, in a tragic accident. Under her stimulating direction, both pupils and teachers worked together. Another good teacher left the school in 2010 to continue her university studies in the capital Yakutsk. She is ambitious and is pursuing a career in linguistics. In spring 2011, two new teachers, inexperienced in language teaching, have taken over their tasks.

Tundra Yukagir and language education

According to G. N. Kurilov (*personal communication*), it was in 1979 that in Andriushkino Anna G. Vyrdylina started teaching TY as a separate subject in primary school. The first TY alphabet developed by G. N. Kurilov appeared only in 1987. Since 1990, the native languages TY, Even, Yakut and Chukchi are taught in primary and secondary school. Nowadays, TY lessons are given from 5 to 6 hours per week in the first four classes, 4 hours per week in the next four classes, and up to 2 hours per week in the last three classes. Besides the native language, pupils learn about the traditional TY culture, rituals, costumes, music, dance, cooking and utensils, and learn how to make handicrafts from, for example, fur and wood. Since 1992, learning TY starts in kindergarten *Podsnezhnik* 'Snowdrop', but, unfortunately, they just play with isolated words like those for relatives, colours and numerals; not even short full sentences are learned. The TY generation between 30–50 years old in 2010, who in their youth were not allowed to use their native language, has on average a poor command of the language, yet they usually understand it quite well. So sometimes young children now learning TY at school speak TY with their grandparents or with the nomadic TY who always lived and still live on the tundra, rather than with their parents. There is no nomadic school in the area and there was, to my knowledge, only one unsuccessful attempt to create one, in 2009. The proposal was accepted by the Ministry of Education, but nothing further happened. I addressed the issue with local teachers, but in their opinion there was no need for a nomadic school, as the few children whose parents live on the tundra always have relatives in the village they can stay with. Some teachers were even against a nomadic school: children should grow up in the village, they felt.

The method used for teaching is the so-called 'translation method'. Pupils translate sentences or words from Russian into TY and the other way round, and frequently write dictation exercises. They answer improvised questions asked by the teachers about the texts they translate. Learning materials are very limited and exercises for practicing items they just learned do not exist. With financial support by UNESCO, a rich collection of audio recordings on CD with tales, poems and songs has recently (2009) been made available to the schools. However, these CDs come without any accompanying texts, transcriptions, directions or annotations. Moreover, in the classroom it is not possible to listen to the recordings, as in school there are no reliable CD-players, and computers work too slowly, don't work at all or have no sound card or speakers. There was no further initiative undertaken by UNESCO or the Sakha Ministry of Education to develop any additional materials for the discs. The available textbooks in the TY language have no translations or exercises to accompany the texts. There is no learner's dictionary and the only very limited dictionary which has both Yukagir-Russian and Russian-Yukagir is, unfortunately, full of errors and lacks many common words (Atlasova 2007). The academic dictionary (Kurilov 2001) has an impractical alphabetical order in the sense that words are presented with their compounds etc. by root and not in a strict alphabetical order. There is also no learner's grammar. I was told by the teachers that the grammar written by Gavril Kurilov (2006) for the higher classes in secondary school is much too difficult. And again, all existing materials have no exercises or practice tasks. Interactive materials are not developed at all.[3] Therefore, teachers prepare teaching materials themselves by drawing tables with, for example, verb conjugations and case inflections and pictures with names of objects on posters they hang on the wall. They make exercises in the classroom or improvise them on the blackboard. So it is thanks to the commitment of the teachers that there exist any teaching materials at all.

Many texts in TY were written before an orthography was actually developed, the official orthography by Gavril Nikolaevich Kurilov existing only since 1990. However, this orthography still leaves a lot to be desired. For example, in the orthography there is no agreement on long vowel /o:/ written by Kurilov as '*oo*', which can be observed as pronounced with a short vowel [o], a long vowel [o:] or a diphthong [uo]. According to Kurilov's orthography, these three different phonemes /o/, /o:/ and /uo/ should be written as 'o', 'oo' or 'uo', respectively. A problem here is also dialectal difference in pronouncing the vowels. The result is, that if in spoken TY a word with /o/ or /o:/ occurs, one will have to check all three spellings '*o*', '*oo*' and '*uo*' in the dictionary to see which one is correct according to Kurilov's orthography, supposing that he has it all right. The same holds for /o/ and /ö/, even if a minimal pair exists. Understandably, for teachers and for children learning the language this confusing spelling is frustrating, as it is for us linguists and our language consultants with whom we register and transcribe spoken TY.

As said earlier, parents and children hardly ever speak the TY language at home. At best it is spoken when children live with their grandparents who speak the language among themselves. This is the most preferable situation for learning to speak

TY, especially if also during the three month summer holiday they stay with their grandparents. Unfortunately, writing skills are as a rule very poor as there is no special need to write the language.

Despite all the negative factors discussed above, pupils are eager to learn their native language. I witnessed their pride during TY lessons. They are aware of their TY identity, but they are also aware of belonging to a minority people of the north and in this sense their awareness of identity is also a collective one. Important in this respect is also the fact that the TY language is now taught in a setting with improving modern facilities. For example, during my last field trip (March 2012), I noticed that language classrooms are provided with computers and more audio-visual courseware has been developed. Teachers would like to have karaoke in the classroom and develop TY rap. The TY language is often considered a traditional language of nomadic people. This attitude should be changed to TY being a modern language, making it much more attractive to learn and practice. Twice a week there is a radio programme by TY writer and artist Nikolai Kurilov, with news, interviews, songs, old recordings, not only about the TY people and is, except for interviews with non-TY people, exclusively in the TY language. All TYs in the village listen to it.

Unfortunately, the local TY community has not been very active in promoting TY language education. Only recently are the TY people and also other peoples increasingly interested in language education and actively support its development. It is therefore disappointing that hardly any financial support from governmental authorities is given or is expected in the near future, as I was told (March 2012). The local authorities cannot be blamed too much for this situation, as they try hard to get financial support and themselves have hardly any means to help the schools.

"What does learning your native language mean to you?" Children express themselves [4]

The following short essays that were written upon my request by pupils in the third class tell about motivation to study TY. The question was: "What does learning your native language mean to you?" Note that the family name *Kurilov* is very common in the area and does not necessarily indicate any kinship between people carrying that name. The short essays were collected in 2009 by TY teacher Anastasiia Kurilova who, unfortunately, paraphrased the texts a little bit to make them, as she suggested, sound better. The texts were translated by the author as close to the original as possible.

> "For me the Yukagir language is important so that when we are gone it is passed on to our children. I want the Yukagir language to live and sound loudly. Each Yukagir must know and love it so that it does not disappear but will always live in our hearts. And our children should not lose it!" (*Igor Kurilov*).

"For us the Yukagir language is a native language. We are Yukagirs. In the old times our great grandparents talked in this language. Everybody must know and love his native language. I like to study the Yukagir language. In each lesson we learn new words, we translate from Yukagir to Russian, we sing in our native language, I know Yukagir writers. I love, respect and preserve my native language!" *(Eseniia Tret'iakova)*.

"The Yukagir language is necessary for conversation, for example, somebody asks you something in Yukagir and you don't know how to answer, that is why the native language is needed. Only few of us are left. Our great grandparents spoke Yukagir from their childhood. And we also must know our native language. If we don't know it, it will disappear, it will die. Preserve your native language!" (*Lena Toiento*).

"I need the Yukagir language in order to know my native language. If we don't know it, few Yukagirs will be left. We will soon be adults, we will know and understand the language, and then we will be proud of ourselves. I want to know my native language!" (*Maria Kurilova*).

"My native language is the Yukagir language. When we are old, our language will be passed on to our grandchildren, will be passed on from generation to generation. I love my native language very much and cherish it. If I didn't know it, then our children and grandchildren will also not know it and they will be ashamed. I will learn my native language!" (*Sergei Nikulin*).

If all TY children are indeed so consciously proud of their native language as stated in their essays, then revitalisation can be considered possible. Unfortunately, as we will see below, only a small percentage of all TY children attend TY language classes.

TY teachers on teaching their native language

During fieldwork in winter 2009, I organised a meeting with TY teachers. The aim was to discuss the present situation of TY language teaching and to make an inventory of unpublished teaching materials written on cards and posters by themselves. We expected that this inventory could serve as a checklist for what exactly is lacking. On the basis of such an inventory a list of priorities could then be made. This was expected to be a difficult task, because the materials are not documented or sorted as to type or level, but are kept in boxes by each individual teacher.

A general complaint of the teachers is that they have no time to develop teaching materials to make these ready for publication, and there is also no money to publish them. They also complain about the fact that there is not enough support by the Ministry of Education, and now they are frustrated and don't try anymore to get support.

They especially need methodological support. Andriushkino is a very remote village, they said, and it is easily forgotten unless villagers raise their voices loudly. The village is extremely hard to reach; sometimes helicopters don't come for months. There is only one helicopter for a region of 30,000 km^2, and it is often only used for urgent transportation of seriously ill people, or of officials. Another complaint is that teachers' wages are very low (in 2010 some 30,000 Roubles per month, approximately 750 Euro) as compared to the quantity of working hours.

The three–hour-long meeting held in Russian was so useful that I will now present some relevant parts of the script of this meeting that I recorded. As can be understood from the fragments below, three obligatory languages are learned in primary and secondary school: Russian as a first language, in which all other subjects including local knowledge are also taught, English as a second language, and a national language as a third language. The third language can be chosen by the pupils themselves, but in practice it is the parents who make the choice. Since Yakut is for them an obvious choice, as Yakut is the national language of the Sakha Republic, and in the future children will benefit most from Yakut, most children are sent to the Yakut group. But children learning in the Yukagir, Chukchi or Even group also learn Yakut, because that language is most frequently spoken among villagers and is the lingua franca of the area. In summertime, when many children live with their parents on the tundra in small settlements or in tents with the herders, the language commonly used is also Yakut. Note that in Andriushkino it is an every-day situation that people of different ethnic groups and language backgrounds come together and have to speak a language they all understand. All children know Russian quite well too, but despite a high degree of motivation their English is very poor, also in the higher classes.

The three teachers involved in the discussion were the late Anna Vyrdylina (linguist, qualified language teacher, classes 9–11; director of the school), Valentina Tokhtosova (non-qualified language teacher, classes 5–8), and Anastasia Kurilova (non-qualified language teacher, classes 1–4). The others attending were PhD student Mark Schmalz (working on TY morphology) and the author (language documentation, prosody, language teaching). The English translation is mine and names of speakers are abbreviated to their initials AV, VT, AK, MS and myself as CO. First the selected fragments are presented, followed by my comments.

AV: "We have no methodology. Of course we need exercises and tasks to go with the grammar."

VT: "I made a TY alphabet in poetry with pictures, but I cannot finance the publication. Can you help me to publish it?"

AV: "Here is a book in which I participated. I compiled texts by TY writers." AK: "You hide your materials from us!" AV: "Yes, of course I hide it from you. (...) These are stories from Kolyma Yukagir which I translated into Tundra Yukagir and I typed the texts myself. (...) Stories, texts and dictations, lots of texts, but we don't edit these texts in a proper way. (...) I don't have the time. (...) Nothing is ready. We have to learn how to edit texts properly (...) in a methodologically correct way."

CO: "Do you have written exercises or tasks for the pupils that they can carry out themselves?" VT: "In the classroom I ask them, for example: find the verb in this sentence." CO: "So you improvise exercises during the lesson?" VT: "In the course of the lesson, yes." CO: "So you would need such materials in written form." AV: "Yes, of course. They read a text, analyse it, and do the exercises during the lesson." VT: "Before school I sit down to prepare the lesson, take the dictionary, translate the TY text into Russian, then think about what to tell the pupils, what meaning the story has, what exercises to do with them."

AV: "Of course nobody works on grammar. We tell the children what we know and have them learn it. (...) In this respect teaching is very difficult for us. Because our children don't know the language. And it will become even more complicated because fewer and fewer people master TY."

AV: "It is probably my fault, but I never have time. I should make a programme, because only I know all eleven classes."

VT: "I understand Yukagir, but I haven't fully mastered the language. I only teach children. It is only my third year. Therefore it is sometimes very difficult for me. Then I go to Anna Gavrilovna who helps me. She plans the lesson, how to run the lesson. Each word, everything she writes down for me. Then I learn it all by heart, go to school and teach how it was written down."

AV: "This is of course the biggest problem. They all have to address me for help. On the other hand, that is not convenient for them. And not for me, because I have a programme, I have it all ready." CO: "In your head?" AV: "In my head, yes, my whole life I have it all, but I did not register it in written form, well, in a scientific way, how would you call it. Well, for example, I will not always teach. They, the young ones, will stay. I am always afraid: who will do all this after me? I am afraid, all the time, it scares me." VT: "That's why I say: everything must be published so that it will be left behind for us." AV: "During my whole life many linguistic expeditions came here, they collected materials. Many times they collected materials at a time when I didn't understand that there is a need to do so. If these materials had been in written form, or phonetically, uh, in a phono-library, then maybe it would be easier. Even I forget some words. I forget them, I don't remember everything, then I have to ask someone. But who?" VT: "Publish everything, so that it is kept." AV: "Nowadays many people work on course books for other subjects. There are so many authors for other subjects, aren't there? We don't have that. In the whole world there are standardised course books, methods. Well, that is exactly what we need."

AV: "There are many minority peoples in the world. Each people has something interesting. Well, such interesting aspects should somehow be taken together, so that each people learns something about the others, if only a little bit. That would be interesting. On the other hand, text materials about modern life are also necessary." (...) "I am happy that we teach conversational speech. But conversational language does not exist without writing. You say a word and it flies away. It's another thing if you have seen its written form or a picture."

AV: "I would like, for example, to have a kind of scientific model and a programme and course books, in the first place for the primary classes. (...) The teaching materials must be interesting, nice, very attractive, in such a way that they learn something new and recognise themselves. (...) We are an experimental school and that requires a good methodologist in all respects, because we must make programmes, produce materials, we must finish our work, but where are we going to do this in this constant rush? That's the problem." (...) CO: "I don't think that text materials is the problem, but how to structure them, so that they become a real course book with exercises and tasks, especially for the first classes." AV: "Exactly. Starting with the first classes, because everything depends on them."

VT: "We have to wake people up. Because a complete degeneration is going on. People somehow go down, down, down and don't want anything. (...) In hospital on the cards you can see that every second newborn is a Yukagir. But they learn Even or Yakut." AV: "That is because of the mixed marriages. If it is lucrative for them, they are Yukagirs. If not lucrative, they are not. It is lucrative where they get certain things for free, like medicine." VT: "Come on, Yukagirs, send your children to the Yukagir group. They say: No, the Yukagir group is so complicated, the child will not be able (to learn the language, C.O.), because it is difficult to pronounce, words are very long." AK: "But in the pharmacy they get their medicine for free." VT: "We must work on the parents. My mother didn't tell that she is Yukagir, my father is Yakut, but my mother is Yukagir. However, she didn't say: Daddy is Yakut so send her to the Yakut group. (...) Let the children learn Yukagir because it is disappearing!" AK: "In the first class half of the children are Yukagir but I have only one pupil (in my Yukagir group, C.O.). Everything should happen in kindergarten and when they come to the first class..."

AV: "Russian is obligatory in all public schools. Yakut is the state language. Our Russian children learn Yakut. We consider English (the second obligatory language, C.O.) necessary as international language." VT: "We are a national school." AV: "Whatever nationality the pupil has, that language he studies. (...) As a national village, languages are studied according to the nationality you have."

MS: "Children choose the language (as a third language, C.O.) they want." VT: "What the parents want, to that group they go." CO: "A third language is obligatory, but which one they choose themselves." AK: "They choose themselves."

The remarks and complaints about teaching materials sound alarming, especially since the death of Anna Vyrdylina. Though there was, according to her, no structure in her materials, they could still be used as a basis to develop a language course, but we don't know where they have gone. All her belongings have been taken away from the school by her family. Particularly alarming is the role of the TY parents, who do not send their children to the TY groups. Very often a TY parent is married to a speaker of another minority language, and so at home they speak mainly Yakut. Yakut is considered the best choice for children with respect to their future education, profession and career. In this respect the strength of the influence of Yakut nationalism should not be disregarded. Language ability, both in Yakut and Russian, gives you even better chances. In the Andriushkino setting this is very understandable given the increasing unemployment in the area. Even if both parents belong to the TY community, they do not know why their children should learn their native language. It is thus highly recommended that parents of newborns learn what it means for their children to learn the native language, and why as early as kindergarten they should send their children to the respective language group. In this group they should not learn only isolated words as is the situation now. Special emphasis should be placed on culture, traditions, nomadic life and nature in the environment of the child, using a methodology that is attractive to them. For example, learning to pronounce words, certainly not difficult at a young age, can be done by repeating words from a recording referring to traditional TY nomadic life with audio-visual illustrations. But, as said earlier (p. 93ff.), it should also be made clear to children that the TY language is a modern language in which modern life as well as traditional life can be expressed. I would also suggest teaching local knowledge in the local languages, not only in Russian as is now done.

In the 2009 situation, not all teachers were equally fluent in their native language, and some had no full education in language teaching and were not well enough equipped for their task, but they all were very motivated. In the 2011 situation things had changed for the worse, because now there was no TY teacher who was fully educated and fluent in all skills.

Teaching and learning TY: is there a future?

Given the disappointing data presented above on TY teaching and learning, it would seem that if parents do not send their children to the TY language group, the TY language will soon disappear as a native language in school and hence in daily-life communication. However, there are examples of minority languages in the Siberian northeast that have enough courseware, but that are not spoken anymore, not even by the older generation. Such an example is Itelmen (Kasten 2008). In the context of TY, today there are only some families left who use their native language in daily communication. The number of TY reindeer herders who live their nomadic life on the tundra is decreasing rapidly. Only three herds are left. Next to the nomads there are some settlements where TY families live. A particularly striking and unique example is the TY Kurilov family with members living on the tundra and in the village, where four generations speak only the native language among themselves, the youngest, Alayii (see *Illustration 14*), being five years old in 2012. Unfortunately, in 2011 she

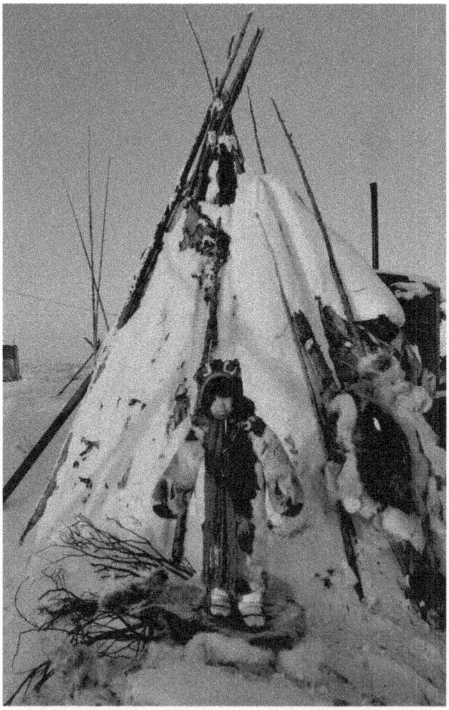

moved to the village and lives with her grandparents. Her grandmother is an Even who understands but does not speak TY. With her grandfather and mother Alayii used to speak TY, but since 2011 she has been speaking Yakut with her friends and grandmother. Since 2011 she has been going to the kindergarten and her grandparents will send Alayii to the TY group in kindergarten where she has the great advantage of understanding TY and knowing nomadic life, but the disadvantage is that the language lessons, in the way they are given, as I pointed out above, will not be much use to her. It only helps her not to forget words that other TY children may not know at all. I met Alayii in March 2012 and

|14| Alayii in front of her tundra dwelling

|15| School children in Andriushkino

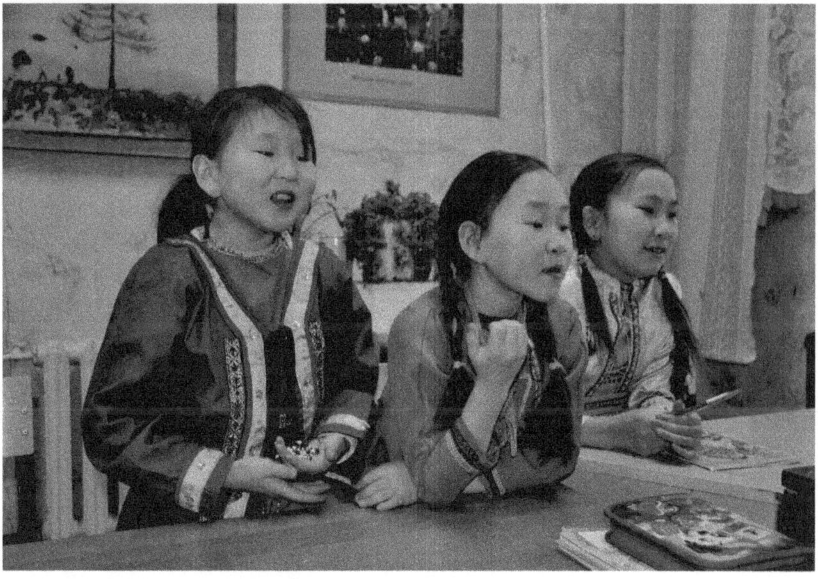

noticed that she understands TY but does not speak it anymore. Her mother, fluent in TY, lives with the herders on the tundra, where little Alyaii seems to be happy too, as I witnessed during my last field trip.

Extra school activities like excursions with a TY would motivate both teachers and pupils. These could take the form of, for example, trips to the Kurilov settlement to spend a traditional day with the family, while only speaking TY, and engaging the students in activities like making a ritual fire, feeding it with tea and food while improvising words that ban evil spirits, cooking a meal, making traditional clothes and decorations, going fishing, etc. The teacher could prepare such a day before setting off to the Kurilov settlement.

Every young TY child in the village has his or her own unique cultural and linguistic background which makes it complicated to develop a language education programme for all TY children. Differentiated instruction in the TY language classroom would be the ideal solution, but in the given situation, as described in the previous sections, is impossible to realise: lack of sufficient qualified teachers, no methodology for language teaching and learning, no appropriate courseware.

The minimal requirement for safeguarding the TY language for future generations would be a specific curriculum development for the Andriushkino situation. It would include, for example, the planning and development of an effective language education programme, organising teacher training courses, writing a learner's grammar and dictionary, developing exercises and tests to add to the existing collection of textbooks and sound recordings. However, developing such a curriculum is unrealistic. As Anna Vyrdylina clearly pointed out during our meeting in 2009: "We are an experimental school and that requires a good methodologist in all respects, because we must make programmes, produce materials, we must finish our work, but where are we going to do this in this constant rush? That's the problem."

Our research project 'Tundra Yukagir' (http://www.tundrayukagir.info) is limited in time (2009–2013). We cannot meet all the urgent needs of the Andriushkino school staff and supply the language teachers with a specialised methodologist. That is the task of the Sakha Ministry of Education and the local authorities in the district, but so far no methodologist has been willing to work in the village and, moreover, there has been no financial support. What we can do is provide teachers with instructions on developing course materials (exercises and tests) for the collection of texts and sound recordings, as well as with our continuing moral support. Informing the authorities and making publications for a broad audience about the situation in Andriushkino would also be desirable.

Very encouraging is the new initiative in March 2012 by TY Vasilii Tret'iakov to create a TY community in Chersky with official statutes, which gives him the possibility to apply for grants. This community of which Vasilii is the chairman now has a board with a secretary and a treasurer. All TY people who accept the statutes can become members, for which they pay a yearly fee of 600 Roubles (15 euro). Vasilii already started a 'Sunday school' in Chersky where TY children learn their native language. So far such a possibility did not exist in Chersky. Unfortunately, as in Andriushkino, the TY teachers suffer from a lack of courseware.

Finally, a main and first requirement for the safeguarding of Tundra Yukagir is informing the parents of the youngest TY children about what their children may win or lose in joining or not joining the TY language group: their native cultural traditions, indigenous knowledge, stories and legends, ecological knowledge. Moreover, they can be proud of their native language which has a unique status, being an isolated language not related to any other language group in the world. And it is language in which culture is expressed. Losing yet another language decreases the diversity in the world, languages and cultures become lookalikes, and non-natives and TY who don't master their language will be unable to access the TY language, history, culture and their vision of the world. That is the message that somehow must reach the TY children in a way they can understand.

Notes

1 The present research is financially supported by the Netherlands Organisation for Scientific Research (NWO).
2 Parts of the first sections are taken from Odé's work in progress on the Tundra Yukagir language.
3 The only person capable of developing and constructing appropriate learning and teaching materials, Anna Gavrilovna Vyrdylina, to whom the present article is dedicated, died at the age of 68 in 2010. For years she was the director of the school in Andriushkino, the TY teacher for the advanced pupils and the 'walking TY encyclopedia' for the younger TY teachers. Her passing is a tragedy for the teaching of TY. In autumn 2009, together with the young teachers, we were just about to make an inventory of learning materials that exist in one form or another and a listing of materials that were most urgently needed. Developing such materials is part of the current TY project.
4 The essays by TY children have earlier been published in Russian in Odé (2011).

References

Atlasova, E.S. 2007. *Slovar' yukagirsko-russkii i russko-yukagirskii* (tundrennyi dialect, 3500 slov.) [Yukagir-Russian and Russian-Yukagir dictionary (Tundra dialect, ca. 3500 words)]. Sankt Peterburg: Prosveshchenie.

Forsyth, James 1992. *A History of the Peoples of Siberia. Russia's North Asian Colony 1581–1990.* Cambridge: Cambridge University Press.

Kasten, Erich 2008. Preserving Endangered Languages or Local Speech Variants in Kamchatka. In *Endangered Languages and Language Learning*, Proceedings of the Conference FEL XII. T. De Graaf, N., Ostler and R. Salverda (eds.), 151–154. Leeuwarden: Fryske Akademy.

Kurilov, G. N. 2001. *Yukagirsko-russkii slovar'* [Yukagir-Russian dictionary]. Novosibirsk: Nauka.

Kurilov, G. N. 2006. *Sovremennyi yukagirskii yazyk* [The Modern Yukagir Language]. Yakutsk.

Maslova, E. 2003. *Tundra Yukagir.* Languages of the World / Materials 372. München: Lincom Europa.

Odé, Cecilia 2008. Teaching Materials on Language Endangerment. In *Endangered Languages and Language Learning,* Proceedings of the Conference FEL XII. T. De Graaf, N., Ostler and R. Salverda (eds.), 147–150. Leeuwarden: Fryske Akademy.

— 2011. Tundrennyi yukagirskii yazyk kak rodnoi v Andriushkinskoi shkole [Tundra Yukagir as a native language at school in Andriushkino]. In *Ulica Ševčenko 25, korpus 2.* Scritti in onore di Claudia Lasorsa. V. Benigni and A. Salacone (eds.), 169–173. Caissa.

Pakendorf, Brigitte 2007. *Contact in the Prehistory of the Sakha (Yakuts).* Utrecht: LOT.

Struchkov, K. N. 2008. Yazyki malochislennykh narodov Severa v obrazovatel'nom prosntranstve respubliki Sakha (Yakutiia). In *Yazyki i fol'klor narodov Severa.* A. N. Myreeva (ed.), 89–101. Novosibirsk: Nauka.

Vyrdylina, A. G. 2006. Ob Andriushkinskoi natsional'noi srednei shkole [About the Andriushkino National Secondary School]. *Tatkachiruk* (2), Nauchno-metodicheskii zhurnal. S. S. Semenova (ed.). Yakutsk.
(http://www.nlib.sakha.ru/knigakan/journals/tatkachiruk_2006_2.pdf)

Yazyki mira. Paleoaziatskie yazyki. 1997. T. Yu. Zhdanov, N. V. Rogova, O. I. Romanova (eds). Moskva: Indrik.

7 ANTHROPOLOGY AND APPLIED ANTHROPOLOGY IN SIBERIA: QUESTIONS AND SOLUTIONS CONCERNING A NOMADIC SCHOOL AMONG EVENK REINDEER HERDERS

Alexandra Lavrillier

Introduction

Designing and implementing a project for language revitalisation is not easy and requires facing many obstacles in various domains, most of which are really unexpected. I will illustrate some of these obstacles on the basis of my own experience as a social anthropologist who never planned to take part in an applied anthropology project, but was asked to by the community. This example can also demonstrate the need for a good knowledge (be it anthropological or not) of the concerned society when carrying out such a project.

From social anthropology to applied anthropology

The path from social anthropology to applied anthropology may contain a certain theoretical contradiction. Keeping in mind, firstly, that in contrast to what some anthropologists tended to describe in the past, societies are not 'frozen',[1] since they were and are changing due to various cultural exchanges, individual or global issues, and secondly, that neither social anthropology nor applied anthropology are 'neutral' in terms of influence over the concerned societies, and thirdly, that current applied anthropology has developed new approaches, there are still important differences between social/cultural anthropology and applied anthropology.

This theoretical contradiction was highlighted in a historical debate between French anthropology and Anglo-Saxon anthropology (between the 1950s and the 1970s), but also between the so called 'ivory-towerish' anthropology in England and the 'practicing anthropology' in the USA. This opposition was based on the following principle. Social anthropology aims to observe and study the society, avoiding as much as possible changing it (even if the lack of influence of the anthropologist in the field, or of his or her writing, is an illusion). In contrast, applied anthropology or development anthropology, willingly involves anthropological knowledge in decision-making processes that are acting on (with) the society, or sometimes somehow deciding for the society (Baré 1995). Indeed, it groups persons from different cultures (i.e. from different cognitive realms) in one common action that can be a source of additional problems. It also transplants onto traditional societies some alien/foreign resources, techniques and knowledge (together with the development). In addition, in contrast with social anthropology, applied anthropology applies the method and theory of anthropology to the analysis and solution of practical problems and often works for non-academic agents such as governments, development agencies, NGOs, tribal and ethnic associations, advocacy groups, social-service and educational agencies, and businesses. In the 1990s, these applications of anthropology were realised in almost every part of the globe (Cernea 1991; Baba and Hill 1997; Hobart 1993; Long and Long 1992). Nevertheless, applied anthropology can have and usually has a consulting role, and ethnography with participant observation are the applied anthropologist's primary research tools (Olivier De Sardan 1995, Lévi-Strauss 1958: 440–443). More recently renamed 'engaged anthropology', applied anthropology redefines its sphere of activity as following: "from basic commitment to our informants, to sharing and support with the communities with which we work, to teaching and public education, to social critique in academic and public forums, to more commonly understood forms of engagement such as collaboration, advocacy, and activism" (Low and Merry 2010). In spite of the development of more participatory methodology and reflexive approaches that avoid some previous approaches that were close to colonialism, Aiello writes that "among the dilemmas that remain unresolved" regarding engaged anthropology "are the ethics of intervention, the appropriateness of critique given the anthropologist's position, and the hazards of working with powerful government and military organisations."[2]

Despite the historical contradictions mentioned above, the link between ethnography or anthropology and applied anthropology is ancient. Except for the involvement of L.H. Morgan in the 19th century in Indian Affairs, the first experiences of applied anthropology date from the 1930s and were initiated by John Collier in some Indian reservations. Some famous western anthropologists took part in applied anthropology, such as, in the 1940s M. Mead and G. Bateson, who created the Society for Applied Anthropology.[3] In the East, from the 1930s to the1950s, the Russian ethnographers were consultants for the Soviet state in order to propose solutions for the economic development of indigenous peoples, to study the consequences of Soviet policies on Siberian societies and, in particular, to create an alphabet and indigenous language manuals; to build up a unified and standard written indigenous language from numerous dialects of one language. In spite of the current development of engaged anthropology in the USA, most French anthropologists are still sceptical and critical of applied anthropology. This situation may change in the future since for instance the University of Paris X has a Master programme with an option in development anthropology and the University of Versailles developed a Master of 'Arctic Studies' that attributed scholarships to Siberian indigenous students.

The contradictions in the French position toward engaged anthropology mentioned above made me feel, in the beginning, embarrassed to be fully involved in the creation of the project for a nomadic school among the Evenk reindeer herders. On the other hand, Evenk in the field often told me that, according to their social logic of gifting and counter-gifting, "You take information from us, we give you a lot, but what do you give to us? You could help us with something". It is also, but in other words, what Fluehr-Lobban defines as collaboration, i.e. "key to the sustainability of anthropological fieldwork and research, and perhaps for anthropology as a discipline," meaning that collaboration helps to gain equality between researcher and 'researched' from its traditional top-down approach (Fluehr-Lobban 2008: 177). In contrast to France, in Anglo-American social anthropology, collaborative and participatory (research) projects have been developed for the last ten years. As an illustration of such a shift in research ideology, the expression 'applied anthropology' was also replaced by 'collaborative anthropology' or 'cooperative anthropology' and the term 'informant' was replaced by 'collaborator', 'co-researcher' or 'colleagues'. A good example is a project that directly addresses the reindeer herder's need for additional data and information in responding to the global and environmental changes called EALAT (2007–2010).[4] It is an unprecedented new reindeer herder-led initiative that is studying the challenges to reindeer herding posed by climate change.

To come back to our concrete case study, from 1996 to 2005, I spent some of the time I had free from social anthropology research helping with a project to create a nomadic school among Evenk reindeer herders in Siberia. After my Ph.D. was completed, I became more engaged in the project in 2005–2006, and devoted time to implementing the wishes of the Evenk nomads with whom I was working. But, from the beginning it was clear to me that my role had to be only to help in the creation of this nomadic school and that, when the project was running well on its own, I would distance myself from this direct involvement.

My way from social anthropology to applied anthropology was as follows. I performed fieldwork among the Evenk (but also among the Yakut of central Yakutia and the Even of northern and north-eastern Yakutia). I studied such themes as shamanism, ritual practices, indigenous concepts of the material and immaterial constituents of the individual, nomadic lifestyle, adaptation of nomadic collective representation to the settled lifestyle in villages, the renewal of traditional rituals after the fall of the Soviet Union, the urban minority *intelligentsia*, indigenous development projects, etc. For that purpose I learned the Evenk language and performed many field projects (in total for a length of six years between 1994 and 2003), mostly among the nomadic Evenk reindeer herders and hunters in two main areas related to the villages of southern Yakutia (Olekminsky and Nerungri *ulus*) and the north-western Amur region (Tyndinsky *rayon*).

Siberian and Evenk cultural and linguistic insights

Before explaining the Evenk nomadic school project, let me give an overview of the Siberian context. Today, most of the Siberian languages are endangered or have disappeared.[5] According to the decree of 2000, Siberia and the Far East of the Russian Federation count 40 indigenous peoples of the North with a population below 50,000 people,[6] for a total population of 250,000 people, which corresponds to 2 % of the whole population of the Russian Federation. Of these, 80 % of the indigenous population live in the villages and/or practise a nomadic lifestyle.[7] We can estimate that nomads represent around 10 to 20 % of the whole population of indigenous peoples of the North.[8]

As we will see from a case study of the south-eastern Siberian Evenk, indigenous languages are often better safeguarded in the nomadic realm and in villages to which a nomadic community is still related. In contrast, in villages where the population was completely settled, indigenous languages are often not used anymore. One of the reasons could be, as I often noticed in the field, that Evenk speakers prefer to use Russian in the village since, as they explain, the vocabulary is more adapted to the rural life (i.e. Evenk language has no term to designate 'administration', 'post office', 'street' or other items). According to the same logic, they prefer speaking Evenk language in the nomadic realm, since Russian has a lot of terminological lacunas for the nomadic lifestyle. So, logically it seems that in the case of the disappearance of the nomadic lifestyle (i.e. when the traditional uses of the natural environment disappear), Evenk language is not needed anymore.[9] Here I must clarify that, in contrast with other Arctic peoples, such as in the West among some Inuit groups, a standard language was not adopted by the population (see *below)* and no effective efforts were made to adapt vernacular language to urban life and technologies, which requires the commission of native speakers to create neologisms and the help of governmental institutions or media to impose the use of those new words.

The language situation seems to be better among some of the indigenous peoples with a population of over 50,000 peoples, such as the Sakha (Yakut), the Altai and the Tuvan.

The Soviet Union brought far-reaching changes to Siberian societies and cultures. Of these, the most important for our argument are the following. The nomadic populations were partly settled in villages built especially for that purpose. Most of the parents and all children received education in Russian in boarding schools and from that period, Russian has been the sole language of school teaching. Between the 1930s and the 1950s, according to the various regions, children of nomads were obliged to live in boarding schools and to be separated from their parents for months on end. In addition, according to the testimonies of the Evenk, until the 1980s it was strictly forbidden to speak indigenous languages within the walls of the boarding school. Some of the informants even remember being beaten by some educators if they were caught speaking their language. At the same time, in the 1930s, for almost every Siberian language – originally oral languages – a standard written language was created by linguists on the basis of one (or two) of the numerous dialects of each language. These Siberian standard written languages are currently taught in most of the boarding schools. Also, Soviet politics allowed for the appearance of an indigenous *intelligentsia* (current teachers, researchers, artists, writers, politicians, administrative workers, library and House of Culture workers, etc.).

The language situation of the Evenk can illustrate the consequences of Soviet politics. The Evenk are 70,000 individuals[10] and live in small groups in Eastern and Central Siberia (38,000 individuals in Russia) and in Manchuria (35,000 individuals in China), in taiga or tundra environments. Their language (divided into 51 recognised dialects) belongs to the Tungus-Manchu linguistic group together with the Even, Negidal, Nanai, Udihe, Ulcha, Orok (Uilta) and Oroch languages.[11]

2010 Russian Census	Evenk	Even	Negidal	Nanai	Udegei	Ulcha	Orok Uilta	Oroch
Population	38,396	21,880	513	12,003	1,496	2,765	295	596
Speakers	4,802	5,656	74	1,347	103	154	47	8

Diagram by A. Lavrillier on the basis of 2010 Russian Census' archives

The Evenk standard language was artificially built, firstly in the 1930s on the basis of a dialect from the Irkutsk region (Nepa dialect) (first in the Latin alphabet, then in Cyrillic) and secondly was changed in 1952 to a standard language based on the dialect of the *Podkommenaia Tunguska* subgroup of Northern Krasnoiarsk region (Poligus dialect).[12] Thanks mostly to G. M. Vasilevich, one hundred books in standard Evenk were already published by 1934.[13] Despite the numerous publications, distributed textbooks and obligatory training at school for several decades, this standard Evenk language is still not accepted by most of the Evenk, but only by a small part of the *intelligentsia*. Worse, this standard Evenk is so different from most of the Evenk dialects in pronunciation, lexicon and suffixes, that according to Evenk speakers, it results in a rejection of Evenk language by children in general. Parents explain that children lose patience: "on the one hand they know one Evenk language from us, on the other hand they learn another Evenk language from school that we cannot understand; we even cannot help them with their homework in Evenk. If they write their homework in our dialect, they get bad marks. So, they are lost between those Evenk languages, they can properly study neither our Evenk nor standard Evenk, so they switch to Russian – that is easier for them. Children need a teaching in our dialect if we want to keep Evenk language". Three other reasons can cause children to lose interest in Evenk language. Firstly, Evenk standard written language is currently taught in boarding school only one to two hours a week and secondly, this language is not highly valued by the village's Slavic social groups. Thirdly, speakers of Evenk dialects still have an oral conception of their language: almost all of them report that they are not "able to read or write Evenk language", while they currently read and write in Russian. Effectively, when I asked them to write something in Evenk, they hardly did it and wrote one word each time with a different orthography. When I gave them some texts to read, they could not understand what was written, but when I read those texts aloud, they understood. So, the problem is cognitive: the speakers have a representation of their language that excludes writing and it probably precludes the appropriation of a written standard language.[14] In addition, except in the official Evenk Autonomous Okrug in Krasnoiarsk region (also called Evenkiia, with a population of only 3,800 Evenk) where standard language is supported by written press and media, the standard Evenk is not spread by any media in other regions where Evenk live.

In 1990, after the collapse of the Soviet Union, there appeared in almost all Siberian villages under the collective idea called by indigenous people themselves 'revival of traditions', a lot of projects initiated by local schools, museums, dance groups, town halls and nomadic families. These projects were aimed at cultural survival or language preservation, but they faced many obstacles and most of them were never implemented.

Siberian specifications in the setting up and implementation of projects

For the last two decades, some factors seem to be curbing language revitalisation projects undertaken after the fall of the Soviet Union. The reasons are diverse. In contrast to most of the other Western Arctic and Circumpolar Regions, in Siberia (in its broad geographical meaning) there are very few aboriginal decision makers. The size of the indigenous minority *intelligentsia* is small and insufficiently represented in governmental institutions. The logistic and financial support of the government (using indigenous language for mass media, official communication in policy and education) is essential to carry out language revitalisation projects efficiently, as the case of Sakha (Yakut) language has demonstrated. In Siberia and the Far East of Russia, there is also poor financial support for projects emerging from indigenous villagers or nomads. The system of non-profit associations which could counteract this lack of financial support is not active because, generally in Russia, the volunteer work groups (associations) are very few and don't act as a social phenomenon (accomplishing tasks that government cannot perform) as they do in the West. Another source of funding of projects for language revitalisation is the foreign funding organisations, such as DoBeS (Volkswagen Foundation), The Hans Rausing Endangered Language projects, Earth Action and so on. But, several phenomena are preventing the indigenous *intelligentsia* from benefiting from this help. Firstly, the majority of the indigenous *intelligentsia* do not even know about those funding institutions. Secondly, they usually have little knowledge of foreign languages and computing (which is essential for submitting proposals). Another fact which is curbing the efficiency of revitalisation projects is the lack of close social interaction and contacts between speaking communities in villages or in the nomadic realm which often have very good projects and field knowledge, and the indigenous *intelligentsia* of the towns which has some power to act and to access some funding.

The origin of the Evenk nomadic school project

This applied anthropology project took place in north-western Amur region, among Evenk nomadic groups administratively related to a village where only Slavic allochtonous population and Evenk live.

From the beginning of my fieldwork in the 1990s, Evenk, but also Even nomads expressed to me the need for a nomadic school in order to keep children with them, and to convey Evenk language and nomadic knowledge to them. They also wanted to ensure their children got a good quality education with knowledge of current technologies and foreign languages. They were very willing for their children to receive the needed knowledge to feel confident and powerful in both the nomadic world and the worlds of the villages and towns. In those regions, some nomads had already tried to convince local authorities to fund their familial nomadic school, and some members of the indigenous *intelligentsia* had also tried to convince local authorities, without any success.

In the late 1990s, members of the local indigenous *intelligentsia* asked me to work out with the nomads during my field work the logistic details of such a school – as an anthropologist supposed to know nomadic communities well, their demography, children's populations, the details of roads travelled, etc. After collecting from the nomads all the needed information and defining the project's specifications, I was asked by the indigenous schoolteachers and pedagogues to help in writing down the parameters of the nomadic school project for the local authorities. Together with them, with the Centre of National schools in Yakutsk, and with the help of RAIPON (CSIPN/RITC),[15] we studied the various cases of already existing 'nomadic schools' in Siberia, most of which were little settled schools (*statsionarnye shkoly*) in remote places in the tundra (as for example Yuri Vella's one) (cf. Dudeck, *this volume*) or in the taiga. The experiences showed that most settled little remote schools were not really attracting the nomads: "It is worse than the village boarding school, because we also need to be separated from our children and the school is badly built, children get cold, and the teaching is not as good as at the village school and we have additional work to prepare wood for the school", explained some parents I met during conferences on that subject. The expensive project with heavy technical equipment seemed also to not be a good option. Indeed, a nomadic school was transporting the teachers from one camp to another by big truck. But after two years, the school had to close because the fuel consumption was too expensive, the truck broke down and no additional money was found. Two other cases helped us in finding the proper organisation. The first one was along the Olenëk River in Northern Yakutia where an indigenous teacher in retirement took her numerous grandchildren with her into the tundra and taught them there, living and teaching in the tent, moving with a nomadic group. The second example took place in the Amur region. In the 1980s, an indigenous teacher and her husband, travelling by helicopter, visited the nomadic camps and taught there. Her teaching experience has shown the great results of educating nomadic pupils. After the collapse of the Soviet Union, this teacher organised the so-called 'taiga school' (*taezhnaia shkola*) which allowed the pupils from 12 to 13 years of age to join their parents in the taiga. There, they were studying on their own with manuals and exercises given by the teachers in the village. In this context, one nomadic mother personally taught all her children and grandchildren on her own in the taiga. The pedagogical results were varied, but all those nomadic pupils became great reindeer herders and hunters, are fluent Evenk speakers, founded a family, and this village (in contrast with most other similar places) did not know such symptoms of social depression as mass suicides among indigenous people. Using all these experiences, we defined a project for a nomadic school that allows children to live continuously with their parents, that uses the cheapest and most secure transport (i. e. the reindeer), that avoids heavy technology and infrastructure and that offers high-quality education. Also, the parents wanted a school that would prepare their children for both nomadic and rural/urban life. Indeed, if some of the parents, thinking that there is nothing good in rural and urban places, wish their children to continue the reindeer herding lifestyle, most of them desire their children to 'be satisfied with their lives,' be it in the taiga, in the village or in the town, or both. By the way, surprising as it may seem to the European mind, to be both nomad and urban is perfectly possible. Effectively, among the Saami, as among Siberian peoples, there are several persons of different generations who are efficient in both the nomadic lifestyle and urban administrative or business tasks. Since the collapse of the Soviet Union, parents think that their children must be able to manage administrative, juridical and business tasks, even if they lead a nomadic lifestyle. So, parents wish their children to be adaptable to both lifestyles and environments in the future.

After the Evenk nomadic school project was defined, the Evenk schoolteachers and pedagogues asked me to defend this project in front of the Russian authorities, thinking that it would be easier and more persuasive coming from a 'French doctor of the Sorbonne'. From time to time over the course of many years, during my free time from research, and in collaboration with Evenk nomads, villagers and townspeople, we wrote a dozen versions of the project for submission to local authorities, and for presentation in numerous local conferences, in order to get funding. We had no success except in 2002 in Moscow, when we obtained a diploma from the Minister of Education of the Russian Federation certifying that this project for a nomadic school was recognised as a federal pedagogical platform, but no funding came with this diploma. Then, with other French researchers, in particular with the ethnomusicologist Henri Lecomte (who edited eleven CDs of traditional music of Siberian peoples),[16] we decided to look for funding from European countries or the USA, and in 2004 we created the non-profit and completely volunteer NGO 'French-Evenk Association Sekalan'.[17] We decided that the first funding for the school would be the little sum of the royalties from the CD of Evenk traditional songs we created together (Lavrillier and Lecomte 2002). We submitted the project to various funding organisations in France and visited various people at the UNESCO headquarters in Paris, and on the advice of RAIPON, we tried without any success to get funding from various organisations such as Sorosoro, the World Bank, etc.

Creation and development of the school

As mentioned above, our purpose was to implement the wishes of a nomadic Evenk group to have a nomadic school. One of its aims is to preserve language by keeping children in the nomadic environment with their parents, who still use the traditional knowledge and speak the Evenk language. In this region, around 70 % of adults are fluent Evenk speakers, but there is a problem of language transmission to younger generations. As I noticed during the fieldwork, Evenk is spoken mostly within nomadic communities, while Russian is spoken in villages (see *above*). In this region, the language preservation situation is exceptionally good, in comparison with the other Evenk regional groups, where for instance in some Amur region villages the Evenk speak only Russian, or in most southern Yakutia villages the Evenk speak only Yakut and Russian. Here we can see that this project's idea is – in contrast with *stricto sensus* revitalisation projects – to maintain language practice and to reinforce intergenerational transmission before the language disappears. Indeed, the present generation of children is a key generation, among which (according to their current knowledge), the language will be lost or maintained.

Before continuing the description of this project, let me clarify a few points on the Siberian language situation. In many other Siberian indigenous peoples' villages, be they Yukagir, Koryak and so on (cf. Odé, Kasten, *this volume*), and among other Evenk villages, the language is not anymore practiced by children and young generation.

The reasons for language loss can be various. Many Evenk assert that one of the consequences of education in the village boarding school is the loss of their language. This point of view can be moderated by several facts. First, let me say that the boarding school is probably not directly the only factor responsible for the disappearance of the language. Indeed, the first generation entering the boarding schools were Evenk only speakers and had to learn Russian language at school. Despite the ban on speaking Evenk at school, they willingly continued speaking Evenk in secret among themselves. But when this generation had children, as the Evenk testified, many of them where ashamed of their language or did not want their children to suffer the same ban, and have not transmitted the Evenk language to their children. In addition, when the ban on Evenk speaking at school disappeared, the one to two hours of standard Evenk lessons were not sufficient to maintain the language. So, indirectly, the boarding schools were to a considerable degree responsible for the reduction in the numbers of Evenk speakers (see also Dudeck, *this volume*).

In addition, nomadic and settled Evenk say that boarding school triggered the appearance of what they call 'a lost generation of children', i.e. a generation which is able to live neither the nomadic lifestyle nor a rural/urban one. They explain that during the short holiday time they were able to spend in the taiga, children could not receive the tremendous amount of knowledge needed for surviving in this extreme environment. In addition, nomadic children tend to develop psychological problems for several reasons. First, they suffer psychological and cultural trauma at the age of 7 years from the abrupt separation from their parents and from the nomadic realm when entering the boarding school. Consequently, they tend to become introverted. Second, as members of an under-appreciated minority surrounded by a Slavic pedagogical team, most of who give them to understand they haven't the same intellectual capacities as Russians (see *below*), they get a negative view of themselves. Those inferiority complexes caused by this social atmosphere don't help those children to feel self-confident in the rural / urban lifestyle. Although this portrait is a bit stereotypical and there are exceptions, it represents well the idea of the 'lost generation'.

The Evenk nomadic school project finally got lucky at the end of 2005, when we obtained the first funding from the German NGO 'ProSibiria',[18] which allowed the school to start for a year. Simultaneously, the Amur region Ministry of Education attributed to this nomadic school the status of 'Regional pedagogical platform'. The school could then start at the beginning of 2006. From the conception of the school project in the 1990s until funding was finally granted, the concerned Evenk lost hope, but the ProSibiria funding resulted in an enthusiastic response by the local authorities and all the participants. Seeing that a foreign institution was funding this project, the local Department of Education immediately decided to help with one teacher's position by funding some equipment and offering some logistic help. In January 2006, while we had not yet received the funding from ProSibiria (because of the time necessitated by the money transfer), we decided to leave for the taiga to help get the school functioning. The participants agreed to receive their salary later, and I spent my last money to buy food for the team. The nomadic parents were also very enthusiastic, helping with transport (lending reindeer), constructing school tables, etc. At that time we did not even know if the school would exist for more than one year, but all involved Evenk, nomads and villagers said: "The most important thing is to start!" So we opened the school for the eight children of one nomadic group.

Some months before, I had applied to the Rolex Awards for Enterprise, not really hoping for success. So, it was a great surprise and joy for all of the participants to see, the helicopter arrive in June 2006 in the nomadic camp in the middle of the forest with the Rolex team to announce to us that we would receive the funding which would allow the school to function for several years longer.

From paper to reality

During the first year we were very aware of how difficult it was to pass from the written version of the project to its realisation. We had to change various logistic details, taking into account all remarks from both the nomads and the local authorities at the Ministry of Education. It appeared that the organisation of the school had to be flexible and needed to be modelled on the nomadic society in order that the school would function successfully. For instance, the first year the staff was too expensive in relation to the number of pupils and transport from one camp to another was too complicated. Now, the organisation, based on alternating direct and indirect teaching (i. e. alternatively, directly with professional teachers and with parent-educators) is the following: if the camps are near each other, the teachers move from one camp to another every ten to twenty days; while, if the camps are too far from each other, teachers stay in one camp for three months before being replaced by another teacher or by parent-educators. During the absence of the teachers, some nomadic parents act as educators to give homework or lectures to the children. Some of them had started a degree in their previous life and are able to teach at a good level.

Thanks to the nomadic school, eleven positions were created: two for the professional teachers, one for the coordinator, one for the cashier-accountant, one for the reindeer herder guide and six for the parent-educators. Monthly salaries vary from 3,000 to 15,000 roubles according to the type of position and the effective working time. I should explain that in the Amur region, thanks to the proximity to the railway network, the cost of living is much lower than in northern Siberian regions, which explains the low salaries.

According to their own system, the nomadic families are making from one to four trips per year to the village in order to obtain fresh supplies, and during this time, they bring the children to the village school in order that their level of education can be checked. Today the school covers eight camps over a territory of 1,200 km^2 and from the beginning 56 children benefitted from this nomadic school. The participants of the project are nomadic communities, the Evenk *intelligentsia* of the village, two Evenk professional teachers from the region's nomadic families (Gabyshev A. I. – educated as a primary school pedagogue at Yakutsk University, Goncharova T. D. – educated as a primary school and Evenk teacher at St. Petersburg University, the Department of Education of the Amur region (Siberia) (Russians) and the Primary school of the village (Russians). Legally, the nomadic school is an administrative subdivision of the village school (boarding school included) which greatly simplifies the expenses and administrative management of the nomadic school and avoids the huge difficulties a nomadic school would have to obtain an education licence. With the agreement of the local Department of Education and the village boarding school, the pupils from kindergarten age up to the fifth class (according to the Russian system) (from approximately four years old to eleven or twelve years old) can attend the nomadic school if their parents wish. After that age, the pupils are obliged to attend the boarding school because of the complexity of the Federal teaching programme.

Let me explain that, in various publications on nomadic school issues, it is said that some parents do not wish their children to study in such original schools. We also faced some scepticism among some parents at the very beginning, because parents worried about the quality of teaching. First of all, parents demanded the teaching of computing and foreign languages in the nomadic school. Surprising as it may seem, while in the beginning all parents asked for the creation of a nomadic school, when we were finally able to start implementing this project, some parents were sceptical the first year and waited for the first year's evaluation results before deciding to join the project. In addition, I argue that it is very important to make such schools non-compulsory, because, as we noticed, at certain times of the year, for instance during the exhausting period of sable hunting (on which the yearly financial budget of the family depends), some parents prefer to leave their children at the boarding school for a month. There is also another advantage, because according to the parents and the local pedagogues, children also need to get used to being in crowded classrooms and to the social atmosphere of the settled lifestyle.

In order to meet the requirements of the parents the pupils have more teaching hours in the nomadic school than in the boarding school. They study all the subjects of the Federal Programme, such as Russian, Mathematics, Life and Earth Sciences, History, Literature and so on, the same as the village pupils. In addition, they learn and practice computing, Evenk and English language in the specific way described below.

Creation of multimedia documentation products

In addition, according to the pedagogical programme of this nomadic school and the willingness to involve children in preserving and documenting their language and culture, the children create multimedia documentation products and have access to some ethnographic archives on Evenk culture (records of songs, stories; videos of technical processes, ritual practices; pictures of ancient expeditions, documentary films, etc).

The nomads didn't want their children, being nomadic school pupils, to be isolated in the role of 'traditional nomads', away from the current technologies. So, we

|16| During the nomadic school process, parents and children access a set of ethnographic multimedia documentation in the nomadic realm.

|17| Sample of language talking manual made in Power Point programme by the children of the French-Evenk nomadic school.

decided to create pedagogical activities according to the principle of two (or more) in one – the children learn current electronic technologies (and foreign languages) through concrete tasks and realisations for documenting language and culture. Since the nomadic families value their own Evenk dialect, it was decided that these multimedia documentation products will be made in their own Evenk dialect and with their own orthography. Children use various tools such as fold-away school tables, laptops, digital cameras, microphones and software such as Power Point, Word with integrated pictures, sound and written texts (see *Illustration 16*). With the help of teachers and parents, children created multimedia manuals with speech examples (see *Illustration 17*), little encyclopaedias, life-journals, Evenk calendars, etc.

Let me now present some positive results as well as questions and found solutions in various social spheres involved in this project: the nomads, the village and town indigenous *intelligentsia*, the local and main regional town authorities in education. All those partners correspond to very different socio-economic, cultural realms and lifestyles.

Positive results

After six years of existence, we can observe diverse positive results, such as the healthy psychological development of the children because of the closeness to their parent's affection. We also noticed that parents took an active part in these education processes. In addition to their active involvement in the logistic organisation, they spontaneously took part in multimedia productions, local epic poetry theatre, nomadic technologies and Evenk language lessons, and in collective games organised by professional teachers.

Obviously, the fact that children live a nomadic lifestyle allows for good maintenance and development of cultural and linguistic knowledge, transmitted through traditional modes of transmission (observation, imitation by playing, implementation). In addition, the educational level (in terms of the Russian Federal programme) of the nomadic school children is often higher than among the village boarding school children, because they receive individualised teaching and because they learn to create their own projects and realise them. Pedagogically, thanks to the direct / indirect way of teaching, the children get used to doing their school work independently.

Besides the creation of eleven jobs, significant in the context of the financial crisis in the villages and among the nomads (see *above*), there are also unexpected positive results such as the creation of a social and psychological dynamism among both children and parents. Children grow to be proud of themselves and self-confident. For instance, they know computing programmes that their village boarding school teachers do not know and also nomads (who are often disparaged by allochtonous institutions) have their own special school. All of this counteracts the hang-ups (see *above*) they had in the village school as members of an ethnic minority. In addition, some of the parents, reassured by their successful experience as educators in the nomadic school, decided to found a little nomadic enterprise (ru. *rodovaia obshchina*) or to study to become nomadic teachers. Others decided to adopt orphans from a neighbouring Evenk village. Among those orphans there was one little Russian girl who was learning in the nomadic school for five years. Even some children living in the village were willing to join the nomadic school, but the nomadic school didn't have the legal status needed to implement this wish.

Questions and solutions

But let me now explain what kind of questions we had to resolve in order to attain these results.

Firstly, we had several ethical questions. The question was from the unsolved dilemmas of applied anthropology: Although one knows that societies are continuously changing and that the social anthropologist has a certain influence on the studied society anyway (see *above*), is it ethically correct for a foreign anthropologist to risk causing changes to a nomadic society by creating such a project? Low and Merry (2010: 211–212) recognise that there is no easy answer to such a dilemma:

> "The first dilemma concerns the extent to which the researcher should act as a participant, including becoming engaged in activism that seeks to reform features of social life to enhance social justice rather than being a disengaged outsider observing and recording social life. Some argue that participation of this kind changes the society being studied and question the ethical right to seek to change other ways of life. Others argue that those who fail to respond to the need for intervention are acting unethically. Some point out that all societies are now economically and politically interconnected such that isolation is not a possibility, and many suffer from the effects of this interconnection. How, and to what extent, the anthropologist should seek change is uncertain."

In our case study, one of the answers to this dilemma was the fact that it was a project of the Evenk themselves. Secondly, this question was resolved by the fact that all the decision-making was led by, or in close collaboration with, the nomads. Regarding the introduction of computers into the nomadic lifestyle and the risk of this changing their society (a critique that I have heard from some anthropologists), I argue that, firstly it was an Evenk decision; secondly, nomads have for several decades used various new technologies, such as radio, communication systems with the villages, music players, and more recently mp3 players, DVD players, and mobile and satellite phones.[19]

Secondly, the organisation of the school was adapted to the nomadic society and did not require any change in the nomads' mobility as the taiga/tundra settled remote schools did. So, this society's organisation did not have to change in order to receive the services of the school. And, through the years, the project management was gradually being transferred to the Evenk themselves. So, while I devoted most of my time to this project for two to three years from 2006 (solving administrative, pedagogical, methodological, logistic, financial and social issues, and being temporary teacher), since 2008 this project is entirely collaboratively led by nomadic families and the village boarding school. Since western financial support is still needed, the French-Evenk association Sekalan is still funding the nomadic school and controls the use of the money, and regularly surveys the level of satisfaction among the project's partners. I argue that it is very satisfying that the applied anthropologist is not needed anymore in this project.

Furthermore, in order to avoid the risk of unintentionally imposing a new 'norm' on 'Evenk culture', during the pedagogical programmes (access to ethnographic archives and multimedia creation), like the Soviet Union had in their Evenk manuals, it was decided to give simple access to the ethnographic and archive data, without further commentaries or directions.[20] It was especially important for me as a western anthropologist showing these materials and teaching multimedia technologies. These materials should be only opened as windows on the archive about some Evenk groups. Furthermore, I argue that it is very important that children and parents decide themselves about the content and forms of the multimedia documentation products. Indeed, Evenk regional groups have all cultural and linguistic specifications which are very important to them. For instance, Evenk dialectal differences, even linguistic innovations based on crossing roots and suffixes from Russian and Evenk, or based on borrowings from Yakut, are all very important markers of regional identities as are differences in motifs decorating clothes and other items (Lavrillier 2005: 436–438).

In the area of politics and governance, we met important obstacles. Firstly, there is an important lack of communication and collaboration between the various governmental institutions of the administrative regions. Indeed, the initial project was to cover all the nomadic camps in a huge area situated in the South of Yakutia and the North of the Amur region. Because of this lack of communication, it was decided to create the school only in the Amur region. Secondly, in another sphere, we had to cope with the lack of communication and mutual understanding between the nomads, the local governmental authorities and the urban indigenous *intelligentsia*. In those relations, as an anthropologist, and a 'neutral' (as much as possible) foreigner, I had to be a kind of ambassador between these social spheres and to act in each of these spheres according to its specific social behaviours, discourse and convincing arguments.

I had the initial feeling that the local government was sceptical of indigenous projects and I guess that the local government might be afraid of a too powerful and organised indigenous society. Indeed, the main stake concerns the lands in use by the nomads that are coveted by the mining enterprises. The state usually seems to avoid funding any project likely to raise decision-making skills among the indigenous people or to create a strong political consciousness and identity. The state funds festivals, cultural and artistic events quite readily (cf. Kasten, *this volume*). Another possible reason for the local government's scepticism can be that the nomads represent a demographic minority in comparison with the more numerous allochtonous population which also meets with serious socio-economic problems and needs government help. In order to cope with this political atmosphere, we had to prove that the project was apolitical and to provide the already obtained foreign funding. Let me insist here on the need for foreign funding for indigenous projects. Here, the figure of a foreign scientist involved in the defence of this kind of project seems to somehow impress the local authorities and help in obtaining support, as some connections from the local government told me.

From a social point of view, we had to resolve various questions. Firstly, there was a lack of such project planning and management among the concerned nomads, so we decided to directly involve the indigenous people in all the project management tasks and decisions. One of the obstacles was the important differences in favourite/recognised modes of communication that allow for the establishment of definitive agreement and decisions among each concerned social/administrative sphere. Among the local authorities, the written texts and official discussions within the framework of the time available are the most valued modes of communication. In contrast, among the nomads, the most valued and usual mode of communication is individual oral discussion with each family at anytime, in any place. For example, most agreements between the nomads and the village boarding school were not made during the official meetings in the school director's office, but at any time, in the middle of the street or at partners' private houses. In addition, most of the nomadic logistic agreements were made between the school team and the nomads, sometimes several months before, in the middle of the forest on the road or in a tent. I must stress the fact that such verbal agreements made in impromptus sites (to the western mind) are strictly respected by the nomads and have the same value for the nomads as a signed document for the school administration. So, here, anthropological knowledge of the rules and behaviours of both social spheres helped in adapting the mode of communication to each specific social realm involved in the project for obtaining agreement and help in communication between nomads and local authorities.

We also had to avoid some situations likely to raise competition and conflicts in various social spheres. Within the realm of the village boarding school classes, the number of children is very small and boarding school teachers are often afraid of not having enough children. In the beginning they were afraid that the creation of the nomadic school would encourage children to leave the village school and make their number of pupils smaller, thereby endangering their positions. So, we had to find an administrative solution to avoid the loss of salary for boarding school teachers. Thus, the nomadic school children remain administratively attached to their village school class, where they must pass school tests anyway and spend some weeks while their parents go shopping or do administrative tasks in the village. Some of the allochtonous boarding school teachers felt seriously offended by the fact that some nomadic parents (who had never completed a degree) were teaching pupils, receiving salaries and having good results, while they themselves had completed degrees and had many years of teaching experience. So, for several years, boarding school teachers were against the nomadic school and tried to discredit it. But seeing that nomadic school pupils got good evaluations, some of them changed their mind. Of course, without the strong support of the director of the boarding school, the opposition of those teachers could have seriously endangered the nomadic school's existence. By the way, the same problem has prevented the creation of a nomadic school in the neighbouring village.

Within the realm of the nomadic society, there is a traditional spirit of competition that may create serious tensions and jealousies between nomadic families. With the collaboration of some indigenous villagers, we found three ways to avoid conflicts. The first is that the nomadic school would provide strictly equal services and rules to all families. The second was to use this spirit of competition in order to improve the performance of the project and the third was to install older indigenous persons (traditionally respected and listened to by all kin groups) as coordinators of the project. In essence, we used the traditional social rules in the project's structure.

While offering a high quality of education in the context of the nomadic taiga, we had, of course, to answer numerous educational questions. One of the biggest problems for all nomadic school projects was the lack of teachers ready to live the nomadic lifestyle.

According to the study of nomadic school projects in Siberia we did in order to create our project (see *above*), the lack of teachers ready to work in nomadic schools is one of the biggest obstacles to the project's success. The UNESCO initiative in late 2006 towards developing nomadic schools in Yakutia, later supported by the Yakut Government, resulted in the creation of a specific section for educating nomadic teachers two years ago at the Yakut State University Pedagogical Institute. This has raised hopes for the development of nomadic schools in general.

No Slavic teacher wants to live this life (considered uncomfortable), they told us. Only Evenk teachers can accept it, because they are used to this lifestyle, but there are very few of them in this region. Let me explain that in this region the number of Evenk having completed graduate studies is low, while in some Evenk villages almost the whole of the village institutional workforce (hospital, administration, museum, school and so on) is Evenk. Here the villagers and the nomadic population, with their very good knowledge of everyone's life and skills, really helped identify potential teachers. Here also, the nomadic mode of communication for agreement was the only one to use. Thus, identifying a potential candidate for the position of nomadic teacher, we usually went to him at home, along with some involved nomadic parents, with relatives and friends of this potential teacher, and started with long collective discussions to convince him/her to take up the position. We argued that they would receive good salary, they would act for the future of their own people, they would lead a healthy life and eat good food from hunting and herding. Besides the salary, one of the successful arguments was that this work would allow them to re-establish their traditional knowledge and relationship with nomadic life, which they often lose in their childhood or in later urban student life. It is quite important because they grew up in the taiga with their own nomadic parents. This loss of knowledge of the nomadic lifestyle can really influence the decision of the potential nomadic teacher. Indeed, we had the case where an Evenk village teacher had to be convinced by the nomadic fathers that they wouldn't make fun of him because he didn't even know "how to approach a reindeer" (according to his own expression), that they would teach him everything.

After two years of work in the nomadic school this teacher knew reindeer herding and hunting tasks well and really liked his work and lifestyle in the taiga. Another way of coping with this lack of teachers was to train the nomadic parents by practice and by funding higher education. Indeed they actively help (at their educational skill level) the teachers in education and some of them asked for additional higher education. During the period of absence of the teachers, and during the whole pedagogical process, the nomadic school also used digital teaching programmes in all subjects (Russian, Math, Sciences and so on) that we found in shops in big towns.

Regarding modern computing training, we had a real challenge, because in small villages in this part of Siberia, computing skills are not developed (the situation is currently improving), even in the village boarding school, and we had to face a real lack of computing knowledge among teachers. But nomads adore technology and we trained the teachers, the parents and the children with concrete tasks.

In order to have electricity, we used small, easily transportable electric mini-stations and one set of solar panels and batteries. In addition, there was the psychological danger of introducing computers to the taiga, as suggested by local pedagogues: i. e. as in the West, children could become addicted to the computer and lose interest in the traditional knowledge and teaching programme. In order to avoid this, we decided to use the computer not as an aim in itself, but as a 'tool' for educational training purposes, for realising various concrete tasks and projects (language and cultural documentation products, life journals, etc).

Regarding the Federal programme, as an ethnic school, we thought teaching all subjects in Evenk language would be very helpful for language preservation (as it was done for instance in Yakutia or in the successful Breton school *Diwan* in France). But there is no standard Russian Federal programme in Evenk language. This is an important issue for all minority languages. On the other hand, in other Siberian examples of ethnic schools, in particular Yakut ones, teaching the federal programme in indigenous languages has shown that such children have adaptation difficulties at university afterwards, as a Yakut State University lecturer explained. Nevertheless, if the teaching of the Federal programme is in Russian, the nomadic teachers keep using Evenk for common words and phrases, such as "listen!, sit down!, be attentive!, don't worry, you will do it" and so on. Teachers say that using Evenk language is very important to create a comfortable familial atmosphere for the children, within which they feel self-confident. Indeed, some of the children started school before the creation of the nomadic school and have been traumatised by the boarding school. One of them even said: "I am not able to do math exercises since I am Evenk, math is for clever Russians, not for Evenk!" Furthermore, some minor changes in the programme were needed, such as translating a math exercise put in terms of jam pots sold in a shop (a bit difficult for a child rarely in the village shop to understand) to the same exercise (with the same numbers and operations) into terms of reindeers that enter or exit the camp enclosure (easier to figure out). In order to help the children understand the village lifestyle, Evenk teachers invented a game in the middle of the camp – the shop game: a shop was represented by items collected from the tents; children played alternatively the seller and the buyer and thus were receiving training in both mathematics and village lifestyle.

As a result of previous decades where children were forced to spend most of their life separated from their parents and culture in the boarding school, as a result also of globalisation whereby children are attracted to new cultural offerings (radio, TV, modern music, electronic games), there was a strain in intergenerational interactions in some domains.[21] In order to reinforce those links and cultural transmission within Evenk speaking communities, nomadic school children take dynamic part in traditional activities throughout the year. In addition, the nomadic school involves older nomadic people in the educational process, for instance by telling stories, leading discussion groups, organising training in traditional techniques and taking part in social education.

In spite of the proven efficiency of this nomadic school, in spite of the huge amount of work already done and obstacles removed, and in spite of the willingness of nomads from other villages of this huge region to benefit from the same nomadic school, after six years of existence, this school is now endangered. During the last few years, the local administration has increased its support to the nomadic school. In 2005, the Department of Education of the region attributed a 'diploma of Pedagogical Platform of the Amur region' and offered financial support in the amount of 10 % of the total annual budget. In 2009, after an academic inspection in the taiga, this Department officially declared this school successful and essential for nomadic people. Unfortunately, the financial support still isn't coming from the centre – the Amur region (as it should be), but from its small and poor district where the school is established. Despite this situation, the local Department of Education is now meeting 40 % of the nomadic school's annual costs, which is quite good (two teacher positions, one parent-educator position, school books, transportation from the edge of the nomadic area to the village, oil for the mini-station and so on). The rest, 60 % of the cost, is met by the French – Evenk Association Sekalan (i. e. the rest of the Rolex funding). The annual operating cost for foreign funding corresponds to a sum of twelve to fifteen thousand euros, depending on the number of pupils and the number of camps covered. In addition, the school currently needs around seven thousand euros to renew the technical material. Nowadays, the rest of the Rolex funding ensures the existence of the nomadic school only to the end of the 2011–2012 school year, and a recent small donation from the Association d'Aide Humanitaire is funding part of the 2012–2013 school year. The French-Evenk association Sekalan is still actively looking for funding in the West.[22]

Conclusion

In conclusion, I argue that risk-free projects do not exist. As this case study has shown, even a simple nomadic school project raises many questions in various spheres (political, ethical, social). It appears that there are three kinds of major difficulties. The first is to convince the local authorities to fully fund an indigenous minority project. The second is to instil into indigenous populations the self-trust in their project management skills so that they can fully lead a project for their community at all levels (discussions with authorities, nomadic logistic organisation, etc.) and the third is to create real communication and understanding between nomads and local government. It is also important to stress the fact that the creation of such a project requires a lot of time and energy, a long presence there for the foreigner, and many trips to villages, nomadic camps and local towns to meet with the concerned authorities. It took me around two to three years of almost continuous work. From my own experience in this nomadic school, I argue that any applied anthropology project needs to be the initiative of the society itself. It is very important also that the project be adapted to the model of the concerned society and not the opposite. Last but not least, foreigners or allochtonous persons involved in a project and the decision makers have to know and understand very well the functioning of the society and of the concerned governmental institutions. For that, anthropological expertise and historical knowledge of the country are essential tools for helping in the creation and development of indigenous projects.

In addition, in order to act efficiently for language revitalisation, such projects should be better supported by the Russian government, which could integrate such indigenous language multimedia manuals within the set of officially and largely used school manuals. Also, several things seem to be indispensable for revitalisation, like intensive training of local teachers in the use of computing tools and creating multimedia pedagogical manuals, as well as funding for scientific collaborative work with local pedagogical institutions (local government and funding institutions).

Notes

1 Fabian 1983.
2 Aiello 2010: 201.
3 For the detailed history of engaged anthropology in the USA, see Low and Merry 2010: 204–207.
4 http://icr.arcticportal.org/index.php?option=com_content&view=article&id=245&Itemid=86&lang=en
5 Cf. link UNESCO http://www.unesco.org/culture/languages-atlas/en/atlasmap.html.
6 Decree of the Russian Government Nr 255 *On the Unified Register of Indigenous Small-Numbered Peoples of the Russian Federation*, 24 March 2000 (Postonavlenie Pravitel'stva RF ot 24 marta

2000 g. N 255 *O Edinom perechne korennykh malochislennykh narodov Rossiiskoi Federatsii* [Russian]) http://base.garant.ru/181870.htm.

7 Suliandziga R. V., Kudriashova D. A., Suliandziga P. V. 2003. Malochislennye narody Severa, Sibiri i Dal'nego Vostoka Rossiiskoi Federatsii. *Obzor sovremmennogo polozheniia*, p. 142.

8 The Russian Association of the Indigenous Peoples of the North (RAIPON) http://www.raipon.info/en/

9 Lavrillier 2005: 436.

10 From 2010 census for Russian data and from 1995 census for Chinese data (quoted in Bilik 1996: 64).

11 For more detailed analysis of the language situation of this Evenk group, see Lavrillier 2005.

12 Bulatova N. and Grenoble L. 1999: 3.

13 Nedjalkov 1997, Vasilevich G. M. 1969: 767–770.

14 Lavrillier 2005: 439–445.

15 Center of support for Indigenous Peoples of the North / Russian Indigenous Training Centre.

16 Buda records, collection 'Siberia' (http://www.budamusique.com/en/search?orderby=position&orderway=desc&search_query=sib%C3%A9rie&submit_search=Search).

17 French-Evenk Association Sekalan: http://ecolenomadeevenk.over-blog.com

18 http://www.prosibiria.de/

19 There are very interesting studies about the use of new technologies by nomads in various places of Siberia, see Stammler 2009.

20 As it is shown in the paper by Kasten, DVD learning tools made and distributed by the Foundation for Siberian Cultures were translated and presented with the same approach.

21 About this issue, see Dudeck *this volume*.

22 A film about this nomadic school was made in the winter of 2008 by Michel Debats with the collaboration of the nomads, H. Lecomte and A. Lavrillier (Debats 2008).

References

Aiello, Leslie C. 2010. Engaged Anthropology: Diversity and Dilemmas: Wenner-Gren Symposium Supplement 2. *Current Anthropology* 51: 201–202.

Baré, Jean-François (ed.) 1995. *Les applications de l'anthropologie. Un essai de réflexion collective depuis la France*. Paris: Karthala.

Baba, Marietta L. and C. Hill 1997. *The Global Practice of Anthropology*. Williamsburg: College of William and Mary Press.

Bilik, Naran 1996. Emotion gets Lost: An Ewenki Case. *Inner Asia, Occasional papers*, I (1), 63–70. Cambridge: Mongolia and Inner Asia Studies Unit.

Bulatova, Nadezhda and Lenore Grenoble 1999. *Evenki*. München/Newcastle: Lincom Europa.

Cernea, Michael M. (ed.) 1991. *Putting People First. Sociological Variables in Rural Development*. New York: The World-Bank-Oxford University Press.

Debats, Michel 2008. *School on the Move*. A film of 52', Lagaptière Production.

Fabian, Johannes 1983. *Time and the Other: How Anthropology Makes its Object*. New York: Colombia University Press.

Fluehr-Lobban, Carolyn 2008. Collaborative Anthropology as Twenty-first Century Ethical Anthropology. *Collaborative Anthropologies* 1: 175–182.

Hobart, Mark (ed.) 1993. *An Anthropological Critique of Development: The Growth of Ignorance.* London: Routledge.

Lavrillier, Alexandra 1998. Écoles nomades en Sibérie. Repenser l'école. Témoignage et expériences éducatives en milieu autochtone, *Ethnies-Documents* 23–24: 143–153.

— 2005. Dialectes et norme écrite en évenk contemporain. In *Les langues ouraliennes aujourd'hui. Approches linguistiques et cognitives,* M. M. J. Fernandez-Vest (dir.), 433–44. Paris: Honoré Champion (éd.), coll. Bibliothèque de l'École des Hautes Études.

Lavrillier, Alexandra and Henri Lecomte 2002. *Evenk: Ritual Songs of the Nomads of the Taiga.* [Introduction text CD 3015792, songs translation]. Musique du Monde, Siberie 8. Paris: Buda Records.

Lévi-Strauss, Claude [1958] 1974. *Anthropologie structural.* Paris: Plon.

Long, Norman and Ann Long (ed.) 1992. *Battlefields of Knowledge. The Interlocking of Theory and Practice in Social Research and Development.* London: Routledge.

Low, Setha M. and Sally Engle Merry 2010. Engaged Anthropology: Diversity and Dilemmas: Wenner-Gren Symposium. Introduction to Supplement 2. *Current Anthropology* 51: 203–226.

Nedjalkov, Igor 1997. *Evenki.* London/New York: Routledge.

Olivier de Sardan, Jean-Pierre 1995. *Anthropologie et développement. Essai en socio-anthropologie du développement social.* Paris: Khartala.

Stammler, Florian 2009. Mobile Phone Revolution in the Tundra? Technological Change Among Russian Reindeer Nomads. *Folklore. Electronic Journal of Folklore*: 47–78. http://www.folklore.ee/folklore/vol41/stammler.pdf

Vasilevich G. M. 1969. *Evenki. Istoriko-etnograficheskie ocherki (XVIII-nachalo XX v.)* [Evenki historical-ethnographic reports (XVIII-beginning XX century). Leningrad: Nauka.

8 CHALLENGING THE STATE EDUCATIONAL SYSTEM IN WESTERN SIBERIA: TAIGA SCHOOL BY THE TIUITIAKHA RIVER

Stephan Dudeck[1]

Introduction

It is common knowledge that indigenous populations who preserve their own lifestyles that are different from the mainstream societies in their home countries face disadvantages in education all over the world. In this regard, Western Siberian reindeer herders of the Khanty, Mansi and Nenets people are no exception (cf. Hairullin 2006; Magga 2005).

The following paper tells the story of an educational experiment, developed and organised by a Forest Nenets reindeer herding family on their ancestral land in the taiga (boreal forest) by the Tiuitiakha River in the Western Siberian Surgutsky *rayon*.

The organisational form and the educational idea of this taiga school challenged the state educational system based on boarding schools in central settlements often hundreds of kilometres from the reindeer herders' campsites. Surprisingly, it was not as much the content of the school curriculum, which was almost the same as that of the boarding school in the village, but the organisation of the educational process and the context of the work of the small taiga school that differed so much from the conventional system of education.

This paper will describe the school project and its educational ideas and place them in the broader context of attempts to reform the educational system for indigenous groups in Siberia and to develop new forms of bicultural education (Kasten 1998) after the breakdown of the Soviet Union.

After thirteen years of existence, the school could not continue its work, not only because of the reluctance of the state authorities to support the experiment further, but also because other obstacles and difficulties arose, which will be described below.

Fieldwork

The paper is based on extensive ethnographic fieldwork from 1993 to 2009 in the Khanty-Mansiisky autonomous district – Yugra in Western Siberia, Russian Federation. The main interlocutors and research partners were indigenous reindeer herders and activists of the indigenous *intelligentsia*. A long time was spent at the reindeer herders' campsite at the Tiuitiakha River where the self-organised taiga school was established by the Nenets activist Yuri Vella (www.jurivella.ru; Niglas and Toulouze 2004). Participant observation as well as collaboration and interviews constituted the main research methods. The author did not work directly for the school but tried to raise awareness for the school in the West and supported the main organiser Yuri Vella in his efforts to defend his land from the oil companies. Before the closing of the school he initiated an open letter (see below) to the authorities to prevent the end of the school project.

History of the Education of Indigenous People

The history of formal education of the indigenous population in Western Siberia goes back to the end of the 19th century when Russian missionaries founded the first schools (Toulouze 1999; Balzer 1999; Toulouze 2011). Education was considered to be the best tool to transform 'primitive pagans' into civilised Christians, who were the only proper humans, according to the stereotypes of Russian settlers about Western Siberian natives, brilliantly analysed by Art Leete (1999). The children of Khanty, Mansi and Nenets reindeer herders, hunters and fishermen were then living with their parents on nomadic campsites in the conical tents called *chum* [2] or in remote seasonal settlements almost never visited by state officials or missionaries. The missionaries had to rely mostly on indigenous orphans who were handed over to them in the Russian settlements, as Roza Laptander writes of the Nenets, in her contribution to the volume. Until the beginning of the 20th century, indigenous inhabitants met with state and church representatives and traders only on the occasion of the annual fair in the Russian cities.

The Soviet administration took over the ideas of the Christian missionaries and considered education as one of the main tools to integrate the Siberian natives into Soviet society and culture. Informed by talented ethnographers, like for instance Vladimir Bogoraz and Lev Shternberg working in the Institute of the Peoples of the North in Leningrad (Bartels and Bartels 1995; Slezkine 1992), early Soviet planners understood that state education had to be adapted to the local lifestyles in order to be successful. Up to the 1930s, plans existed to organise mobile schools that whould travel together with the nomads and their herds (see the chapters by Roza Laptander and Elena Liarskaya, *this volume*). But the reality was different in the Khanty area called Ostiako-Vogulskii national district at that time, which later became Khanty-Mansiisky autonomous district – Yugra. As far as I know, no nomadic schools were established in the area, probably because of the semi-nomadic lifestyle and scattered family settlements of Khanty, Mansi and Forest Nenets people, and probably because of negative experiences with this school-type in other regions (see Laptander and Liarskaya, *this volume*). The young Soviet state decided to establish stations called 'kul'tbaza' (ru. *kul'turnaia baza* – cultural centre) on the territories of the indigenous population all over Siberia and to collect the children from the taiga (boreal forest) and tundra (boreal steppe) to educate them in residential schools located in these stations. As a result, a *kul'tbaza* was established in 1930 for the Khanty on the Kazym River. Ten persons in three groups travelled 330 km through the surrounding forest tundra and collected 17 Khanty children in 1931, the first year of the school (Sheveleva 2009).

This was only a small part of the local Khanty community's children. Most of the parents were reluctant to give their children to the Russians, and not without reason, as they were afraid their children would suffer bad nutrition and be infected by different diseases. This forced relocation of children recalled the colonial *amanat* system when Russian Cossacks abducted natives as hostages to force their relatives into submission and often to Christianise and culturally assimilate the captured Khanty (Forsyth 1992; Balzer 1999). The local conflict escalated in 1933 when state officials desecrated the most important sacred site of the region, Lake Num-To, and locals took a group of Russians hostage. These were killed after an ultimatum to lower taxes, withdraw from the sacred site and release the children from school. These events and the following punitive expedition became famous as the so-called 'Kazym uprising' (Ernychova 2003; Leete 2004). Open resistance and opposition were finally put down in 1934 by Soviet troops, and the residential school became compulsory for all indigenous children.

Language Development

Knowledge of indigenous languages dropped in Siberia from 75 % in 1959 to 53 % in 1989 (Zhirkova 2006). There are no statistics for demographics or number of speakers for Forest Nenets and Eastern Khanty languages, which are subsumed under the Nenets and Khanty in general. Below I provide some data for these groups in general. They show that the number of Khanty and Nenets has grown significantly over the last fifty years. Nenets have one of the highest birth rates among all ethnic groups in Russia. Another factor explaining the extraordinary growth, especially of Khanty and Nenets between 1989 and 2002, is the affirmative action measures taken by the state since the 1990s that motivated a lot of children from mixed ethnic families to register as indigenous. The change in the number of speakers is difficult to estimate because the questions provided to record knowledge of the native language in the census were formulated differently in 2002 and 2010 and in the former censuses (Sokolova and Stepanov 2007). Especially the 2002 figures seem to be inflated because the census asked only about some knowledge of the indigenous languages, not full proficiency. Especially for the Khanty the language loss is dramatic. The speaker community has lost one quarter of its speakers in the last 20 years. Recent personal communication with Khanty journalist Reonalda Olzina revealed that less than half of Khanty school children study their native language as a subject at school and less than

5 % of the indigenous preschool children have the possibility to learn or speak their native language in the preschool facilities. Indigenous school children taking part in the school subject 'native language' in the Khanty-Mansiisky autonomous district – Yugra diminished from 2,610 in the year 2008, to 2,056 in the year 2009, 1,476 in 2010, and 1,595 in the year 2011.

	1959	1970	1979	1989	2002	2010	Growth 1989 to 2002	Living in cities	in rural areas
Nenets	22,845	28,487	27,294	34,190	41,302	44,640	+20.8%	21.4 %	78.6 %
Khanty	19,246	21,007	20,743	22,283	28,678	30,943	+28.7%	38.4 %	61.6 %

Table 1. Demography of Khanty and Nenets in the Soviet and post-Soviet censuses according to Sokolova and Stepanov (2007), www.perepis2002.ru and www.perepis-2010.ru

	1970		1979		1989		2002		2010	
Nenets	23,844	83.7 %	22,081	80.9 %	26,730	77.7 %	31,311	75.8 %	21,926	49 %
Khanty	14,516	69.1 %	14,126	68.1 %	13,548	60.8 %	13,568	47.3 %	9,584	31 %

Table 2. Dynamics of the number of speakers of the Khanty and Nenets languages according to Sokolova and Stepanov (2007), www.perepis2002.ru and www.perepis-2010.ru

Criticism of Soviet Schools in the North

The Tiuitiakha school experiment becomes understandable only in light of the background of the educational system that was introduced during the Soviet Union, the criticism it has met since the time of *perestroika*, and the awakening of a plurality of ethnic revitalisation movements in Siberia (see Laptander and Liarskaya, *this volume*).

Mainstream scientific and popular literature about the Soviet boarding school system after *perestroika* denounced Soviet education as one of the main factors contributing to the ongoing cultural transformation in northern indigenous communities (cf. Hairullin 2006; Zhirkova 2006; Eremin and Traskunova 1989; Liarskaya 2005; Bloch 2004). These transformations were described in terms of destructive social processes that resulted not only in the extinction of native languages and loss of traditional knowledge but also in russification and maladaptation to the local living conditions. And one cannot deny that these processes took and take place. But there are also other developments that put the transfer of knowledge and language in danger.

Sedentarisation and 'Gender Shift'

Collectivisation and resettlement in central villages caused a depopulation of the taiga and tundra in many regions of Siberia, which then became a male working sphere of hunters and reindeer herders. Sedentarisation deprived the reindeer herders of the place and mechanism needed to transfer the predominantly implicit and unwritten knowledge of the indigenous lifestyle to the younger generation. The subsequent loss of prestige and status of the indigenous men accompanied by alcoholism, high suicide rates, migration to central settlements and towns and a high degree of mixed marriage was described as a 'gender shift' in Siberia (Vitebsky 2010; Liarskaya 2009a; Povoroznyuk, Habeck, and Vaté 2010; Liarskaya 2010).

Introduction of the Boarding Schools

This picture contradicts the way in which the bright future of the so-called 'small people of the North' was depicted in official statements in Soviet times. Boarding schools there were seen as the corner posts of progress that let northern peoples participate in the most advanced achievements of technological progress and let them become doctors, soldiers, technicians or cosmonauts.

The Soviet educational programme tried to fight indigenous socialisation in an active way and to replace it with a modern lifestyle and Soviet values. Indigenous culture was treated as a folkloristic ornament, a collection of elements of material culture detached from the original context, manipulated by Soviet cultural specialists, and administered by professionals in official cultural institutions. This concept of culture is still very much alive among cultural workers in the indigenous settlements and towns (see Habeck 2007; Volkov 2002).

The use of native language in the boarding school even in free time was often forbidden, and clothing, diet and organisation of the living environment were adapted to Soviet standards. Separation from parents served as an important tool for the replacement of habits and norms and was a traumatic experience for children as well as their parents (cf. the chapters of Laptander and Liarskaya, *this volume*). The authors own recent fieldwork among the European Nenets relativised this general picture. The pressure on native language and culture varied in different schools and at different times, probably being the harshest after the Second World War and diminishing by the 1980s. It also had different effects on different people, according to their family background and profession after school (see also Liarskaya 2005; Liarskaya 2009b on the Yamal Nenets).

Effects of Boarding Schools on Language and Culture

The intended educational effect yielded various results. On the one hand, the Soviet school system produced an indigenous *intelligentsia* which subsequently became the harshest critic of the system itself, irrespective of the fact that they profited the most from it. Their situation was paradoxical in yet another sense: their educational carriers let many of them become specialists in cultural institutions like village houses of culture, the public media, local museums, schools and universities. The indigenous culture that was taken away from them by the educational system often became their most important resource in that very educational system or in their cultural institutions. Some specialists in indigenous languages and indigenous linguists had to relearn their native language, because they were inhibited to use them from the age they entered school up to university (personal communication by Roza Laptander for the Nenets). The feeling of cultural and often also language loss was one of the major motivations for the indigenous intelligentsia to become the protagonists of the cultural revivalism and the preservation projects that have spread throughout Siberia since the time of *perestroika* in the 1980s (see Laptander, *this volume*).

Northern boarding schools on the other hand often provided only an inferior education in comparison to the schools in larger Russian settlements. Remote villages experience difficulties in attracting well-trained staff. The reindeer herders' children that live and learn in the boarding schools experience prejudice even from village youth. The drop-out rate is quite high and today nobody enforces compulsory attendance anymore. Especially in the 1990s, quite a lot of parents living in the taiga withdrew their children, often the girls, after some initial grades from the boarding school, and took them back home. In interviews, Khanty blamed the boarding school for the bad habits the children had learned at school, like drinking, smoking and swearing, instead of anything useful. Magga et al. speak about subtractive education, whereby instead of adding knowledge, the effect of formal school education is to diminish the knowledge, skills and language proficiency acquired by indigenous children in their primary socialisation, while not giving the same level of education that children of the dominant social group receive (Magga et al. 2005; Magga 2005).

Indigenous Response to Boarding Schools

Elena Liarskaya (2005) has shown that, in the example of Nenets residential schools, the blaming of the boarding school for all evil is as wrong as the belief that state school education is the panacea for all desired change. She concludes, "that residential schools first, were unable to completely break off intergenerational ties and channels of cultural transmission, and second, became 'inscribed' into ethnic cultures"(Liarskaya 2005: 76).

The positive effect of the negative influences of boarding school education could be found in the resistance strategies that native youth developed towards 'total institutions', to use a term by Ervin Goffman (Goffman 1961; cf. also Williams 2009). I would argue that Soviet state institutions and their practices to enforce the subordination of indigenous peoples under official language and ideology in places like school, army, administration, and party resulted in indigenous people learning how to veil their values and avoid open conflict (cf. Yurchak 2003). Indigenous inhabitants of the taiga developed strategies to safeguard their own cultural norms in the realm of the informal (the taiga) and to maintain a public façade conforming to the official ideology (cf. Oswald and Voronkov 2003).

One could say that a Soviet bi-culturalism, a double reference frame, allowed indigenous reindeer herders to move between the realm of their own autonomy and the settlement, dominated by what they often call 'the world of the Russians'. It allowed indigenous youth to open up choices for career and lifestyle decisions and in that way broaden the economic basis for indigenous families.

Elena Liarskaya described this effect of boarding school education on the Yamal Nenets (Liarskaya 2009b). In the Nenets case, compulsory school education was introduced only at the end of the 1950s. The quantity and structure of the tundra population on the Yamal peninsula did not undergo serious changes, the family type reindeer herding is still predominant and the language has a firm stand. During the last 70 years the number of Nenets on Yamal has doubled. But half of the population is now living in the newly established settlements. Norms and rules are different if not contradictory in these settlements in comparison with the tundra. Settlement life is sedentary while tundra life is nomadic.

Liarskaya (2009) stresses that the eight years of education in the settlement is considered by most scientists as the main reason behind the alienation from tundra life and from reindeer husbandry of the younger generation (see Laptander, *this volume*). Liarskaya interprets the situation in a slightly different way. According to her view, life in the settlement became just another option for the Nenets who were born in the tundra. They just chose another 'life scenario'. If education plays a significant role in this choice, then one would expect that people who acquire higher education are more likely to stay in the settlement and not choose a nomadic life in the tundra. Liarskaya discovered that this was not the case. She suspects other reasons behind the decision to live in the settlement or in the tundra. It's a rule in Nenets culture that the oldest children help their parents bring up the younger ones, and the youngest children stay with their parents when they grow old. So, the oldest and youngest are more likely to become tundra dwellers, while the middle children have more freedom to choose between the tundra and the settlement. Liarskaya's analysis of about 300 cases shows that, roughly speaking, a third choose a settlement life, a third a life in the tundra and a third change their lifestyle during their life cycle. Liarskaya's conclusion is therefore that there is nothing like two different cultures, but rather a complex cultural system in which tundra life and life in the settlement are connected to each other, even if the norms and values inherent in each are sometimes quite contradictory (Liarskaya 2009b).

But Liarskaya is not numb to the traumatic experiences of Nenets children in the boarding schools. She describes for instance how painful it is for young Nenets to undress and be washed in front of strangers when they first come to the boarding school. And also the changing of clothing from their usual to the European style is experienced as a violation of the Nenets norms for the human body. The different relation to clothing becomes a marker for the different lifestyles, but the different clothes don't stand in a clear hierarchical relationship. European clothing is not considered to be more cultural. The relationship is more complex than that. What is true for the changing of clothing is also true for the change of language when moving between tundra and settlements.

Liarskaya describes convincingly that, though the boarding school system aimed to change Nenets lifestyles and values, it did not lead to assimilation, but enabled the Nenets to choose and to switch even within the lifespan of one person between life in the tundra and in the settlement and between lifestyles with sometimes not only different but contradictory norms and values.

I agree with Liarskaya that the situation of the eastern Khanty and Forest Nenets in the Khanty-Mansiisky autonomous district – Yugra is much like that of their Nenets neighbours in the Yamal-Nenets autonomous district. Though the number of reindeer herders living on traditional seasonal family campsites in the taiga is even higher than before the Soviet sedentarisation campaign, more than half of the Khanty in total now live in the central villages. The Khanty reindeer herders developed various strategies to retain the autonomy of their norms and cultural practices in the forest and keep the colonising influence out of their taiga settlements without getting into conflict with the official policy. The boarding school experience was probably a crucial one in that respect.

But notwithstanding the positive effects of the boarding school system on the resilience of indigenous communities in the Russian North and Siberia, one should not forget that reindeer herders are, like almost all nomadic communities in the world, disadvantaged in respect to education in comparison with the majority population, as was already stated in the UN 'World Declaration on Education for All' (Dyer 2010). The main problem in Siberia is not the lack of formal schooling, as in a lot of Asian, South-American and African countries. Indigenous people in Siberia are suffering from a low quality of formal education and the worsening of the conditions for the transmission of the traditional indigenous knowledge[3] which is usually transmitted outside school.

Tiuitiakha Taiga School

A lot of the indigenous activism in Siberia during and after *perestroika* was directed towards education. Language loss was identified as one of the most visible markers of the social marginalisation of indigenous people, and educational reforms were considered most important to fill the gap in the transmission of knowledge between generations. The school was, besides the local village administration, the most visible institution of the state in indigenous settlements, and the state was blamed for being the force behind the assimilation process and subsequent loss of indigenous identity.

In view of this background, it's no wonder that the 1990s were the decade in which the indigenous Siberian *intelligentsia* developed a broad range of educational ideas and projects, from radio education to ethnographic summer camps. A prominent idea among these projects was a nomadic form of school that whould follow the reindeer herders in their annual movement and thus put an end to the separation of parents and children. Roza Laptander describes in her chapter an attempt to establish such a school in the Yamal-Nenets autonomous district.

Since the 1990s, I have tried to collect information about existing nomadic schools throughout Siberia, but with the exception of a rumour from the Evenkiiskii autonomous district, I have hardly found any information. Only in the last few years did I learn about the nomadic school for Evenki children initiated by French anthropologist Alexandra Lavrillier (see her contribution in this volume) and some other examples for Evenki and Chukchi in the Republic of Sakha (Yakutia) (ELOKA; Zhirkova 2006).

The only attempt to realise a similar idea in western Siberia was undertaken by the Nenets poet and reindeer herder Jurii Kylevich Aivaseda (known under his pseudonym Yuri Vella).[4] In the wake of indigenous activism at the beginning of the 1990s, he tried to revive the lifestyle of his forefathers and returned with his family and a small reindeer herd to the forest tundra several hundred kilometres from the settlement where he and the majority of the indigenous people of the Agan River resided at that time (Dudeck and Ventsel 1998). One of the main motivations for his grown daughters not to follow his example, but instead to stay in the village, was their reluctance to give their offspring to the boarding school and to be that way separated from their education.

To establish a school in the reindeer herders' campsites in the taiga was therefore one of the priorities of the revivalist project that he planned as an exemplary model for the neo-traditionalist movement and as a 'living museum' of the reindeer herder lifestyle. Neo-traditionalism is used here as the term for the *intelligentsia's* activism aimed at a return to their 'roots' and native traditions, and is slightly different from its use by Alexandr Pika (Pika and Grant 1999). In 1996, Yuri Vella succeeded in establishing a small school for his own children and the children of the neighbouring reindeer herders in a building that looked similar to the usual log houses of the Eastern Khanty winter settlements. The first teacher was an anthropologist from Moscow who agreed to live at the campsite for one school year. But the greatest challenge was to convince the bureaucrats in the education department of the *rayon* administration to accept the school as equivalent to the usual village school. Yuri Vella came to an agreement that the school would be considered a branch of the school in the village in Var'yogan, in the Nizhnevartovsky *rayon* of the Khanty-Mansiisky *avtonomnyi okrug* – Yugra, where the taiga inhabitants were registered, and that the teachers of the taiga school whould be on the payroll of the department of education of the Nizhnevartovsky *rayon*. The building was maintained by the Vella family at their own cost, but the department financed some equipment and in some years even some food for the school children.

The model for this kind of nomadic school was adapted to the way of life of reindeer herders and fishermen in the Western Siberian taiga, which differs considerably from the tundra zone further north. The northern nomadic reindeer herders live in tents and migrate with their big herds of several thousand reindeer across huge distances up to several hundred if not thousands of kilometres. The taiga inhabitants have up to four seasonal settlements not far from each other consisting of log houses and different other buildings. The type of school adapted to this way of semi-nomadic life differs therefore from the one for tundra reindeer nomads. Therefore, I will call it in the following not a nomadic school but a taiga school.

There was one permanent problem standing in the way of the official recognition of the school. The Tiuitiakha is a tributary of the Agan River, one of the tributaries of the main water artery of the region – the Ob River. Ethnic boundaries of the indigenous population were maintained within the river basins. And the administrative subdivisions of the district followed the same rule. The Agan River basin was part of the Nizhnevartovsky *rayon* and the indigenous people were bound administratively to two central villages on the shores of the Agan River. When the district became one of the main producers of crude oil in Russia, some of the administrative borders were adjusted to meet the needs of the oil companies. Near the Tiuitiakha River, a huge oil field, called Povkhskoe, was explored and supplied from the newly established oil town of Kogalym. The Tiuitiakha River basin thus was administratively transferred to the Surgutsky *rayon* which Kogalym belongs to. Reindeer herding families in the region appeared to be administratively registered in the Nizhnevartovsky *rayon* but their land belongs to the Surgutsky *rayon* now. Traditional seasonal settlements of reindeer herders are officially not considered settlements at all. In the case of the Tiuitiakha School, the school appeared to territorially belong to the Surgutsky *rayon* but hosted children from the Nizhnevartovsky *rayon*. Both *rayon* departments of education thus had a reason to refuse funding and support for the school. As described above, in the end Yuri Vella succeeded in convincing the Nizhnevartovsk authorities that his school should be considered part of the boarding school of the village of Var'yogan.

Through the first years, the school existed in one log house on the winter settlement, which also served as the teachers' home. The house was divided for that purpose with a wooden wall. After some time the teachers got their own cabin. They used the same facilities as the two or three indigenous families living on the site. There was a toilet outside, a sauna, water from a nearby lake and supplies from the village brought by Yuri Vella himself with his all-terrain vehicle *UAZ*. Electricity was produced by a little generator in the evenings or during the day when it was needed for the computers in the school. Subsequently another school building was established on the late summer and autumn settlement. It was a wagon formerly used as living quarters by oil workers. All school children were taught in the one room. The parents of the school

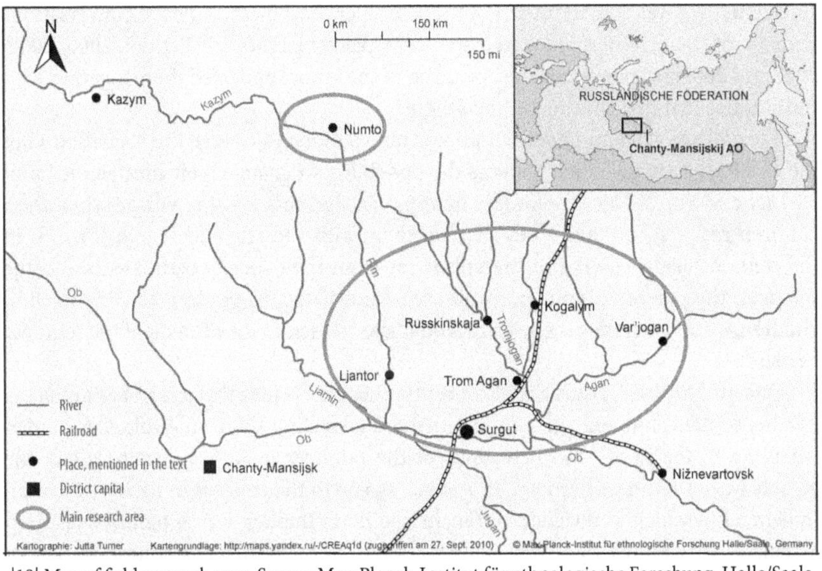

|18| Map of field research area. *Source*: Max-Planck-Institut für ethnologische Forschung, Halle/Saale

children heated the school building in the morning and teachers and students maintained the buildings and prepared firewood. In 2008, Vella's family decided to move to a new winter settlement several kilometres away from the old one. The older school children reassembled the school building in the new place. For the teachers there was a separate little cabin there.

Yuri Vella explained to me in an interview the further plans for the school which could not be realised because the school was closed after two of the elder children left the settlement for further studies in 2009. Teachers and parents developed a project for such a small school on a taiga settlement which would meet the conditions of the Khanty and Forest Nenets type of reindeer herding. School, teachers' flat and a sleeping room for the children of neighbouring settlements would be joined in a log house heated by a common stove. Electricity would be delivered by a small generator or from a neighbouring oil field. Besides the teachers, there would be one additional educator or housekeeper to care for the children and the school. As Yuri explained, such a small school and dormitory should be even cheaper than the residential school in the village because the school did not need so much technical staff and it could use local resources like firewood and fresh fish.

Concept of the Taiga School

Yuri Vella explained to me his thoughts about the school in several interviews, and the Forest Nenets poet and political activist was the 'master mind' behind the school.

Additionally, I was able to interview three teachers and meet and have conversations with six of them. When I visited Yuri Vella's place in 1996, 1997, 1999, 2000, 2006, 2008 and 2009, I experienced the operation of the school and lived there together with the families that had children in the school.

The educational aim of the school was not so much to change the socialisation of the children as to give their parents the possibility to change their lifestyle. A lot of Khanty and Forest Nenets reindeer herding families move to the village when their children reach school age. They give up their taiga lifestyle and search for jobs in the central villages. Living in the village far from their former settlements and the reindeer, the parents cannot transmit their knowledge of reindeer herding to their children, even when they themselves would later return to the lifestyle of the reindeer herders.

One of Yuri Vella's educational concepts relies on the idea that it is not as much the parents or educators but the reindeer that are educating the young reindeer herder. Adapting to the needs and behaviour of the reindeer is an important skill in the Nenets way of reindeer herding. This idea links up to the concept of native education in general in which knowledge is transmitted in an implicit way. Cognitive research associates this knowledge with the processual memory of behavioural sequences storing predominantly habitual knowledge like practical skills and habits (Anderson 1976; cf. also Derlicki 2004). Only a small part of traditional knowledge belongs to the so-called declarative memory, where facts, meanings and events are memorised. But this knowledge stays connected to the memory of practical skills and behaviour sequences and cannot be transmitted unless the learner takes part in and observes these practices. As a Khanty proverb says: "You have eyes: see! You have ears: hear! You have hands: do! You have legs: go!" (Vagt 2012).

This knowledge, Yuri was sure, cannot be transmitted in formal schooling. The only place to learn to live as a reindeer herder is the reindeer herder's settlement. On the other hand, he is not a revivalist in the conservative sense. He always stressed that he would love to see his grandchildren become doctors or lawyers. Important from his perspective was to keep the ability alive, so that children could become reindeer herders, fishers or hunters if they wanted to. The idea of the school on the Tiuitiakha River was to give the children a formal education on the same level as every school in Russia. The school curriculum should not contain local or traditional knowledge, which is almost impossible to integrate into the usual school teaching process. This knowledge should be transferred in everyday life together with the reindeer and the parents in the taiga.

Another important aspect of the relation between so-called indigenous and school education was not explicitly stressed by Yuri Vella, but became obvious in talks with the parents and the teachers. The symbolic relationship of the school-book knowledge and indigenous knowledge is determined by the relation of taiga versus urban lifestyles. In the settlement, the lifestyle of reindeer herders has low social prestige and is

|19| Yuri Vella, the founder of the school ↑

|20| Schoolboy in the classroom ↓

often considered to be less cultural and less advanced by the people living there. Reindeer herders' children feel marginalised by that dominant opinion, which is supported by the way culture, history and progress are presented in school books. The situation in the taiga is different. The value of indigenous knowledge is obvious there, while the superiority of school-book knowledge is not at all self-evident. This dependence on the norms and rules of forest life was sometimes a big challenge for teachers trying to adapt to life on the reindeer herding settlement. This was already the experience of the first nomadic school experiments in the 1920s, as Roza Laptander describes in her chapter. From the perspective of the mainstream concept of school education in Russia, the parents' educational function is completely secondary. Education is delivered by formal schooling, not through the upbringing by parents. If the parents fail to transfer certain knowledge or values, it is the school which should take over this function. Being trained in such an environment, it was quite difficult for some of the teachers to recognise their own sometimes marginal position on the taiga settlement. They had to follow the same everyday routines, eat the same food and obey to the same religious taboos as everybody else there. They experienced the culture shock that indigenous children usually experience when they are transferred to the boarding school.

To sum up the concept and contrast it with other alternative schooling programmes, one could stress that it pursued not the 'integration' of indigenous knowledge into the school curriculum, but the adaptation of the school itself to the conditions of the reindeer herding lifestyle. The same could be said about the school project described by Alexandra Lavrillier (*this volume*). In this way, the school circumvented the value conflict between different knowledge that is taught in one curriculum. The content of the curriculum was identical to that for all other children, but the institution itself and the teaching process had to be integrated into the everyday life on the indigenous settlement.

According to my interpretation, Yuri Vella did not believe in the reformation of the institution from within. He did not believe that indigenous knowledge could remain alive and valuable to manage everyday life if it was transferred to the formalised learning process at school. On the other hand, he was well aware of the importance of the formalised knowledge and the educational methods of the school system for an urban lifestyle and for communication with mainstream society.

Teachers' Adaptation to the Taiga

Most of the teachers adapted quite well to the taiga conditions. But almost none of them stayed more than one or two school years in the taiga school. Their motivations were quite different, and as well, they experienced many difficulties. Some were interested in the salary, others mainly in the exotic experience. Some had to cope with loneliness, some had personal conflicts with some of the parents, and others were asked to leave after an evaluation by the parents themselves. In the first years, mostly non-professionally trained school teachers were hired as teachers. Some anthropologists and some intellectuals interested in the experience and the educational experiment agreed to live for one school year at the Tiuitiakha River school. Later, Yuri Vella hired teachers from the region itself. I witnessed this hiring procedure twice. He put an advertisement in the local newspaper. The booming oil cities of western Siberia are popular places to live in Russia. But changing demographics and educational politics produced unemployment among the teachers in the district. So it was not difficult to find teachers from the oil towns who would be interested and agree to live one year in the forest.

This was of course an exceptional situation which was very different from almost all other regions in Russia inhabited by indigenous people (see Alexandra Lavrillier, *this volume*). I was quite surprised at why indigenous students or teachers were not applying for the job. Pedagogy is the most popular subject among indigenous students and there is a lot of state support for indigenous youth who want to study at local universities in Surgut, Khanty-Mansiisk or Nizhnevartovsk. But I learned that the main motivation of indigenous students to get a higher education is to change their lifestyle and become urban dwellers. None of them wants to go back to the small villages some of them came from and even more not to the taiga settlements. This is all the more noteworthy because in other regions going back to the small settlements or nomad camps seems to be still an option for some students, as the article by Alexandra Lavrillier in this volume shows. New educational experiments in the Khanty-Mansiisky autonomous district will hopefully prove that the situation can change. Even if students know the rules and norms of the life of the reindeer herders, they don't aspire to live and work in a small taiga school. There is only one example of a young teacher from a northern Khanty village who is married to a reindeer herder and almost agreed to come to the Tiuitiakha, but unfortunately she had to refuse because of personal circumstances.

Changing Conditions in the Taiga School

In the meantime, the taiga settlement has a mobile phone connection. In emergency cases, the next town, with a modern hospital and airport, could be reached in several hours, or even a helicopter could be called. In the last two years of the existence of the school it was possible to access the internet via satellite through the "multimedia point" that was established there.

The plan was originally to collect children from the neighbouring settlements to the school at Tiuitiakha River. The settlement is located between Forest Nenets and Eastern Khanty reindeer herding territories. There are five or six neighbouring families. Some of the Forest Nenets families have kinship ties with the Vella family, and Yuri thought they would be interested in sending their children to their relatives. But most of the time only the children of two of his daughters were attending the school. The reasons for that were manifold. One very shy boy from a neighbouring Khanty family was hiding in the forest during the daytime or running away to his parents' settlement. The lack of enforced discipline which is usual in the boarding school made this behaviour possible, and nobody tried to force him back to school.

Obstacles and Difficulties of the Taiga School

Some of the neighbours were not convinced that the taiga school could provide the children with the same level of education and the same experience of enforced discipline as the boarding school that would be necessary for them to survive in the hard world of wage labour outside the forest, or in case of the boys, the tough experience of army service. The contributions of Cecilia Odé and Alexandra Lavrillier (*this volume*) mention also the often overlooked motivation of parents to secure future chances for their children by the mainstream form of education. Additionally, the high degree of what I would like to call individualism got in the way of Yuri Vella's plans to attract neighbouring children. Khanty and Forest Nenets reindeer herding families live with a high degree of competition that against all obligations of solidarity sometimes leads to mistrust and quarrels between neighbouring families, even if these families are linked by kinship ties.

Another quite serious obstacle was the resistance of the official educational bureaucracy. I've already told the story of the administrative difficulties the school had to deal with. The project was met with varying responses on the part of the authorities. Many of them saw it as just another attempt by the indigenous population to get additional subsidies and benefits, summarily called '*lgoty*' in Russian. Others feared that the establishment of a small school so far away would cause them to lose control over resources and political power. Yuri Vella tried to convince them that the school would not cost so much and that it would be under the permanent supervision of the main school in the village of Var'yogan. Teachers had to report regularly to the village school and the pupils had to pass exams at the end of every school year to prove that the school provided the same curriculum. As far as I know, educational progress was always above the average of the village school (see also Alexandra Lavrillier, *this volume*).

Appropriating Media Competence

But there was also open support from some of the authorities, which saw the school as an opportunity to gain additional resources for innovative projects. The regional department of education in the Nizhnevartovsky *rayon* gave their approval in 2002 for the existence of the school under the supervision of the village school, and agreed in 2005/6 to finance the salary of the teachers. The institute of language, history and cultures of the Ugrian people of Yugra University in the regional capital of Khanty Mansiisk supported the establishment of a multimedia centre in the school, financed by UNESCO. Information about the project is available at two websites (UNESCO-doc, UNESCO-Moscow)

The project provided the school with a satellite phone and access to the internet, and encouraged the inhabitants to communicate with other indigenous communities and the wider world via the internet. The project was launched in 2007, but when I visited the school in 2008 and 2009, it was still in the starting phase, as teachers and children were getting acquainted with the new technologies. Technicians had to travel a whole day from Khanty-Mansiisk to fix technical problems. And the children were using the computer mainly to play ego-shooter computer games. They had just started to use a video camera and a photo camera to produce little reports about their life in the taiga and put them onto the internet. Due to the restructuring of the University in Khanty-Mansiisk, the institute of language history and culture was unfortunately closed, along with the websites, so the content was lost. My personal impression was that even if the planned educational effect of the multi-media centre probably failed, one cannot underestimate the overall media competence the youngsters got by playing around and experimenting with the computer, the internet and audio-visual devices. I was impressed by their self-awareness in front of a camera and by the quality of their own photographs. The process of acquiring media competence is now one of the biggest challenges native communities face, and it will change the way they are able to defend cultural diversity seriously (see for instance Stammler 2009; Miller 2006; Horst and Miller 2005).

In 2009, I witnessed three pupils learning in the school at the Tiuitiakha, but two of them graduated the same year, and Yuri could not find enough children to prolong the existence of the school.

Foreign Support

The support and advocacy of scholars and activists for indigenous rights played a significant role in the establishment of and struggle for various reform projects in ethnopedagogy in the Russian North. Generally speaking, one could distinguish three parties that joined forces in the process of the establishment of new forms of schooling for the indigenous people: the native *intelligentsia*, parents who remembered their problems with the boarding school system and wanted to spare their children some of the side effects of that system, and as a third party, activists and scholars from outside the indigenous communities. Therefore, I consider it necessary to shed some light on my own involvement in the school project. The focus of my research and my plans of study did not allow me to consider working in the school as some Russian scholars did. But, as a known foreign visitor paying extraordinary attention to the project of Yuri Vella, mentioning the school in talks and papers, and being present at the official celebration of the 10th birthday of the school in 2006, my presence had some effect on the life of the school.

Only once did I decide to take a more active step in supporting the school, when I visited the school together with my colleague Carolin Grosse and her two children and the German translator of Yuri's work, Ines Baumgartl, in November 2008. As an example of the engagement of foreign anthropologists in such projects, I will describe our involvement briefly in the following paragraph.

Yuri Vella heard 2008 about the *Law on nomadic schools in the Republic of Sakha (Yakutia)*. I helped him to download the text of the law: *Zakon Respubliki Sakha (Yakutiia) ot 22 iiulia 2008 g. 591-3 N 73-IV 'O kochevykh shkolakh Respubliki Sakha (Yakutiia)'* – from the internet (www.chebgym5.ru/federal/regional_law/016.rtf). The law described in detail the functions and different forms of schools for indigenous people according to their specific lifestyle, such that the education of children next to the living place of their parents would be possible, even if they led a nomadic way of life.

Thereafter, he tried to initiate a similar law in the Khanty-Mansiisky autonomous district to give his own school legal basis and force the regional government to support it. He was backed by a member of the regional *Duma* (parliament), Aleksei Andreev, in this effort. Later on, the regional *Duma* accepted the initiative. The law on nomadic schools for the Khanty-Mansiisky autonomous district was still in the process of getting support by a special working group of specialists in 2010, and probably still will be until the publication of this book.

I asked Yuri Vella at the same time if I could support the school with some public action such as, for instance, an open letter. He agreed with the idea but refused to give me any hints as to what he would like to have written. He explained to me that the effect of such a letter would be even greater if the form and content including spelling mistakes would prove that the foreigners themselves were really the creators of the letter. He only provided me with the address of the head of the administration of the Nizhnevartovsky *rayon*, Boris Aleksandrovich Salomatin, and the head of the department of education in the administration, Shermadin Yasonovich Gogoshidze.

Carolin Grosse, Ines Baumgartl and I drafted the letter and then used the internet connection available at the Tiuitiakha settlement at that time to send it to some colleagues and friends we thought would agree to sign the letter. Johannes Rohr, who was at that time the coordinator for the work with the indigenous people in Russia at the international NGO IWGIA (International Working Group for Indigenous Affairs), and Florian Stammler, the leader of the Anthropology Research Group at the Arctic Centre of the University of Lapland, agreed very quickly to be co-authors of the letter. They then asked the group members of the Anthropology Research Team of the Arctic Centre, Nuccio Mazzullo, Anna Stammler-Gossmann, Alla Bolotova from the St. Petersburg Centre for Independent Social Research, Pekka Aikio, the former president of the Finnish Saami Parliament and coordinator of the Saami higher education and research programs in Lapland, and Professor Bruce Forbes from the Arctic Centre, to support the letter.

The main purpose of the letter was of course to support the idea of the legislative initiative, but also to secure further financing of the school by the local authorities. Our main argument was the role of this specific school type for the maintenance of indigenous cultures and the specific socialisation of children and its effect on the development of responsibility and self-reliance in the school children. We tried to provide the ethno-pedagogical idea of the school with scientific legitimisation by stressing our competence in indigenous education issues and our own experiences with the tundra school. An important point was also to emphasise the role of the new communication technologies available at the school that linked the remote settlement with the surrounding world.

The letter was sent on November 19th, 2008 to the administration of the Nizhnevartovsky *rayon* and published on the internet on Yuri Vella's homepage: http://www.jurivella.ru/index.php/2009-09-01-06-41-19/127-kiri-koolist-2008.

Unfortunately, there was never a direct or public reply to the letter, but I am sure that the responsible people in the administration took notice. In order to keep a low profile, we did not involve any regional or international media in the publication of the open letter. It's hard to estimate the effect the letter had, because the school was closed a year later when two of the school children left the school and there were not enough children to replace them. The legislative process is still ongoing and much depends on the policy of the new governor, Natalya Komarova, who came to power in the district in March 2010.

Other Educational Initiatives

What is the place of the above-described educational experiment in the overall picture of the attempts to reform indigenous education, and how did it contribute to them?

First, I will try to sum up the educational reform initiatives in the region itself, and then give an outlook on educational projects for indigenous and nomad groups in general, and to then compare them with the approach of the Tiuitiakha School.

As already mentioned in the beginning and described in the contribution of Laptander in this volume, indigenous voices became louder during *perestroika*, claiming that the younger generation in Siberia was losing its cultural knowledge and native languages, and that educational programmes should be initiated to reform and adapt the school curriculum to the special needs of northerners.

The KASh

The first project to be realised was the '*Kazymskaia kul'tur-antropologicheskaia shkola*' (khanty: *Kasum KASh* – Kazym River cultural-anthropological school), founded in 1991. The first experiment to reform state education was undertaken by some Khanty scientists and teachers at the place of the first Soviet *kul'tbaza* and the first open acts of resistance against state education. The idea was to find completely new forms of education adapted to traditional indigenous ones. Instruction was executed in ethnically homogeneous classes and in the native languages, Khanty, Russian and Komi (Kravchenko s.a.). But one of the main ideas of the school was also to reform the boarding school system without abandoning it. The project developed new ideas like the establishment of 'social parents' for the children who came from distant reindeer herder settlements. Social parents meant in that case that the traditional role of educators based on discipline and subordination was changed to a relationship built on trust and emotional support. The educator was meant to become in that way a supportive confidante, a person a lot of boarding school children are missing.

The main purpose of reforming the curricula was to adapt them to what the educators called the 'ethnic worldview'. Taboos and behavioural conventions of the reindeer herders were to be maintained and even taught in the boarding school. The school was closed in 1998 due to the refusal of further support by the authorities of the Khanty-Mansiisky autonomous district. Since then, the teachers and activists around the school are organising summer camps for school children and youngsters, where they try to pursue their ethno-pedagogical ideas. Indigenous religious practices and world views, like the bear-feast or traditional crafts and hunting and fishing skills, lie within the focus of this ethno-pedagogical endeavour. Summer camps for the indigenous village youth are now quite common all over the region. But the focus group of these educational projects is children who lack native socialisation in the taiga or tundra and the knowledge of reindeer herding or shamanism. Their outreach is not so much to the children who have grown up in reindeer herding families. The ethno-pedagogical ideas that were developed in the region for reindeer herders' children, like for instance, a system of distance education by radio, never reached the stage of realisation, as far as I know.

Conclusions

Language Preservation

The starting point for almost all ideas to develop alternative educational ideas for native northerners is the problem of language preservation. The ubiquitous processes of language loss seem to be the most visible sign of the loss of indigenous knowledge and subsequently identity and social prestige (Jääsalmi-Krüger 1998; Jordan and Filchenko 2005; Toulouze 2003). On the other hand, language is considered to comprise the way of thinking (Anderson 1976; Basso 1992). To use an ethnically distinct language is therefore considered to be naturally the first step towards establishing an ethnically distinctive teaching (Kasten 1998; Pikunova 1998; Ball 2004; Deyhle and Swisher 1997; but, challenging that concept, see also Henze and Vanett 1993). This language-oriented approach is often pursued by activists coming from the indigenous *intelligentsia*, many of them trained linguists. It is also understandable in view of the background of available financial resources for research on endangered languages in the scientific funding environment. Applied scientific projects in the field of ethnopedagogy face here a similar dilemma to people active in nature conservation projects.

The aim of these advocating projects is to support people in their everyday struggle for survival. A distinct language is only one element in a whole complex of culturally distinct practices and knowledge that help to retain social cohesion and solidarity and to survive in a specific natural environment. Institutions like kinship or complex ecological knowledge are other elements. But the concept of a native language fits so well the Western perception of ethnic identity and makes the tragedy of a dying language understandable to public discourse in Western nation states that it is much easier to present the need for support of indigenous people as a need for the preservation of a dying language. In this way, one could compare nature conservationists who have to present a beautiful dying-out species, something like the snow leopard, to justify their projects to save complex ecosystems, with applied anthropologists. The tragedy of the death of an exotic language is easier to represent to a western public and to funding institutions than the complex cultural and economic changes indigenous people have to cope with.

Mainstream Ethno-Pedagogics

To describe the mainstream concept of ethno-pedagogics in the Russian North I will quote here the paper by Sargylana Zhirkova about nomadic schools in Yakutia: "The main goal of a nomadic school is to preserve the traditional culture, minority language and traditional way of life" (Zhirkova 2006: 39) and "the aim of the nomadic school is to keep the language as part of traditional culture even if the language is not officially used" (Zhirkova 2006: 42). Hairullin even states that, "the curriculum ... must introduce children to the world of their own ethnic culture" (Hairullin 2006). The educational programmes of state institutions often lack any imagination of the role of the primary socialisation given by parents to their children. I would interpret this ignorance as being a result of the still existing conceptual division between the world of the official and that of the informal in which 'culture' is considered part of the official and therefore part of what state education has to provide. But, as for example the Russian linguist Olga Kazakevich reported, attempts to transmit the mother tongue outside the family in Ket, Selkup and Evenki villages were not successful (Kazakevich 2009: 12).

But besides this linguistic focus, ethno-pedagogy is often also focussed on the educational content of the curriculum. It aims at the development of alternative subjects based on indigenous folklore and crafts (cf. Derlicki 2004). The state concept of development of education for the indigenous people still favours the splitting of the educational programme: one for the indigenous population oriented towards the traditional forms of economy and one for those oriented towards an urban lifestyle. Subsequently, these two groups are taught with different educational ideals and different educational content (Hairullin 2006). It seems to me that this approach cemented the differences and the disadvantages of indigenous people in education.

Ethnic Components

Another less radical approach is the introduction of an ethnic and regional component to the school curriculum. But the very concept of 'component' deals with cultural forms as detachable objects that can be included in conventional forms of teaching. Culture is here presented in a musealised form, as a collection of elements of so-called 'material and intellectual culture' that are detached from the original social context and transformed into teachable knowledge or sometimes mere ornamentation. Ethnicised pictures in school books, local elements in examples and paradigms and some additional information about the local environment and history are some ways in which these types of objects serve as ethnic and local components. The danger of the content-oriented educational projects in general is that they remain a pure ethnic decoration to the usual schooling procedure, not changing the disadvantages and shortcomings of inferior rural education for indigenous people. The role of this ethnic ornamentation in the school curriculum should on the other hand not be underestimated. It serves as an official legitimisation of cultural difference and emphasises the equality of different ethnic belonging and identity. There is a clear positive effect of the inclusion of knowledge of the local indigenous cultures and their language in the school curriculum on children that grew up without direct contact to the reindeer herders' lifestyle. But the everyday reality in northern villages shows that these components have no power to call into question the existing vernacular hierarchy of ethnicities, which positions Russians on top of the civilisation scale.

Other Nomadic School Examples

Unfortunately, information about the evaluation of existing alternative school models in the Russian North is not easy to obtain. Scientific literature on this topic is all but missing or remains in a very generalised form. Analysis of concrete examples and a critique of different pedagogical approaches are still rare. Most of the nomadic schools were founded in the Republic of Sakha (Yakutia) during the 1990s, and this was also the region where the first regional law on nomadic schools was drafted, this after federal Russian legislation had already allowed indigenous nomadic groups to have such schools (cf. Hairullin 2006, Robbek et al. 2009). I can refer here to the paper by Alexandra Lavrillier (*this volume*) for the description of the situation in the Sakha Republic concerning nomadic schools and for the situation of Evenki reindeer herders on the border of Yakutia, in particular.

Another Evenki nomadic school is mentioned by Sargylana Zhirkova: the *Amma* nomadic school in the Aldan *ulus* in the Sakha Republic (Zhirkova 2006). It is, as in the case of the Tiuitiakha School, a sub-branch of the ordinary rural school in the village called *Khatisdir*. Zhirkova mentions another nomadic school supported by the *Snowchange projec*t in the Chukchi community of Nutendli. She describes it as "one of the well-organised nomadic schools in the Republic of Sakha" (Zhirkova 2006: 48). It was initially deprived of state financial support but later got financial help from outside sources. Similar to the school initiative of the Vella family, the school fostered strong involvement of the local community in the organisation of the school, and this was a precondition of the success of the school (ELOKA; Snowchange Cooperative 2007). Konstantin Klokov describes the school in a slightly different way, which shows how contradictory the information about nomadic schools is at the moment: "The community was formed on the basis of one extended Chukchi family that included parents, several brothers and sisters, and many grandchildren. The economy of the community is based on reindeer husbandry (it has about 2000 reindeer) and fishing. The main part of the income is derived from state subsidies. The community is settled 20 km from the nearest neighbour village. There are two houses (a dwelling house and school), slaughterhouse, garages for snowmobiles, ice-house, bath-house, and hen-house with about 50 hens. The school was established in the autumn of 2003 and it includes a kindergarten. There are 11 children in the school; 6 in the first grade and 5 in the kindergarten. The school-staff comprises two persons: one teacher and one educator. It is financed by the state (50 %) and the Nutendly community (50 %). One day a week, everybody speak the Chukchi language in order to practice their mother tongue. The fathers of some of the children are herders and move with the herd around the community at distances from 20 to 80 km. Other children in the school are from Chukchi families that live in indigenous villages far away from the Nutendly community. Thus, in reality the 'nomadic' school is a tundra indigenous boarding school where children receive common primary education" (Klokov 2007).

I found some information about a project of nomadic school project that was opened in October 2008 on the Taimyr Peninsula and was initiated by the local college in the town of Dudinka. The small schools were opened in the Ust'-Eniseisky *rayon* in the Polikarpovska and Tukharska Tundra. There is no more information available than that about "equipping the single teacher in the school with a field telephone and two laptop computers" (Grenoble 2010: 81).

According to Zhirkova (2006), exams are passed in the main school in the village in a similar way to the practice of the school on the Tiuitiakha River. The main advantage of these nomadic schools is to avoid the separation of the children from their home community and to allow them to live under the same living conditions as their parents. In the Sakha Republic the curriculum of these schools includes, besides special native language courses, special subjects like reindeer breeding, fishing, hunting and crafts (Zhirkova 2006).

Challenges for the future

Ole Henrik Magga (2005) provided some keywords that mark the preconditions of successful solutions for the problems indigenous communities have with existing state education. Among them was the participation of the people concerned in decision-making as well as employment in the school itself. This was one of the main conditions of the Tiuitiakha School and probably also the main reason for the conflict with the conventional educational system. The participation of indigenous groups and especially parents in decision-making and management of education seem to be still one of the biggest challenges for state bureaucracies, as you can also see in the contributions of Cecilia Odé and Alexandra Lavrillier (*this volume*).

As a second important point, he mentioned the equal access of all indigenous persons to the same level of school education. In a situation where some indigenous parents decide for different reasons not to send their children to the boarding school in the village, the nomadic school could be a way of giving these children the possibility to have equal access to education.

But I would also like to summarise here the main challenges the school on the Tiuitiakha River posed to the conventional educational concepts:

1. The Tiuitiakha School challenges the prevalent hierarchy of urban versus rural schools in Russia, in which the latter provide only inferior education. The individual attention given to the children and the social embedding of the school give reindeer herders' children better chances to adapt to the usual school curriculum.
2. It challenges the clear hierarchy of lifestyles which is presented in the formal school curriculum. The dominant lifestyle in the environment of the school is not the urban one presented in the school books as the norm. The contradiction between life as presented in school books and the everyday reality in the settlement facilitates a more relativistic view of different lifestyles.
3. The school concept challenges the prevalent concept of an ethnic component in school education. Ethnicity is the everyday identity in the social environment and does not become a folkloristic ornament for some special events.
4. The concept of the Tiuitiakha School challenged the dominance of a language-oriented approach. Its only language of instruction was Russian because it recognised the role of the parents as the ones who should provide the children with their mother tongue. The nomadic school should render it possible to transfer traditional knowledge and indigenous languages in the natural way in everyday life (see also the Evenki nomadic school presented by Lavrillier in this volume).
5. The biggest challenge was probably that the parents at the reindeer herder's settlement took over the initiative and direct control of the school, and thereby put implicitly into question the power of the educational bureaucracy in the urban centres and the influence of scientific advisers.

To conclude the lesson learned from the experiment at Tiuitiakha River, I would say that the problems that nomadic schools are facing are not in the content of the curriculum or the adaptation of content to the nomadic way of life. The purpose of the school curriculum in the narrower sense is neither the preservation of language nor the transmission of traditional knowledge. The setting of the school itself enables the primary socialisation by parents to fulfil its proper function.

But the main problems that have to be addressed by projects to establish nomadic schools for reindeer herders in the Russian North are:

- the set-up and financing of infrastructure;
- the recruitment and education of the teaching staff;
- the resistance of the state educational bureaucracy;
- and the participation in and control of education by the nomadic communities themselves.

Notes

1 I must gratefully note the support of the Max-Planck Institute for Social Anthropology, Halle/Saale, Germany and the Finnish Academy ORHELIA project, funding decision 251111 of 2011.
2 The term *chum* is used in the Russian language for the conical tent of nomadic reindeer herders in Western Siberia. The name has its origin in the Komi language. It is now besides the reindeer one of the main symbols of indigenous culture in the Russian North.
3 This is also called TEK – traditional environmental knowledge in policy documents and scientific literature.
4 The following information about the Tiuitiakha School derived from numerous interviews with Yuri Vella and fieldtrips to his settlement between 1996 and 2009.

References

Anderson, John Robert 1976. *Language, Memory, and Thought*. Hillsdale: Lawrence Erlbaum.

Ball, Jessica 2004. As If Indigenous Knowledge and Communities Mattered: Transformative Education in First Nations Communities in Canada. *American Indian Quarterly* 28 (3/4): 454–479.

Balzer, Marjorie Mandelstam 1999. *The Tenacity of Ethnicity: a Siberian Saga in Global Perspective.* Princeton: University Press.

Bartels, Dennis and Alice Bartels 1995. *When the North Was Red: Aboriginal Education in Soviet Siberia.* Montreal: McGill-Queen's University Press.

Basso, Keith H. 1992. *Western Apache Language and Culture: Essays in Linguistic Anthropology*. Tuscon: University of Arizona Press.

Bloch, Alexia 2004. *Red Ties and Residential Schools: Indigenous Siberians in a Post-Soviet State.* Philadelphia: University of Pennsylvania Press.

Derlicki, Jarosław 2004. Ethno-Pedagogy the Curse or the Cure? The Role of the School Among Youth in Nelemnoe (Yakutia). *Sibirica* 4 (1): 63–73.

Deyhle, Donna and Karen Swisher 1997. Research in American Indian and Alaska Native Education: From Assimilation to Self-Determination. *Review of Research in Education* 22: 113–194.

Dudeck, Stephan and Aimar Ventsel 1998. Do the Khanty Need a Khanty Curriculum? Indigenous Concepts of School Education. In *Bicultural Education in the North*. E. Kasten (ed.), 89–100. Münster: Waxmann Verlag.

Dyer, Caroline 2010. Including Pastoralists in Education for All. *Commonwealth education partnerships* 2010/11: 63–65. London: Commonwealth Secretariat.

ELOKA. Snowchange Oral History: Nutendli. http://eloka-arctic.org/communities/russia/nutendli.html.

Eremin, S.N. and M.M. Traskunova 1989. Problemy vospitaniia i obrazovaniia molodezhi narodnostei Severa [Educational Problems of the Northern Peoples]. In *Narody Sibiri na sovremennom etape: natsional'nye i regional'nye osobennosti razvitiia. Sbornik nauchnykh trudov* [The Peoples of Siberia in the present stage: National and Regional Development features]. V.S. Shmakov (ed.), 114–122. Novosibirsk: Nauka.

Ernychova, O.D. 2003. *Kazymskii miatezh: ob istorii Kazymskogo vosstaniia 1933–1934 gg.* [The Kazymsk Mutiny: about the history of the Kazymsk Rebellion in 1933–1934]. Novosibirsk: Sibirskii Khronograf.

Forsyth, James 1992. *A History of the Peoples of Siberia: Russia's North Asian Colony 1581–1990*. Cambridge: Cambridge University Press.

Goffman, Erving 1961. *Asylums*. New York: Anchor Books.

Grenoble, Leonore A. 2010. Language Vitality and Revitalization in the Arctic. In *New Perspectives on Endangered Languages: Bridging Gaps Between Sociolinguistics, Documentation and Language Revitalization*, J.A.F. Farfán and F.F. Ramallo (eds.), 65–92. Amsterdam/Philadelphia: John Benjamins Publishing Company.

Habeck, Joachim Otto 2007. Enacting 'Culture' and 'Culturedness': Why People May or May Not Want to Spend Their Free Time in the House of Culture. *Kultura: Russian Cultural Review* (1): 14–18.

Hairullin, Ruslan 2006 *Development of Educational Systems for Northern Peoples in Russia*. http://www.ankn.uaf.edu/curriculum/Articles/Rouslan/index.html

Henze, Rosemary C. and Lauren Vanett 1993. To Walk in Two Worlds: Or More? Challenging a Common Metaphor of Native Education. *Anthropology & Education Quarterly* 24 (2): 116–134.

Horst, Heather A. and Daniel Miller 2005. From Kinship to Link-up: Cell Phones and Social Networking in Jamaica. *Current Anthropology* 46 (5): 755–778.

Jääsalmi-Krüger, Paula 1998. Khanty Language and Lower School Education: Native, Second or Foreign Language? In *Bicultural Education in the North: Ways of Preserving and Enhancing Indigenous Peoples' Languages and Traditional Knowledge*. E. Kasten (ed.), 101–111. Münster: Waxmann Verlag.

Jordan, Peter and Aleksandr Filchenko 2005. Continuity and Change in Eastern Khanty Language and Worldview. In *Rebuilding Identities: Pathways to Reform in post-Soviet Siberia*. E. Kasten (ed.), 63–89. Berlin: Dietrich Reimer Verlag.

Kasten, Erich (ed.) 1998. *Bicultural Education in the North: Ways of Preserving and Enhancing Indigenous Peoples' Languages and Traditional Knowledge*. Berlin: Waxmann Verlag.

Kazakevich, Olga 2009. Pre-School and Outside School Mother Tongue Educational Programmes in the Contexts of Selkup, Ket and Evenki Communities. In *Conference on Multilingualism, Regional & Minority Languages: Paradigms for 'Languages of the Wider World' 16th - 17th April 2009*. Book of Abstracts. 12.

Klokov, Konstantin 2007. Reindeer Husbandry in Russia. *International Journal of Entrepreneurship and Small Business* 4 (6): 726–784.

Kravchenko, Olga s.a. *Kazymskaia kul'tur-antropologicheskaia shkola* (Kasum KASh). Zemlia Koshach'ego Lokotka. http://kazym.ethnic-tour.ru/kazym/kazym/publ/kash.html.

Leete, Art 2004. *Kazymskaia voina: vosstanie khantov i lesnykh nentsev protiv Sovetskoi vlasti.* [The Kazymsk War: Rebellion of the Khanty and Forest Nenets to the Soviet Power]. Tartu: Kafedra Etnologii Tartuskogo Universiteta.

— 1999. Ways of Describing Nenets and Khanty "Character" in 19th Century Russian Ethnographic Literature. *Folklore: Electronic Journal of Folklore* (12): 38–52.

Liarskaya, Elena Vladimirovna 2005. Northern Residential Schools in Contemporary Yamal Nenets Culture. *Sibirica: Journal of Siberian Studies* 4 (1): 74–87.

— 2009a. *Zhenshchiny i Tundra. Gendernyi sdvig na Yamale?* [Women and the Tundra. Gender Shift in Yamal?]. Unpublished paper at the workshop 'Gender Shift in Northern Communities of Russia' 2 - 6 May 2008, Max Planck Institute for Social Anthropology, Halle (Saale).
http://www.eth.mpg.de/events/current/pdf/1208422529-02.pdf.

— 2009b. Settlement Nenets on the Yamal Peninsula: Who Are They? *Folklore: Electronic Journal of Folklore* (41): 33–46.

— 2010. Women and the Tundra: Is There a Gender Shift on Yamal? *Anthropology of East Europe Review* 28 (2): 51–84.

Magga, Ole Henrik 2005. Indigenous Education. *Childhood Education* 81 (6): 2.

Magga, Ole Henrik, Ida Nicolaisen, Mililani Trask, Tove Skutnabb-Kangas and Robert Dunbar 2005. *Indigenous children's education and indigenous languages. Expert paper written for the United Nations Permanent Forum on Indigenous Issues.*

Miller, Daniel 2006. The Unpredictable Mobile Phone. *BT Technology Journal* 24 (3): 41–48.

Niglas, Livo and Eva Toulouze 2004. Yuri Vella's Worldview as a Tool for Survival: What Filming Reveals. *Pro Ethnologia* 17: 95–114.

Oswald, Ingrid and Viktor Voronkov 2003. Licht an, Licht aus! "Öffentlichkeit" in der (post-) sowjetischen Gesellschaft. In *Sphären von Öffentlichkeiten in Gesellschaften sowjetischen Typs. Zwischen partei-staatlicher Selbstinszenierung und kirchlichen Gegenwelten.* G. T. Rittersporn, M. Rolf, J. C. Behrends (eds.), 37–64. Frankfurt am Main: Peter Lang Verlag.

Pika, Alexander and Bruce Grant 1999. *Neotraditionalism in the Russian North: Indigenous Peoples and the Legacy of Perestroika.* Edmonton/Seattle: University of Washington Press.

Pikunova, Zinaida 1998. Politics, Education, and Culture: A Case Study of the Preservation and Development of the Native Language of the Evenkis. In *Bicultural Education in the North: Ways of Preserving and Enhancing Indigenous Peoples' Languages and Traditional Knowledge.* E. Kasten (ed.), 123–137. Münster: Waxmann Verlag.

Povoroznyuk, Olga, Joachim Otto Habeck and Virgine Vaté 2010. Introduction: On the Definition, Theory, and Practice of Gender Shift in the North of Russia. *Anthropology of East Europe Review* 28 (2): 1–37.

Robbek, Vasilii A., Feodosia V. Gabysheva, Rozalia S. Nikitina and Natalia V. Sitnikova 2009. Promoting Educational Access for the Indigenous Reindeer Herders, Fisherpeople and Hunters in the Nomadic Schools of Yakutia, Russian Federation. In *Traveller, Nomadic, and Migrant Education.* P. A. Danaher, M. Kenny, J. R. Leder (eds.), 74–86. New York: Routledge.

Sheveleva, Marina Mikhailovna 2009. *God za godom... (iz istorii Kazymskoi shkoly)* [From year to year... (From the history of the Kazym school)]. Kazym. Zemlia Koshach'ego Lokotka.
http://kazym.ethnic-tour.ru/kazym/kazym/publ/shkola-istoria.html

Slezkine, Yuri 1992. From Savages to Citizens: The Cultural Revolution in the Soviet Far North, 1928-1938. *Slavic Review* 51 (1): 52–76.

Snowchange Cooperative 2007. *Nomadic School Cooperation Between Inari School and the Nutendli Nomadic School in Sakha Republic.* http://www.snowchange.org/2007/09/nomadic-school-cooperation-between-inari-school-and-the-nutendli-nomadic-school-in-sakha-republic/.

Sokolova, Zoia Petrovna and Valerii V. Stepanov 2007. Korennye malochislennye narody Severa. Dinamika chislenosti po dannym perepisei naseleniia. *Etnograficheskoe Obozrenie* 5: 75–95.

Stammler, Florian 2009. Mobile Phone Revolution in the Tundra? Technological Change Among Russian Reindeer Nomads. *Folklore: Electronic Journal of Folklore* (41): 47–78.

Toulouze, Eva 1999. The Development of a Written Culture by the Indigenous Peoples of Western Siberia. Arctic Studies 2, *Pro Ethnologia* 7: 53–85.

— 2003. The Forest Nenets as a Double Language Minority. Multiethnic Communities in the Past and the Present. *Pro Ethnologia* 15: 95–108.

— 2011. *'Nomads and School: The Experience of Russia's North' presented at the WORLD ROUTES 2: Arctic Workshop of University of Tartu, May 27*. Tartu. www.ut.ee/CECT/docs/wr2/Abstract_Toulouze.pdf.

UNESCOdoc, http://unesdoc.unesco.org/images/0015/001592/159200m.pdf

UNESCO-Moscow, http://www.unesco.org/fileadmin/MULTIMEDIA/FIELD/Moscow/pdf/two_community_multimedia_centres.pdf

Vagt, Christian 2012. *Before the snow*. Documentary Film. http://www.christianvagt.com/before_the_snow.html.

Vitebsky, Piers 2010. From Materfamilias to Dinner-Lady: The Administrative Destruction of the Reindeer Herder's Family Life. *Anthropology of East Europe Review* 28 (2): 38–50.

Volkov, Vadim 2002. The Concept of Kul'turnost': Notes on the Stalinist Civilizing Process. In *Stalinism: New Directions*. S. Fitzpatrick (ed.), 210–230. London: Routledge.

Williams, J. Patrick 2009. The Multidimensionality of Resistance in Youth-Subcultural Studies. *The Resistance Studies Magazine* 1: 20–33.

Zhirkova, Sargylana 2006. *School on the 'move'. A case study: Nomadic schooling of the indigenous Evenk children in the Republic of Sakha Yakutia (Russian Far East)*. Master Thesis. Master of Philosophy in Indigenous Studies. Faculty of Social Sciences University of Tromsø.

9 BOARDING SCHOOL ON YAMAL: HISTORY OF DEVELOPMENT AND CURRENT SITUATION*

Elena Liarskaya

Introduction

This article is dedicated to the analysis of the relationship between the school system education and the indigenous population of Yamal in the modern period and to a short review of the history of these relations. This article is based on data and materials collected on the school at the Yamal cultural centre, which was created in the Yamal tundra in the early 1930s. This school still exists; now it is a boarding school in the settlement of Yar-Sale – the biggest boarding school in Russia.

The modern system of education on Yamal is not new. It was formed as a result of lengthy development, and it is very difficult to understand the many peculiarities of the modern state of these schools without consideration of the ways in which they have developed. That is why I will dedicate the first part of my article to the historical background – to the review of the main stages of development of the educational system in the North. I will base my review – and would like to honestly notify the reader – on a simple but rarely articulated idea that Soviet policy in the field of education in the North, though it seems unified and integrated, is in fact not homogeneous and full of discrepancies. It was not integrated in time and was differently realised in space.

When we speak about education in the North we immediately visualise boarding schools and children forced into these schools against the will of their parents, torn from their native environment and culture into a completely new environment, where, due to strict russification, they are forbidden to speak their own language and their teacher's culture is different from their own. Of course, this image complies in part with reality but with the reality of a certain period, and we should not apply it to the modern situation without additional research. Boarding schools differ and to enhance this idea, I will apply the phrase 'classical boarding school' to educational establishments of the late 1950s until the mid-1980s.

The aim of the article is not to describe the whole system of education in the North. My work is based on my own field data gathered on Yamal, on historical research which I conducted when preparing my Ph.D. thesis (Liarskaya 2003) and on archive materials from the 1930s from the Fund of the North Committee at the State Archive of the Russian Federation.[1]

Soviet policy in regards to school education for the peoples of the North: consistency and contradiction.

The history of the formation and reformation of the modern system of education in the Russian North began after the establishment of the Soviet Union, and is still going on. Nevertheless, this history has, as it should, its own pre-history. This pre-history was the missionary schools. They affected neither the level of education of Siberian natives, nor their way of life and culture,[2] but they are of a certain interest from the point of view of school organisation and detecting the weak points of this process.

The task of the missionary schools was not the proliferation of literacy or positive knowledge but raising Christians and the propagation of Russian Orthodoxy among barbarians. Correspondingly, children in such schools first of all studied prayers, basic Christian notions, the basics of Christian history and, if possible, basic literacy.[3] Such schools enjoyed neither popularity nor respect nor even minimal trust on the part of the parents, this being one of their main problems.

However, wide proliferation of education in the North started, as I have already mentioned, after the establishment of the Soviet Union. The reform of school education and the introduction of new educational principles, such as the availability and universality of education, started almost immediately all over the country, together with the creation of a wide network of public schools for the whole population of the country. Available education was always an important integral part of Soviet ideology. So, creation of schools in the North was a part of this process.

The history of northern schools can be divided into four periods:

1 First period – the 1920s until the beginning of the 1930s: creation of first separate schools, experiments with the form and content of education.
2 Second period – the mid-1930s until the end of the 1950s: beginning of the development of school education as a system, creation of a network of elementary schools for native children of the North, unification of school curricula.
3 Third period – the end of the 1950s until the mid-1980s: period of 'classical boarding schools'. Introduction of universal compulsory secondary education, strict execution of the law on universal schooling, period of maximal activity of the system of boarding schools, the domination of the Russian language in educational establishments.

This period can be subdivided into two steps:

3a From the end of the 1950s until the mid-1970s: a stricter regime; the time when, in fact, native languages were totally prohibited; in many districts all children were forced into boarding schools, even in cases when their parents were not nomads but lived in the same settlement.

3b The mid-1970s until the mid-1980s: the regime grows a little softer; the majority of settlement children return from boarding schools to their homes (for example, in Chukotka), several concessions were also made to native languages.

4 Fourth period – the mid-1980s to the present: softening of the conditions set in the previous period, appearance of new programmes and new forms of education and less consistent and rigid execution of the law on universal schooling. At this time the state stopped managing school education strictly, and the policy towards school education in the Far North ceased to be unified: there appeared possibilities for independence at the local level. And what is especially important is that in this period the changes happened not from above, but from below.

I will emphasise here that the difference between these stages is not only in the amount of pressure from the state onto local minorities and the breadth of involvement. I suppose that the idea of the existence in the USSR of a unified and consistent policy in the field of education for local minorities is not as correct as the idea that schools in the North were always based on the same 'Soviet' principles.

Soviet educational policy in the North[4] is a heterogeneous and inconsistent phenomenon, and it is very difficult to speak about it being consecutive or continuous. On the one hand, there were several principles that were stable during the entire Soviet epoch (such as universality and secularity), and some tendencies and processes that started in the first stage which were really consistently developed during the whole history of Soviet schools in the North. On the other hand, several principles of school organisation (no less fundamental than universality and secularity) changed from time to time, sometimes into directly opposite ones (i.e. the position of the state towards pupils' native language or their culture and way of life).

Concealing these contradictions and the idea of unanimity arise, to my mind, mainly from Soviet official rhetoric which never announced any change of course and always presented one-hundred-eighty-degree turns as a forward movement of the same 'Lenin national policy' in a new stage.[5] It is quite important for us not to get into this rhetoric trap.

Not to be ungrounded, I will give several instances of both consistent and inconsistent phenomena and processes.

A Examples of consistent processes:

As an example of a stable and consistent tendency we can name the gradual growth in school attendance (the percentage of northern children attending school was growing steadily up to the end of the Soviet period).

As another example of consistency we can mention purposeful work on the creation of a northern minorities *intelligentsia*. The first step in this direction was made by P.G. Bogoraz who created a *rabfac* (university faculty for working people) for northern minorities (for details see Slezkine 1996, Voskoboinikov 1958: 50–61). Then there appeared a network of national teaching schools and colleges for cultural workers, and a system of various incentives for northern children to enter institutes. This system included not only free education and enrollment privileges, but also social security for students belonging to northern minorities, which undoubtedly boosted the accessibility of higher and secondary special education. This activity did not stop even when native languages were banned in schools and all ethnicity was rendered obsolete. I do not know of any serious changes in this policy in the Soviet period. The result of these activities was the creation within a 50-year period of a rather numerous stratum of people with higher or secondary special education who became activists in national movements in the 1980s and started working on the conservation and restoration of native culture.

B Examples of inconsistent policy:

The brightest example of this kind is the attitude towards native languages. (Here it is very important to remember that the history of the attitude towards northern languages is just a particular case of the history of the attitude towards minority languages in the USSR in general).

It is well-known that in the 1920–1930s, state policy was directed at the development and support of northern languages. Teaching children in their native language was considered to be the only worthy decision and the ideal to strive for. And they did strive for it, creating literacy, textbooks, ABC-books. Teachers were required to study local languages and even a special training of teachers for northern schools was begun (Voskoboinikov 1958). Of course it happened very often in the 1920s and1930s that teachers in fact did not speak the children's native language or spoke it poorly, but it was considered a temporary phenomenon.[6] In situations where it was impossible to organise teaching in the children's native language, teachers were asked to pay maximum attention to encouraging pupils not to forget their language, to communicate with each other in it. Teachers were emphatically recommended not only to study the pupils' native language, but also to delve into their way of life, learn about their culture and maintain close connection with the parents. Thus, in the 1920s, teaching in the native language was an independent value, a means for furthering the development of a harmonious personality. In the 1930s, it was officially stated that "teaching in pupils' native language is a very important political and pedagogical task" (Bazanov, Kazansky 1939: 33), and the occasional tendency to transfer teaching in national schools into the Russian language was officially called harmful (the Decree by CC of CPSU[7] and *Sovnarkom*[8] from March 13 1938).

During the 1940s and 1950s, the position of native languages were gradually changing: the share of Russian in the curricula increased, while the volume and repertoire of literature in minority languages decreased. By that time the practice of teaching Russian from the very beginning to children of different minorities in northern

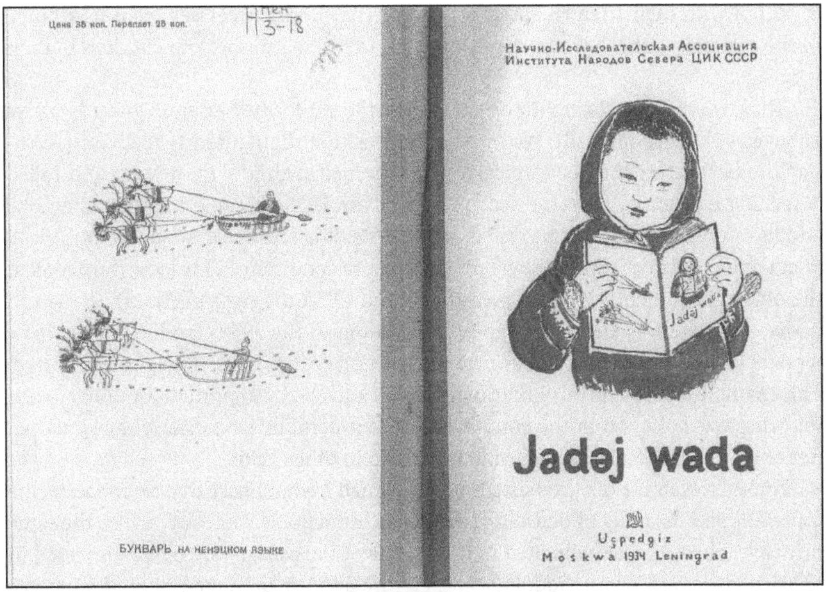

|21| ABC book in Nenets language, 1934.

schools (i. e. in Chukotka) had been commonly adopted. The same took place also for those minorities whose literacy had not been created (Boitsova 1958: 294–295). By the end of the 1950s, teacher's books for northern school teachers said nothing about the harmonious development of a personality in the case of teaching in the native language, and the only pragmatic value attributed to studying it was that literacy in the native language was a guarantee for good acquisition of Russian and, as a result, good academic results in high school (Tsintsius 1958: 89). However, the former rhetoric about the importance of native languages was still used.

At the end of the 1950s, a radical change took place in the state's attitude towards native languages. Officially in the USSR, the right to receive education in one's native language was always proclaimed. However, in that period education in native[9] schools began to be criticised. The logic was as follows: teaching in a minority language hampers good knowledge of Russian and insufficient knowledge of Russian, in turn hampers good education. This led to a sharp decrease in the number of schools teaching in native languages all over the country, and in the North native languages were even banned, not only as the language of instruction or as a subject of teaching, but also as a means of communication among children. This practice, in existence between the 1950s and 1970s, was completely opposite to the state policy of the 1920s and 1930s.

Concessions started, as is known, only in 1970s (Vakhtin 1993: 39–40), but in the Soviet period native languages never became official languages of instruction; even in linguistically happy regions, children were prohibited to speak their native language at school with their friends, and it was never considered necessary (as it used to be in the first half of the 20th century) for a Russian teacher to speak to children in their language.

Thus, we see that during the Soviet period the authorities' attitude towards native languages changed radically. We saw that the position stigmatised as chauvinist, erroneous, not meeting the pedagogical and psychological aims of knowledge and called 'wrecking education', after the second half of the 1950s became the prevailing one and its opponents began to be called nationalists. It is obvious that one cannot speak about any consistency in language policy in these conditions! However, if we look at the official documents, it will appear that in the USSR the right to education in one's native language was always recognised, including in the 1960s, and nowhere was a tendency towards russification or non-recognition of the rights of languages allowed. This example is very typical of the Soviet Union and is very important for understanding what was going on in the country, because it demonstrates clearly the situation, not only in the field of language policy, but also in other fields.

Another example of inconsistent policy, which I would dare to cite, concerns the functions and meaning of boarding schools within schools. Here we can see the same principle: changes that happened in the middle of the century are never discussed in either pedagogical or methodological literature and are presented in all documents not as a change in course but as a logical continuation of the previous stage.

Initially in the 1920s and 1930s, the boarding school appeared as a hostel at a school, without which it was sometimes impossible to organise normal education. As at that time schools in the North were not intended to solve the problem of russification or isolation of children from the harmful influence of the parents' environment, boarding schools were given a rather important but auxiliary function. It should be said that it is quite interesting that in post-revolutionary pedagogics there was a rather popular idea that for the creation of a new personality, all children were to be brought up by the society and the upbringing should be passed on from a family sphere into the sphere of the state, etc. However I have never met with this idea in any texts dedicated to the creation and development of northern schools. On the contrary, the majority of articles and directives of the 1920s and 1930s were full, not of the requirement to take a child out of the family, but of reminders that school should not tear a child from his or her environment, and that it should be based on parents, 'local mass' and so on.[10]

Up to the 1940s, the system of boarding schools within schools was the dominant, but not the only form of education. In the 1950s, small-sized schools were liquidated step by step, nomadic schools disappeared completely and there was practically no alternative to boarding schools. However, a form of boarding school began to be viewed as possessing a set of teaching advantages: it allowed children to study better, secured a "healthy lifestyle and organised cultural leisure for children through the long, dark polar night, in blizzards, in severe frosts" (Krongauz 1955: 91). However, then it was not a closed educational establishment aimed at intensive russification and saving children from a dangerous life in the tundra.

Sharp changes in the attitude towards boarding schools happened at the end of the 1950s (let's mark that as the time of the beginning of great shocks and changes in the North which would last up to the 1980s, and the changes in the sphere of education as just a part of those shocks).

Surprising though it may be, the over-estimation of the role of boarding schools and the announcement that they were the most advanced form of teaching, happened at the end of the 1950s, but were not connected directly with the North. This idea was expressed in an open speech by N. S. Khruschev at the famous 20th CPSU Congress.[11] Khruschev said that the country was making a "historical leap from a lower stage of communism to its upper stage" and that this would require the state to help schools and families in children's upbringing. He reminded the listeners of the experience of closed aristocratic boarding schools which existed in Russia in the past, and proposed the creation of such schools, not for the establishment, but for all. Children were to be sent there according to their parents' wish, but communication with the family was to be limited to holidays, vacations and extra-curricular time. "It is difficult to over-appreciate the great meaning of this system of upbringing. We should not spare our means and efforts because they will be repaid a hundredfold" (Khruschev 1956: 97).

Naturally, after this speech, a campaign started all over the country to create 'boarding schools' as the most progressive form of education, and they didn't spare means or effort. Such educational establishments appeared both in big cities and in the countryside. And then the boarding schools which had been working in the North for a long time began to be regarded not as auxiliary means or hostels at schools but as those advanced educational establishments mentioned by N. S. Khruschev. Later, education in the North was of course supposed to develop only as a system of 'boarding schools', thus implementing the progressive policy of the party and the government.

This new estimation of the role of boarding schools coincided with the introduction of the new law on education (1959), which established universal compulsory secondary education for all citizens of the USSR, and strengthened state paternalism in the North (1957). As a result of these acts, all northern children of school age had to (independently of the will of their parents) enter the full state security in boarding schools (there were already no alternatives to them in the North). In many regions of Siberia this system involved even children of settled parents residing in the same settlements where the boarding schools were located. Unfortunately this coincided also with a radical change in the attitude towards ethnic cultures and languages. Thus, the boarding school in fact turned into an instrument of russification, the consequences of which were even more severe because at the moment of its implementation children were completely torn away from their parents and resettled among teachers mainly belonging to another culture. So the boarding school changed from a hostel at a school necessary for the organisation of education into a classical boarding school – the central element of the wide, well-organised system of teaching, which greatly increased the state's role in education and socialisation of northern minorities and seriously limited the family's role in this process. This situation remained stable from the late 1950s up to the 1980s. The ideology and practice of education at a boarding school in the late 1950s and 1960s seriously contradicted what the state proclaimed as its goal in the 1920s and 1930s. Similar to the case of changing the course of language policy, these shifts were not thought as a change in the course of either pedagogical literature or mass media.

The next important step began in the mid-1980s. At that time people began to discuss openly the 'problems of boarding schools' and the consequences of their existence. The point of view was expressed both by the local population (and this was for the first time) and by teachers and scientists. The majority agreed that because boarding schools tear children away from their families, they are unacceptable, and it is better to refuse them if there is any possibility and to replace them by ordinary day schools, to restore small-sized schools in settlements or to resurrect the experience of nomadic schools. Where boarding schools remained for certain reasons (this happened on Yamal), the attitude towards them changed radically, even on the part of Russian teachers. Boarding schools are now officially perceived, not as a neutral means to education, as they were in the 1920s, and not as a progressive form of teaching, as they were in the 1960s, but rather as a necessary evil. And if it is impossible to avoid them, all efforts should be made to minimise the consequences.

This transformation of a boarding school from a hostel into a progressive form of school and then into 'a necessary evil' demonstrates to us once again the absence of consistency and direct continuity between the different stages of Soviet school policy.

I hope that the examples cited above demonstrate clearly that it is impossible to speak about any unified Soviet policy in the field of education in the North, a policy one stage of which is logically connected with another and arises from it consistently. It is a mirage created by the rhetoric of Soviet texts. There was no consistency in many important spheres and the main breaks to see, fall at the end of the 1950s and in the middle of the 1980s.

School system on Yamal

Everything written above was typical of Soviet policy concerning the organisation of school education for all minorities of the North all over the territory of Russia. Soviet government and community in a certain sense perceived these population groups and these territories as something homogeneous and thus did not focus their activities on specific ethnic groups or specific territories. There was no separate policy for Chukchi or Khanty, for Amur district dwellers or tundra dwellers; the policy was thought to be unified in regards to the entire region. But the Peoples of the North is a collective name [12] which unites groups of people who from the very beginning seriously differed from each other, and in the period studied were in different conditions and interacted with the state with different levels of intensity. To understand how the policy was realised, we need to consider not the whole North together but to analyse concrete examples and compare them with each other.

One of the most interesting and instructive cases is Yamal.[13] This example, I believe, can be interesting not only for those studying western Siberia. Why?

On the one hand, the history of education here has passed through all the classical stages typical of other regions as well. From the end of the 19th until the first half of the 20th century, the tundra of Yamal was inhabited only by nomads (mainly Nenets and a small number of Northern Khanty), who were engaged in reindeer husbandry, hunting and fishing. There was practically no settled population. In the 19th century, missionaries tried to work there and encourage natives to send local children to their school in Obdorsk. This had no result and at the beginning of the Soviet Union, practically the whole tundra population was illiterate. In the 1930s, a standard *cultbase* was created here – a *cultbase,*[14] around which the settlement of Yar-Sale was built. One of the most important parts of this base was the school with a boarding school within it, which in the 1960s was transformed into a classical boarding school, where children were forcibly gathered from all over the tundra. This school continues to work, being the biggest boarding school in Russia. The overwhelming part of Nenets and Khanty of Yamal younger than 60 have gone to this boarding school. Thus, the history of education here is rather typical of many northern regions.

But the condition of the native dwellers of Yamal today, their language and culture, seriously differ from other minorities of the North. For example, nomads not only have remained here, but in 2006 there was practically the same quantity of nomads as in the 1930s, that is, before intensive contacts with the Soviet power. Very important is that not only male reindeer-breeders live in the tundra, but women, children and the elderly as well. Here, as distinct from other regions of the North, there was no collapse of reindeer husbandry in the 1990s; on the contrary, the reindeer herds are constantly increasing. Due to a high birth rate, the number of Yamal indigenous people has doubled in the last 50 years, and half of them live in the tundra. The other half now live in settlements and are enganged in activities absent from nomadic culture. Both halves maintain constant and intensive contacts with each other. Let us note that Yamal Nenets and Khanty have retained their native language better than other minorities, and continue teaching it to their children. This means that there was no separation of Nenets from their traditional way of life, occupations and world outlook, and the prestige of tundra living is still rather high among the natives.

So, the history of education here is the same as in other parts but its results are not very typical of the North. This makes the situation extremely interesting to analyse. It is obvious that even the classical form of boarding school of the 1960s until the 1980s was not able to prevent the communication of traditional knowledge and skills or to undermine the prestige of tundra living.

To understand how this could have happened we have to carry out a whole historical research project. For us more important is what has happened – it makes Yamal a unique research field. I propose to focus on a comparison of tasks and targets of education on Yamal (as well as of the methods for reaching those targets) in the moment of the organisation of the first school on Yamal tundra (during the1930s) and in the modern period (since 2000). In fact, we are trying to compare how the answers to the two main questions "Who needs education" and "Why is education needed" have changed in past decades.

The first Soviet schools of the 1930s and the heritage of missionary schools: methods, principles and specifics of the organisation of teaching.

The education which was created in the 1930s had an important peculiarity: organisers had to act, not in a vacuum, but were forced to contrast themselves to what had been before.

I have already mentioned that even before the Soviet Union there was a Russian Orthodox mission on Yamal and a school at it, whose purpose was to teach nomadic children. This school did not influence the level of literacy among Nenets and Khanty and did not enjoy parents' trust. The analysis of works dedicated to missionary activities on Yamal (Irinarkh 1906: 142–143; Bazanov 1936: 75–79), enables us to compile a list of the main reasons why parents did not want to send their children to those schools.

1 Parents did not see any sense in education: their child wouldn't adjust to living in the taiga or tundra and wouldn't get any useful skills or knowledge.
2 Parents were afraid of russification and suspected the schools of weaning their children from 'traditional' life and teaching them to despise their elders.
3 Parents did not want to be separated from their children.
4 Parents justified their refusal by the fact that if they sent their children to the missionaries, they would lose working hands necessary for the household.
5 The conditions in those schools had a bad reputation. It was thought that children there often got sick and even died.

So we can say that parents saw no benefits from the school, but rather much harm and danger. This can explain why Nenets and Khanty voluntarily sent children to school only in the case of extreme poverty (Shemanovsky 2005).[15]

The organisers of new Soviet schools faced the same attitude to their initiative and it was important for them to show that the new schools were completely different from the missionaries', that they had other targets and methods, and the knowledge they gave to children was very necessary for them and their nation.

Analysis of the texts describing the creation of schools in the North in the 1920s –1930s shows that the new schools were theoretically opposed to missionary ones all over Siberia and the North, both for the organisers of education and for ordinary teachers. The old missionary school in these texts turns into the symbol of everything negative that should not exist in a new Soviet school. From this point of view, it is not so important how the missionary school looked in reality; it is more important that the description of the new Soviet school was construed by a rejection of missionary techniques: the missionary school was religious, the Soviet one was secular, the missionary school taught prayers and catechism, the Soviet one gave literacy and the basics of positive knowledge, the missionary school was russificationary, the Soviet one taught in the native language and tended not to separate children from their culture, the missionary was based on mindless drilling, the Soviet on new achievements in pedagogics, et cetera.

If we return to one of our central questions, "Who needs education?", we will notice that alongside all differences between these two types of schools there is a fundamental similarity: neither parents nor potential pupils saw any sense in school education, and education was needed only for school and state.

In principle, the target of education in both kinds of schools was always to raise the cultural level of a person and a nation and their involvement in world culture. Only the missionary school[16] saw the ultimate goal in bringing the aborigines up as good Christians so as to secure their closer ties with Russia, tried to raise their cultural level through russification and saw, as an ideal, their school-leavers as clerks rather than hunters and reindeer- herders,[17] while the Soviet school at that moment wanted to bring them up as USSR citizens and set the goal to promote the development of language, culture and economy of the native population. It saw, among its most important tasks, the propagation of hygienic norms and new handicrafts necessary for the nomad's everyday life.

But good intentions were not enough and parents, as they had done before, did not want to send their children to the Soviet school, but instead hid them, sent the agitator off, taught children to pretend to be epileptic, etc.

In such a situation it was possible either to force (which they did not do, unlike in the 1960s), or to gradually persuade parents of the necessity of education, thus building a friendly relationship between the school and the population.

The second way was chosen by missionary schools and the first Soviet ones as well. We cannot but admit that Soviet schools were much more successful and the result of their activities much more notable.

The purpose in the first years of Soviet school on Yamal was to prove to parents and the surrounding population that it did not aim at tearing children from their family and culture, that it gave education to the tundra and not to a city; and to this end, all possible methods which one can imagine were used.

To begin with, the Soviet school, in contrast to the missionary one, did not try to take children from the tundra into a Russian village (like Obdorsk), which natives (and not all of them) visited once a year for the fair, but moved into the Yamal tundra inhabited by Nenets and Khanty. This fact immediately made the school closer to the local population and, on the one hand, gave it some advantages. However, on the other hand, the position of school and *cultbase* workers was extremely vulnerable. The relationship of trust and cooperation gradually appearing around the base was easily destroyed, in which case not only the school activity but even the mere lives of base workers were endangered. A sad example of such a scenario is given by the event of the Kazym uprising (Leete 2004). Fortunately, it never happened on Yamal, partially because the base workers initially avoided making inflammatory actions. The task of the *cultbase* team was, according to one of its creators, M. M. Bridnev, "to treat kindly the Nenets' customs, to help in reorganising their household, everyday life, and culture painlessly for the local people, without sudden changes and extremes" (Brodnev 2008: 237).

All the school work was set in such a way as to shatter the parents' existing anxieties and to prevent new ones. Thus, the children of course were given mainly European food and were taught to cook these dishes, but also a reindeer was slaughtered several times a month, especially for children to eat raw venison, as they were used to. To dispel distrust between tundra dwellers and school, they employed two Nenets women, after which all pleasantness and unpleasantness in the pupils' lives quickly became known to their parents. According to the teachers, this helped the school development very much (Brodnev 2008: 242–243). Besides, the parents could come to the school at any time, visit their children, watch the lessons, speak to the teachers – the school was at that time maximally open to the parents.

To prove that they taught children skills useful for the tundra, they opened workshops at the school to teach children new crafts necessary for tundra life: netting, bench work;[18] boys could fix traps for their fathers, for example. There were guns and traps for polar foxes and children didn't stop hunting during their studies under the supervision of a *cultbase* worker.

Though in her first year at the school the teacher could not speak the Nenets language, she began studying it immediately and in next few years tried to speak with the children in their native language (Brodnev 2008: 243; Verbov 1936; Stankevich 1934). And all my informants of the older generations recollect with respect that at that time teachers tried to speak 'our language'.

The measures named above established a certain level of trust between the school and the community. It is well-known that the main mission of the *cultbase* was to acquaint the 'retarded' tundra population with the achievements of culture. For this the *cultbase* had a very specific structure: along with the stationary school, hospital, the Nenets' house, the local museum, centres for veterinary and zootechnical assistance in the settlement, there were moving divisions (for example, the so-called 'red tents'). These moving groups had to cure people and reindeer of illnesses, tell about the Soviet

Union and its laws, show films in the tundra where people were living, while at the same time promoting specific settlement services by giving information and raising the level of trust. This form of mobile service for tundra dwellers remained on Yamal for rather a long time and the system of moving medical attendants (specially trained medical workers who lived together with tundra dwellers and treated the nomadic population) still exists. What is very important is that these two ways of working with the population – stationary and mobile – did not contradict but rather supplemented each other, accomplishing the same tasks. In the 1930s, the school was among the services possessing both stationary and mobile forms. Besides the school-boarding-school in the settlement, there were in the first years two constantly working nomadic schools at the *cultbase* (in the north and in the south) and in summer additional ones were opened. According to the existing documents of the cultural base, their task was not to give children education directly in the tundra, they were to interest children, to persuade their parents of the necessity of studies and to help man the school in the settlement. If we believe the report of the *cultbase* to the North Committee, these schools fulfilled this task rather successfully (Stankevich 1934; Shmyryov 1935).

In order to get the school closer to the community where it worked, an unusual step was undertaken in 1935. In January and February, the school together with the pupils and teachers left the settlement for one of the Nenets nomadic camps and worked there. The children lived in a separate school tent, cooked their meals, held regular classes, participated in the everyday life of the nomad camp, led a nomadic life and at the same time received guests showing them their achievements, holding talks and giving reports on recent domestic home and international events. During the period of its existence the school was visited by more than a hundred guests from neighbouring and far-off nomadic camps. The report on practical work which I have at my disposal shows that the school seemed to have two most important tasks: the first was to increase the level of awareness and trust, and the second was a mere *kultträger* one – to teach dwellers of the nomad camp to observe the norms of hygiene. Children took separate tents and explained to adults why it is necessary to wash hands, brush teeth, wash floors, do laundry and wash babies, and tried to accustom them to doing it regularly. A tidiness competition was held between tents and the winners were given valuable prizes (Stankevich 1935).

The fact that the school managed to persuade Nenets and Khanty of the necessity of studies is also proven by the numbers: in the beginning of the first academic year there were only five children in the school; by end of that year there were already 22; the next year, 35, the third one, 55, the fourth, 100 (Brodnev 2008: 243; Stankevich 1934).

For our topic it is very important to stress that at that moment the school strived to destroy the barrier between itself and parents, to maximally increase the level of trust on the part of the population, and to persuade them of the necessity of education for their children. To reach these goals it used various methods: it adjusted the content of education to the parents' needs, made the children's life as open as possible, and demonstrated by all means respect towards the native population's way of life and language. Reviewing the methods undertaken by school education on Yamal since then, we can characterise the period of the 1930s as the time of the most correct and respectful attitude on the part of the organisers of education towards the native population.

One of the methods of informing the people about the school and of destroying the distrust on the part of the population was the creation of a nomadic school. I would like to stress that it is wrong to speak of an opposition between the nomadic school and the boarding school (for instance, "the former was respectful of the traditional way of life and the latter tried to tear the child away from that life and accustom him or her to the new values") at that time on Yamal.

On the one hand, the nomadic school of that period did not have the special task of retaining the natives' language and skills (as it does now); support and development of the existing culture of the native population and its language was the aim of both forms of school, and both renounced vigorously the intention to tear children away from their natural environment. At that time these two forms of school did not compete with, but rather complemented each other, achieving the same task.

On the other hand, at that time it was difficult to make a clear separation between the nomadic and the stationary school: those who in summer attended a nomadic school, in winter could study with the same teacher in the settlement. And those studying in the settlement could appear in a nomad camp in winter, where their regular studies continued in the tent with their Russian teachers (as it happened in 1935).

It is very likely that the contemporary opposition between boarding school as estranging children from traditional life and the nomadic school, allowing them to live in harmony with their ethnic culture arose much later, after the sharp turn in school policy, as a reaction to the traumatising experience of the classical boarding school with its strict russification techniques and violent recruiting of children.

If we get back to the list of reasons why parents did not trust their children to a missionary school and did not see any sense in it, we will notice that as a result of laborious and well thought-out work, most of the items were losing their validity in the new conditions of the1930s.[19] Parents could see that the school did not teach children to despise their families, did not wean them away from the tundra, children were not subjected to russification, they knew what their children were eating and how they were living and could even see the benefits of the knowledge given to their children at school.

Inevitable were only the separation from the parents (though its term was minimised due to the transfer of the school to Yamal tundras) and the loss of working hands. Of course these were very important obstacles for the school education and they were not to be avoided. The necessity of help in the tundra still had priority over education, but the problem with working hands was solved by the Nenets for a long time in a rather interesting way. My analysis of family histories of Yamal Nenets shows that, trying to retain working hands in the tundra, parents tried to keep the eldest and the youngest, but middle children often went to school. As one of the informants born in the early 1930s told me: "I was the fourth in the family and from the tundra point of view the most useless, so they sent me to school". Thus, typical was a situation where a part of the siblings never studied and a part studied and finished the full school course. Often these people retained connections with each other for the whole of their life and rendered help and support to each other.

Modern schools on Yamal: key changes

It is in comparison with the situation of the 1930s that the specifics of both the classical boarding schools and of the modern state schools is the most obvious.

Let me remind the reader that as a result of the introduction of a classical boarding school system with its strict recruitment at the end of the 1950s, practically all Nenets people younger than 60 went through Yamal boarding school. I have already mentioned many times that these boarding schools in their essence were very different from the schools of the 1930s, and in their russification aims and tasks and, by their attitude towards the native population's way of life and culture, they were much closer to missionary schools.[20] Since the 1980s, the system of northern boarding schools has started to be criticised, but the organisers of education on Yamal failed to find another way to give nomadic children full education, and boarding schools in this region were retained, though they are now treated as a necessary evil.

In reality, classical boarding schools began to change in approximately the 1970s, when the second generation of tundra dwellers came to study there. At the same time people who started working there were representatives of the first generation of school-leavers who had themselves experienced boarding schools, and that is why they could more easily understand the children of tundra dwellers. By that time Russian teachers, who had been working in the boarding school for a long time, had accumulated quite significant experience, and many parents personally knew the teachers and realised who would teach their children.

During the time since the 1930s, great changes have taken place both in the population of Yamal and their way of life. I have already mentioned that half of the ten thousand of today's Nenets and Khanty of Yamal do not lead a nomad's life but live in settlements. They have formed a specific settlement variant of native culture, which has much in common with the tundra variant, but is opposed to it in several attributes. The majority of younger Nenets possesses both variants and know the rule for switching from one to another (for details see Liarskaya 2009). As a result of the changes every child going to the boarding school today has these or those close relatives living in the settlement. So when entering the school in the settlement, the child is not isolated from Nenets and their culture. This fact radically differs from the situation of the missionary school in Obdorsk and even from the school at the *cultbase* of the 1930s. Yar-Sale, with several buildings around the trading station and *cultbase* in the middle of the tundra, has turned into a busy district centre with a population of several thousand people of different ethnic groups. It is quite symbolic that the school and the hospital are so far in the centre of the settlement. So, not only have the boarding schools changed, but also the environment in which they exist.

In the new conditions, the answers to the questions: "Why is education needed?" and "Who needs a school?" are changing.

Based on the field materials which I have gathered since the end of the 1990s, I can state that, first, education onYamal is acquiring an independent value, and modern parents consider that it is good to study in general and it is bad to be uneducated (I was told this not only by representatives of the *intelligentsia*, but by reindeer herders as well).

In the new conditions, the school on Yamal is starting to fulfil a number of functions which it did not have, either in the 1930s or in the 1950s and 1960s. I will dwell on some of them in detail.

Today, staying at boarding school for the children of tundra dwellers is a specific way to study the interaction with the world of 'Russians', with the world which exists outside the tundra, and to study Russian well. A boarding school is also the place to acquire the 'settlement' variant of culture and to form the ability to behave in the settlement way when in the settlement and in the tundra-way when in the tundra, all the while remaining Nenets or Khanty. The inability to use either of these variants or to switch between them is now considered a violation of the norm.[21]

Another important function of school is that it gives children the possibility to choose a profession and way of life in the future. The mere possibility of such a choice gives tundra dwellers some freedom and makes their future more stable as they are ready for different variants of events. This is well-realised by tundra-dwelling parents: "What if his life makes him live in a settlement?" – This is what I was told by my informants – reindeer herders who dream that their son will continue their occupation. Another mother, who lives in the tundra, explained to her daughter, who wanted to leave school for the tundra: "Study. What if you have to live in the settlement, would you like to be a cleaner and wash toilets?" These my observations seem to coincide completely with the attitude towards education found by Stephan Dudeck and Alexandra Lavrillier (see *this volume*).

One more principal difference between the situation of the 1930s (and even of the early 1960s) and the modern one lies in the fact that before, when a child went to school, it was an outstanding event, whereas now it is a routine thing, a part of the normal life scenario known in advance by children and parents and thus less scary (see Liarskaya 2004). This has a very important, though not so striking consequence: the attitude towards childhood has changed gradually: it is now longer and regarded as a period for special education (this is the process that has concerned not only the North but also all of rural Russia). Children have turned from workers and breadwinners into creatures in need of training and looking after. It can be borne out by the fact that one of the most popular reasons in the past why not to send children to school, 'working hands are needed,' is now mentioned rarer and rarer (though oftener than in European Russia).

The modern boarding school has received some functions which, it seems to me, were never planned by its creators. For example, tundra families have many children, and since education became compulsory, many siblings and cousins are usually together in boarding school, helping each other and taking care of youngsters. Thus the boarding school has unintentionally boosted intergenerational ties between relatives. On the other hand, having gathered together so many children of a similar age, the organisers of the boarding school have created a specific (and heretofore absent) children's environment, in which a lot of traditional information is transferred. I know examples of the spreading among children of different beliefs, rules of behaviour in specific situations, folklore texts and even a case when children who did not know the Nenets language studied it from their peers when entering the boarding school.

Another important change that has happened is that modern natives don't consider themselves only as Nenets or Khanty, dwellers of the peninsula of Yamal, but also as residents of the big country of Russia, who know about life in other places and have mainly the same cultural background as residents of St. Petersburg, the Far East or Kamchatka. This is a principal change, in which school has played a great role.

An important peculiarity of Yamal is that neither tundra dwellers nor settlement dwellers in their majority consider the boarding school a threat to the Nenets or Khanty way of life. If there is something to connect the threat with, it is the construction of the railway and the industrial development of the region, which endangers both reindeer husbandry and reindeer-herders (see Novikova et al. 2011).

What should a school teach, according to parents? It should give high-quality education of the European type. As far as my materials allow me to judge, no parents expect school to teach children reindeer tending or hunting or to give them the basics of Nenets religious ethics or the so-called tundra laws. My informants, as well as the informants of Stephan Dudeck from the Khanty-Mansi Autonomous *okrug*, believe that these are taught by absolutely different means and not through formal school education. How? In the tundra, by relatives before school, during summer vacations or after studies; in the boarding school, in informal surroundings by other children and teachers, tutors and technical workers of Khanty or Nenets origin, working there and living in the settlement. Judging by the fact that tundra life has some prestige for native residents, reindeer husbandry is developing successfully and the Nenets and the Khanty languages are retained well and widely used on Yamal, the native residents have managed to cope with these tasks rather well.

We can say that of the old problems of the boarding school, only one has remained unsolved – separation from parents. And though it is not the most popular question for discussion in the region, every person telling me about the start of studies mentioned this traumatic experience (though all admitted that it is necessary to study). This is the reason why many parents try to send their children to school a year or two later than is required by the law, believing that older children find it much easier to handle the separation. One should admit that it is not a specific problem of northern boarding schools but of the closed form of education in general wherever it is practised – in Russia, England or Switzerland.

The key to understanding the modern situation lies, I think, in the answer to the question: "Who needs school education?". Before, it was needed only for school and the state, but today, for Nenets and Khanty, tundra dwellers and settlement dwellers themselves want their children to go to school. In the 1990s, the organised recruitment of children to school with the help of helicopters was practically stopped. Then many people thought that in this situation children would stay in the tundra, but as it happened, practically all parents brought their children themselves (without any pressure on the part of the state). School has stopped being something outside the life of the natives. It is no longer made by Russians for Nenets and Khanty, who don't need it. Natives now put their hopes and expectations in it and start to actively participate in the process of discussing the future and present of school. This creates a principally new situation which was never possible in a missionary school, in the first Soviet schools, or when introducing mass boarding school teaching. Before, the local population used to be only an object of educational system impact, whereas now natives have turned into partners of the school and in the present correlation of school and society on Yamal, have to be based on absolutely different grounds. And this is very important.

Conclusions

In making some conclusions, I would like to return to some important ideas: As I was trying to show, there was never a unified Soviet policy in the field of education in the North; rather, this policy was complicated and inconsistent in time and space.

The 'classical boarding school' is just one of the stages in the development of the system, whose ideology in many ways contradicted the previous (epoch of the 1930s) and following stages of the development of education.

With the example of Yamal we have seen that in the 1930s, boarding schools were not in principle opposed to nomadic schools, but acted together with them, complementing each other and serving the same goals; sometimes it is impossible to draw a line between these two forms of education.

The Yamal experience shows us that during the time since the beginning of school education, the relationship between the native population and the boarding school has changed radically. The main change consists in the fact that modern parents want their children to go to school. Boarding school now fulfils many important functions in modern Nenets and Khanty society, and one of the most important is to give children the possibility of choosing their future life.

Today's Yamal school faces absolutely new tasks and new problems and these are important to be regarded in preparation for any reform of education. Any changes in the form of education and its content must correspond not only to the wishes of the reformers or the Ministry of Education and their ideas about children's benefits and the future of the culture, but also to the functions which are really fulfilled by the school in the modern society of Yamal and to the parents' opinion concerning the future of their children.

Of course in speaking about the Yamal case we should always remember that it is quite unique: many elements of the native culture are retained, are developing and exist in the full sense here, and that is why the conclusions which I have made based on Yamal material cannot be automatically transferred to other northern regions. But perhaps the analysis of the processes which took place here in the sphere of education will help to clarify what goes on in other regions as well.

Notes

* The article had been translated from Russian by Irina Liskovets.

1 I am grateful to EU SPb, which supported my research in the North for many years and the Max Planck Institute for Social Anthropology (Halle, Germany), which granted me the possibility to work with archive materials of the North Committee (State Archive of the Russian Federation, Moscow).

2 Thus, for example, in 1868 in the whole huge Tobol gubernia there were only three schools. In the next 50 years their number increased a little. We can estimate the number of pupils in such schools by the fact that in 1902 even the school at the Obdorsk mission, which specially worked on the organisation of a school for nomadic children and the recruitment of children for that school, had 15 pupils (5 Khanty, 3 Nenets and 10 Komi-Zyryans). (Bazanov 1936: 74, 82; other details: see Shemanovsky 2005).

3 In Russia there were two types of missionary schools: 1) the first and the most popular type – with instruction in Russian language. Such schools were considered as openly russificatorical ones by both teachers and parents. Usually children who started school did not know the teacher's language and the teacher did not speak their language. 2) The second type – schools using the system proposed by Kazan University professor N.I. Il'minsky. According to this system, the teaching of literacy was done in the pupils' native language. They appeared in the second half of the 19th century and influenced greatly the development of education in the Volga region and among Yakut. At the end of 19th century this system was supported officially as a model for the creation of schools in the North, but in reality there were very few schools of this type for the minorities of the North and they existed for only a short time (Bazanov 1936: 3–111).

4 In respect to national schools in general.

5 Similar observations on the inconsistence of Soviet policy, but towards minority languages, were described by the researchers (compare: Alpatov 1997: 8, 121; Vakhtin 2001: 25–28)

6 In 1927, Narkom of Education A.V. Lunacharsky wrote: "We know how ugly and unpedagogical it is to teach children in Russian but nothing can be done here as there are almost no teachers speaking children's native language and these small nations don't have their own *intelligentsia*."

7 Full name: Central Committee of the Communist Party of the Soviet Union.

8 *Soviet Narodnykh Komissarov* (Council of People's Commissars) – at that time the government of the USSR.

9 *natsionalnaia shkola*, a Soviet term of the 1920s and later referring to a school where all or majority of the children belong to a local ethnic minority, with a special curriculum emphasizing teaching in the minority language.

10 On the other hand I have never seen in the texts written at that time about the first schools any discussion of the fact that placing children into a boarding school is traumatic and creates problems in education. These texts generally abound, on the other hand, in detailed descriptions of everyday life and the difficulties and problems which the authors had to face. It is possible to think that this topic was not the focus of attention.

11 This was the same congress at which Khruschev first disclosed Stalin's cult.

12 About the history of the notion 'Peoples of the North' (see, for example, Vakhtin 2001: 24).

13 This work first of all deals with the Yamal region of Yamal-Nenets Autonomous District (centre – Yar-Sale) located on the Yamal peninsula.

14 called "Kultbaza" (ru. *kulturnaia baza* – cultural centre).

15 Besides, the same attitude to missionary schools was popular far outside western Siberia.

16 It was true also for the turn of the 20th century, when the mission school worked according to the so-called *Il'minsky* system, i.e. they tried to organise teaching in the native language.

17 It is difficult not to see that the russification ideas and techniques of these schools (with the exception of religious ones) were ideologically much closer to the ideas of classical northern boarding schools of the 1960s and 1970s than to Soviet schools of the 1920s and 1930s. This ideological resemblance, as far as I know, was never an object of reflection in pedagogical and methodological literature.

18 This craft was not well-known in the tundra.

19 It is silly to state that in a society with no tradition of formal education even the most successful policy can lead to universal schooling in two to three years after the start of schools. Everything takes time.

20 With one principle exclusion – Soviet education was only secular.

21 In some cases parents, due to family conditions, have to take children into the tundra before the end of secondary school, some children leave school themselves and go to the tundra. But elementary education is now received by practically all children. To my mind this is directly connected with this function.

References

Alpatov V.M. 1997. *150 yazykov i politika: 1917–1997* [150 Languages and policy: 1917–1997]. Sotsiolingvisticheskie problemy SSSR i postsovetskogo prostranstva [Sociolinguistical problems of the USSR and of the post-soviet space]. Moskva: Institut Vostokovedeniia RAN [Institute of Oriental studies at the Russian Academy of Sciences].

Bazanov A.G. 1936. *Ocherki po istorii missionerskikh shkol na krainem severe Tobol'-skii sever)* [Studies of the history of mission schools in the Far North (Tobol North)]. Leningrad: INS Glavsevmorputi.

Bazanov L.G., Kazansky N.G. 1939. *Shkola na Krainem Severe* [The school in the Far North]. Leningrad: Uchpedgiz.

Boitsova A.F. 1958. *Shkola narodov Krainogo Severe: Natsional'nye shkoly za 40 let* [The schools of Minorities in the Far North: National schools during 40 years]. Moskva: Izdatel'stvo APN.

Brodnev M.M. 2008. *Nov' Yamal'skoi tundry: 'Sava lutsa' khoroshii chelovek* [News from the Yamal Tundra: "Sava lutsa – a good man]. L.F. Lipatova (ed.). Tiumen: Stit-press [first publication in *The Red North*, 1963].

Irinarkh 1905. Obdorskie ostiaki i samoedy i arkhangel'skie zyriana v otnoshenii k svoim detiam [Obdorsky ostyaks and samoeds and archangelsk zyryans and their attitude towards their children]. *Pravoslavny blagovestnik* 1 (January), 35–36.

Irinarkh 1906. *Istoria Obdorskoi dukhovnoi missii 1854–1904* [History of the Obdorsk mission 1854–1904]. Moskva: Pechatnaia A.I. Snegirevoi.

Khruschev N.S. 1956. *Otchetnyi doklad TsK KPSS XX s"ezdu KPSS* [Summary report of the central committee of the CPSU to the XX Congress of the CPSU]. Irkutsk: Pravda.

Krongauz F.F. 1955. *Nekotorye voprosy vospitaniia v internatakh shkol narodov Severa: V pomoshch' uchiteliu shkol Krainego Severa* [Several problems of upbringing in boarding-schools for the Northern peoples: To assist the teachers of the schools in the Far North] Issue 5, 91–101. Leningrad: Uchpedgiz.

Leete A. 2004. *Kazymskaia voina: vosstanie khantov i lesnykh nentsev protiv sovetskoi vlasti* [The Kazym war: Uprising of Khanty and Forest Nenets against soviet power]. Tartu: University of Tartu.

Liarskaya E.V. 2003. *Severnye internaty i transformatsiia traditsionnoi kul'tury (na primere nenetsev Yamala)* [The Northern boarding-schools and the transformation of traditional culture (on the example of the Yamal Nenets). Sankt Peterburg: Ph.D. Dissertation.

— 2004. The Place of Northern Residential Schools in Contemporary Yamal Nenets Culture. *Sibirica: Journal of Siberian Studies*, 4 (1): 74–87.

— 2009. Settlement Nenets on Yamal Peninsula: Who Are They? Generation P in the Tundra: Youth in Siberia. *Folklore* 41: 33–46.

Novikova N.I., Martynova E.P., Vasil'kova T.N., Evai A.V. 2011. *Korennye malochislennye narody i promyshlennoe razvitie Arktiki: etnologicheskii monitoring v Yamalo-nenetskom avtonomnom okruge* [Native small minorities and industrial development of the arctic: ethnological monitoring in the Yamal-Nenets Autonomous District]. Moscow/Shadrinsk: Izdatel'stvo OGUP, Shadrin Dom Pechati.

Shemanovsky I.S. 2005. *Izbrannye trudy.* [Selected publications]. L.F. Lipatova (ed.) Moskva: Sovetskii Sport.

Shmyryov 1932–34. *Otchet o deiatel'nosti Yamal'skoi kul'tbazy* [Report on the Activities of Yamal Cultural Centre]. State Archives of the Russian Federation f. 3977, rec. 1, d 1138.

Slezkine, Yuri 1996. *Arctic Mirrors: Russia and the Small Minorities of the North.* Ithaca: Cornell University Press.

Stankevich C. 1934. *Kratkii otchet o rabote shkoly -internata kul'tbazy za 1933–34 gg.* [Short report on the work of boarding-school at the cultural centres for 1933–34]. State Archives of the Russian Federation f. 3977 rec. 1 d. 1137 s. 1–4 (ob.). Manuscript.

— 1935. *Otchet o rabote shkoly chuma, shkoly-internata Yamal'skoi kul'tbazy* [Report on the 'tent school', the boarding-school at the Yamal cultural centre] 22/1 - 20/2 193. State Archives of Russian Federation f. 3977 rec. 1 d. 1137 s. 5–8. Manuscript.

Tsintsius V.I. 1958. Rodnoi yazyk v nachalnoi shkole narodov Krainego Severa. [Native Language in Elementary School of the Peoples of the Far North]. *Prosveshchenie na Sovetskom Krainem Severe* 8: 76–89. Leningrad.

Vakhtin N.B. 1993. *Korennoe naselenie Krainego Severa Rossiskoi Federatsii.* [Native Population of the Far North of Russian Federation]. Sankt Peterburg: Evropeiskii dom.

— 2001. *Yazyki narodov Severa v XX veke. Ocherki yazykovogo sdviga.* [Languages of the North Minorities in the XX century. Studies of language shift]. Sankt Peterburg: Dmityr Bulanin.

Verbov G.D. 1936. *Polevoi dnevnik 1936 rukopis'* [Field Diary of 1936 manuscript]. Archives of Peter the Great Museum of Anthropology and Ethnography (Kunstkamera) f. 2, rec. 1, d. 69, s. 3–4. manuscript.

Voskoboinikov M.G. 1958. *Podgotovka v Leningrade pedagogicheskikh kadrov dlia shkol narodov Krainego Severa* [Training of the teaching staff in Leningrad for schools of the Far North]. *Prosveshchenie na Sovetskom Krainem Severe*, 8: 48–75. Leningrad.

10 MODEL FOR THE TUNDRA SCHOOL IN YAMAL: A NEW EDUCATION SYSTEM FOR CHILDREN FROM NOMADIC AND SEMI-NOMADIC NENETS FAMILIES

Roza I. Laptander

Introduction

This article describes the modernisation of the education system for the indigenous people of the North by providing an example from the Yamalo-Nenets Autonomous District (YNAD). In 2010, the District's Department of Education started an experimental education system for reindeer herders' children. In this experiment, children have the possibility to get primary education in the tundra, where they live with their parents. This model for the Tundra School (*kochevaia shkola*) was introduced by the Nenets writer Anna Nerkagi. It is a new experiment for the District, because in other places in Yamal children still study in boarding schools. These boarding schools have a double impact on the indigenous children[1]. On the one hand, they provide them with education, but on the other, they have a negative impact on their native language and culture. This is not only the case in the Yamalo-Nenets Autonomous District, but also in the whole of the Russian North, Siberia and the Far East.

This paper is intended as a report on my personal contribution to this work, which is rather modest. I had to prepare papers and to write about the Tundra School project with Valentina Niarui, a specialist in teaching methods from Salekhard. We had to apply to the Yamalo-Nenets Department of Education for official support for this project. An interesting aspect of this work is the fact that the Tundra School is not a completely new education concept in the tundra. There have been attempts to try it before, but they did not succeed. This time the participants are hopeful that this school will have the right to exist and that it will bring good results into the process of education for the tundra children. During our meetings we used to talk to Anna Nerkagi and other teachers of the Laborovaia School, and we asked them how they are working at their school and what is different there from ordinary schools.

As a result, we were able to compose a document about the development of this new type of school and its way of teaching children whose parents have a nomadic way of life or live in places difficult to reach in the tundra. This Tundra School is officially called the 'Model of Nomadic Education for Indigenous Children of the North in the Yamalo-Nenets Autonomous District', whose parents follow the nomadic or semi-nomadic way of life. In this paper, we shall consider it as an example of the Municipal system of education in the Priuralsky County (*Raion*) in the Municipal Educational Institution, the Primary Comprehensive School in Laborovaia.

The location of Yamal in the Russian Federation and its inhabitants

The Yamalo-Nenets Autonomous District (Okrug) is one of the 89 federal districts of the Russian Federation. It is located in Western Siberia. The indigenous population of Yamal consists of the Nenets, Khanty, and Selkup people. They form approximately 8.2% of the whole district's population, and only a small number of them speak their native languages in everyday life. The majority of the population consists of people of many other nationalities who migrated to this region from different parts of Russia. Most of them moved here in the 1990s from central Russia, Ukraine and other former Soviet Republics because of the development of the gas and oil industry in the district.

Nowadays Yamal is one of the richest regions of the Russian Federation, with high salaries and good living conditions. This is very attractive for incoming people from central parts of the country and from former Soviet Union republics. As a matter of fact, this process is surely still changing the whole population structure of the district, which is illustrated by the following table.

Ethnic group	1979 Census		1989 Census		2002 Census		2010 Census	
	Number	%	Number	%	Number	%	Number	%
Nenets	17,404	11.0 %	20,917	4.2 %	26,435	5.2 %	29,772	5.9 %
Khanty	6,466	4.1 %	7,247	1.5 %	8,760	1.7 %	9,489	1.9 %
Komi	5,642	3.6 %	6,000	1.2 %	6,177	1.2 %	5,141	1.0 %
Selkups	1,611	1.0 %	1,530	0.3 %	1,797	0.4 %	1,988	0.4 %
Russians	93,750	59.0 %	292,808	59.2 %	298,359	58.8 %	312,019	61.7 %
Ukrainians	15,721	9.9 %	85,022	17.2 %	66,080	13.0 %	48,985	9.7 %
Tatars	8,556	5.4 %	26,431	5.3 %	27,734	5.5 %	28,509	5.6 %
Others	9,694	6.1 %	54,889	11.1 %	71,664	14.1%	74,625	14.3 %

The Nenets people form the most numerous northern nation among all indigenous peoples of the Russian Federation. According to the 2010 census of the Russian Federation, there are 44,640 Nenets people. They live in three national districts: the Nenets Autonomous District (as part of the Arkhangel'sk Province), the Yamalo-Nenets Autonomous District (as part of the Tiumen' Province) and the Taimyr Autonomous District (as part of the Krasnoiarsk Region).

In the past, there existed a widespread multilingualism among the local people in Yamal, where one of the above-mentioned indigenous languages was dominant. Local people only used the Russian language for trading and for communication with Russians, Komi or Tatars. This situation changed markedly after the 1930s.

Moreover, intensive oil and gas development in huge areas of the Yamal peninsula is a main reason for many nomadic people (who were living in the tundra with reindeer and still used their native language in everyday life) to move to settlements, where they have to use Russian. In many families the next generation will shift to the use of Russian, which is due to the fact that Russian is the official state language of the whole Russian Federation, and therefore it is the language of communication, education and official mass media. This situation is a common feature everywhere in Russia, except that in several parts of the country the local national languages also have official status, such as in the Sakha Republic (Yakutia) or the Republic of Tatarstan.

Why it is important to modernise education for aborigines

For the history of the tundra schools, we refer to the article by Elena Liarskaya (*this volume*), which describes how the northern minority nations of Russia had a negative experience with boarding school education. Not all ideas were optimal under the working conditions of Tundra Nenets. However, here we should mention that in the 19th century there were some examples of migrating schools (*shkoly peredvizhkie*) accompanying the children of the families that followed their reindeer herds (see Toulouze 1999: 56). Other solutions were developed in the first part of the 20th century. These schools did not really follow nomads on their migration but they were situated on the routes of migrating families (Toulouze 1999: 65). The idea was that these migrating schools would bring education to children who lived in areas difficult to reach. Such schools started to work in the early 1930s, but it was found that such methods of education did not work well in the conditions of a permanent nomadic life. Unfortunately, we do not have many materials about these schools, but Elena Liarskaya wrote about them (Liarskaya 2005; *this volume*). Some articles mentioned that teachers used to travel with reindeer herders to the tundra and tried to teach children and their parents there. This work did not yield good results (Golovnev and Osherenko 2000).

It is clear that the reindeer herders' traditional way of life depends very much on reindeer. This means moving with the herds and looking for good pastures all the time. Nenets migrate all year round from the south to the north and back, a distance of several hundred kilometers. The children of these families travel with adults, and by living this life, they learn their inherited language and culture. They do not just watch how their parents work, but they also learn by taking an active part in their families' lives, and helping the adults with the reindeer and the household work. We know that there was a strong political movement to bring literacy and education to all 'wild northern tribes' and to make them members of the Soviet Union. For this purpose, the children of the northern aborigines were taken away from the tundra to study in boarding schools with Russian as the only language of education for all school subjects. We know about this from the stories of people who used to study at that time (Dudeck 1998; *this volume*).

Because of this fact, there is nowadays an important group of indigenous people who live in settlements and towns and speak predominantly Russian, whereas only a small number of them speak their native languages. All of them were taken to boarding schools from the tundra, and from primary school age they felt that they were different from Russians because they spoke a different language and used to live in 'uncultured' life conditions. When we had our interviews with representatives of this group of people, some of them were from settlements, whereas others continue to live a traditional way of life in the tundra. Both of these groups have their own problems, but at the same time they are happy in their own way. On the one hand, there is the life in warm houses of the settlements with a small regular income, but under the pressure of a bigger nation, and on the other hand, there is the life in the primitive conditions of the tundra, but with a strong feeling of freedom. In many cases, these people have the same negative memories. They did not have a personal life in their childhood, but were more or less considered as property of the Soviet state. They were fed, clothed and provided with education according to state rules, while their parents were partly replaced by teachers. Such an education programme does not build up the children's knowledge of their own ethnic background or their own place in it. No one can learn specific national skills outside his or her own community. Even nowadays, when pupils come from the boarding school back home to the tundra, they are not completely members of their community but, at the same time, they are still not completely Russians. They are citizens of the Russian Federation, educated by the same programme as for instance pupils in Moscow and other places of the Russian Federation. Unfortunately, they do not know much about their own culture, nor do they have the same proficiency in Russian as Russians have. For them it is difficult to switch into Nenets society and to be Russians at the same time.

In the Yamalo-Nenets District, quite often, Russians pejoratively call aborigines *natsionaly*. This word derives from the name of the federal national districts, which appeared in the 1930s. It means 'people who do not completely belong to the Russian society and are not fully competent in their indigenous culture'. Nenets called them by themselves *jodej ter"* – 'new people', or settled aborigines, who moved from the tundra to live in villages for many reasons. Some of them drink and they do not have any fixed income; mostly they live on an unemployment benefit. Most of them do not have any professional qualifications other than a school diploma. Quite often, they live in the poor parts of the settlements, in old and ramshackle houses. This group of aborigines cannot integrate completely into the settlement's life. It is even difficult for their children, who were born in villages, because they are somehow halfway in between Nenets and Russians, and they do not know these cultures well. Maybe here I could relate an example from my own childhood.

My own attitude about Nenets culture formed chaotically. In my early childhood I spoke only Nenets and I lived with my parents in the tundra. Sometimes we used to come to Russian settlements, where our relatives lived. My parents were at that time private reindeer herders and lived in the Baidaratskaia tundra in Yamal. I went to the boarding school when I was six. In my class were mostly Khanty children. We had one primary school teacher who spoke Khanty and Russian. She taught us the Russian language. In the beginning she used to speak Khanty with pupils, introducing step-by-step the Russian language until the children started to understand it and tried to speak it as well. Therefore, I learned Russian with the help of the Khanty language, and I started to speak it quite fast. The next school year my aunt moved me to the settlement class to study with Russian children. In the boarding school we had Khanty language classes every week, but my parents thought that the Russian language was more important for my future and I had to speak it well. Well, then I started to study in Russian with Russians.

Our settlement class was international: there were also children from mixed families, but most of them were Russians. It is interesting that when I was with my Khanty classmates I knew that I was different but it was not a shame to be Nenets, but in the Russian class, I always felt uncomfortable about my Nenets origin. So, I had one period of my life when I tried to hide my connection with Nenets culture. When my Russian school friends asked me if I spoke Nenets I used to say 'no' just because I wanted to be closer to Russian society. Of course, it was a deception, but in such a way I wanted to be more like the settlement's children and to be closer to their life. During summer, when other children used to go for their vacation to the South, I travelled in the opposite direction, to the tundra. At first, it was difficult to return there, but in a few days I would become a tundra child again, speaking just Nenets language. It meant that I always used to live between two cultures, but they were always at a distance from each other and they never mixed. It was good for me, and this made me somehow follow Nenets and Russian rules and not mix them together. Therefore, among settlement children, I was like them, and among tundra children, I was also not so different. It is a question, why I tried to hide my provenance. Maybe, because quite often my Russian schoolmates gave me names. Some of them were from so-called 'low class settlement society', and often their parents did not have a good education. They could easily call me *khantejka*[2], which is another variation of national, but with a more humiliating meaning.

Why was it so? I think the explanation for it is that there is a lack of information among Russian speaking inhabitants, which is quite a serious problem. Many of them do not think in a positive way about the northern aborigines. The problem is also that most of the Russian language speakers who moved to the North have no interest in getting information about the culture of the locals and their traditions. This situation leads them to tell different disparaging jokes and anecdotes about local indigenous people, mentioning how stupid they are and how they are not able to follow 'normal rules of behaviour'. Of course, there are cultural centres, museums, and libraries where it is possible to get some information about the indigenous cultures and traditions, as is also described in Stephan Dudeck's contribution to this volume. There are many cultural folklore events in the Yamalo-Nenets district, but they are mostly modernised and are presented in quite an artificial and funny way. In reality, they do not show so much of the real life and values of the indigenous population. The painful part of this situation is that most of these *natsionaly* who live in towns or settlements do not value their own culture, but instead think that inclusion into Russian society is more important and will make their children more successful.

It is also a problem that for ex-boarding school pupils it is more difficult to find their place, either in the native or in the Russian society, and to realise their full potential in adult life. As a result, there is a high level of alcoholism and suicide among the minority peoples. Could this be caused by the separation of these people from their traditional living conditions, to which they were accustomed for centuries? For a long time people in Yamal did not talk about this inconvenient subject. It was somehow like a taboo. It became open in the 1980s, after the publication of the book *Aniko from the Nogo clan*, by the Nenets writer, Anna Nerkagi.

The Tundra School of Anna Nerkagi

Anna Nerkagi was born December 12th, 1952, in the Polar Ural tundra and lived there with her parents. When she was six years old, she was taken to a boarding school, as many other Nenets were. She returned to her family when she was already a young woman. In her novel, she described her own experience of schooling and then returning to the tundra to her Nenets culture after studying at the industrial institute in Tiumen and living in Russian society. The most anguished part of her book is about her childhood in a boarding school when she was not allowed to live with her parents and speak her native language. All indigenous children there had to be ashamed of belonging to their nation. She said that at that time they were brought up in school like soldiers and that it was part of their destiny that they were indigenous.[3]

Anna Nerkagi is not only famous as a writer, who has won many literary prizes for her novels.[4] She has a very authoritative character and is a strong leader in her community in Laborovaia. She used to be a regional deputy of the Priuralsky County, where she worked on protecting the Nenets' rights. We should also state that Anna is very religious. The forerunner of the Tundra School was her orthodox camp 'The Land of Hope'.

In the 1990s, Nerkagi already organised a primary school for local Nenets children in the Laborovaia village, which is situated 200 km from Salekhard – the Yamal District's capital city. Laborovaia village is located in the Priuralsky municipality and has a population of about 20 families living with their children who are of preschool or school age. There are about 47 camps of reindeer herders in the tundra near the village and in the Polar Ural Mountains.

|22| Laborovaia village.

|23| Children in the winter tundra.

By the way, Anna is by nature a big pessimist. Even in her novels, we can read about her feeling of hopelessness about the Nenets future. When working with the Tundra School project, I feel as if Anna Nerkagi tries somehow to turn back the huge wheel of history. She tries to correct its consequences by taking the young generation of Nenets back to the tundra, as if by doing so she could somehow correct a big mistake of the former Soviet empire's political regime.

When she presented her idea for the first time, she said that it is most important for children from indigenous families to have the feeling of self-sufficiency. This is the main way in which they realise their personal, psychological and social identity. When Nerkagi, as a leader of her project, provided information about the Tundra School project, many people (teachers, parents and children) reacted to it in different ways. People have quite a careful attitude to Anna Nerkagi. Nenets people know her not just as a writer, but also as a strict leader of their society. Most of them are afraid even to have any contact with her, because they never know how it will be to meet her personally, because this depends very much on Anna's mood. At the same time – although she lives in the little Laborovaia village – she travels once or twice a week to the capital city Salekhard and to the district centre Aksarka.

When Anna came for the first time to the Department of Education in Aksarka with her idea about the Tundra School, nobody knew how to work with it. There were no documents about it or examples of how it would be possible to realise this idea. Authorities were not so enthusiastic about Tundra education, because most of them were quite happy that there was just one way of educating children from nomadic families, one which showed its value over time: the boarding schools. Nevertheless, Anna's strong character and the clearness of her idea made bureaucrats take this idea seriously. I met Anna when the head of the Department of Education in Aksarka, Sergei Boichenko, asked me to work with the Tundra School documents and to prepare them for an application to the Department of Education in Salekhard. My first impression about this school was quite chaotic. There was not so much information about the way this school would work. We found some information about nomadic schools in the Sakha (Yakutia) and Evenki areas, but that was all.

On the internet we discovered a few documents about the Tundra and the Taiga Schools in other places. This information was very useful and it introduced the idea of an alternative way of giving education, different from boarding schools. We should say that for some teachers in the district it is still difficult to accept the idea of the Tundra School. The majority of them have already fixed models of the basic traditional education at schools or in boarding schools, which are formed by years of working practice and for them it is difficult to imagine how to try this completely different way of education.

In comparison to the last century, the living conditions in the Yamal tundra are changing dramatically. Therefore it is time to also try to change the old way of educating aborigines. Nenets people still follow their traditional way of life, the reindeer herding culture. It is somehow a mystery how they managed to save it. At the same time they are very open to changes and new technologies, like the telephone and internet, which make communication faster and easier (see Stammler 2009). Besides that, Nenets people are very much interested in new ways of teaching that can help them to save their native language and will give their children the chance to preserve their culture and to learn about their traditions, history and cultural knowledge from early childhood.

When we asked Valentina Niarui, the coordinator of this project as a representative of the Regional Institute for the Development of Education in Salekhard, for her opinion of Anna Nerkagi's school, she gave a very positive evaluation of the Tundra School and said that it is a new level of education. Niarui used to work for a long time as a supervisor of the teaching of the Nenets language at school, and she wrote many teaching books for indigenous children. Nowadays it is possible to put new methods of teaching into practice because there are good telephone connections and internet in the tundra. Many difficulties, which used to exist before, are not relevant or present anymore. It is possible to start the Tundra School. "By the way", added Niarui, "Anna Nerkagi developed this idea a long time ago, and when she came out with it, it was clear that the necessity and reality to try it in real life have a future".

When Anna Nerkagi started her Tundra School project, she based it on the fact that the education system of a district cannot ignore the culture and lifestyle of reindeer herders, hunters and fishermen. When their children live with them, they learn the essential quality of self-sufficiency and the virtue of looking reality in the eye (Ready 2000). "Of course," said Anna, "they would not become political leaders or famous people, this is not my aim, but I hope that my children will never become confirmed drunkards or scum of society because they are educated by labour."

Most of the children who live with her were from orphanages. Anna does not have children of her own. Her adopted children lack relatives beside Anna herself who are responsible for them. It is also interesting that in old times it was difficult to find Nenets children in orphanages, because in the Nenets culture it was a big sin to treat orphans badly. The Nenets believe that orphans bring good luck to their family. Some of Nerkagi's children are from families with social problems, whose parents were deprived of their right to child custody. They had a tough childhood and therefore have difficulties integrating into life under tundra conditions without proper education and training. It is right that children with problems should have an education which is different from the ordinary one. At the same time children from local tundra families, who have a completely different life, still study at Anna Nerkagi's school, in the settlement of Laborovaia.

Anna organised the process of studying in an unique way. She divided her school into three sections: one is in the village – it is a primary school; another one is in a camp not far from Laborovaia, where children learn in theory how to work with reindeer. Later, when they know this, they will move to the third camp. This camp is in the mountains quite far from Laborovaia, with tents and reindeer. Mostly all young people work there with reindeer in the traditional way of life and live in the tundra most of the time.

Place of the Tundra School in the education system of the YNAD. Why the Yamal government accepted Anna Nerkagi's idea.

The problem of the integration of boarding school children and their socialisation is not new. Several years ago a different approach was made to facilitate their integration into the education process. The system of the boarding schools in the Yamalo-Nenets district introduced a new project to make a family type boarding school. Brothers and sisters from the same family were allowed to live together in the same sector of the boarding school, just to make it similar to family living. This change had a positive impact on the process of adaptation of school children to the education process, and later other boarding schools in Yamal adopted it (Sotrueva 2003). Here we mention some aspects:

Positive aspects of boarding schools:

- They give the possibility to children, whose parents live in the tundra and migrate all year round, to get free primary and secondary education in stationary schools;
- In boarding schools children get food and clothes, school books, exercise books and other writing materials for free;
- After finishing school, children have the possibility to study for a profession at colleges or at university level.

Negative aspects of boarding schools:

- They are a cause of language and culture loss, for from the very beginning children were not allowed to speak their native languages or to wear traditional clothes;
- Children are separated from their family for the period of nine months.

We could surely say that young indigenous people who finish studying at a boarding school are the most vulnerable group of people. They have to integrate into another social system which differs from their boarding school experience. Therefore, the need to try to provide good education in the tundra is very clear. One way to realise it is a new experimental Tundra School, which is officially called a New Model of Education in Yamal.

In December 2010, the governor of the Yamalo-Nenets Autonomous District signed a document about Anna Nerkagi's experimental project on developing a new model of education for children from reindeer herders and fishermen families. This school is called in Russian *kochevaia shkola* which means that this school is nomadic. The name 'Tundra School' fits well because it works mostly in the tundra. This form of education should teach all school subjects according to the Russian Federal Educational standards. The main aim of the Tundra School is to save the language speaking ability of Nenets children and moreover, to encourage them to use their traditional cultural knowledge in different natural (traditional) life situations. Children learn how to live according to their traditions; they know and respect their culture, history and nation.

This act shows that the authorities of the Yamal-Nenets Autonomous District were introduced to the culture and lifestyle of the indigenous people, who are reindeer herders, hunters and fishermen. Their children, studying and living in boarding schools, cannot integrate easily into modern society because they lack knowledge of basic skills such as cooking, cleaning or working to earn money. Children are not taught how to do elementary things for themselves because, according to Russian state health standards, children in the boarding school are not allowed to do these things. They live in an artificial world and as a result, we observe a low level of socialisation after finishing such schools.

As I was told, the Laborovaia primary school is very different from all other schools in the Yamalo-Nenets Autonomous District. In this school, children do not just study school subjects, but they are also taught how to fish, hunt and work with reindeer in natural conditions. Nowadays, 37 children study at this experimental school. The original idea of the Tundra School, which combines school, family and tribal education, is to make children familiar with their culture and with working skills in the tundra. It is the first time educational methods of the Nenets traditional pedagogic have been officially recognised. Why has this happened? Probably one of the reasons is connected with the 'Concept of Sustainable Development of Indigenous Peoples of the North, Siberia and the Far East of the Russian Federation' (4 February 2009 N 132), which the Russian Government adopted in 2009. It focusses on the idea of the socio-economic, ethnic and cultural development of the minorities and on the modernisation of education in the North. The change of the level of educational politics encouraged people to start to discuss new ways of teaching indigenous children that are different from the boarding school system.

Future planning of the new experiment

The changes in educational level make it possible to organise new forms of teaching, where teachers are willing to work in the tundra and teach children in their traditional living conditions. If this Tundra School project were successful, other schools in the district would be ready to work in the same way. According to the idea of this project, the main language of education would be one of the district's indigenous languages. Nevertheless, Russian would also be introduced to pupils as the language of teaching. This bilingual (possibly trilingual) education would help to skip the language barrier and would assist pupils to get primary education both in their native languages and in Russian as well.

The original idea of the Tundra School is that parents and teachers in collaboration give the children the basic primary education and provide them with knowledge about their traditional way of life in the tundra. This tundra project is still an experimental model for the contemporary education of children from nomadic families in the Yamalo-Nenets Autonomous District. Therefore, it is under the supervision of two official education centres: the Departments of Education of the Priuralsky County and the Yamalo-Nenets Autonomous District.

Official papers dealing with the experimental model of the Tundra (nomadic) School state that this model is based on the following facts:

- the traditional way of life is one of the components of the Arctic civilisation, which has its own customs and values;
- the separation of primary school age children from their parents is detrimental to their psychological health and leads to a low degree of adaptation and socialisation to new living conditions;
- young people are not prepared to live in modern society after finishing boarding school, due to their lack of skills in leading an independent life in the village (or town) or in the tundra.

The Tundra School has the following objectives:

- to organise for the educational process such a situation for indigenous children that they are adapted to the natural living conditions of migration in the tundra;
- to guarantee the possibility to continue education at the secondary school level;
- to develop innovative teaching methods for the Tundra School which are based on the Nenets ethno-pedagogical ways of teaching and on modern teaching methods with the use of internet and telephone communication;
- the education process should work to maintain the connection between generations of nomadic families, in order to ensure the preservation and further development of the traditional way of life and ethnic culture of indigenous people;
- to train professional teachers to work in the tundra.

What does it mean to study in a 'nomadic' or 'migrating' or 'tundra school'? This method of teaching is not yet specified. I understand it as a way of education that provides such knowledge, which allows children to use and practice it in real life situations. Of course, 'nomadic' means a process of permanent migration, mobility and seasonality. For that purpose, the tundra school's classes should be organised not like the ones in ordinary schools and not only by teachers, but also by the parents, who play an active and important role in the education process.

Summary

This experimental model of education for children from nomadic and semi-nomadic indigenous families is the new contemporary education system of the Yamalo-Nenets Autonomous District. Today the living conditions of the Nenets are much better than they were previously: there are telephone and internet connections in the tundra and electricity generating stations. People use these modern facilities quite actively.

I hope that this Tundra School project will have a positive outcome and that it will be a good model for many other places of the Yamalo-Nenets District, where nomadic reindeer herders live. Nowadays there are completely different ideas about what members of society need to have, different from a century ago. It is a pity that at the beginning of the 20th century, the human factor hindered the success of the Tundra School project. At that time the indigenous people were not yet ready to accept the idea of education, which is possible nowadays. This is understandable, because people had simply to survive in the severe conditions of the tundra.

Today, under the circumstances of scientific and industrial development, people have more possibilities, even in the tundra, and they do use all achievements of technical development. Yes, some innovations cause painful experiences and people have to cope with them, but returning to the old experimental ways of education would not work.

The Tundra School project is just starting to work, but it is becoming clear that its main problem is the lack school books, which are only written in the Russian language. All available books in Nenets are quite old and were made in the 1950s to 1970s and reprinted in the 1990s after the collapse of the USSR. Today children are Russian and Nenets bilinguals. The question remains, how to follow the standards of the Russian State Education school programme without special books for native education. A lot has been done by local teachers in the Tundra School who teach in both the Russian and the Nenets languages. If this experiment works well, we could say that the Tundra School provides such an education for children, which is adapted to the national traditional education and preserves the traditional way of life and the Nenets language.

To summarise, we should remember that Yamalo-Nenets Autonomous District is one of the most expensive places in the Russian Federation, where prices are based on the high level of oil and gas workers' salaries. These prices for food and everyday goods are so high that it is hard for ordinary people without a regular income to survive in the region. It is especially hard for those Nenets families who do not have reindeer and therefore cannot sell their meat. This means that they do not have any income of their own. Nowadays there are so many huge industrial projects inland of the Yamal Peninsula, which completely change the ecology, land and human environment. Anna Nerkagi said herself that children should work and get an education that would help them to survive in the tundra. The question remains, how long they will live in the tundra. It is also important for them to learn how to survive in the aggressive environment of industrialisation. It is probably possible to live in a balance between these completely different spaces of the tundra and oil, gas and industrial areas. The Tundra School is taking its first steps, and I think that the young people who finish it learn by themselves how to use their traditional knowledge in modern situations for their life and work. If this is successful, then we will have the Nenets culture and language safeguarded for a longer time and for more Nenets generations.

Notes

1 Project *Socio-cultural change of Uralic minority languages in 20th–21st century Siberia, analysed through Nenets life histories* (KONE foundation grant 2010, number 18-4665; KONE foundation grant 2011, number 27-6407, Finland).
2 From the word Khanty, which is a name for the Khanty ethnic group. It is used both for women and men.
3 One of the stories of a woman who used to study in a boarding school and who lives now in a village is told in a film of Anastasia Lapsui and Markku Lehmuskallio *The last in the line*. Illume OY, Finland, 2010. www.sukunsaviimeinen.fi.
4 *Ilir* (1975), *The white lichen* (1995), *The Silent* (1996).

References

Dudeck, Stephan and Aimar Ventsel 1998. Do the Khanty Need a Khanty Curriculum? Indigenous Concepts of School Education. In *Bicultural Education in the North*, E. Kasten (ed.), 89–100. Münster: Waxmann Verlag.

Golovnev, Andrei V. and Gail Osherenko 2000. *Siberian Survival. The Nenets and Their Story.* Ithaka, NY: Cornell University Press.

Grenoble, Leonore A. 2003. *Language Policy in the Soviet Union.* Dordrecht: Kluwer Academic Publishers.

Harrison, K. David 2007. *When languages die. The Extinction of the World's Languages and the Erosion of Human Knowledge.* Oxford: Oxford University Press.

Liarskaya, Elena 2005. Northern Residential Schools in Contemporary Yamal Nenets Culture. *Sibirica: Journal of Siberian Studies* 4 (1): 74–87.

Ready, Oliver 2000. Taking Back the Tundra. *The Moscow times* (1), November 2000.

Sotrueva, Zoia 2003. *Adaptatsia mladshikh shkol'nikov k novym usloviiam v internate semeinovo tipa Yamala-Nenetskogo avtonomnogo okruga.* [Adaptation of the youngest school children to the new life conditions in the family type boarding schools in the YNAD], Report.

Stammler, Florian 2009. Mobile Phone Revolution in the Tundra? Technological Change Among Russian Reindeer Nomads. *Folklore: Electronic Journal of Folklore* 41: 47–78.

Toulouze, Eva 1999. The Development of a Written Culture by the Indigenous Peoples of Western Siberia. *Pro ethnologia* 7: 53–85. Tartu.

Vakhtin, Nikolai 2001. *Yazyki narodov severa v 20 veke: Ocherki yazykovogo sdviga* [Languages of the Peoples of the North: Essays on Language Shift]. St. Petersburg: Dmitrii Bulanin.

Web sites:
http://en.wikipedia.org/wiki/Yamalo-Nenets_Autonomous_Okrug
http://www.ethnoconsulting.ru/cntnt/presscentr/koncepciya.html

11 TOWARDS A DIGITAL INFRASTRUCTURE FOR KILDIN SAAMI[1]

Michael Rießler

Finnish, as a language of education and literature,
would not produce other than ABC-literature.
If you believe in the possibility of a Finnish literature,
then you would even believe in the possibility of the
foundation of an Estonian and a Saami nation and literature.
(*Nervander 1845, cit. Kuusi-etal. 1983: 9*)

Introduction

The introductory quote is taken from a letter written originally in Swedish by the Swedish-speaking scientist from Finland Johan Jakob Nervander to Johan Vilhelm Snellman, a *fennoman* philosopher and statesman who was central in the establishment of Finnish as the second national language in Finland beside Swedish. The quote nicely illustrates several points relevant to the discussion in the present paper. As we all know, Estonia eventually became a nation state and Finnish and Estonian are in fact well-established languages of education and literature. As national languages they function similarly to Swedish today. Even the Saami are catching up on their Northern European neighbours' nation building processes. In a similar way to other nations, Saami construct their ethnicity and nationhood on the basis of land, tradition, history, culture, etc. Ethnic and national symbolism is well-illustrated in pan-Saami discourses on, for instance, *Sápmi* (North Saami designation for the Saami 'homeland'), *duodji* (North Saami designation for Saami 'traditional' (artisan) handicraft), *joiking* and *reindeer herding*, or national institutions leading these discourses (e.g. ethnic Saami museums in all Nordic countries or the ethnic Saami University College in Guovdageaidnu).

Thus, Nervander's disbelief in the 'national capabilities' of Finns, Estonians and Saami was proven wrong by history. However, the Saami case is different because there is no Saami nation state. Members of the Saami nation are united under one flag and one national anthem, they celebrate February 6 as national day for all Saami and feel represented by the pan-Saami Parliamentary Conference uniting Saami parliamentarians from four countries. Nonetheless, the perhaps 150,000 Saami are scattered as mini minorities over territories belonging to the four northern European nation states, Finland, Norway, Sweden and Russia. There is no single national language for all Saami, either. Instead, the ten living Saami languages form a group of very closely related but not mutually comprehensible idioms. Six of them have standardised written forms based on different orthographic principles.

Nevertheless, today's Saami languages are continuously transforming from media of mere 'ABC-literature' to true media of education, of literature and of everyday digital communication. The most developed Saami language is North Saami, spoken in a vast area across the northernmost parts of Finland, Norway and Sweden by about 16,000 (Aikio 2003: 35) speakers. Besides being the primary language of everyday communication in several municipalities with a strong proportion of North Saami inhabitants (especially in Kárášjohka/Karasjok and Guovdageaidnu/Kautokeino in Norway as well as in Uhcejohka/Utsjoki in Finland), today North Saami is also used as a medium for education in preschools, primary and secondary schools, and even in professional and academic education. It is used in fine arts and popular culture, in official documents at the local, national and even European administrative levels, it is the language of political debates and, last but not least, of different kinds of printed, broadcast and internet based mass media.

This paper describes one of the more minor Saami languages, Kildin Saami, which is only starting to become a language of education, literature and written communication.

Current language situation of Kildin Saami

Kildin Saami[2] (Endonym *kīllt sām' kīll'*) belongs, along with Ter Saami, to the peninsula group of the East Saamic languages (Sammallahti 1998: 26–34). Originally, Kildin Saami was spoken all over the central inland parts and the central coastal parts of the Kola peninsula. Four dialects of Kildin Saami are still maintained: the Kīllt dialect, the Koarrdegk dialect, the Lujavv'r dialect and the Arsjogk dialect. The neighbouring Saami dialects in the Northwest belong to the Skolt Saami language. Ter Saami dialects were formerly spoken in the eastern parts of the peninsula, but there are practically no Ter speakers left in these areas today. The third neighbouring Saami language, Akkala Saami, was originally spoken in the Southwest of the Kildin Saami dialect area, and has repeatedly been reported to be extinct since 2003 (Rantala et al. 2009), but there are likely Akkala Saami who speak the language at least passively (Elisabeth Scheller p. c.). Since the Kola peninsula is the traditional homeland of the four Saami languages of Russia, they are normally referred to as Kola Saami.

Kildin Saami is the most vital and most developed Saami language in Russia today. The densest Kildin Saami settlement is found in the village and municipal centre Lovozero (Kildin *Lujavv'r*) with 700–800 ethnic Kildin Saami among a total village population of approximately 3,000. Other Kildin speakers live spread over all parts of the Kola peninsula, both in rural and urban settlements, one of them being the

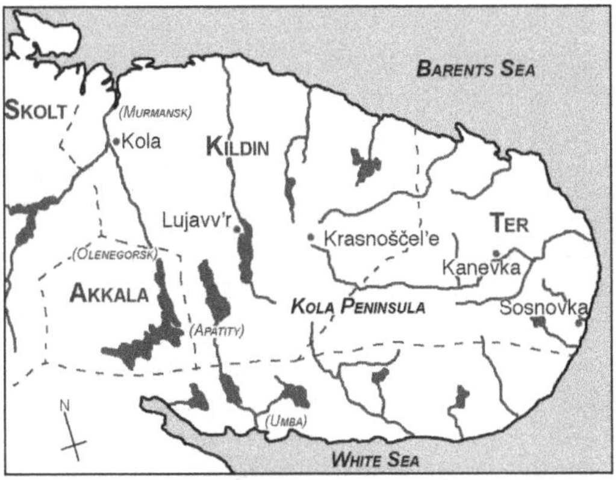

|24| Map of Kola peninsula

administrative centre of the Murmansk area. There is also a considerable Kildin Saami diaspora population, with several speakers among them, who live elsewhere in Russia or in other countries.

Kildin Saami is critically endangered as the result of a very intense language shift to Russian. Today, the language has only about 100 active and perhaps 600 passive speakers (Scheller 2011: 88, 89, 91). Active language use here refers to fully proficient speakers who use the language on a daily basis and in communications which are not restricted to special thematic domains. There are also fully proficient speakers among the group of passive language users who do not, however, use the language regularly today. The language proficiency of other passive speakers, in Scheller's terminology, might even be restricted to a few expressions or symbolic language use.

|25| Training course on *Archives, Technology and Tools for Kola Saami* (19.–22. October 2011) at the computer lab of the vocational school PU-26 in Lovozero. In the foreground participants Svetlana Danilova (left) and Mariia Medvedeva (right) with the teacher Jeremy Bradley, in the background participants Viktor Danilov and Elisabeth Scheller.

All Kildin Saami speakers are bilingual in Russian. In fact, Russian is the dominant language in all domains of Kildin Saami society, and Kildin Saami is hardly ever heard in public life. Currently, there are hardly any children acquiring Kildin Saami as their first language. The youngest first language speakers belong to their parents' generation. However, there are a few young adult Kildin Saami who are trying to learn and use the language again. Language courses and other resources are not offered in great number, but are available nonetheless. In general, Kildin Saami individuals are interested in revitalising and maintaining the language and a few representatives take an active role in practical measures and relevant projects. For more detailed information on the current situation of Kildin Saami and ongoing revitalisation, see the descriptions in Rantala 1994, Sergeeva 1995, Sergeeva 2002, Scheller 2004, Scheller 2012 and further references mentioned there.

History of research and standardisation

The history of Kildin Saami standardisation is closely tied to the linguistic research history for the whole group of East-Saami languages. The following sections provide an overview focussing on contemporary written Kildin Saami. For a more detailed historical description of Kildin Saami literacy development, see Siegl et al. (in print). A comprehensive description of linguistic research history on Kildin Saami is in the works by the present author, and outlines are found in Sergeeva 2000 and Rantala 2005.

Orthography

Kildin Saami has been written since the end of the nineteenth century. However, the contemporary written language is not the result of a sustainable development of continuous modifications, because earlier standards were abolished in order to reintroduce completely new orthographies in the 1930s and 1970s. The history of Kildin Saami writing also includes a back and forth shift from Cyrillic to Latin to Cyrillic.

A translation of the Gospel of Matthew was the first book printed (partly) in Kildin Saami. It was written, with the help of native speaker consultants, in Cyrillic orthography by the Finnish linguist Arvid Genetz, in 1878. During the early Soviet period, a new, Latin-based orthography was successfully introduced. This new Kildin Saami written language was used in several textbooks for different subjects in the school education of Saami children[3] and in communist propaganda texts.[4] However, teaching Kildin Saami and the production of materials written in the language came to a complete standstill for decades when the official Soviet doctrine shifted away from minority language support in the late 1930s. The second new Cyrillic orthography for Kildin Saami was developed in the 1970s and 1980s by a working group of

Saami teachers and language activists led by the non-Saami educationalist and linguist Rimma Kuruch. This orthography (cf. *table*, p. 205) has since been used, in different variants, in dictionaries, in textbooks for elementary schools, as well as in several published literary texts for children and adults, and most recently even in the internet. An extensive presentation of Kildin Saami media history, including print and other written media, is included in Rießler (in print).

Documentation and description

Arvid Genetz was also the first researcher to work on an extensive linguistic documentation and description of Kildin Saami. Based on his Bible translation and a few other collected texts, he published a Kola Saami descriptive dictionary in 1891. Even the first short grammatical sketch of Kildin Saami (written in Hungarian and including comparative data of all Kola Saami languages) by Halász (1883) is based on Genetz' text collection. The first Kildin Saami grammar was written by Endukovskii (1937). The aim of this grammar was to support the training of Saami teachers. Consequently, the author applies a moderately prescriptive approach and uses the orthographic standard of that time, i.e. the Latin-based alphabet mentioned above.

T. I. Itkonen's (1958) comparative Kola Saami dialect dictionary (written in phonemic transcription and with translations into Finnish and German) is the most comprehensive source for Kildin Saami vocabulary. It comprises about 7,200 word stems, which are listed with all known cognate forms from different dialects of the four Kola Saami languages. A comprehensive descriptive grammar of Kildin Saami was produced by Kert in 1971. Other fragments of theoretical linguistic descriptions and several text collections (written in phonemic transcription and with translations into either Russian, Finnish or German) have also been published, mostly by researchers from Estonia, Finland, Hungary and Russia. Kildin Saami is thus not undocumented. Still, lexical and grammatical descriptions are incomplete and there is not much data available which reflect current language use.

Prescriptive dictionaries and grammars

There are three user's dictionaries of contemporary Kildin, published as Afanasyeva et al. 1985 (comprising almost 8,000 Kildin lemmas with Russian translations), Kert 1986 (a Kildin-Russian-Kildin school dictionary with about 3,000 lemmas in both directions)[5] and Sammallahti et al. 1991 (a Kildin-North Saami-Kildin dictionary with approximately 2,500 headwords in both directions).

The first two dictionaries mentioned above have more recently been combined and re-published as the *Electronic Saami dictionary* (Yur'ev 2003).[6]

The only user's grammar available for the modern Kildin Saami written standard is the grammatical sketch by Kuruch (1985). This prescriptive grammar contains a short but comprehensive phonology, all main inflectional paradigms of nominals and verbs and a few very basic syntactic rules. The monograph on Kildin Saami orthographic rules by Kuruch et al. (1995) could in principle also be considered a prescriptive grammar because it includes detailed and almost complete descriptions of Kildin Saami phonology, morphophonology as well as (inflectional and derivational) morphology. The Sammallahti et al. (1991) dictionary includes a short appendix with basic inflectional paradigms.

The available printed dictionaries and grammars are clearly insufficient from both linguistic and pedagogical points of view. However, altogether they would still form a relatively solid base for teaching. The corpus of teaching materials even includes a few textbooks. Although those target elementary school pupils and the remaining few materials are practically useless for self-teaching by adults, interested Kildin Saami teachers have in fact a store of teaching materials at their disposal for preparing classes on different levels beyond elementary school level. Note that even today almost all active Kildin teachers are fluent L1-speakers with academic training. Today there is also funding available from different (Russian and non-Russian) sources for organising teaching at different places, including teacher compensation. According to my own observations, one important reason for the lack of progress in the quality of teaching is the generally low degree of basic pedagogical knowledge, combined with a lack of interest among teachers and the loss of attraction for learning the language among potential students, rather than the lack of contemporary teaching materials or funding (cf. also Scheller 2011: 101–102).

History of language planning

Language planning means the conscious interference in the development of a language in order to further advance its use in new domains (cf. Janich 2007). Consequently, Kildin Saami, a language which originally was only transmitted orally, was promoted as a written language, first in the 1930s and later in the 1970s, in order to become a functional communication device in Soviet society. The status of the language in society was supported by teaching it to children at school and using it in printed texts (status planning). To accomplish this task, a normalised written standard and new vocabulary adapted to modern society had to first be created (corpus planning).

The prescriptive dictionaries and grammars mentioned above are a product of the last fruitful period of language planning for Kildin Saami under the active participation of native speakers. In the 1970s, the language working group had already started producing preliminary teaching materials for Kildin Saami children. The aim was to create a linguistically and didactically well-founded written standard as the basis for a set of textbooks for different levels, as well as for dictionaries and didactic guides for Saami teachers. Although this ambitious goal was not reached completely (for different reasons), a considerable amount of materials has been produced, the most important being the large Kildin Saami-Russian dictionary edited by Rimma Kuruch and co-workers (Afanasyeva et al. 1985), and a set of textbooks for grades 1 through 3, including accompanying didactic materials. Even the other Russian-Kildin-Russian school dictionary written by Georgii Kert (1986), the North Saami-Kildin Saami-North Saami wordlist written by Pekka Sammallahti and Anastasiia Khvorostukhina (1991) and other materials created recently by Kola Saami language activists (e.g. Sharshina et al. 2008) would not have been possible without the groundwork in language standardisation and orthography development by the Kildin Saami language working group.

Unfortunately, systematic work with language planning stopped in the late 1990s, when the Kildin Saami language working group at the Saami division of the Murmansk branch of the Russian Academy of Sciences disbanded. Reasons for terminating work included the lack of administrative and financial support after the collapse of the Soviet Union (Nina Afanasyeva, Rimma Kuruch p.c.), but perhaps also the ongoing tension between group collaborators and Saami language activists elsewhere. A sound description of the history of Kildin Saami language planning during the 1970s through the 1990s, including the founding, development and breakup of the Kildin Saami language working group, its achievements and its conflicts with outside language planners, has yet to be written. It can only be stated that true linguistic reasons, such as the prescription of dialectal forms not accepted by all speakers, are scarcely the trigger for the current conflicts. Unfortunately, all insider descriptions have so far been exclusively polemic, cf. a chapter in a book on the topic *The alphabet and orthography of the normative Kildin Saami language: History of the question* (translation MR) (Kuruch et al. 1995: 175–186) or personal statements provided to the present author in interviews or unpublished documents (e.g. by Aleksandra Antonova, Nina Afanasyeva, Ekaterina Korkina, Rimma Kuruch and Ekaterina Mechkina). Several scientific investigations of Kola Saami society also deal with this topic, but are rather biased in that they mainly portray the conflicts with the non-Saami researcher Rimma Kuruch, but disregard the fact that the history of the Kildin orthography has been quite successful overall (cf., e.g., discussions in Scheller 2004 and Øverland et al. 2012).

As a matter of fact, there is no professional infrastructure available today at a local level which could systematically support ongoing revitalisation attempts and continue the work with Kildin Saami language planning. Currently there are two local institutions evolving which could potentially fulfill this task. The first institution is a Saami research group called 'the Saami laboratory' led by the linguist Olga Ivanishcheva at the Murmansk State Humanities University.[7] Although Olga Ivanishcheva and her students conduct research on Kildin Saami, none of them has active proficiency in this (or any other Saami) language. So far they predominantly work on theoretical questions of Saami lexicology and terminology related to culture and society. It seems also unfavorable from a language planning perspective that the research group has neither Saami collaborators nor any close collaboration with Saami organisations.

The other institution, called the *Centre for Saami Competence,*[8] is itself a Saami institution located in Lovozero. It is provisionally led by the historian Maksim Kuchinskii and was officially registered as a nonprofit organisation in December 2011. According to project descriptions, practical language work will be but one target area of the centre's future work. Although the successful implementation of this aim hinges on the availability of permanent funding (which has not yet been provided) and the professional expertise of participating personnel, the centre should have the best requisites for also including a 'language centre', due to its close administrative and personal ties both to the local Saami community and to Saami representative organisations, as well as to Saami and non-Saami educational and academic research institutions in Russia and elsewhere.

A non-local research institution dealing partly with issues of Kildin Saami language planning is the *Centre for Sámi Language Technology* (Giellatekno)[9] at the University of Tromsø in Norway. Giellatekno provides, among other things, computer applications such as proofing tools, text processing tools, language learning programmes and digital dictionaries for Saami and other languages, and builds digital written language corpora for these languages.

Although North Sámi is the language that Giellatekno (the name actually means 'language technology' in North Saami) originally worked on and has most intensively researched, other Saami and even other northern languages have also always been the focus of work. Systematic work with Kildin Saami started in 1999 when Giellatekno launched a collaborative project between Trond Trosterud, Michael Everson and Rimma Kuruch to help provide the Kildin Saami language working group in Murmansk with the necessary digital infrastructure for using Kildin Saami on computers (cf. Everson 1999). Earlier, Everson and Trosterud had already proposed the addition of the Cyrillic Saami characters to the Unicode standard (ISO/IEC JTC1/SC2/WG2 N1744 and N1590). Giellatekno also collaborated (together with Juhani Lehtiranta) on the creation of new fonts specifically for printing Kildin Saami at the Saami publishing house Davvi Girji in Kárášjohka[10] and (together with Everson) on the standardisation of character sets for Saami languages. Giellatekno's current work with Kildin Saami will be described below.

The Kildin Saami written language

The most fundamental achievement of Kildin Saami language planning has been the creation of a written standard that basically all Kildin Saami language users agree on today. A considerable corpus of printed texts using this standard is even available to future language planning activities, and this corpus is continuously growing.

The following section describes the standardisation of the Kildin Saami alphabet as an essential prerequisite for the creation of any digital infrastructure. Note that 'alphabet' refers to a set of graphic symbols (letters) representing sounds, whereas 'orthographic rules', which are not the topic of the present paper, are needed for combining the letters of an alphabet into words, word forms and larger text units in order to represent the written language in a conventionalised way.

After the introduction of the current Kildin Saami alphabet in the 1970s, it underwent several revisions reflecting improvements based on new and better insights into Kildin Saami phonology and morphophonology (for a description of the alphabet's history, including all revisions, see Kuruch et al. 1995: 175–186). The first, preliminary version of the alphabet was used in the Kildin Saami primer by Aleksandra Antonova (1982) and the dictionary by Georgii Kert (1986). The table *(p. 205)* presents the full set of characters after the last linguistically motivated revision leading to the version used in the comprehensive Kildin Saami-Russian dictionary (Afanasyeva et al. 1985).[11] The two letters in parentheses (14' and 18') are simply typographic replacements previous to the last orthography revision. This revision was meant as a compromise to settle a dispute over two alleged non-Cyrillic letters (Kuruch et al. 1995: 183). Although this most recent orthographic version has been used in the vast majority of published books up to today (i.e. in most textbooks published by the Kildin Saami language working group, in the North Saami-Kildin Saami-North Saami wordlist (Sammallahti et al. 1991), and in all Kildin Saami books published by Davvi Girji in Norway during the 1990s), the two replaced letters were later abandoned again and this alphabet variant seems to be completely out of use today. A third orthographic variant, used by several current authors, does not include either letters 14, 18, 14' or 18' and is similar to the initial variant introduced in print by Antonova (1982).

Shortcomings, gaps and open questions in the standardised alphabet

The Kildin Saami alphabet is the result of the continuous groundwork completed by the Kildin Saami language working group since the 1970s. Saami teachers and activists were included in this work under the leadership of the non-Saami academic Rimma Kuruch (see also the section on language planning above). The successful creation and establishment of a written norm is a major achievement in the history of Kildin Saami revitalisation. It is the most fundamental basis for all recent, current and future work with language planning and language technology. The following discussion of possible shortcomings, gaps and questions does not intend to diminish the efforts by Kuruch and her collaborators. On the contrary, the new creation of an alphabet is far from trivial and in most cases its practical implementation will need a sustained period of evaluation and possible revisions.

Linguistic shortcomings. From a linguistic perspective, this alphabet with a number of modified letters, like the vowels with macron (marking length, e.g. э̄) and diaeresis (marking so-called 'half-palatalisation', e.g. ӭ) or the consonants with tail (marking devoicing, e.g. ҋ) and hook (the velar nasal ӈ) seems unnecessarily complicated because some marginal oppositions in Kildin Saami phonology are overemphasised, e.g. the length of vowels and the voicelessness of sonorant consonants. On the other hand, some rather relevant phonological distinctions are represented unsystematically. This is especially true for the difference between palatalisation as a secondary modification of consonants and the primary place of palatal articulation of other consonants. This important phonological distinction is completely blurred by the unsystematic use of the palatalisation and half-palatalisation marks or di- and triglyphs for representing the respective sounds (cf. Kuz'menko et al. 2012). It is most likely that the alphabet creators' original intention was to stress the linguistic differences between Russian and Kildin Saami, as they are perceived by native Saami speakers, who are also fully literate in the majority language Russian. Incomplete and even wrong linguistic analyses from that time also seemed to have played a role. For Saami members among the working group, who were all well-educated and fluent bilinguals, the alphabet was surely a useful tool for representing their native language in written form. However, teaching Kildin Saami pronunciation as a foreign language with the help of this alphabet is clearly a didactic challenge. The introduction of a typographically complicated alphabet, in combination with missing linguistic advice and the teachers' generally poor knowledge of multilingual education, has likely caused severe difficulties in Kildin Saami language education from the beginning until today.

Typographic shortcomings. A high level of creativity in the construction of new letter symbols was generally typical of minority language planners in the Soviet Union (Trosterud 1996). [12] From the point of view of standardisation, the large amount of special letters in the new Cyrillic alphabet for Kildin is definitely a challenge, both for language learners and language technologists. The Kildin Saami alphabet (main variant, see *table* on p. 205) contains eight letter bases which are not included in the Russian alphabet. Adding a macron on the vowels adds another nine letters, plus two more letters with diaeresis. Altogether, the additional 19 special Kildin Saami letter symbols increase the basic modern Russian alphabet's 33 letters by more than 50 %.

The high number of Kildin Saami special letters and their typography has already resulted in technical shortcomings affecting work with written Kildin Saami in the pre-digital age. The resulting problems concern mainly the input of letters with different technical devices but sometimes even their typographic appearance on the output side.

The special Kildin Saami letters were created according to different principles. In most cases, a Russian letter was typographically modified. Thus, for instance, adding a diacritic MACRON (¯) as a marker of vowel length was clearly borrowed from a similar rule used in phonemic scripts. Several other modified letters also borrowed their meaning from other known alphabets, for instance the CYRILLIC LETTER EN WITH HOOK (Ӈ ӈ), which marks a voiced velar nasal in different Uralic (and several other) languages. The CYRILLIC LETTER SHHA (Һ һ) and the CYRILLIC LETTER JE (Ј ј) were also borrowed from existing alphabets of other languages. The former is used in the Cyrillic alphabets of several Turkic languages, where it also marks a voiceless fricative sound. The latter comes from the Cyrillic alphabets of Serbian and Macedonian, where it marks an entirely different sound. Note that in current non-professional arguments against these two letters, one of the main reasons for not using them is their alleged status as 'Latin letters'. This is obviously not entirely true, even though they are certainly better known from the Latin alphabet.

A few other letters are inventions rather than borrowings, such as the CYRILLIC LETTER SEMISOFT SIGN (Ҍ ҍ) for the (phonologically misinterpreted) so-called half-palatalisation. This letter resembles the Old Slavonic CYRILLIC LETTER YAT (Ѣ ѣ), but is typographically slightly different from it.[13] The use of diacritic DIAERESIS (¨) for the (phonologically mis-interpreted) so-called half-palatal vowels CYRILLIC LETTER A WITH DIAERESIS (Ӓ ӓ) and CYRILLIC LETTER E WITH DIAERESIS (Ӭ ӭ also follows a principle which the creators of the alphabet had developed themselves.

1 А а 0410 0430	2 А̄ а̄	3 Ӓ ӓ 04D2 04D3	4 Б б 0411 0431	5 В в 0412 0432	6 Г г 0413 0433	7 Д д 0414 0434
8 Е е 0415 0435	9 Е̄ е̄	10 Ё ё 0401 0451	11 Ё̄ ё̄	12 Ж ж 0416 0436	13 З з 0417 0437	14 Һ һ 04BA O4BB
14' (') 02BC	15 И и 0418 0438	16 Ӣ ӣ 04E2 04E3	17 Й й 0419 0439	18 Ј ј 0408 0458	18' (Ҋ ҋ) 048A 048B	19 К к 041A 043A
20 Л л 041B 043B	21 Ӆ ӆ 04C5 04C6	22 М м 041C 043C	23 Ӎ ӎ 04CD 04CE	24 Н н 041D 043D	25 Ӊ ӊ 04C9 04CA	26 Ӈ ӈ 04C7 04C8
27 О о 041E 043E	28 О̄ о̄	29 П п 041F 043F	30 Р р 0420 0440	31 Ҏ ҏ 048E 048F	32 С с 0421 0441	33 Т т 0422 0442
34 У у 0423 0443	35 Ӯ ӯ 04EE 04EF	36 Ф ф 0424 0444	37 Х х 0425 0445	38 Ц ц 0426 0446	39 Ч ч 0427 0447	40 Ш ш 0428 0448
41 Щ щ 0429 0449	42 Ъ ъ 042A 044A	43 Ы ы 042B 044B	44 Ь ь 042C 044C	45 Ҍ ҍ 048C 048D	46 Э э 042D 044D	47 Э̄ э̄
48 Ӭ ӭ 04EC 04ED	49 Ю ю 042E 044E	50 Ю̄ ю̄	51 Я я 042F 044F	52 Я̄ я̄		

The current Kildin Saami alphabet, including capital and lowercase letters.
The subscript number to the left of each letter pair is used for reference elsewhere in this paper. The Unicode (Hex) is given below each letter. If there is no Unicode, the letter has to be composed either with the COMBINING DIAERESIS (Unicode Hex 00A8), or with the COMBINING MACRON (Unicode Hex 00AF).

The input of the large amount of special letters not available on commonly used digital writing devices continues to be the main challenge. Earlier, special letters or letter modifiers (tail, hook, etc.) not available on the Russian typewriter were often added manually afterwards in the manuscript. This solution is still sometimes used in combination with a computer (e.g. in the second issue of the journal *Sām'* 'Saami', published as Samizdat by Korkina and Galkina in 2005). For manuscript creation by the Kildin Saami language working group, a tailor-made typewriter including all needed letters was produced (Aleksandra Antonova, Nina Afanasyeva p.c.). In the computer age, especially after the breakthrough of the international standard Unicode (cf. Allen 2011) in practically all commonly used applications (office programmes, internet browsers) this coding problem is solved, in principle. However, inputting the special Cyrillic letters of the Kildin Saami alphabet, combined with incomplete or typographically non-appealing fonts on the output side, remain the most crucial problems.

Regardless of all linguistic and typographic shortcomings in the large inventory of Kildin Saami special letters, I believe that any attempt to revise the orthography 'from above' would create even more confusion and perhaps conflicts. Computational problems with Unicode, font typography and input devices will likely be solved soon. The teaching of complicated (or even linguistically unsystematic) writing systems is in principle possible, as several cases from other parts of the world show. Note also that Saami teachers and other language users seem to identify themselves with the alphabet specifically developed for their native language. The outside researcher working with language planning should thus concentrate on the provision of the necessary basis for revitalisation (such as adequate linguistic description and language technology), rather than interferring in orthography revisions.

Sorting order. Although the typographic shape of Kildin Saami letters has been standardised and all letters and diacritics are included in Unicode, a standardised sorting order for all letters was never suggested explicitly by the authors of the alphabet.

The standardised letter inventory of the Kildin Saami alphabet can be found in different textbooks for schools (e.g. in Antonova 1990: 130–131), in the three dictionaries (Afanasyeva et al. 1985: 16; Kert 1986: 9; Sammallahti et al. 1991: 6), as well as in the monograph on Kildin Saami orthographic rules (Kuruch et al. 1995: 7). Deducing from the alphabets presented there, authors agree on a general sorting order similar to the modern Russian alphabet, with the Kildin modified letters following the respective basic letters. However, although the two vowel letters with diaeresis are included, following the non-modified vowel letters, vowel letters with macron are not listed. Instead the macron is explained separately as a marker of vowel length.

It would in principle be possible to exclude the vowel letters with a macron from the alphabet, i.e., to not handle them as separate letters.[14] A standardised sorting order is nevertheless needed, not only for lemma lists in dictionaries, but also for sorting routines on the computer.

In the table *(p. 205)*, I propose a sorting order in which all vowel letters with a macron directly follow the respective plain vowel letters but precede letters with diaeresis. A very similar ordering of letters with macrons and diaereses was also suggested by Everson (2002).[15]

Infrastructure for endangered languages in the digital age

Written language production and reception in the computer age has become unthinkable without the internet. Therefore the survival of written languages hinges on the availability of the relevant digital infrastructure. However, computer technology and the internet is not exclusively a threshold that a language must exceed to survive modernisation. On the contrary, these technologies also offer valuable resources for vitalising active production and perception and thus reversing language shift. The internet (including e-mail, social networks, etc.) is an excellent long-distance communication device and is constantly becoming cheaper and more widespread. The internet's role as a local information channel is growing fast as it is becoming more easily available to more people. Last but not least, the internet makes text production easier as it lowers publication costs. One and a half decades ago (long before Wikipedia and Facebook where launched), Trosterud (1996) explicitly described these important characteristics of the future internet as a crucial resource for vitalising the endangered Northern languages. Trosterud was perhaps too optimistic about how fast this development would take place. However, the developments during the last 15 years bear out his vision.

Basically, 'general digital infrastructure' means technology that makes it possible to use a language in today's computerised society, especially in the governmental context, in education, or in modern publishing activities. Any general digital infrastructure must thus include: (1) computer fonts covering all letters of the specific language in question, (2) keyboards for input of these letters on the common computer platforms, (3) annotated language corpora as data pools for language technology, (4) multi-language dictionaries in electronic form, and (5) proofing tools for the most important office programmes.

In the Soviet context, many written minority languages were traditionally used in schools and partly also in cultural life. However, today most minority languages of the former Soviet Union have practically no access to language technology resources (with very few exceptions). Without a digital infrastructure in place, these languages will not make the necessary transition to being functional in modern information and communication technology, and will thus fall out of use in public life. In the same vein, any official statements about recognising and supporting a minority language are only empty declarations as long as we are not able to use computers to write letters in the language, or to correct text or find the correct terminology. Until this happens, the language cannot be put into use in the administration of modern societies.

Available digital infrastructure for languages can be divided hierarchically into three main levels, each building on the previous one. On the first level is the generation of languages which have keyboard layouts, fonts, sorting routines, as well as time and date formats already available. Kildin Saami is only in a preliminary stage of becoming a member of this language generation.

Spellcheckers, automatic hyphenation and electronic dictionaries characterise languages of the second generation, to which North Saami already belongs. South and Lule Saami have also recently made the jump to this generation and have these tools available now.

Building on that, electronic thesauri, machine translation and speech technology can be created for third generation languages, such as Russian, Swedish, Finnish and Estonian.

To make the work on the mentioned infrastructure and tools a sustained base for further development, it is most crucial that the applications created are open source, without any third party owning even part of the source and able to block similar efforts in the future. That means that all gathered knowledge should be made explicit by providing an open project documentation. Furthermore, knowledge inside the relevant language communities has to be fostered. A permanent and sustained infrastructure as defined here is important in preventing existing results from being wasted in the long term. It should be possible for everyone, with reasonable effort, to pick up the thread again at any later point and continue to build on the work already done.

Computer literacy. Creating and providing digital infrastructure for an endangered language is useful for revitalisation only if the targeted users, i.e. members of the endangered language community, can access and use it. Purely technical restrictions, like access to computers and the internet, will hopefully be irrelevant in the near future of Kildin Saami. Although computerisation in rural communities of the Russian North is slower than optimistic forecasts earlier suggested, there is still clearly continuous progress. A much more serious problem – and one rarely addressed in connection with revitalisation and the pedagogy of endangered languages – is the degree of computer (and general digital) literacy among language users.

Computer skills are a logical precondition for using any kind of digital linguistic infrastructure. Since most Kildin Saami individuals who can read and write their native language use computers (at least occasionally) nowadays, this precondition is generally met. In the current Kildin Saami context,[16] however, computer literacy is restricted to a very basic level and computer skills are almost exclusively restricted to the use of very specific applications and a few very well-defined simple tasks. Most typically, these include writing and formatting shorter text documents in Microsoft Word for Windows, browsing the internet – including web-based social networks and e-mailboxes – with Microsoft Internet Explorer as well as using a few multimedia applications included in Windows. Needless to say, any additional knowledge and ability beyond basic skills would constitute a significant asset in using digital resources more efficiently and hence more successfully for revitalisation.

Note that the problem of computer illiteracy is far from being specific to Kildin Saami or other endangered language communities. On the contrary, feeling uncomfortable with using anything other than a few familiar applications for a restricted set of specific tasks seems rather common, even for many people using computers professionally every day. However, working less efficiently as a linguist, for instance, by formatting a research paper in an office programme manually from paragraph to paragraph or inserting and formatting each reference individually and by hand seems trivial compared to computer illiteracy in the endangered language context, where ignoring the very few available resources for revitalisation is much more crucial.

It is definitely the case that the creator and provider of any sustainable digital linguistic infrastructure should also put effort into promoting computer literacy among native language users. For Kildin Saami language activists and potential collaborators in future language technology projects, training has been provided occasionally both by 'Kola Sami Documentation Project' *(*KSDP) and Giellatekno. Participants had very different levels of computer literacy, ranging from using the computer for the first time to being well-acquainted with office programmes and internet-based communication such as e-mail, instant message programmes and social networks. Teaching thus ranged from a general introduction to working with computers (the difference between an operating system and an application running on that system, installing and using common applications for language work) to introduction to Unicode and the proper use of character encoding in applications and fonts, as well as the use of internet-based communication software (Skype, Google, etc.) for file sharing and long-distance collaborative work. Courses even dealt with general database structure and text technology applied for instance in wiki-markup language or XML-based lexicography.

Documentation and technology. Documentary linguistics is a relatively new and evolving field primarily concerned with language documentation as a comprehensive, multi-faceted and multi-purpose record of linguistic practices characteristic of the investigated speech community (cf. Himmelmann 2006: 1 and other contributions in Gippert et al. 2006). Although documentary linguistics evolved from traditional field linguistic methodology with the primary aim of providing more and better data on the world's linguistic diversity for future research in theoretical linguistics, the field is currently developing into a linguistic sub-discipline of its own. Among the most important purposes of language documentation is the provision of data for further research on and for endangered languages, for both further theoretical and applied research, as well as for direct use by the investigated language community. Ideally, the data pool provided by the documentary linguist includes a comprehensive, deeply annotated and easily accessible multimedia corpus of a spoken language. Recent calls for project grant applications, e.g. by DoBeS[17] or HRELP,[18] and numerous recent conferences or workshops organised by a variety of institutions dealing with documentary linguistics, also explicitly include technical, methodological and theoretical issues connected to endangered language revival. If this collaborative approach to documentary linguistics is to be more than just window-dressing, language documentation must first of all also aim at working together with and obtaining useful results for the investigated community.

Beside methodologies and techniques related to archiving and corpus building, which belong to applied research per se, documentary linguistics interfaces with different aspects of language planning and language technology for endangered languages. Here, language technology is understood as the functional application of computational science as it is aimed at analysing and generating natural language in various ways and for a variety of purposes. Machine-based translation or automatic language analysers are but two examples of such practical applications. Whereas the documentary linguist provides language corpora and linguistic analyses necessary for the computational modeling of the language in question, the language technologist applies formal-descriptive linguistic and corpus linguistic methods to the programming of machine readable morphological, syntactic and lexical descriptions of the relevant languages, and thereby creates tools for effectively analysing language corpora and carrying out better linguistic documentation and description.

Although all combined efforts between language technology and documentary linguistics are also directly profitable in the revitalisation of endangered languages, these two fields rarely meet in practice today. One possible explanation is that documentary linguistics predominantly deals with the documentation of spoken language, whereas applications created in language technology are almost exclusively based on written language corpora. Another point is that mainstream approaches in documentary linguistics still predominantly focus on the improvement of methodologies and techniques for field- or corpus based empirical data analyses of endangered languages, rather than specifically including applied research towards providing data and revitalisation.

The theoretical bias in documentary linguistics, which is likely a relic of the typologically oriented theoretical-functional linguistic school from which most current documentary linguists descend, is well-illustrated in the overemphasised need for thorough morphosyntactic analyses in corpus annotation (frequently carried out by researchers manually). While such annotations can be quite precise, they require a lot of time and leave much room for inconsistencies and mistakes. Mostly, a basic transcription, a basic translation into the main lingua franca and a basic grammatical description accompanying the corpus seem sufficient in order to make the language documentation useful, i. e. readable and accessible to further linguistic analyses or practical applications. This is especially true for languages like Kildin Saami, which already have an established orthography and a basic linguistic description available. Rather than providing our corpus with phonological and morphosyntactic analyses and English translations, like many other similar documentation projects would do, we believe that transcriptions using the established Cyrillic writing system and providing Russian translations is entirely adequate from the perspective of making our documentation useful for the broadest possible future applications, including language technology, while also utilising the limited time and financial resources we have at our disposal for maximum effect.

Building a digital infrastructure for Kildin Saami

Regarding digital infrastructure, Kildin Saami is still at the starting block. However, a comprehensive annotated multimedia corpus is in the works by KSDP. Fonts and preliminary keyboard layouts are already available and pilot work on digital corpora, electronic dictionaries and even grammatical analysers has been done. The step to a sustained second-generation infrastructure (similar to what is currently being done for Lule and South Sami, as well as Komi-Zyrian) is the short-term objective of KSDP and Giellatekno. Later, even more advanced tools will hopefully be created by us or other projects.

The remaining sections briefly describe work in progress on the creation of an improved digital infrastructure for Kildin Saami, in which the present author is involved.

Kildin Saami keyboards. Work on functional and effective keyboards for Kildin Saami is currently being carried out as part of the 'Barents keyboard project' (which is itself part of a pilot project on 'Digital infrastructure and language technology for indigenous languages of Northwest Russia').[19] Although there are keyboard solutions available which make it possible in principle to produce text in Kildin Saami on the computer, the praxis shows that better keyboard drivers for the most common platforms are needed in order to further support active use of written Kildin Saami on the computer.

The keyboards currently developed build on standardised designs based on the existing Russian keyboards. They need to be user-friendly during installation on all common platforms (Windows, Mac, Linux) and will be equipped with a user guide in Russian. Furthermore, it is important to provide two variants: one variant uses Russian as the main language and has all special Kildin Saami letters available only through key combinations. The other keyboard, focussing on the minority language, has the most frequent Kildin Saami letters visible on top (replacing non-frequent Russian letters).

This work is planned to be finished in summer 2012. Besides publishing keyboard drivers for free downloading, the project will also propose official keyboard standards to be submitted to the Russian standardisation body. The envisioned goal is to introduce the keyboards into the most important operational systems, like the keyboard drivers for Saami languages in the Nordic countries, which are included in Windows, Mac and Linux.

Note, however that our keyboard solutions can only solve the problem of character input with the correct Unicode. Serious problems with the representation of Kildin Saami on the computer remain, but are out of our hands to deal with. Many common fonts still miss several (or all) of the Kildin Saami special glyphs, and show squares instead. Another problem is that many applications do not combine diacritics with the respective letters.

Kildin Saami digital language corpora. Although many hours of recorded Kildin Saami spoken language are stored at different archives, mainly in Estonia, Finland, and Russia, the first linguistic documentation focussing on digital data was the Kola Saami Documentation Project, a DoBeS project led by Jurij Kusmenko and the present author (cf. Rießler et al. 2007).[20] The project created a multimedia documentation of Kildin and the other Kola Saami languages.[21] Although the regular funding period for the project ended in 2010, the present author continues to work on archive building.

Currently, most archived text recordings are only provided with cataloguing metadata and preliminary orthographic transcriptions. In its current state, the corpus can only be further annotated, presented and searched using the tools created and implemented by the Language Archiving Technology team at DoBeS/MPI Nijmegen.[22] These tools have been created specifically to meet the needs of quite divergent linguistic and anthropological documentation projects. In this, it is crucial, and in accordance with current methods in documentary linguistics, that annotations are linked to multimedia, discoverable via rich metadata and accessible via user-friendly interfaces.

One significant difference between KSDP and common practice in other documentation projects is that we use orthographic representations of spoken language data rather than phonological transcriptions. It is our plan to benefit from methodologies and computational linguistic infrastructure and tools created by Giellatekno specifically for the preparation of a searchable corpus by automatised annotations. The spoken language corpus will later be able to be joined with corpora of written texts. This will result in a significantly higher volume of texts for improved corpus research in the future. Finally, the resulting larger corpus infrastructure will later also be able to provide better resources for future (theoretical and applied) research. For example, lexical resources, such as word form frequency lists, letter frequency lists, and part-of-speech frequency lists will be created automatically. The corpus can also be lemmatised and parsed automatically and thus be used for improving any future lexicographic work.

Last but not least, the multimedia corpus, including acoustic and video data, might in the future also provide a basis for contemporary teaching materials.

Kildin Saami dictionary project. The basis of Giellatekno's digital dictionary infrastructure for Kildin Saami[23] is identical to the Kildin Saami-Russian part of Yur'ev's (2003) *Electronic Saami Dictionary* (see also above), which the author kindly shared with us in digital form. The digital dictionary shows some drawbacks in regard to content, usability and availability. Among other things, the dictionary is not distributed freely, it can be installed only on Windows systems with a Russian language localisation, and its search function needs a special font due to the incompatibility of the dictionary with Unicode. Therefore, we decided to focus on transforming the existing data into a lexicographically better structured XML database, which will later allow the application of XSLT-scripts to export into different kinds of platform-independent dictionary or other teaching applications, for which Giellatekno already has the necessary infrastructure available, see, for instance, the LEKSA programme for teaching vocabulary[24] or the online multi-lingual dictionary portal for a variety of languages.[25] It will also be possible to extend the database with example phrases from the automatically analysed text corpora (see above).

Yur'ev (2003) consists of lexical data found in the two printed Kildin-Russian dictionaries and translations in both directions. However, while data from both sources (i.e. Afanasyeva et al. 1985 and Kert 1986) are included in the Russian translations, the reverse translations are restricted to the Russian-Kildin Saami part of Kert 1986. We plan to complete the Russian-Kildin translations by converting the much larger Kildin-Russian part of the dictionary. In fact, a comprehensive dictionary translating from Russian into Kildin Saami or explanations in Kildin Saami is needed most urgently by students or other language users who are not fluent first-language speakers for creating texts. Needless to say, merely reversing a dictionary will not automatically result in an adequate dictionary, unless the lexicographer has put a great deal of manual effort into refining the resulting database (cf. also Trosterud 2001).

Conclusion and prospects

"Rather than being written for the average American web surfer, the future web page will be written for well-known customers, fellow citizens, or for neighbours. Thus, future web pages will reflect human life on this planet in all its colourful varieties" (Trosterud 1996).

The wish, manifested in this quote from only fifteen years ago, to reflect our world's linguistic variation in the digital world, has already come true if one thinks about the many threads posted on digital social networks every day in Saami and other minority languages, or about the globally free and collaborative internet encyclopedia project hosting Wikipedias, not only for the 'average American web surfer', but also for speakers of much smaller national languages and even non-national minority languages like North Saami.

Quite recently, a Kildin Saami test Wikipedia was launched. Let us make it possible for the Kildin Saami language to become fully functioning as a language of education, fine arts and communication in our digitally globalised world, following the path of other formally alleged 'minor languages' like North Saami, Estonian and Finnish, and finally disprove Nervander's disbelief in the 'capabilities' of small languages.

Notes

1 Kristina Kotcheva, Beverley Stewart, Nick Thieberger, Joshua Wilbur and the editors of the present volume provided valuable comments and suggestions on earlier drafts of this chapter. Special thanks are due to Sjur Moshagen and Trond Trosterud for discussing specific issues on digital infrastructure for Saami languages. Needless to say all remaining errors are my own.

2 Other common spellings are Sámi or Sami.

3 E.g. Popova 1934: *Olghš škola varas arifmetika opnuvəm kniga* 'Textbook in arithmetics for primary school'.

4 E.g. Valerštejn 1934: *Mi lij mogka industrializacija jemnest* 'Industrialisation of the country – what does this mean'.

5 But note that the subtitle on page 1 states '4000 words', which is not exactly true.

6 This dictionary, together with a keyboard driver and the font RuSaDic (both non-Unicode), are distributed by the author, on CD-ROM, or via the website http://saami.su/saami/rusadic.html.

7 http://www.mshu.edu.ru/

8 http://saami-tied.ru/

9 http://giellatekno.uit.no/

10 http://www.davvi.no/

11 In the Kildin Saami community and for some researchers, this dictionary is also often referred to as *Kuruch's dictionary* – after the leader of the working group and main editor (Russian: *redaktor*) – or as the *Red dictionary* – after the hard cover version's prominent red colour (perhaps also with an allusion to the included extensive Soviet terminology created for the first time for Kildin Saami?). According to common standards the authors are listed here alphabetically, just as in the imprint on page 4 of the dictionary.

12 A similar situation has led to the same kind of consequences for today's language learners and language technologists concerning the Skolt Saami alphabet developed by linguists in Finland in the 1970s.

13 According to Aleksandra Antonova (p.c.) this difference was intentional.

14 Similarly, letters with (optional) accent diacritics in Norwegian, like in *òg* 'also' and *vær̂* 'weather' are never listed as separate letters of the alphabet.

15 Note that the order of a few other letters in Everson's document is different from the other alphabets mentioned and published in Afanasyeva et al. 1985; Kert 1986; Sammallahti et al. 1991; Antonova 1990 and Kuruch et al. 1995.

16 This is according to my own observation. To my knowledge, there is no statistical data available, as surveys on computer literacy in connection to general language use and revitalisation are scarcely ever included in language sociological research.

17 http://www.mpi.nl/dobes/

18 http://www.hrelp.org/

19 Project leaders are Sjur Moshagen (Norwegian Saami Parliament) and Trond Trosterud (Giellatekno), see http://giellatekno.uit.no/plan/barents/doc/barentspresentation.eng.html and the project documentation at http://victorio.uit.no/cgi-bin/wiki/index.php/Barents_keyboard_project/.

20 Other collaborators contributing to this language documentation were Anna Afanasyeva, Anja Behnke, Svetlana Danilova, Andrei Dubovtsev, Elena Karvovskaya, Kristina Kotcheva, Elisabeth Scheller, Nina Sharshina, Ganna Vinogradova, Joshua Wilbur, Evgeniya Zhivotova and Nadezhda Zolotuchina.

21 http://corpus1.mpi.nl/ds/imdi_browser?openpath=MPI363060%23

22 http://tla.mpi.nl/tools/tla-tools/

23 The project is carried out in collaboration between Ciprian Gerstenberger (Giellatekno) and the present author.

24 LEKSA is only one part of the teaching platform Oahpa!. For the North Saami version, see http://oahpa.no/davvi/

25 http://victorio.uit.no/webdict

References

Afanasyeva, Nina E., Rimma D. Kuruch, Ekaterina I. Mechkina, Aleksandra A. Antonova, Lazer' D. Jakovlev and Boris A. Gluchov 1985. *Saamsko-russkii slovar' = Sām'-rūšš soagknehk'*.[Saami-Russian dictionary]. Moskva: Russkii yazyk.

Aikio, Ante 2003. The Geographical and Sociolinguistic Situation. In *Siiddastallan: from Lapp communities to modern Sámi life*. J. Pennanen and K. Näkkäläjärvi (eds.), 34–40. Publication of the Inari Sámi Museum 5. Jyväskylä: Siida Sámi Museum.

Allen, Julie D. 2011. *The Unicode Standard, version 6.0*. The Unicode Consortium, Mountain View. http://www.unicode.org/versions/Unicode6.0.0/.

Antonova, Aleksandra A. 1982. *Sām bukvar': dlia 1 klassa saamskikh shkol.* [Saami ABC book for the 1st class of Saami schools]. Leningrad: Prosveshchenie.

— 1990. *Sām' bukvar': dlia 1 klassa saamskikh shkol.* 2e izdanie, dorabotannoe. [Saami ABC book for the 1st class of Saami schools, second revised edition]. Leningrad: Prosveshchenie.

Endiukovskii, Aleksandr G. 1937. Saamskii (loparskii) yazyk [The Sami (Lappish) language]. In *Yazyki i pis'mennost' narodov Severa I: yazyki i pis'mennost' samoedskikh i finno-ugorskikh narodov.* [Language and writing system of the Samojed and Finno-ugric peoples]. G.N. Prokof'ev (ed.), 125–162. Trudy po lingvistike. Nauchno-Issledovatel'skaia Associaciia Instituta Narodov Severa imeni P.G. Smidovicha. Moskva: Gosudarstvennoe uchebnopedagogicheskoe izdatel'stvo.

Everson, Michael 1999. *When is a Descender not a Descender: Kildin Sámi Voiceless Consonants.* Expert Contribution.
http://www.hum.uit.no/a/trond/kildinbackgr.pdf

— 2002. The Alphabets of Europe: Kildin Sami. Manuscript.
http://www.evertype.com/alphabets/kildin-sami.pdf

Genetz, Arvid 1878. *Mah'tveest Pas'-Evangeli: Samas = Evangelie ot Matfeja (na russko-loparskom yazyk)* [The Gospel of Matheus (in the Russian-Lappish language)]. Izdannoe Obshchestvom Rasprostraneniia Biblii v Veliko-Britanii i v drugikh stranach [edited by the British Society for distribution of the Bible in other countries]. Translation A. Genetz. Helsinki: British and Foreign Bible Society.

— 1891. *Kuollan lapin murteiden sanakirja ynnä kielennäytteitä = Wörterbuch der Kola-Lappischen Dialekte nebst Sprachproben*. Bidrag till kännedom af Finlands natur och folk 50. Helsinki: Finska Vetenskaps-Societeten.

Gippert, Jost, Ulrike Mosel and Nikolaus Himmelmann (eds.) 2006. *Essentials of Language Documentation*. Trends in Linguistics. Studies and Monographs 178. Berlin: Mouton de Gruyter.

Gröndahl, Satu 2009. Eposet som nationalsymbol bland finsk-ugriska folk [The epic as national symbol among Finno-ugric peoples]. *Annales Academiæ Regiæ Scientiarum Upsaliensis* 2007–2008, 37: 55–72.

Halász, Ignácz 1883. Orosz-lapp nyelvtani vázlat [An outline of Russian-Lappish grammar]. *Nyelvtudományi közlemények* 17: 1–45.

Himmelmann, Nikolaus P. 2006. Language Documentation: What is it and what is it good for? In *Essentials of Language Documentation*. Trends in Linguistics. Studies and Monographs 178. J. Gippert, U. Mosel and N. Himmelmann (eds.), 1–30. Berlin: Mouton de Gruyter.

Itkonen, Toivo Immanuel 1958. *Koltan-ja kuolanlapin sanakirja = Wörterbuch des Kolta- und Kolalappischen*. Vol. 15. Lexica Societatis Fenno-Ugricae. Helsinki: Suomalais-Ugrilainen Seura.

Janich, Nina 2007. Sprachplanung. In *Angewandte Linguistik: ein Lehrbuch*. K. Knapp (ed.), 481–501. Tübingen: Francke.

Kert, Georgii M. 1971. *Saamskii yazyk (kil'dinskii dialekt): fonetika, morfologiia, sintaksis*.[The Saami language (kildin dialect), phonetics, morphology, syntax]. Leningrad: Nauka.

— 1986. *Slovar' saamsko-russkii i russko-saamskii*. [Saami-Russian and Russian-Saami dictionary]. Leningrad: Prosveshchenie.

Kuruch, Rimma D. 1985. Kratkii grammaticheskii ocherk saamskogo yazyka. [Short grammatical summary of the Saami language]. In *Saamsko-russkii slovar' = Sām'-rūšš soagknehk'* [Saami-russian dictionary]. N. E. Afanas'eva et al. (eds.), 529–567. Moskva: Russkii yazyk.

Kuruch, Rimma D., Nina E. Afanas'eva and Iraida V. Vinogradova 1995. *Pravila orfografii i punktuatsii saamskogo yazyka* [Orthographic rules of the Saami language]. Murmansk: Murmanskii sektor lingvisticheskikh problem finno-ugorskikh narodnostei Krainego Severa Instituta Yazykoznaniia Rossiisskoi Akademii nauk.

Kuz'menko, Yurii [Jurij Kusmenko] and Mikhael' Rissler [Michael Rießler] 2012. K voprosy o tverdykh, miakhkikh i polumiakhkikh soglasnykh v kol'skosaamskom [On the problem of hard, soft and half-soft consonants in the Kola Saami language]. In *Acta Fenno-Lapponica Petropolitana*. Vol. 8: 1. N. V. Kuznetsova, V. S. Luleshov and M. Z. Muslimov (eds.), 20–41. Trudy Instituta lingvisticheskikh issledovanii RAN [Proceedings of the Institute of linguistic research of the Russian Academy of Sciences]. Sankt Peterburg: Nauka.

Øverland, Indra and Mikkel Berg-Nordlie 2012. *Bridging the Divides: Ethno-Political Leadership among the Russian Sámi*. Oxford: Berghahn Books.

Rantala, Leif 1994. Samerna på Kolahalvön: deras situation i dag. *Suomalais-Ugrilaisen Seuran Aikakauskirja* 85: 200–204.

— 2005. Saami studies: Russia/USSR. In *The Saami: a Cultural Encyclopaedia*. U.-M. Kulonen et al. (ed.), 363–365. Suomalaisen Kirjallisuuden Seuran toimituksia 925. Helsinki: Suomalaisen Kirjallisuuden Seura.

Rantala, Leif and Aleftina Sergina 2009. *Áhkkila sápmelaččat: Oanehis muitalus sámejoavkku birra, man maŋimuš sámegielalaš olmmoš jámii 29.12.2003* [Akkala

Saami: a short history about a Saami group, whose last speaker died 29.12.2003]. Roavvenjárga.

Rießler, Michael (in print). Le same de Kildin face aux médias, une revitalisation de la langue? In *L'Image du Sápmi 2*. K. Andersson (ed.). Humanistica Oerebroensia. Artes et linguae. Örebro: Örebro universitet.

Rießler, Michael and Joshua Wilbur 2007. Documenting the Endangered Kola Saami languages. In *Språk og språkforhold i Sápmi*. T. Bull, J. Kusmenko and M. Rießler (eds.), 39–82. Berliner Beiträge zur Skandinavistik 11. Berlin: Humboldt-Universität zu Berlin.

Sammallahti, Pekka 1998. *The Saami Languages: an Introduction*. Kárášjohka: Davvi girji.

Sammallahti, Pekka and Anastasiia Khvorostukhina 1991. *Unna sámi-saam' saam'-sámi sátnegirjjáš = Udc' sámi-saam' saam'-sámi soagknegka* [Small North Saami-Kildin and Kildin Saami-North Saami dictionary. Ohcejohka: Girjegiisá.

Sharshina, Nina S., Elizabet Sheller [Elisabeth Scheller] and Aleksandra A. Antonova 2008. Sām'kilsyjjt (ōxxpnuvvemtyj): 1. grammatika: 2. leksika. Unpublished script. Lujāvv'r.

Scheller, Elisabeth 2004. *Kolasamiska - språkbyte eller språkbevarande? En sociolingvistisk studie av samernas språksituation i Ryssland*. M.A. thesis. Umeå: Umeå universitet.

— 2011. Samisk språkrevitalisering i Ryssland - möjligheter och utmaningar. *NOA:* 27 (1): 86–119.

— [in print] 2012. Kola Sami Language Revitalisation - Possibilities and Challenges. In *L'Image du Sápmi 2*. K. Andersson (ed.). Humanistica Oerebroensia. Artes et linguae. Örebro universitet.

Sergeeva, Elena 1995. The Situation of the Sami People in Kola. In *Indigenous and tribal peoples' rights - 1993 and after*. E. Gayim and K. Myntti (eds.), 17–188. Juridica Lapponica 11. Rovaniemi: Institute for Environmental and Minority Law.

— 2000. The Research History of Kola and Skolt Sami Folklore and Religion. In *Sami Folkloristics*. J. Pentikäinen et al. (eds.), 155–188. NNF Publications 6. Åbo: Åbo Akademi.

— 2002. The Eastern Sámi Languages and Language Preservation. In *Samiska i ett nytt årtusende*. E. Mørck and T. Magga (eds.), 103–116. Vol. 717. ANP. Köpenhamn: Nordiska Ministerrådet.

Siegl, Florian and Michael Rießler (in print). Uneven Steps to Literacy - the History of Dolgan, Forest Enets and Kola Saami Literary Languages. In *Equally Diverse: Comparing Linguistic and Cultural Minorities in the Russian Federation and the European Union*. Reihe: Uralica Helsingiensia. H. Martin, J. Saarikivi, R. Toivanen and M. Rießler (eds.). Helsinki: Helsingin yliopisto.

Trosterud, Trond 1996. *Funny Characters on the Net: How Information Technology may (or may not) support Minority Languages*. BAR-IT conference, Apatity, 16.-

20.9. 1996. http://www.hum.uit.no/a/trond/barit.html.
— 2001. Review of Kåven, Brita E. (red.) 2000: Stor norsk-samisk ordbok / Dárusámi sátnegirji. Davvi girji, Kárášjohka. In *LexikoNordika* 8: 283–306.
Yur'ev, Aleksandr 2003–2007. *Elektronnyi saamskii slovar' = Electronic Saami dictionary*. RuSaDic. Ver. 2.0. CD-ROM.

12 BUILDING YI (M)OTHER TONGUE: VIRTUAL PLATFORMS, LANGUAGE MAINTENANCE AND CULTURAL AWARENESS IN A CHINESE MINORITY CONTEXT

Olivia Kraef

Introduction

In this chapter I discuss current developments regarding language loss and corresponding language revival activities among the Yi (Nuosu) of China. The so-called Yi ethnic minority ranks sixth in size among the officially recognized 55 ethnic minorities of the People's Republic of China (MOFCOM 2009). The Yi are an extremely heterogeneous group consisting of different branches or tribes which are distributed in China's southwestern provinces of Yunnan, Guizhou, Sichuan, and Guangxi. Yi cultural and linguistic heterogeneity, paired with the lack of a unifying, vibrant religious-linguistic culture, such as Tibetan Buddhism or Islam in China, co-determine a process of acculturation and language switch/loss, which has been increasingly evident with the Nuosu subgroup in semi-urban and urban, as well as in semi-rural contexts.

The new Constitution of the People's Republic of China in 1982 granted ethnic minorities far-reaching legal, political and cultural autonomy. It also signified for the Yi an incentive to re-assess issues of language reform and education, whose foundation had been laid in the 1950s, and which had come to a forced standstill during the ten turbulent years of the Cultural Revolution (1966–1976). Nevertheless, the languages of the Yi, like those of other ethnic minorities in China, are in a state of crisis. In an ironic twist of events, this situation may be co-determined precisely by measures propagated to preserve language, such as the Yi language reform.

I argue that the mechanisms which determined and emerged as a consequence of the Yi language reform, can be conceived in terms of an ongoing process of superscription (Duara 2009), which has gained a different and potentially much more far-reaching dimension over the past ten years. The unparalleled speed with which the internet, and corresponding new means of virtual information-sharing, have been developing in China has generated new types of Yi language learning materials, which are primarily proliferated online, and which emerged only rather recently as part of what I define as an 'Yi language revitalisation' movement. This movement employs the notion of a heterogeneous 'Yi mother tongue' (*yizu muyu*), and sometimes a 'Yi mother tongue culture' (*yizu muyu wenhua*) to advance language learning and maintenance among young Yi in urban and semi-urban contexts in China. An analysis of the current and the future design and potential of Yi language learning materials requires an assessment and understanding of the 'Yi Mother Tongue' language movement. As part of this assessment I present and analyse contemporary Yi (Nuosu) language materials in their primarily virtual manifestations (internet), especially in regard to their genesis and potential for language maintenance.

The Yi (Nuosu) of Liangshan and the current situation of 'Yi language'

The Nuosu are the largest of several subgroups (Harrell 2001a), or branches, of the so-called Yi ethnic group, which was established by Chinese sociologists and ethnologists in the 1950s. As allegedly one of the oldest (MOFCOM 2009) *minzu*, or officially recognised Chinese ethnic minorities, the Yi are distributed over Sichuan, Yunnan, Guizhou and Guangxi provinces. Today, around 2 million Nuosu live in what is known as Liangshan Autonomous Prefecture, a mountainous area in southwest Sichuan Province, as well as increasingly in translocal urban centres such as Chengdu and Beijing. Until the Communist takeover of the area in 1956, the Nuosu were organised in a rigid caste-clan system, with a ruling caste of the nobility, or Black Yi at the top, underneath these the serf case of the White Yi, and two serf/slave castes in the bottom stratum. This social structure was branded by official ideology and Han-Chinese scholars as the only 'slave society' (*nuli shehui*) in feudalistic China. The term Liangshan, 'cold mountains', was coined by Han Chinese. Originally the area encompassed a much larger total territory than remains in today's Liangshan Autonomous Prefecture. In their own language the Nuosu call their homeland *nimu*, or *nuosu muddi*, which literally means 'land of the Nuosu' (Harrell 2000: 3).

The Nuosu speak a variant of what has come to constitute 'the Yi language' in post-1949 China. Recent scholarship classifies 'Yi' as belonging to the Tibeto-Burman language family, and as being closely related to Burmese (Bradley 2011; Hu 2010: 3). In the 1950s six major 'Yi' dialects were identified, e.g. the Northern, Southern, Western, Eastern, Central and South-Eastern dialects. Most of these are mutually unintelligible (ibid.). The Liangshan Yi, who call themselves 'Nuosu', or simply 'people' in their own language, speak what has become classified as the Northern Yi dialect. According to Hu (2010: 3), there are nearly 2.8 million speakers of Nuosu dialect(s), including those outside of Liangshan Prefecture. Like the other 'Yi' dialect groups, the larger Northern Dialect group consists of smaller linguistic units, which Bradley (2001: 202) refers to as subgroups. The Northern Dialect is generally divided into three such subgroups, namely the 'large trousers', or *Yynuo* (Chinese, *Yinuo*); the central 'middle trousers', or *Shynra* (Chinese, *Shengzha*); and the southern 'small trousers,' or *Suondi* (Chinese, *Suodi*),[1] with a subdivision into western *Adu* and eastern *Suondi* (Bradley 2011: 203, 204). "*Yynuo* and *Shynra* are mutually intelligible, but speakers of *Suondi* must make a considerable effort to learn *Shynra*" (ibid.). Among the Yi (Nuosu) of Liangshan, differences in language also always go hand in hand with cultural differences, such as dress, headdress, and women's jewellery.[2]

A common feature of Yi Northern Dialect is its own traditional script, with which this language has purportedly been recorded for about 500 years (see for instance http://www.ancientscripts.com/yi.html; and longer according to other sources, such as http://www.babelstone.co.uk/yi/script.html; both sites last accessed on 22 November 2012). This script consists of a pictographic system of 8,000–10,000 glyphs, with each glyph representing a basic lexigraphic unit that developed independently from the (Han) Chinese script. According to Hu (2010: 3), it is also unrelated to the alphabetic scripts of neighbouring peoples such as the Tibetans or the Burmese. These characteristics might evoke a sense of a homogeneous Yi script for all Yi dialects and areas. This, in fact, is not the case. As early as 1913 Mueller (1913: 51f.) discusses the parallel existence of several such scripts among different Yi-related groups in Sichuan and neighbouring areas of Yunnan and Guizhou.[3]

An understanding of the reasons behind both the 'Yi language' crisis and language maintenance thus necessitates not only a cultural and linguistic differentiation between different branches of 'Yi', but also between the notion of 'Yi' and 'Nuosu' spoken and written language, as the main cultural-linguistic group focused on in this chapter. In traditional Nuosu society before 1956, spoken and written language belonged to different dimensions of daily life. Written language was associated almost exclusively with the realm of religion, e.g. the *Bimo* (priest or religious practitioner), whose extensive scriptures and rituals accompany every Nuosu through life. Use and proliferation of written language in sacred contexts stood in contrast to the orality of mundane cultural transmission of songs, ballads and poetry, as well as orally transmitted classical 'texts' with social and ethical instructions, such as the *Hmatmop teyy*, or 'Book of Teachings' (see excerpt at: http://faculty.washington.edu/stevehar/bkhmamu.html).

Bradley (2001: 197ff.) and others have written extensively about the project of Chinese ethnic classification and corresponding language issues between 1956 and 1958. According to Bradley (2001: 199), determining the standard variety within each officially designated ethnic minority group was the most difficult and controversial aspect of language policy – a process whose outcome "was largely determined in advance, but the consultative process was seen to be carried out in full" (ibid.). For the Yi of the now so-called Northern Dialect group, the *Shynra* speech of Liangshan's Xide County was selected as standard (Bradley 2001: 206). From the existing Yi script in Liangshan, a "new syllabary of 819 syllables and one diacritic (representing a tone that arises mainly from *sandhi*) was chosen from the traditional characters in their Xide pronunciation"(ibid.). However, official approval of this new syllabary was substantially delayed by the Cultural Revolution (1966–1976). In the mid-1970s "a group of Nuosu cadres and intellectuals, sensing an opening amidst the declining radicalism of the last years of the Gang of Four, began to agitate for using the Nuosu language once again as a medium of instruction" (Harrell 2001b). Without their own script, they argued, the rate of illiteracy and school attendance could not be improved (Heberer 2001: 230). Their efforts resulted in the ratification of "a modified version of the traditional Nuosu script used by the *bimo* priests" on 1 October 1980 (ibid.).[4] According to Heberer (2001: 230) the

> "reintroduction was, at the same time, an expression of the failure of the policy to compel the Yi and many other people to use the Chinese language, along with Chinese script, as their own language. The Yi were clearly not ready to undertake the unlearning of their own language in favour of a foreign tongue."

Since its ratification in 1980, the new script has been widely used and proliferated by an "entire corpus of elementary and secondary textbooks for a wide range of subjects, [... and] bilingual education in elementary and later in secondary schools" (ibid.). Due to these developments up to 100 percent literacy has been claimed in some areas (Bradley 2001: 206).

Parallel to the standardised Liangshan variant of Yi script (which is also used in the *Shynra*-speaking part of northwestern Yunnan's Ninglang County), other Yi groups in Yunnan and Guizhou devised their own models of script reform. For Guizhou, "the decision was to retain and standardise the traditional characters, but not to impose a standard pronunciation" (Bradley 2001: 207, 208). Although their own learning materials were published in the early 1980s, the Guizhou standardised Yi script variant has not gained in popularity to date. One major reason for this may also be that most Yi areas in Guizhou have been sinicised for quite some time, and therefore lack the necessary human resources to teach and proliferate spoken and written Yi in a school environment. Others lament the fact that the old generation of Yi-speaking or literate Yi intellectuals has died out, and that the younger generation has not been able to live up the former standard of spoken and written knowledge.

For other groups in Yunnan, a "somewhat unusual" (Bradley 2001: 208) policy was employed for script reform. Misleadingly, this new script is, like the new Liangshan syllabary, also known as *guifan Yiwen* (lit. 'standard Yi'). These two scripts are usually only distinguishable by the adjunct 'Liangshan', 'Sichuan', or 'Yunnan', which precedes them in related online sources. According to Bradley, the Yunnan version was "devised between 1982 and 1987 by a committee of Yi working at the Yunnan Nationalities Commission, and approved for use from 1987 in most areas of Yunnan" (ibid.). It is based on a "character-by-character compromise between Eastern, Southern, Southeastern, and Northern Yi characteristics" (ibid.). With some 2258 selected characters the sheer vastness of the new script may have been one of the many 'complicated reasons' which determined 'setbacks' in its implementation to date (LJF 2010).

From reconfiguration to superscription: the crisis of 'Yi language'

As part of the realisation of Chinese ethnic minorities' rights to political and cultural autonomy, the Nuosu/Yi language and script reform ostensibly reconciled the notion of Nuosu and Yi as well as the gap between traditions of spoken and written language realms, and is therefore generally regarded as a success by those who participated in the reforms and the resulting canonisation and proliferation of language materials and instruction. Perhaps ironically, these reforms have not been without their cultural repercussions for the language and culture they have purportedly attempted to help sustain. For the Nuosu as well as Yi groups in Yunnan, the reforms that came to constitute the notion of a monolithic 'modern Yi language and script' initiated a process which could well be read in light of what Prasenjit Duara (2009: 79ff.) has described as superscription. In Duara's interpretation, superscription is part of a complex balancing between worldly powers and dimensions of (spiritual) meaning within a religious context. Specifically, he describes how during the late years of the Qing dynasty (1644–1912), local Qing administration was able to contain, and thus control, (potentially deviant) local power structures in villages in Hebei Province through the expansion of the canon of deities in local Guandi (God of War) temples by Confucian principles (statues). Through this strategic move, the Qing connected to existing structures, which were potentially politically challenging unless conquered, but without usurping or obliterating their original set-up. This strategy proved highly beneficial for maintaining local social and cultural stability.

Although a one-to-one transcription of Duara's concept to minority language mechanisms is not possible per se, the process of superscription certainly bears interpretative validity if understood in terms of a mechanism of ruling, or power discourse. Applied to the Yi/Nuosu language situation, this process entailed (similar to Duara's example),

1 a premeditated, politically determined top-down incentive to contain local identity (minority diversity with official rights to political and cultural autonomy), while having to secure the dominance of socialist state control (in Duara's case, empire).
2 In containing local structures, members of the local ruling elite are integrated in the decision-making process and become actively involved in shaping the canon of their local cult and/or culture.
3 These groups do not regard the interference of the state as an infringement on their rights because they are actively involved in the process by the state, and because the expansion of a canon, or in this case the reform of a language and a script, does not undermine their position of power at the local level. Quite the contrary, it expands, parallel to the state's (empire's) sphere of influence, their own political position within both their (local) culture and vis-à-vis the state (empire).

4 As for the cult or language at stake, an expansion of its canon, or accompanying changes in structure, do not overtly diminish its symbolic power of cohesion.

Interpreted in light of superscription, then, the specific case of 'Yi language' in its 'Northern Dialect standard Yi' variant entailed both the (random) legal identification of a standard dialect for all speakers of the Yi Northern Dialect regardless of their 'mother tongue', and for all students, both Yi and non-Yi, wishing to acquire Northern Yi Dialect. More importantly, it involved both a formal and ideographic reform of 'Yi' written language in its then diverse manifestations[5] into a standardised, homogenised 'Yi' script (a thorough description of which can be found in Bradley (2001: 206, 207). Both aspects of language reform were initiated by the state and reinvigorated with the new Chinese Constitution in 1982, which granted extensive rights to minorities in regard to their political and cultural-linguistic-religious autonomy. Moreover, Yi language reform was implemented in coordination with the new academic and political Nuosu elite. Hence, language reform manifested itself as an immediate, positive effect of the new rights to cultural and political autonomy, but maintained the power of local ethnic authorities and elites.

Generally, the popularity which the new (standardised) language and script have enjoyed speaks for the success of this unique model of language reform in China.[6] Since it came into effect more than thirty years ago the new standard Yi script has been widely popularised via language tools and the media in Liangshan Prefecture, Ninglang County in Yunnan Province (home to *Shynra*-speaking Yi communities) (Bradley 2001: 207) as well as at university level in semi-urban and urban contexts, primarily Xichang, Chengdu, and Beijing. At the time of Bradley's (2001) comprehensive appropriation of the Yi/Nuosu language situation in the 1990s there was

> "extensive publishing of school textbooks up to university level [...], adult literacy materials, traditional literature, new literature in traditional and modern styles, translated Chinese literature, agricultural and political materials, and even a daily newspaper. Regular radio broadcasts and public notices in the Yi areas of Sichuan are bilingual, and much of public life can be conducted in Yi. One result is rapidly increasing knowledge of the standard variety by speakers of other varieties, derived from its use of a lingua franca and language of education and the media. There are type fonts, including various ornamental ones, typewriters, and a computer font, for this script. In addition, a standard Romanised phonetic form for Shynra has been agreed upon, though it is mainly used for teaching Yi to Chinese and others or in citing linguistic examples in scholarly literature" (Bradley 2001: 206).

A study of bilingual education at a middle school in Liangshan in the same time period (Schoenhals 2001) also affirmed a strong sense of ethnic and cultural pride in young Yi students who were speakers of Nuosu (subdialects) while receiving Chinese language state education.

These developments notwithstanding, both written and spoken Yi are currently on the decline. This is true for translocal (migratory) and urban Yi contexts as well as for the language situation at different levels in Liangshan Prefecture. The apparent bilingualism which Bradley observed at the end of the 1990s stands in stark contrast to the current language loss among young Yi, as discussed by Hu (2010). Regarding the language situation in Liangshan Prefecture, a place which has over the past years advanced to a position of role model par excellence for Yi culture and language maintenance, Hu found that many young Yi in rural, semi-urban and urban contexts and regardless of their social background, now frequently speak a more sophisticated version of what is sometimes jokingly referred to '*tuanjiehua*' (lit./iron. 'ethnic unity speech'): local Yi dialect invested with a fair share of Sichuan dialect loan words and Chinese grammar (see also Wu 1992).

The ongoing loss of domains for spoken Yi (Nuosu), and the deterioration of mother tongue use and knowledge among Yi in Liangshan and across China are attributed to a variety of factors, most pertinently: the fundamental dilemmas of bilingual education in Liangshan and at university level;[7] the crisis of China's higher education system;[8] the influx of national television, broadcasted national culture and the generalised access to the internet in semi-rural/semi-urban Liangshan;[9] and intensified labor migration from Liangshan and other Yi areas to non-Yi urban environments, and back.

The implications of a crisis of colloquial Yi have thus come to outweigh by far those of the 'loss' of a written language, considering that this new script has yet, despite its official standardisation, to become a universal means of communication among Yi groups of China. Bradley (2001: 207) asserts that the standard dialect and script have also created new hurdles for Yi/Nuosu language acquisition and literacy among the Nuosu:

> "A speaker of *Yynuo, Suondi*, or *Adur* (or even a speaker of a local variety of *Shynra*, where the rules are slightly different) must learn standard *Shynra* as a second dialect to achieve literacy, and will have considerable trouble learning all the arbitrary extra forms in their correct phonetic spelling; this problemwould not have arisen if the characters had remained semantic rather than syllabic."

A major issue of this script is that "it is based on the phonetic form of the standard *Shynra* dialect" in "which there is a semiproductive tone *sandhi* process that changes a midlevel [33] tone and in some environments a low falling [21] tone into a lower-high [44] tone" (ibid.).[10] Rather than providing a means to sustain Yi language in its original domains, then, the new script may actually signify the first step on the road to a de-contextualisation and subsequent deterioration of Yi language. (Yi) Scholars' main criticism mentions the discrepancy between the original socio-cultural function of written language, and its (modern) representation. As Hu (2010: 3) notes, literacy and writing in Yi script in traditional, pre-1956 Liangshan were almost exclusively restricted to the ruling caste (Black Yi) and to the use of the *Bimo* (religious practitioner) clergy.[11] Although a "number of works on history, literature, religion and medicine as well as genealogies of the ruling families written in the Yi script are still in circulation in Yi areas today," a large percentage of old *Bimo* religious scriptures were burned during the Cultural Revolution (1966–1976). Also, most of the older written sources, or hand-copied newer versions of old Yi script sources existent in Liangshan today are not to be mistaken with the new syllabary described above, but have in turn been influenced by it (Bradley 2001: 206, 207). In this sense, the apparent ruptures in transmission of traditional written Yi script and an accompanying, rapid decline in traditional scriptures as hand-copied and transmitted by the *Bimo*[12] (allegedly the traditional keepers of Yi script) are not exclusively a byproduct of the advent of modernity via television and bilingual education for their children in rural areas of Liangshan.

Criticism is also increasingly audible from the ranks of those wishing to learn Yi for both study and for (re-) affirming their ethnic and cultural identity. This critique is largely based on the earliest, and most comprehensive, Yi textbooks so far. These were developed by and for the specific use of Yi language instruction within university departments, and have since served as the basis for all other learning materials available, both written and increasingly online.[13] I have heard (and read online) numerous complaints from young, male Nuosu regarding *Shynra* as the only dialect available to learners of 'Yi', and regarding the reformed script. The latter, one young Nuosu man told me in 2007, is dismissed by many young Yi on the grounds that it is a 'fake' script, which has been abstracted and devalued, and imbued with new meanings by a commission of scholars, as opposed to being inherent to the tradition of a group of people. The young man said he refused to learn a script which was not 'his language' anymore, but construed by policies and strategies leading towards eventual cultural assimilation of the Yi. Along similar lines, many Yi from Liangshan wishing to achieve fluency in their purported mother tongue are restricted to the standard *Shynra* dialect.[14] In light of these developments, questions regarding available, and standardised, means for language transmission, their quality and effectiveness, have become more pressing.

Media and language maintenance

Although the Yi (Nuosu) language and script reform may be considered a completed project, recent developments, such as language loss and new studies on language domains and cultural maintenance, have been increasingly contesting its theoretical-methodological legitimacy. Superscription of the Yi language is not (yet) a process under closure. Those realities of language loss, which have been co-determined by the initial superscription through language and script reform have more recently co-determined the advent of a Yi language revival movement among Yi *intelligentsia* and artists. This 'Yi mother tongue' movement may prove an even stronger force for superscription, as it merges artistic pursuits (pop songs, poetry) with the political-cultural agenda and (post-) modern media, primarily the internet.

Through media such as television, karaoke and, rather recently, internet and mobile telephone internet access (3 G), the process of superscription of Yi language has gained in momentum and complexity. In her very detailed study of public and private domains, in which 'Yi' is still spoken in Liangshan today, Hu (2010: 8, 16) emphasises the overall importance of media in the process of transmission and awareness-raising for the cause of endangered languages, and culture in general. In her study, in which Hu investigated five domains of language transmission in Liangshan (family, education, religion, work, media), media are limited to conventional media in Liangshan, such as Nuosu-language newspapers (Liangshan Daily) and television programmes (Chin. *Yi Xiang Feng*; Engl. lit. 'Yi Hometown Winds'). Hu (2010: 8, 9) noticed that the duration and contents of these programmes were "fairly limited as compared to their Chinese language counterparts, thus limiting the use of Yi, and the limited broadcasting times affect their rankings in assessments of language vitality." In many rural and semi-rural contexts in particular, Nuosu have regular access to television. The Nuosu (Yi) language television programme in Liangshan has a clear focus on Nuosu culture. The standard broadcast language is *Shynra*. A large share of broadcasts, including national and international news, are in *Shynra*; movies are dubbed in *Shynra* dialect to cater to Nuosu audiences. Also, the Nuosu language channel of Sichuan People's Broadcasting Station features programmes in *Shynra*; traditional music from the Liangshan heartland; and international and national news for six hours daily. The channel, which celebrated its 30th anniversary in 2009, claims to have a regular listening Yi audience in China of over 400,000, and an overseas or southeast Asian Yi community (among these in Thailand and Vietnam) of 100,000.[15]

Hu's media domain somewhat coincides with the platforms identified in Harrell's (2001b) assessment of traditional (in-group) and 'modern' Nuosu media, although Harrell's outline is more concerned with the development of traditional and modern media as a means for sustaining culture towards the in-group, and, later towards the state. Harrell also mentions Nuosu pop music as one such media platform, whose distinct performance, style and content, and of course language of performance, present for him "an interesting amalgam of different mediation processes" (ibid.). At the time of Harrell's appropriation, many modern media in China were still in their fledgling stages. Pop and rock music had just moved out of the tape realm and into new dimensions of CD, VCD (ca. 1998) and DVD (ca. 2003) production, and the Chinese internet was still in its fledgling stages. Since then these realms have witnessed a rapid development to include not only a multitude of new mechanisms for distribution, but new contents, platforms and functions for ethnic minority cultural causes.

The internet in particular has been rapidly expanding and adopting new roles and functions in the process of language, cultural maintenance and awareness-building for China's ethnic minorities (see also Kraef 2012b, 2012d). It has enabled the communication, networking and merging between a tremendous amount and diversity of information, information sources, and different modern media platforms and devices.

And it allows for own, and potentially reversed representations as opposed to former representations by the state through television and film in particular (see Senz and Zhu 2001). These characteristics have led to a sense of empowerment for China's ethnic minorities in particular, and have also made it an attractive platform for Yi causes across China. In 2001 the first Yi-related website, www.yizuren.com, was launched and has been gradually expanded as an information tool both for Yi internet users and those interested in the Yi. At the same time, this platform has contributed significantly to giving voice to cultural concerns among Yi groups in China, and has thus served as a spearhead for all later, similar websites, which are available for networking and resources to young Yi internet users across China today (Kraef 2012 b). These include a vast array of Yi-related websites and local government websites of local Yi areas, and an increasing linkage to Chinese-language blogs, online chat forums, and, most recently, microblogs.

Their new potential for transmitting cultural (and political) causes of ethnic minorities notwithstanding, the content and quality of information available as well as the merging function of the internet do present challenges to the success of precisely these causes. The 'real' threat to a revival, which has become a main cause for cultural concern among Yi internet users may not lie so much in the alleged influx of mainstream (Han-Chinese) language and culture into geographically, culturally and linguistically distinct contexts, where they impact, shape and potentially superimpose language behaviour among young Yi with internet access in particular. Rather, it could lie within the dilemma of the ambivalent role, which some of the main proponents and distributors of the superscribed version of Yi language, are now taking on as 'virtual' advocates of the protection of a 'Yi mother tongue'.

The poetics of virtual 'Yi mother tongue' revival

It is difficult to determine where the idea of a universally valid 'Yi mother tongue', or the recent manifestation of this idea as a full-fledged 'Yi mother tongue' activism, first originated. The significance of this discourse lies in its use of the internet as a means to join the urban to the rural Yi, and to unite modern Nuosu/Yi media (Harrell 2011b) under a common banner. Individuals from translocal academic and artistic Yi groups, most notably Jike Qubu, frontman of *Shanying Zuhe* ('Mountain Eagle'), the most famous Nuosu and Yi pop trio ever, and Nuosu poet Akup Wuwu (Luo Qingchun), have come to act as major agents in this process.

The beginning stages of yizuren.com coincided with the release of *Shanying Zuhe's* seventh album, *Youshang de muyu* (lit. 'Distressed Mother Tongue'). As a reflection of a sense of cultural loss by those Yi who have chosen to make a living for themselves in China's urban centres, it signifies a reproach to 'go back to the roots', a new cultural rhetoric, which is evident in the album title, the text on its accompanying leaflet, and the repertoire of songs performed exclusively in Nuosu, as well as in the album's strong connection to themes of Nuosu language and identity, and its strong message to a young Nuosu (and Yi) audience. In 2002, *Shanying Zuhe* were already looking back on an impressive musical career. Founded in Liangshan in the early 1990s and supported by the local political-cultural elite, the group allegedly became the first all-male minority pop trio in China. Most of their earliest songs were in the Northern Dialect, which earned them musical cult status among (young) Nuosu in Liangshan. The trio later switched to almost exclusively Chinese language-lyrics when they signed with a Guangdong-based record company in 1996. This 'cultural reorientation' to adjust and open themselves to the Chinese market may have co-determined a long-term identity crisis marked by artistic silence between 1997 and 2000.

The release of *Youshang de muyu*, its musical impact among young Yi, and the new karaoke craze sparked by the song *Qopbbop*[16] not only signified another milestone in *Shanying Zuhe's* career. It also marked a change in course and spirit, evident in the way Jike Qubu, an active speaker of Yynuo and grandson of a renowned *Bimo* of Meigu County, conceived of his role as an artist. After 2002, Jike Qubu became increasingly vocal in ways which transgressed the realm of music. Asked in a television interview[17] in 2003 if his calling out to Yi audience in-between songs to take care of their culture and maintain their mother tongue, did not go beyond a singer's responsibility, Jike Qubu answered:

> "The outline [sic] of my blood determined that I was born a Yi of Da Liangshan. The scriptures that I recite, and the mother tongue I speak have determined that I had such a language, such a script, that I am this ethnic group. As an ethnic minority and if you love this country, then you should carry on your own culture, scientifically (*kexue de*) carry on your ethnic culture (*minzu wenhua*). So, where do we start to carry on ethnic culture? We start with mother tongue. So, calling for the use and protection of mother tongue is an occasion for me to express the deep love for my people (*wo de minzu*). We do not only wish to be singers, but want to move beyond that and be 'bards' (*gezhe*), that means that we wish to use our singing voices to testify to these times, to this ethnic group of people, to the people […]."

In the 1990s, and between 2000 and his relocation to Xichang (government seat of Liangshan Yi Autonomous Prefecture since 1979) in 2008, Jike Qubu was strongly affiliated with Yi academic and media networks in Beijing. In 2004/2005 he began participating in Yi-steered, semi-governmental efforts to promote development and poverty alleviation in Liangshan. Until his relocation to Xichang in 2008, Jike Qubu also acted as host and support for several Yi student and community events with Minzu University of China (*Zhongyang Minzu Daxue*, former Central University for Nationalities), which continues to serve as a major platform for Yi diaspora in Beijing. At many of these occasions and similar to the interview quoted above, Jike Qubu would emphasise his ethnic background and sense of pride and belonging.[18] Although his role as spokesperson of young Yi has somewhat faded into oblivion, much of the activities (music, cultural promotion) he is involved with in Xichang now are the result of the translocal network and discourse he was part of while still in Beijing.

Nuosu poet Akup Wuwu (alternately spelled *Aku Vuvu*; Chinese name, *Luo Qingchun*) is another key figure of the 'Yi mother tongue' revitalisation movement. Born in Liangshan Prefecture's Mianning County in 1964, Akup has been part of the Yi (Nuosu) urban diaspora (particularly Chengdu) for many years. He is a member of the Chinese Communist Party, and currently professor for ethnic and Yi literature at Southwest University for Nationalities and Sichuan University in Chengdu. Akup is a long-term acquaintance of Jike Qubu and amply supported the album *Youshang de muyu* by providing textual references for its songs. Since 2004 Akup has been visiting Beijing frequently, where he has also become a regular feature at Minzu University's Yi new year celebrations. His poem *Zhaohun* (calling back the soul), an impressive Yi-language cultural 'wake-up call' that is dedicated to his ethnic identity and his people, has since moved urban Yi audiences (and myself), and signifies Akup's entrée into the limelight of Yi cultural and political activism as a spokesperson for Yi literature and language.

In 2005, Akup began organising so-called Yi Pen Club meetings (*bihui*), the first of which took place in August 2005 in Meigu County, Liangshan Prefecture. In 2007, he convened the First Yi Mother Tongue Culture and Art Festival (*Xide Shoujie Yizu muyu wenhua yishu jie*, CZG et al. 2007) in Liangshan's Xide County. In early 2009, he extended the scope of these meetings to include other realms of Yi culture and language, and related individuals, perhaps to proliferate a common cause, and also to streamline related efforts under a common banner. On 13 February 2009, Akup Wuwu and Jike Qubu jointly convened the *Conference for the Development of Yi (Ethnic Minority) Mother Tongue Literature and Arts* (*yizu muyu wenxue yishu fazhan yantaohui*) in Xichang.[19] According to its organisers this conference was designed to advance theoretical research on the protection of Yi mother tongue *culture* [my emphasis], on ways of language transmission, and dissemination of this 'culture'. Another aim was to develop the creative industry revolving around the production of 'Yi mother tongue' literature and the arts in the new century. The supplement 'the arts' did justice to Yi music as represented at the conference by Jike Qubu and Emu Shama, an amateur singer-songwriter and former teacher with the Liangshan Yi Language College (*Liangshan Yiwen Xuexiao*)[20] in Xichang. As actual conveners, the ethnic language department of Minzu University was listed, among others.[21]

In 2009, Akup began extending his language activism to encompass joint conferences and meetings with renowned scholars from the departments of archeology and literature at Beijing University, with the intent of discussing the relationship between Yi script (as it is still evident in its Guizhou and Liangshan variants today), and the findings at the Sanxingdui sites near Chengdu. So far, two such conferences took place in Xichang. (PD 2010; CB 2010; conference languages: Mandarin, Sichuan and Yunnan Dialects, Nuosu, English) The prefecture government provided substantial financial support for both events.

Concrete academic results of both conferences are still pending,[22] but their relevance may actually lie in the fact that they were organised by Akup with the, albeit unspoken, intent of upgrading the standing of Yi language, and consequently 'Yi culture' on the national scale of Marxist cultural hierarchy and Chinese hermeneutics. With what is considered to be dominant Han-Chinese culture centred around a sophisticated written culture and tradition, much of what continues to constitute feelings of cultural/racial supremacy towards both China's ethnic minorities as well as towards other cultures around the world is based on the ancient history of Chinese writing and written history. The designated media support for the first conference was surprisingly prestigious and substantial (national television station China Central Television (CCTV); and the local TV and newspaper). Also, heated academic debate among the 100 invited delegates and participants, some of whom teach at departments as renowned as the Chinese studies and archeology departments of Beijing University, underlines the sensitivity of the topic, which remains clad in historical implications but which in fact bears much wider-reaching consequences for the cause of ethnic minorities, and particularly the 'Yi' in China.

Akup's events have also attracted international attention, most notably that of UNESCO (United Nations Education Science and Culture Organization). At the *Conference for the Development of Yi (Ethnic Minority) Mother Tongue Literature and Arts* in 2009, then UNESCO Myanmar Bureau delegate and alleged US-anthropologist Baihaisi (English name not provided), reiterated UNESCO's recent policies in regard to protection of ICH (intangible cultural heritage) and language issues.[23] She discussed plans for the filling of a Nuosu-language television series or TV drama for the purpose of promoting knowledge on the prevention of drug addiction and HIV/AIDS in Liangshan. UNESCO's presence at the conference can be seen in light of China's official launching of the drive for the protection of its ICH as part of UNESCO's international policy. The ICH drive has been providing new financial incentives and means to all of China's ethnic minority groups and local Han Chinese cultures for cultural and political development (Kraef 2012a). For the Yi this has so far led to new measures for cultural maintenance and protection in Liangshan (ibid.; also Kraef 2012b), as well as to an unprecedented hermeneutic re-appropriation of *Bimo* scriptures as means for cultural and identity reaffirmation and political repositioning (Kraef 2012c).

Akup's enhanced internet presence over the past six years runs parallel to his increased presence as organiser of Yi language events. On 13 August 2006, he created his first blog called 'Holding ground in the face of Disappearance' on China's most popular blog provider, Sina.com (http://blog.sina.com.cn/u/1249476222). On 16 August 2006, Akup created a parallel blog presence on China's other main blog provider, Sohu.com.[24] The Sina blog has since been out of use.[25] All entries on Akup's blogs are in Chinese. The entries on his Sohu blog have been filed under four different categories, including that of 'mother tongue anxiety'. Between 18 August 2006 and 5 April 2007, Akup filed six entries under this category. On 14 March 2007, he announced the publication of his translated English poetry volume 'Tiger Traces'. The commentary section underneath the entry and an image of the book reveals the deep reverence and emotionality which many young Yi with internet access harbor for Akup's work. Blogger 'Transformed cicada' (*tuibian de chan*) writes:

> "I don't want to say too much, I just want to tell you, that in my and our lives, and in our endless ethnic culture and within countless, entangled ties and numerous ways, what you and your works have released is not only feelings and hurt or misery, but a kind of unprecedented inspiration and stimulation and motivation and spiritualisation; the function of this kind of inspiration and stimulation lies in making many people who don't know who they are understand who they are [...]"

So far, the poem ('Magnificent Mother Tongue'[26]), which Akup wrote as a 'title poem' for the *First Yi Mother Tongue and Culture Festival* in Xide County, seems to be his most popular entry. Also, several discussion threads on www.yizuren.com's chat forum feature a debate on Akup's poetry performances and on the implications of his (poetical) message, for instance in regard to issues of ethnic identity, and a search for ethnic roots (YRLT1/2).

With the advent of microblogging in China, Akup started tweeting on China's favorite microblog, Sina's microblog site Weibo[27] on 8 June 2011. Since its launch by Sina Corporation on 14 August 2009 as the web domain t.sina.com.cn, but more markedly since the inauguration of the new domain http://weibo.com on 7 April 2011, an increasing number of young Chinese (and Yi) in urban and semi-rural contexts have been using microblogs to connect, inform and be informed. My assessment of Weibo so far revealed that the greater percentage of information shared between users with varying degrees of Yi cultural background is Yi- and Liangshan-related. Akup's microblog at http://weibo.com/profile.php?uid=2128010833&page=4 has generated 3975 followers so far.[28] Akup's first tweet ever contains an allusion to the title of his blogs: Mother Tongue, holding ground in the process of disappearance (*muyu, xiaoshi zhong de jianshou*). Like his blogs, his Weibo account runs under his Yi name *Akup Wuwu*, and features regular (sometimes daily) entries with unpublished materials.[29]

'Mother tongue', ethnic pride, and the 'soul' as selling points

Despite their very different biographies and backgrounds, the connection between Jike Qubu and Akup Wuwu and their 'language activism' is obvious. Because they share a common interest, or because Jike Qubu may have streamlined some of his ideas to fit into Akup's general scheme of language and culture protection, similar vocabularies and semantic fields of meaning exist within both artists' rhetoric. Firstly, there is the depiction of 'mother tongue' as homogeneous and 'pure' in an almost primordial sense, and the stubborn (as illustrated by Akup's blog names), female entity, which is located in opposition to a threat of disappearance of non-specified, abstract origin. Yet, and as a second characteristic of both artists' cultural rhetoric, the protection and maintenance of mother tongue is not overtly removed from a sense of responsibility towards the state and its populace (see above interview with Jike Qubu). On the contrary, mother tongue rhetoric is always part of national rhetoric. This also becomes evident in a video of one of Akup's performances of the poem Zhaohun (Chin., lit. 'Calling back the soul'), which is perhaps his most famous poem and which has made him famous on Beijing's Yi stages in particular. The video was uploaded onto Sina Video (http://video.sina.com.cn) by user Mahai Wuda on July 1, 2010 under the heading 'Mother tongue–Calling the Soul' (http://video.sina.com.cn/v/b/34918507-1678562817.html, retrieved on November 22, 2012; 2200 hits so far) and shows a performance of Zhaohun for an audience of probably mixed Yi and non-Yi background people. After the ensuing applause, Akup gives a brief Chinese translation of the literal meaning of the poem, which he always performs entirely in *Shynra* dialect, his native tongue: "Return, mother; return, soul of the mother tongue; return, soul of the Yi people; return, soul of the great Chinese nation/race, return!" [30] (Followed by great applause.)

A third characteristic, which Jike Qubu and Akup Wuwu share in common, is a strategy of merging the promotion of mother tongue with a sense of ethnic pride. Stigmatised for decades by surrounding ethnic groups and, more recently, the Chinese state, as primitive and backward, and, in case of the Nuosu, as a 'slave society', Yi of all Yi areas in China have often incurred these negative vocabularies, in which they now conceive of themselves and of their culture. For Jike Qubu, who received only rudimentary state education but underwent the rigid regimen of *Bimo* training by his grandfather and father, this pride is transported through an assertion of identity and cultural knowledge via his music. Not surprisingly, his recent projects are geared to the preservation of local culture and musical instruments, such as the Nuosu mouth harp (Kraef 2012c), and to public appearances. As a Nuosu intellectual, academic and writer, Akup's recent efforts at renaming the approach of and to ethnic literature in terms of an academic discipline ('anthropological poetry', 'religious anthropological poetry') can also be seen in light of ethnic pride. Moreover, Akup has initiated an (at least on his microblog) outspoken drive towards an increased 'internationalisation' of the cause of Yi mother tongue poetry, which again creates a sense of an active process of redefining not only the terms a language is conceived in, but also its sociocultural environment.

Language activism, the internet, and Yi language learning materials

On the internet, Yi language revival efforts merge with popular platforms frequented by young Chinese internet users of all ethnic, educational and rural/urban backgrounds and contexts. The 'Yi mother tongue' activism and enhanced virtual presence of Jike Qubu and especially Akup Wuwu have 'virtually' influenced a whole generation of young Yi students and their greater social networks extending all the way from urban contexts to Yi communities in China's Southwest, and back – and beyond a mere musical, written, and classroom presence. Indirectly and directly these two individuals have come to act as special interfaces between major institutions of higher education in China, which offer courses in Yi language, literature, history and culture, and young Yi internet users, who may very well become tomorrow's local and translocal ethnic elites.

At the praxis level of language maintenance, initiatives by Yi students and internet users for young Yi of all cultural and social backgrounds to acquire Northern Dialect and the reformed script reflect the language materials distributed in the wake of Yi script reform, and the ethnic spirit which has since become a strong motivating force in language acquisition. When I was a student of Yi (Nuosu) language at Minzu University of China from September 2005 to February 2006, Yi students from different departments within the university had already begun organising free Yi lessons for interested students and young people from outside the university environment, including Yi of Sichuan, Yunnan, Guizhou, and urban-translocal backgrounds, as well as non-Yi. These lessons were held at the university every weekend, and were taught by Yi graduate students from Liangshan.[31] The learning materials were the same that had been used by the former Yi language department at the same university. The department was eventually closed. Like other Yi community events in Beijing, the extracurricular language activity was strongly advocated and supported by the main internet platform for all things Yi in China, www.yizuren.com (see also Kraef 2012b; 2012c). Its main initiators and operators are Yunnan-born Yi Mao Fahu and Pu Zhongliang. Mao, whose current professional life as vice section chief of the security division of Beijing University of Civil Engineering and Architecture (*Beijing Jianzhu Gongcheng Xueyuan*) is only peripherally related to his cultural concerns, and Pu, CASS (Chinese Academy of Social Sciences) scholar, have been very active both on- and offline since 2004, and have revamped the site several times in order to do justice to an ever-expanding diversity of categories, materials, people, and services. They have also built a solid network of people and topics, which are not only regularly featured on yizuren.com, but they use and are used by the website both directly and indirectly to create an interface between the growing communities of (young) Yi in China's urban centres, those in Liangshan, and the Yi cultural, academic, and artistic elites.

Although yizuren.com does not actively promote the cause of Yi language, its own online chat forum reveals a long list of related threads. The online chat 'Mother

Tongue Inn' (Chin., *muyu kezhan*: http://bbs.yizuren.com/forumdisplay.php?fid=8, last accessed 22 November 2012) so far features 24 pages of related chat entries. In one of these from 25 March 2006, user Lucky (*ruyi*) states that she

> "sincerely sympathise[s] with those friends here who cannot speak 'mother tongue'. I don't know how the term 'mother tongue' is defined in linguistics, but I think that if somebody cannot speak a language they can at all call 'mother tongue', then that is something quite ridiculous. [...] There are some Yi, who don't speak Yi, because their parents were sinified (*hanhua*), and they therefore lacked the necessary language environment. But another reason for the not being able to speak Yi is their lack of ethnic pride (*minzu zihaogan*); they have no sense of ethnic self-respect (*meiyou minzu zizunxin suozhi*) [...]."

Despite the difficulty of tracing the varying identities of the users of these chat forums, it is very likely that many of the Yi who are active in the chat forums of yizuren.com and yizucn.com are at least partially congruent with users of Yi-language related materials on other major Chinese websites.[32]

Apart from these online chat forums, information and materials related to Yi learning can be found on individual blogs. On 22 July 2010, user Aniu Yifu launched his blog (http://www.yizucn.com/blog-3814-2933.html) via another popular Yi- website, yizucn.com. His entry from 3 March 2011 is titled 'Learn Yi characters, speak Yi language' (*xue yiwen shuo yiyu*), where he invites "friends wishing to learn Yi characters and Yi language" to use his space blog ('The characters I love with all my heart'), with which he wishes to help "promote the culture of our Yi ethnic group." His platform features phrases and images, which he provides in (modern) Yi script, phonetic script, and Chinese. His page has received 987 hits so far.[33] Blogs by presumably young Yi (judging from user names and profile pictures) also fulfill an important function in the proliferation of online Yi language learning video materials. Proliferation of such a set of videos posted on the Chinese video/audio site tudouwang.com in 2007, for instance, can be found on the sina.com blog platform of user *Musen Haifan* (http://blog.sina.com.cn/s/blog_48b9196301000b0c.html).[34] The three tudou.com Yi lessons (I to III), which he posted on 30 June 2007 were hit 665 times so far, received 6 comments (one comment posted twice), were 'collected' twice, forwarded seven times, and appreciated three times.

Most of the blogs and pages promoting Yi language learning materials feature semi-professional, instructional Yi language video clips, whose origin can be traced to one of China's currently most popular video sites, tudouwang at www.tudou.com. A page titled *Yiyu 600 Ju* (Yi Language in 600 sentences), which can be found at http://www.tudou.com/playlist/id/1634046/ (retrieved 22 November 2012), lists seven Yi learning videos, with lengths ranging from 1:30 min. to 5:35 min., and which were all uploaded by user *Linmu Gujie Yizu CG Gongzuoshi* (Linmu Gujie Yi CG Studio) on 3 September 2007. With 306965 hits so far, this user's tudou.com profile page at http://www.tudou.com/home/jsag/ can be considered a real treasury of Yi online/video learning materials.[35] It also features a link to two clips with simple cartoon clips for children's Yi language learning (retrieved 22 November 2012 at http://www.tudou.com/playlist/p/l1634118.html). So far, all of the online and DVD format video materials found were produced by the *Linmu Gujie Yi CG Studio* (see references to this chapter). One of these videos was recorded in a classroom environment and features a young Yi woman and man acting as teachers, and one other young Yi man and two young Yi women, all in Yi attire, acting as students. The video is 5:35 minutes in length, and teaches words, phrases and simple dialogues in the *Shynra* dialect. It was viewed 4662 times[36] so far, which suggests that it is in fact used as a means to acquire and review basic proficiency in Yi. In a short heading on this 'language' page within his repertoire of materials, user *Linmu Gujie Yi CG Studio* notes that Liangshan Television Station and Xichang College were actively involved in the compilation of language teaching materials and in the production of the video clips.

The comment section underneath the list of videos reveals that these materials are not equally helpful to all users. Although many viewers comment on the good support provided by these materials for self-learning purposes, some voice legitimate objections. User *Guanguang Tudou* notes on 5 October 2010 at 23:31:02 that they

> "primarily need something to learn Yi characters with. This material differs too much from our dialect, some pronunciations are the same, but others are completely different, and I am therefore at a loss as to what to do. It would be great to have language learning videos for each dialect. […]
>
> [T]he simplification of the Yi script has gone a bit over the top, to the extent that some of these characters are in fact '*tongjiazi*'![37] Considering the fact that there are over 80,000 Yi characters, then these surely cannot be completely accommodated by the simplified circa 1000 characters; I really wish to learn the 'authentic' (*yuanzhi yuanwei de*) Yi language and script!"

Several users voice their hope that more such videos will be available in future, and comment that there are not yet enough such learning materials available. Returning to the intricate relationship between language maintenance and ethnic pride, user *Shaochaomin* writes on 10 November 2007 at 17:35:59: "Come on everyone, support the profoundness of our ethnic culture!!!!" Many similar comments can be found on the message board of user *Linmu Gujie's* tudou.com user page http://www.tudou.com/home/jsag; last accessed 22 November 2012). Yet the true impact of such platforms is questioned by the fact that the video, which received the most total views (14881 views! Last accessed 22 November 2012 at http://www.tudou.com/programs/view/_rP42T7qz8o/) on Linmu's page is a music video featuring the Yi (Nuosu) language song *Liangshan Amo* (lit. 'Mother Liangshan') by Yi pop quartet Liangshan Yi Shili Group, with subtitles in Yi script.[38] Nevertheless Linmu Gujie is, to my knowledge, the first one to produce young Yi language movies. These mainly semi-professional slapstick comedies in Yi, which feature amateur actors and tell everyday stories of the lives of young Yi in Liangshan and translocal contexts, are also available on the studio's tudou.com page.

Apart from the operators of popular Yi websites, which now promote and distribute these Yi language materials, the potential of online platforms also seems to have motivated some young Yi individuals in translocal contexts to explore new ways of distributing material, and of networking. One such example is user *Zuzu Puwu* (first name in real life: Wage), who lives in Chengdu, and currently works for a Chinese company that produces fruit juice.[39] On 21 July 2010, Wage set up a Sina blog (*Yizu wenxian ziliao dianzihua xiaozu*; lit. 'Yi digital archive group') at http://blog.sina.com.cn/u/1676595877 (retrieved 22 November 2012) with the intent of building a digital archive for collecting and sharing digitalised sources on Yi history, language, and culture. Perhaps because Wage has been too busy with work this page hasn't been updated since 22 July 2010. Wage is also using other (related) forums, for example Sina's file sharing platform http://ishare.iask.sina.com.cn for the uploading and distribution of materials, such as the original Yi language manual *Yiyu 600 Ju* (see *above*). It remains to be seen if and how networks like Wage's can expand in future, or what potential they bear for an optimised distribution of Yi language instructional and other materials to online Yi communities.

The Yi language phone may prove to be another (digital) information platform, which may prove crucial in the applied use, and thus maintenance, of Yi language. For a while now the rumor of an Yi language phone (*Shynra* standard Northern Dialect and simplified Yi/Nuosu character writing function) has been a topic of discussion among young Yi, primarily in Liangshan. In the online Q&A forum by baidu.cn, *tieba baidu*, we find a post by user *Yingzu Lamo* (lit. 'Lamo of the eagle tribe') from 18 May 2011, asking where such a phone could be bought, which he heard could "send Yi language text messages, speak Yi language, which one can listen to Yi songs with, and which is used by Yi people" at http://tieba.baidu.com/f?kz=1082902700, retrieved 22 November 2012. So far, Lamo received a total of 14 responses, which judging by the icons and/or user names, all belong to the greater Yi group in China. These responses range from users stating that they, too, would like to buy such a phone, to that they have found it difficult to buy the phone despite numerous people having seen numerous related advertisements (around Liangshan in particular), all the way to an analysis of the current user potential of such a phone. Like all other forums I analysed, users demonstrate varying degrees of knowledge regarding Yi culture and language. About the Yi phone user Wind – *Qixi* asks: "Yi writing is kind of like *jia guwen*,[40] or? That writing on the phone screen image looks a bit like that."

My personal search for more information on such a phone revealed many online references to a Beijing-based company, which allegedly produced and issued this phone in October 2009 (for instance http://lib.cqvip.com/qk/80606B/200910/30643892.html, last accessed 22 November 2012), and even a video featuring such a phone (retrieved 22 November 2012 at http://v.ku6.com/show/Tlt14yW3hqvFxgbc.html). So far, I have not been able to verify this information. In personal communication with the author in 2010, young Nuosu in rural, semi-rural and semi-urban contexts in Liangshan stated that they considered the concept of a Yi phone to be quite 'cool', as this device would finally allow them to compose text and chat messages in Yi script, without always having to rely on Chinese characters to act as phonetic placebos. Online chats in particular frequently read like the subtitles to popular Yi songs in local Liangshan karaoke bars: the Yi lyrics are reproduced by using Chinese characters to signify pronunciation, thus providing textual passages, but not their actual meanings.

Conclusion

To date, the Nuosu of Liangshan are sometimes considered to be a sort of cradle of whatever may have come to constitute 'Yi culture' in the minds of younger generations of rural and urban Yi. For many urban Yi in particular, Liangshan has come to signify the heartland of Yi culture, and a prototype for ways to preserve this culture. Relatively untouched by early Han-, empire-, and later state-led attempts at intervention, the Nuosu preserved until 1956 their linguistic and cultural independence both from the ruling power structures, and in relation to other groups, which would later join them to constitute 'the Yi minority'. It may have been this relative cultural and political independence or, put differently, seclusion, which despite harsh setbacks during the Cultural Revolution, determined the long-term successful implementation of the revised editions of language and script after 1980 at all levels of Liangshan, and also at the urban diasporic level in Chengdu and Beijing. Certainly, the purported success of this language reform would have also been unthinkable without a group of early-day vociferous Nuosu specialists, academics, and intellectuals.

These developments can well be interpreted in a positive light, and regarded as having created new chances for linguistic cultural, and also political, autonomy for the Nuosu – and perhaps even a model to emulate for other Yi branches in Yunnan and Guizhou. Yet, 'Yi language', or rather the remains of it, are today in a state of crisis. There are manifold reasons for this development, whose complexity by far transcends the realm of this chapter. Nevertheless, there were and are several mechanisms involved in the process of language development, both as a top-down policy approach and as part of a 'natural' communication between native tongue speakers, which co-determined both the present crisis of the language, as well as its prospects for future development. An appropriation of the 'Yi language' reform in light of Duara's notion of superscription seems justified, both by the notion of Yi script as an interface between religious and worldly/sociocultural matters (*Bimo*), as well as by questions pertaining to order and power structures in traditional societies. Most importantly, I suggest that Duara's concept of superscription also always involves a process of 'decontextualisation' or 'cultural decentring' (Kraef 2013). In Duara's example, an integration of Confucian ideals into a primarily Guandi context expanded the religious canon and thus, by necessity, diversified attention without ruling out the centrality of Guandi's significance for local religious culture and power structures. Similarly, the restructuring and reconfiguration of Yi script and language, which superficially suggest a potential for language (and cultural) sustenance, are in fact creating a new order of language culture. The balance of this new order, which by definition favours some aspects of language and language culture over others, necessitates a homogeneous, clear-cut policy model. In Duara's example, the new balance of empire and local power became a potent unit all the way until its, according to Duara (2009), fateful abolition by the Guomindang during the Republican era. For 'Yi language', too, the incongruence between language reform policy and activism, and speaker reality, is creating an environment that undermines what it was purportedly designed to maintain – all reports of its success notwithstanding.

The media may very well signify the final step in the superscription of Yi language, or Liangshan 'standard Yi'. This is quite ironic when the media have also proven vital, as in Hu's study (2010), for the maintenance and proliferation of standard spoken Northern Dialect in particular. In light of the new platforms for information-sharing and interaction, which it has created for (ethnic) minority groups such as the Yi, the recent, substantial development of the internet in China underlines its huge potential for the proliferation of a budding canon of language instruction materials, which are especially devised and multiplied for an online Yi community. At the same time this function has ironically become threatened by the very same, new strand of superscriptive rhetoric, which can be considered at least partially responsible for these language materials and related discussion forums for young Yi in all geographical, social and cultural contexts of China. The drive for the protection of a postulated notion of 'Yi mother tongue' by a very ambiguous, very vocal, and ethnically affirmative language activism represented by artists and intellectuals such as Jike Qubu and Akup Wuwu, underlines the ambiguity of a set-up, in which language activists and speakers of and for their people are at the same involved in state power structures (government, party organs, universities), which sustain the original overt policies by which their culture, in this case language, was defined and superscribed. Their language goals, and personal interests, are muddled. It seems ironic that those agents signifying superscription are now attempting to continue superscribing Yi language, and the means by which it is conceived and perceived, under the auspices of protection and maintenance, and according to their own terms. As an example, an internationalisation of the Yi language cause via USA-China poetry and research exchange as pursued by Akup may be a welcome and vital development for the proliferation – and thus lifelines – of his mother tongue literature and related audio and video materials. But much of what Akup has actively engaged in over the past ten years is too much focused on his own cause, e. g. promoting himself as a Yi poet. Conferences focused on Yi literature, with the same core group of people attending each time, can probably contribute little to the structures which a language requires in order to be appreciated, cared for, and applied by its speakers. The drive for 'Yi mother tongue' thus creates an abstract environment, which features a debate that actually centres around internet platforms, but whose positive effects on speaker reality among both urban and (at least semi-) rural Yi are pending. These doubts regarding the language revival movement are further highlighted by the varying, and partially low quality of available online learning materials, and the lack of some sort of standardisation of online and print learning materials.

Also, creating a language drive among college or university students (who are avid followers of their professors' ideas, and especially so in a Chinese or Asian context) as the future Yi intellectual elite may not prove to be the most effective way to attain the desired goals. After all, many students who are now graduate students in Yi studies end up in some other business or field which has little if anything to do with their original studies. Moreover, many do not wish to return to their place of origin within Liangshan for professional and financial reasons, and often end up marrying into a language community other than Yi, where any form of language maintenance becomes ever more difficult to maintain. On a different note, and as is the case with many Yi living in urban contexts today, the problem of language switch has introduced a trend which in the long-run may entail Yi or Shynra being completely replaced by Sichuan dialect, even within all-Yi circles.

The propagation of seemingly homogeneous concepts, such as 'Yi language' and 'Yi mother tongue', or the even trickier notion of a 'mother tongue culture', or announcing a drive for 'mother tongue protection', which no one actually defines or re-embeds within the original linguistic and cultural context of 'the Yi', adds to the general confusion that comes hand in hand with the attempt to apply this terminology to one's own language situation. Many young Yi in both Liangshan and beyond, who are not speakers of the proclaimed Yi 'mother tongue' Shynra dialect but wish to either connect back into or share in what is manifesting itself as a collective Yi cultural identity, are unhappy with the limited options available for secondary language acquisition, or future development of language aptitude. Their strongest point of criticism refers to, again, the fact that whatever has been superscribed as 'mother tongue' is in fact nothing of the sort for as heterogeneous a group as 'the Yi', nor could it ever be at least a common denominator of or surrogate for a sense of ethnic belonging.

In conclusion, if the 'Yi mother tongue' revival movement is, as it implies, in fact targeting the maintenance, preservation and revival of language, then it needs to be separated from its twin – the meta-cultural discourse, which members of the ethnic elite are propagating as an alternative to state discourses. Yet the fact that the new set of vocabularies geared to language maintenance is not 'organically grown', but represents yet another set of top-down concepts generated from 'above', could very well prove its downfall. Consequently, the Yi (Nuosu) language revival movement as it can be traced since the year 2002, already seems to be past its zenith. Reasons for this are twofold. For one, the movement will never be able to escape the linguistic (and policy) restrictions within which it came into being. In other words, as long as the vocabularies with which 'Yi language' has been superscribed or at least circumscribed by the state and the minority administrative structure since 1956 are not openly and critically re-assessed, or even reconfigured, and Yi languages, dialects and subgroups of dialects objectively re-assessed and 'updated' (e.g. by means of new and standardised learning materials for Yi as a second or foreign language, etc.), then all other activities relating to language maintenance among the Yi need to be critically assessed. Along the same lines, attempts at re-evaluating and re-estimating the 'worth' of a culture within the rigid, state-defined hierarchy of ethnic cultures, such as the internationalisation of Yi poetry, literary discourse and 'mother tongue death', as well as joint, high-profile, and again international conferences on new historical insights involving age-old 'Yi culture' may be a praiseworthy first step towards reconsidering notions of political dominance and possible shifts in cultural dominance, but not a real indicator of 'progress' in language maintenance. As long as the vocabularies remain the same, or new vocabularies are simply grounded on old ones, suggesting ethnic heterogeneity where there is in fact hardly any, then these efforts cannot be sustainable. Moreover, the willingness to learn Yi, and to practice and maintain it, cannot be instigated as a top-down movement, even if policy makers or activists such as Akup Wuwu are still counting on an elitist – and, towards the state, culturally apologetic – approach to ethnic revival. This model is, even in combination with the joint effort of language, literature and music activists, proving unable to sustain any emotional hype around Yi language learning in the long run.

Nevertheless, what the personal investment of Akup Wuwu and Jike Qubu may have triggered, especially vis-à-vis young, educated Yi internet users, is the willingness to discuss, reflect and share in issues related to the protection or at least maintenance of their own culture and language. Despite the fact that Yi language learning materials are still hard to come by, and multimedia and video materials, which present easier, time-efficient ways of language acquisition as compared to classroom lessons based on written materials, are still sparse, the fact that they exist could already be regarded as a small success. Adding to that the seemingly unlimited potential of internet usage in China, one could very well imagine a scenario in which the collective discussions on the future of Yi culture and language could generate, at least among younger generations of Yi users, an awareness for the necessity of a cultural future. More ideally yet, some linguistically versed individual will come up with a set of learning tools which are applicable to different dialect areas, and which can accommodate linguistic differences while maintaining a sense of ethnic belonging. Such developments, though, also require a re-appropriation of the needs of the younger generation of Yi growing up in Liangshan and beyond, and, as a first step, the definition of younger, more flexible, and more realistic ethno-cultural role models.

Notes

1 In the Chinese transliteration of the local names for these subdivisions, we can see the habit of copying these into Chinese language via standard Mandarin Chinese (*putonghua*) syllabary. This method has since also been mainly employed for subtitles in karaoke videos, as well as for transliterating Nuosu family and personal names, most pronouncedly after 1956.

2 This habit is on the decline, though, even in everyday life in rural areas of Liangshan.

3 In his outline of what is considered Yi script today, Mueller (1913) relies heavily on the findings of Paul Vial's Dictionaire Francais-Lolo, which was published by Impr. de la Societe des mission-etrangeres in Hong Kong in 1909.

4 This date is provided in English-language sources (Bradley, Heberer, Harrell) as opposed to 1 August 1980 inffsace Chinese/Yi sources (for ex. Munai 2011).

5 Not only was the Nuosu script type declared as standard for a multitude of Yi scripts (for ex. Ramsey 1989). Already in 1913 Herbert Mueller (Mueller 1913) commented on the great variety of the then existent Yi script variants, which were later subsumed under the category of 'Yi'.

6 'Yi' is the only language among China's minority languages which has and uses its own, complex character script (as opposed to 'foreign' origins of Uygur, Tibetan, Mongolian, and Korean script).

7 Recent developments and the current status of bilingual education among the Nuosu of Sichuan Liangshan Yi Autonomous Prefecture have been thoroughly documented (Teng 2001; also Heberer 2001: 231; Schoenhals 2001: 242f.; Qumu 1999). In personal communication with the author on 20 August 2011 in Beijing, Chinese scholar Teng Xing, professor, ethnolinguist with Minzu University of China in Beijing, described bilingual education in Liangshan as 'having failed'.

8 The abolition of a top-down allocation of translation jobs for students of minority languages in state departments and academia in 1996 may have contributed to the drastic decline in incentives to learn Yi, especially at university level. The new policy particularly affected the Yi language studies programme at Minzu University of China (former Central University for Nationalities, Central Institute for Nationalities) in Beijing. Together with the Southwest University for Nationalities (former Southwest Institute for Nationalities) in Chengdu, these schools were the only top-level colleges which offered a B.A. degree as well as graduate and doctoral studies in Yi language and documents (historical sources, religious texts in the Yi script). As Hu Suhua related in personal correspondence with the author in April 2012, the Yi language department at Minzu University of China was closed a few years ago. Since then, there has been no option for specialisation in Yi language for undergraduate students. According to Hu however, a specialisation in Yi-Burmese is still possible for undergraduate students. Minzu University currently counts a larger number of graduate students and Ph.D. candidates with a focus on Yi language, culture, society and education. These students are pursuing their degrees in the school's respective departments, e. g. department of minority languages, dept. of literature, dept. of anthropology, and so on.

9 As touched upon by Liu (2007: 325) in his chapter on information transmission among young rural Yi in Liangshan.

10 Bradley here refers to Bradley, David. 1990. 'The Status of the 44 Tone in Nosu.' *La Trobe Working Papers in Linguistics* 3: 125–137; also (in Chinese) in *Proceedings of the International Yi Linguistics Conference*, Xichang, 1991.

11 See also Ramsey 1989: 258ff., who notes that Yi writing is not used as a means for communication, but for divination purposes by the *pimu* priest (essentially the same as *Bimo*). Although Ramsey considers the script reform in Liangshan in his treatise, only limited information in regard to its distribution and usage was available then.

12 Interview with the head of the Meigu Bimo Research Centre Gaha Shizhe Meigu County, Liangshan Yi Autonomous Prefecture, 5 August 2011.

13 See appendix to this chapter, where I list common, written teaching materials for Northern Dialect/Shynra. A common problem with the acquisition of minority languages in China is that there are basically no corresponding tapes/audio materials.
14 This situation can sometimes lead to admonishing remarks in a classroom situation, as I have witnessed myself as a student of Yi Northern Dialect at university level, and was also told about by Nuosu students taking similar courses to achieve literacy in Northern Dialect script.
15 http://v.youku.com/v_show/id_XMTM1NTkyNDQ4.html, uploaded 30 November 2009 by user SRT (Sichuan Radio and Television); retrieved 22 November 2012.
16 Perhaps the most popular song ever among young Nuosu (and Yi) in local Liangshan and translocal contexts: *Qopbbop* (chin. *pengyou*, 'friend').
17 'Mother Tongue – True Record of a Shanying Zuhe Television Interview'.
18 For instance: http://222.210.17.136/mzwz/news/11/z_11_2908.html. In interview with the author in Beijing in November 2007, Qubu confirmed that his self-perception as an artist had changed, and that he felt an increasing responsibility towards his people and his culture.
19 See http://blog.sina.com.cn/s/blog_51ee23290100d19r.html, posted 13 June 2009, last accessed 22 November 2012, and http://iel.cass.cn/news_show.asp?newsid=7948&pagecount=0, posted 31 March 2009, last accessed 22 November 2012.
20 Due to the abolition of the classic job allocation system for students with majors in Yi language, the school was on the verge of closing in 2006.
21 These details are part of the official conference invitation, which Akup Wuwu first published on his sohu.com blog on 6 February 2009. Reposted at Southwest University for Nationalities website *yixuewang* (Yi Studies Net) on 7 February 2009. Retrieved 22 November 2012.
22 Judging by comments (personal communication) of scholars and participants, the first conference in particular had raised new hopes regarding the unraveling of the mystery which Sanxingdui continues to pose for scholars in ancient Chinese history and archeology.
23 http://iel.cass.cn/news_show.asp?newsid=7948&pagecount=4, Last accessed 22 November 2012.
24 Akup Wuwu's sohu.com blog http://akuwuwu.blog.sohu.com/10084065.html. Last accessed 22 November 2012.
25 Akup's sina blog was deserted after 16 October 2006 with only eleven entries (but still total 4,527 hits so far), last accessed 22 November 2012.
26 For complete poem (Chinese): http://akuwuwu.blog.sohu.com/70576937.html, retrieved 22 November 2012.
27 Chin. term for 'microblogging'.
28 Last accessed 22 November 2012. Follower statistics on Chinese microblogs are unreliable as evidence for popularity among Yi netizens though, since many 'users' of this microblog are 'zombies'/virtual machine identities, which can be bought and sold to increase popularity for market purposes. (TE 2012)
29 Personal communication with Akup on 10 September 2011. 'Who is the arch-criminal' is a series of essays, which have not been published in print format yet.
30 '*Muqin guilai, Muyu zhihun guilai, Yiren zhihun guilai, zhonghua minzu weida muqin zhihun, guilai!*' English language excerpts at: http://akuwuwu.i.sohu.com/blog/view/149657176.htm.
31 My class was an official class taught within the Department for Ethnic Minority Languages by teacher Munai Reha.
32 This would require long-term observation, also because many users change names when using different online platforms. User *Zuwu Puwu*, is an exception.
33 Last accessed on 22 November 2012. On September 8, 2011 the page had had 250 hits.
34 Last accessed 22 November 2012, with a total 72,582 hits. I first visited this page on September 8, 2011. Then Yunnan-born Yi Musen Haifan's page had received a total 63,464 hits (since its launch on 22 March 2006).

35 Last accessed on 22 November 2012. I first accessed this page on 10 September 2011, when there were comparatively a mere 11587 hits.

36 Last accessed 22 November 2012. When I first accessed this video on 11 September 2011, it had been viewed 4026 times.

37 Interchangeable characters (from www.dictall.com; retrieved 22 November 2012). A "Chinese character that is borrowed to replace a character that should have been used; this kind of borrowed character which has the same or similar pronunciation with the replaced one is called tong jia zi." (retrieved from www.nciku.com on 22 November 2012)

38 This video was posted as part of their second album *Xungen* (lit. 'Searching for roots'), which was produced by Linmu Gujie Yi CG Studio.

39 Personal communication with the author, 21 August 2011.

40 "The earliest characters ever found in China are the inscriptions on bones or tortoise shells, which have a history of more than 3,000 years." From: http://www.nciku.cn. This user comment reveals the identity of the user – she or he is presumably either Han Chinese or sinisized Yi – in that it re-capitulates a common Han Chinese preconceived notion, which I have heard numerous times, even from scholars, upon seeing Yi script: it is considered to look like an early-stage or primitive version of complex Chinese characters.

References

Blum, Susan D. 2001. *Portraits of Primitives: Ordering Human Kinds in the Chinese Nation*. Boston: Rowman & Littlefield Publishers.

Bradley, David. 2001. Language Policy for the Yi. In *Perspectives on the Yi of Southwest China*. S. Harrell (ed.), 195–213. Berkeley: University of California Press.

Chen Baoya (CB) 2010. *Guyi Wenhua Tanyuan Guoji Xueshu Yantaohui Xueshu Zongjie*. Posted 31 August 2010 at http://www.yizuren.com/plus/view.php?aid=8998. Last accessed 22 November 2010.

Chen Zongguo et al. (CZG et al.) 2007. *Xide Shoujie Yizu Muyu Wenhua Yishujie Longzhong Kaimu*. [The first Mother Tongue Culture Day solemnly opens in Xide]. Originally in: *Liangshan Ribao* [Liangshan Daily]. Posted on 9 November 2007 at http://www.yizuren.com/plus/view.php?aid=4492. Last accessed 22 November 2012.

Duara, Prasenjit 2009. *The Global and Regional in China's Nation-Formation*. Oxon: Routledge.

Dwyer, Arienne M. 2005. *The Xinjiang Conflict: Uyghur Identity, Language Policy, and Political Discourse*. Washington: East-West Center.

Fong, Vanessa L. and Rachel Murphy (eds.) 2006. *Chinese Citizenship: Views Form the Margins*. Oxon & New York: Routledge Studies on the Chinese Economy.

Harrell, Stevan (ed.) 2001a. *Ways of Being Ethnic in Southwest China*. Seattle and London: University of Washington Press.

— 2001b. *Perspectives on the Yi of Southwest China*. Seattle and London: University of Washington Press.

— 2001c. *The Yi and the Media*. Unpublished document. Retrieved at http://faculty.washington.edu/stevehar/bktext.html. Last accessed 22 November 2012.

Harrell, Stevan, Bamo Qubumo and Ma Erzi 2000. *Mountain Patterns –The Survival of Nuosu Culture*. Seattle and London: University of Washington Press.

Heberer, Thomas and Anja-Desiree Senz (eds. and comps.) 2006. Chinas Volk der grossen kühlen Berge – Die Yi gestern und heute. Duisburg: Kultur- und Stadthistorisches Museum Duisburg.

Heberer, Thomas 2011. Nationalities Conflict and Ethnicity in the Prople's Republic of China, with Special Reference to the Yi in the Liangshan Yi Autonomous Prefecture. In *Perspectives on the Yi of Southwest China*. S. Harrell (ed.), 214–237. Seattle and London: University of Washington Press.

Hennock, Mary 2010. In China, Learning to the Government's Tune. *The Chronicle – Higher Education*. Posted 19 September 2012 at http://chronicle.com/article/In-China-Learning-to-the/124434/. Last accessed 22 November 2012.

Hu Suhua 2010. *Assessment of the Social Functions and Vitality of the Yi Language from the Perspective of its Domains of Use*. Harvard: Harvard-Yenching Institute Working Paper series. Downloadable pdf-file at: http://www.harvard-yenching.org/sites/harvard-yenching.org/files/assessment-of-the-social-functions-and-vitality-of-the-yi-language-from-the-perspective-of-its-domains-of-use.pdf. Accessed and downloaded 1 September 2011.

Huang Xing (HX) 2003. *Minority Language Planning of China in Relation to Use and Development*. Retrieved at http://www.sil.org/asia/ldc/parallel_papers/huang_xing.pdf, 22 November 2012.

Humes, Bruce. *'The Last Quarter of the Moon': Evenki Place Names Behind the Hanzi*. Posted at http://www.bruce-humes.com/?p=5773, Retrieved 22 November 2012.

Jike Qubu. *Yizren Muyu Qingjie* [Yi People Mother Tongue Complex]. http://v.26vv.cn/s_tudou_programs/view/1wyeDcFHrus, Retrieved 22 November 2012.

Kraef, Olivia 2012a. Spiel mit dem Feuer – Chinas immaterielles Kulturerbe und der Schutz von Minderheitenkultur am Beispiel des Liangshan Yi Fackelfestivals. *Das Argument*, Heft 296 (2012/1-2), Schönes neues China. W. Adolphi u.a. (Hg.), 154–166. Hamburg: Argument Verlag.

— 2012b. Wangluo dui Yizu (Nuosu) wenhua de baohu zuoyong – Cong (liuxing) yinyue de jiaoluo lai tan [The Function of the Internet in Preserving Yi (Nuosu-Yi) Culture – The example of (pop) music]. In *Liangshan Minzu Yanjiu*, [Liangshan Nationalities Studies], October 2012 (Serial No. 22), 191–196.

— 2012c. Strumming the 'Lost Mouth Chord' – Discourses of Preserving the Nuosu-Yi Mouth Harp. In *Music as Intangible Cultural Heritage: Policy, Ideology and Practice*, K. Howard (Hg.), 77–98. Surrey: Ashgate Press.

— 2012d. The Yi and the Internet – Promoting Ethnicity and Ethnic Identity in Chinese Virtuality. *Pacific Geographies (formerly Pacific News)*, 39: 26–30 (January/February 2013). Hamburg.

— 2013. 'Rescuing Bimo from Religion' – The Cultural Predicaments of Nuosu (Yi) 'Bimo Culture' (Working Title). In *Religious Revival and Chinese Ethnic Minorities*, Liang Yongjia (ed.). Oxon: Routledge (*Forthcoming*).

Liang Yongjia 2012. Superscription Without Encompassment: Turning Gwer Sa La Festival into Intangible Cultural Heritage. In *Religious Revival and Chinese Ethnic Minorities.* Liang Yongjia (ed.). Oxon: Routledge (*Forthcoming*).

Li Jinfa. *Liangshan Guifan Yiwen Shishi Chenggong dui Quanguo Yiwen Tongyi de Yiyi* [The implications of the successful implementation of Liangshan standard Yi for a national, unified Yi script]. 2010. Posted 18 September 2010 at http://222.210.17.136/mzwz/news/9/z_9_43090.html. Last accessed 22 November 2012.

Lin Yi 2006. Choosing between Ethnic and Chinese Citizenship: the Educational Trajectories of Tibetan Minority Children in Northwestern China. In *Chinese Citizenship: Views Form the Margins.* V. L. Fong and R. Murphy (eds.), 41–67. Oxon & New York: Routledge Studies on the Chinese Economy.

Liu Zhengfa 2007. *Liangshan Yizu Jiazhi Wenhua Chuancheng de Jiaoyu Renleixue Yanjiu* [Educational-Anthropological Research on the Transmission of Clan/Family Culture among the Yi of Liangshan]. Beijing: Zhongyang Minzu Daxue Chubanshe [Minzu University Publishing House].

Ma Rong 2013. Another 'Dual Structure' in Contemporary Chinese Society. In *Religious Revival and Chinese Ethnic Minorities*, Liang Yongjia (ed.). Oxon: Routledge (*Forthcoming*).

MOFCOM (Ministry of Commerce of People's Republic of China) 2009. *Population and Ethnic Groups of the People's Republic of China.* Reposted 22 March 2009 by Economic and Commercial Counsellor's Office of the Embassy of the People's Republic of China in the Kingdom of Norway at http://no2.mofcom.gov.cn/aarticle/aboutchina/nationality/200903/20090306117655.html. Retrieved 22 November 2012.

Mueller, Herbert 1913. Beiträge zur Ethnographie der Lolo. In *Katalog der Sammlung Weiss im Königlichen Museum für Völkerkunde zu Berlin*, H. Mueller (Hg.), 38–69. Berlin: Dietrich Reimer Verlag.

Mullaney, Thomas S. 2010. *Coming to Terms with the Nation – Ethnic Classification in Modern China.* Berkeley: University of California Press.

Munai Reha 2011. *Zunzhong Lishi. Zunzhong Ben Minzu Renmin de Yiyuan he Xuanze – 'Yiwen Guifan Fang'an' Dansheng de Lishi Guocheng* [Respecting History, Respecting the Will and Choice of the Yi People – The Historical Process of the Genealogy of 'Standard Yi']. Originally published in Zhongguo Minzu Bao. Reposted at http://www.chinesefolklore.org.cn/blog/?uid-2-action-viewspace-itemid-20964 on 21 January 2011. Last accessed 22 November 2012.

D'Ollone, Henri Marie Gustave 1911. *Mission d'Ollone, 1906–1909. Les Derniers barbares: Chine, Tibet, Mongolie, par le commandant d'Ollone.* Paris: P. Lafitte. Downloaded at http://classiques.uqac.ca/clas-siques/ollone_henri_d/derniers_

barbares/ollone_barbares.pdf. Last accessed 22 November 2012.

Pushi Daling (Pu Zhongliang) (PD) 2010. *'Shoujie Guyiwen yu Sanxingdui Wenhua Tanyuan' Xueshu Yantaohui zai Xichang Longzhong Zhaokai.* [The first academic conference on ancient Yi script and Sanxingdui culture held in Xichang] Posted 21 April 2010 at http://www.yizuren.com/plus/view.php?aid=7024 last accessed 22 November 2012.

Qumu Tiexi 1999. Liangshan Yizu Zizizhou de Shuangyu Jiaoyu [Bilingual Education in Liangshan Yi Autonomous Prefecture]. In *Minzu Jiaoyu Yanjiu* 1999/2. Retrieved http://www.yizuren.com/plus/view.php?aid=4459 on 22 November 2012.

Ramsey, Robert S. 1989. *The Languages of China*. New Jersey: Princeton University Press.

Schoenhals, Martin 2001. Education and Ethnicity among the Liangshan Yi. In *Perspectives on the Yi of Southwest China*, S. Harrell (ed.), 238–255. Berkeley: University of California Press.

Senz, Anja-Desiree and Zhu Yi 2001. *Von Ashima zu Yi-Rap: Die Darstellung nationaler Minderheiten in den chinesischen Medien am Beispiel der Yi-Nationalität.* Duisburger Arbeitspapiere Ostasienwissenschaften, Universität Duisburg-Essen, Institut für Ostasienwissenschaften.

Shanying Zuhe ('Mountain Eagle') 2003. *Youshang de Muyu.* ISR: CNG040331200. Issued by: Chengdu Yinxiang Chubanshe.

Teng Xing 2001. *Wenhua Bianqian yu Shuangyu Jiaoyu: Liangshan Yizu Shequ Jiaoyu Renleixue de Tianye Gongzuo yu Wenben Zhuanshu* [Culture Change and Bilingual Education A compilation of fieldwork and written sources from Yi communities in Liangshan]. Beijing: Jiaoyu Kexue Chubanshe.

The Economist (TE) 2012. *The Power of Microblogs: Zombie Followers and Fake Retweets – The state is responding to microblogs and the rumours they start.* Posted 17 March 2012 at http://www.economist.com/node/21550333, retrieved 22 November 2012.

Wang Yuxiang and JoAnn Phillion 2009. Minority Language Policy and Practice in China: The Need for Multicultural Education. *International Journal of Multicultural Education,* 11(1): 1–14.

Wei Anduo (ed. and comp.) 2004. *Liangshan Yizu Wenhua Yishu Yanjiu* [The Research of the Culture and Art of Yi Nationality in Liangshan]. Chengdu Sichuan Minzu Chubanshe [Sichuan Minorities Publishing House].

Wu Da 2003. Yuyan Wenzi yu Liangshan Yizu de Wenhua Rentong. [Language and Script and Cultural Identification]. In *Zhongguo Yixue, Di er ji* [Chinese Yi Studies, Volume 2], Dai Qingxia (ed.), 64–86. 2003. Beijing: Minzu Chubanshe [Nationalities Publishing House]. Reposted by Southwest University of Nationalities Net on 3 March 2012 at http://222.210.17.136/mzwz/news/2/z_2_53990.html, 171 hits so far. Retrieved 22 November 2012.

— 1998. "Han Yi 'Tuanjiehua' he Yi Han Shangyu Jiaoxue" [Han-Yi 'Tuanjiehua' and Yi-Han Bilingual Education]. In *Shuangyu Jiaoxue yu Yanjiu, Di yi ji* [Bilingual Education and Research, Volume 1], Zhu Chongxian and Wang Yuanxin (eds.), 118–130. Beijing: Zhongyang Minzu Daxue Chubanshe [Minzu University Publishing House].

Xibu Xinwen [Western News] (XX). *Jike Qubu – Wo shi yige Yiren* [Jike Qubu: I am an Yi]. Interview with Jike Qubu. Posted 1 September 2007 with Southwest University for Nationalities Net at http://222.210.17.136/mzwz/news/11/z_11_2908.html, Retrieved 22 November 2012. Views so far: 230. Repost of China Central Television (CCTV) Interview with Jike Qubu on 3 August 2004, posted on cctv.com at http://www.cctv.com/west/20040803/101251.shtml. Retrieved 22 November 2012.

Yiren Luntan (YRLT1/2). *Online chat forum for young Yi* (http://bbs.yizuren.com); retrieved at http://bbs.yizuren.com/archiver/?tid-54576.html and http://bbs.yizuren.com/archive1r/?tid-50697.html. Last accessed 22 November 2012.

Zhu Wenxu, Munai Reha and Chen Guoguang 2006. *Yiyu Jichu Jiaocheng* [Basic Yi]. Beijing: Zhongyang Minzu Daxue Chubanshe [Publishing House of Minzu University of China].

13 BILINGUAL INTERCULTURAL EDUCATION IN THE ANDES

Teresa Valiente Catter and Michael Dürr

Introduction

The main aim of this article is to present the practice of intercultural bilingual education in Latin America, focussing on the Andes and the varieties of Quechua. We will discuss some central political, organisational, social and economic aspects of intercultural bilingual education, as well as the actors and their discourses, following the lines of this volume to supply the reader with a comparative perspective.[1]

In the Andean highlands of Peru and Bolivia, and in parts of Ecuador, the indigenous peoples still form the majority of the population. Among the languages spoken there, the most prominent are the various varieties of Quechua, showing such a diversity that it may be even appropriate to speak of 'Quechuan languages', with a total of approximately eight or possibly up to ten million speakers. Moreover, in the Amazonian regions in the east of these countries, there are scores of smaller languages belonging to various linguistic families, including varieties of Quechua, each with between a few dozen and some tens of thousands of speakers.

In the 16th century, the region came under the influence of Spanish colonial administrative and missionary efforts, resulting in the establishment of Spanish as the dominant and most prestigious language. Nevertheless, language policy also meant conversion to Christianity in the various indigenous languages until 1770, when Charles III enacted a law stating that Spanish was to be used exclusively as the language of communication all over his possessions in the Americas. As a principle of this policy, at least in theory, all indigenous subjects had to speak Spanish, and the use of indigenous languages in education and religious service from then on was forbidden – a ban surviving the colonial era and lasting into the 20th century.

Educational programmes aimed at the various indigenous languages started systematically by the foreign Summer Institute of Linguistics (SIL) as late as 1945 in Peru and in the early 1950s in Ecuador and Bolivia, since then varying in intensity, methodology, and in their pedagogical and political goals. Unfortunately, even in the case of Quechua, all these efforts could not avoid a considerable language shift to Spanish: "What the shift amounts to is an increase in the amount of bilingualism, coupled with a sort of collective decision not to hand on the language to the next generation" (Adelaar 2006: 14–15).

The role of indigenous language in the national education systems

Previous discussions and efforts of anthropologists, linguists, language planners and politicians culminated in 1975, when in Peru Quechua became the second national language along with Spanish, and a unified alphabet was established.

What results can be found after 35 years of implementation of bilingual intercultural education in the Andes? The main components are pedagogical innovation, intercultural perspective and a methodology starting with the indigenous language as the first language, later turning to Spanish as the second and national language and finally to English as the foreign and international language. Participation of the indigenous organisations in the decision process is granted. Such proposals have to be viewed against the background of a rural educational reality with high dropout rates, low yields, and frequent repetition and over-age in the school years.

Quechua as the first language of most children in the rural areas of the Andes became the starting point for teaching reading and writing, thus becoming a vehicle of education.

But except for teaching materials, for the most part restricted to primary education, and official texts, such as the constitution, occasional short articles in newspapers, and a few religious texts, little was published in Quechua – as printed books in general, even in Spanish, are hard to find in rural areas. Some radio and a few TV programmes in Quechua, mostly presenting folklore on a regional level, are broadcasted regularly, but national and international productions in Spanish, such as the telenovelas, are far more popular and leave their mark on individual and collective longings.

In primary schools, the first two years focus on Quechua, whereas the dominant language Spanish is introduced only gradually as a second language by listening and memorising just single words and phrases. Teaching becomes more and more bilingual in the third or fourth grade, and reading and writing experience a shift towards Spanish. The goal is to achieve bilingualism in Quechua and Spanish according to the so-called maintenance model, i. e., the use of both the indigenous language and Spanish throughout the primary years, depending on the subjects and the grade.

Although all official statements refer only to this maintenance model, many actors – politicians as well as members of the indigenous communities – consider this phase as crucial for switching to Spanish as the only language suited to preparing children for their future life in a national and global context. These actors implicitly or even sometimes overtly prefer a transitional model of education that results in the children giving up their first language as a vehicle of communication.

In fact, except for a few programmes using Quechua up to university level, all higher levels of education, through secondary, high school and university, make use of Spanish exclusively. And even in primary school from third grade on, mathematics and science tend to be taught in Spanish.

Developing bilingual intercultural curricula

An adequate curriculum has to be the starting point of all considerations to design the educational process. Such a curriculum is mandatory as the guideline for the preparation of textbooks, teaching and learning materials, and for the training of teachers. Questions as to the what, how, when and by whom of learning are vitally important to be answered by the curriculum (von Gleich and Valiente 2005).

In most cases, teaching materials for Quechua follow the lines of the national curriculum and are slightly modified versions translated from Spanish. A point discussed in Ecuador, Bolivia and, at least for Amazonia, in Peru since the 1990s, is the necessity to develop specific indigenous curricula and to increase the degree of participation of indigenous groups in such development. The influence of participation and the relevance of indigenous curricula in educational practice may vary considerably on the national or even regional level from one legislative period to the next, as can be most prominently seen from the developments in Bolivia since the assumption to the presidency of Evo Morales in 2006.

Sometimes, curricula have been specifically developed by indigenous language experts for Quechua (Adelaar 2006: 14): "Best known are the experimental programs of bilingual education, [...], that were operational in Puno (Peru) and in Quito (Ecuador) during the 1980s and 1990s, as well as the current intercultural bilingual education program PROEIB Andes in Cochabamba (Bolivia)." These curricula reflect Andean cultural concepts focussing on the local way of life the children are familiar with. In 1988, indigenous educators from Ecuador declared the following criteria essential for creating a curriculum (von Gleich and Valiente 2005):

- elaboration of a curriculum that respects and preserves indigenous knowledge and that is in line with the indigenous way of thinking.
- inclusion of indigenous schemata, classifications, and concepts, e.g. of space and time, in the content of the various subjects.
- design of curricula and programmes that are related to the needs, interests and aspirations of indigenous peoples.

In the curriculum, an Andean world view is presented, in part reflecting the discussions of anthropologists, that often simplifies and generalises indigenous concepts to a Pan-Andean level of abstraction. As in the case of the curriculum currently used in Ecuador, this may lead to refusal by the indigenous families, but also by the indigenous teachers (Valiente 2011: 106): "Many teachers also reject the application of a curriculum incomprehensible in meaning and function, and return to the established curriculum." [2]

Important for developing curricula and school materials is the interdependence between the languages involved and the teaching and learning content. Which language will be apt for a given curriculum content? The natural and social environment of the children is presented in the indigenous language. As these topics are in focus in the first three years of school, this orientation neatly fits with the necessity to start teaching with the first language. The more elaborate curriculum content from the fourth grade on, such as for mathematics and science, starts to be introduced at least in part translated or paraphrased from Spanish, to be later substituted by Spanish texts in the higher classes.

In the intercultural approach, the complementarity of different perspectives of knowledge plays an important role in the development of learning content. How do we relate knowledge developed from the experiences of everyday life to the principle of 'universal' science? Answering this question implies recognition of various forms of knowledge and the need for epistemological decentralisation: a) knowledge for solving problems of everyday life, i. e. the development of practical knowledge and genuine forms of abstraction and b) knowledge as a process of abstraction from concrete experiences based on inquiry, observation, measurement, comparison, interpretation and speculation. Thus the knowledge acquired empirically is exposed to stimulating reflections and innovation skills. Intercultural processes take place (von Gleich and Valiente 2005: 147) as follows:

- in the interaction of indigenous people with mestizos (in technical Spanish as a second language),
- in the mastery of concepts and practices of mestizo culture in solving problems of daily life (e. g. in mathematics),
- in the application of local knowledge and the adaptation of other elements of indigenous knowledge to the needs of the communities (in natural history)
- and in the search for the reasons for the current social conflicts and for a new social order based on traditional Andean values (in social studies).

Until recently, these indigenous curricula have been dedicated to, but from an intercultural perspective also restricted to, rural regions characterised by an indigenous majority. With the new education law of 2010, education in Bolivia is officially proclaimed to be a national issue and intercultural bilingual curricula are to be established for the whole country, expanding their realm to the indigenous as well as the mestizo population living in the urban centres. Thus, indigenous languages are starting to be taught as a second language to Spanish-speaking children, including aspects of indigenous knowledge.

Cultural and linguistic routines not only vary between Spanish and Quechua, but also within Quechua. It is therefore crucial to choose a well-suited variety as the standard for the written teaching materials to be printed.

In Peru, with its numerous different dialects of Quechua I and II, there was no possibility to establish a single written standard because the differences are so great that some varieties are mutually unintelligible. Therefore, in 1976, six dialect clusters were identified as the basis of the written regional varieties of Quechua (from the

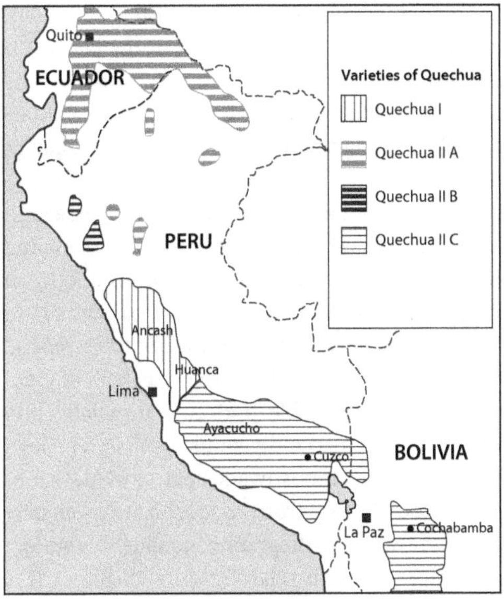

|26| Map showing the main varieties of Quechua in Ecuador, Peru, and Bolivia.

North to the South): San Martín (II B), Cajamarca (II A), Ancash (I), Huanca (I), Ayacucho (II C) and Cuzco (II C). These standardised varieties used in education are compromises resulting from the generalisation of more or less mutually intelligible dialects with similar phonemics, morphology and lexicon. The choice of the respective teaching materials is a political and administrative decision, liable to be reconsidered, as in the case of the Quechua II C varieties, that by now show a tendency to be treated as a single variety. And, of course, local dialects do not in every case correspond with administrative boundaries. As a result, in some communities in Peru the school books do not represent the local variety spoken by the children, thus causing difficulties in teaching and in the perception of the children. Some non-governmental organisations, such as the Summer Institute of Linguistics, preferred to produce strictly local materials in editions of very few copies. From the local perspective, this might be the most appropriate solution, but such an alternative turns out to cause not only an administrative burden and high printing costs, but also leads to a cleavage in language identity.

The regional varieties of Quechua in Ecuador (II A) and in Bolivia (II C) do not differ as significantly as in Peru, so that it was possible to create a single written standard for the whole of each country. For the Bolivian varieties, the official orthography was issued in Cochabamba in 1983, and has been used since then as the single unified written standard, although some variation in practice may be found, in part resulting from regional varieties, and in part from non-linguistic or non-pedagogical reasons. In Ecuador until 1998, a so-called ethnophonemic spelling was used, but since then, the general spelling conventions for Quechua are more or less the same in all three countries.

Ethnophonemic spellings follow the lines of the orthography of the national language, for Spanish most notably in the case of the phoneme /k/, which is written with <qu> before /e/ and /i/, and with <c> elsewhere. This convention was also used in the indigenous languages,[3] e.g. Ecuadorian Quechua <quiru> for /kiru/ 'tooth'. But now, in all official orthographies for Quechua, the phoneme /k/ is represented by the single grapheme <k>. Such ethnophonemic spellings that were also used in Peru and Bolivia before the establishment of the official orthographies in the late 1970s and 1980s, have often been advocated for minority languages, as the same writing conventions for the national language and for the minority languages may facilitate learning of the second language, regardless of whether or not this is the national or an indigenous language.[4]

Sometimes, the phonemic systems of the languages involved lead to a pedagogical dilemma. Should orthography be based on the three phonemic vowels /i/, /u/ and /a/ of most Quechua varieties, excluding the allophonic variants [e] of /i/ and [o] of /u/ from writing, or should it represent the five vowels <i>, <e>, <u>, <o> and <a> to make the learning of Spanish as second language easier, as ignoring the /i/ vs. /e/ and /u/ vs. /o/ distinction of Spanish is a typical error made by native speakers of Quechua, e.g. the loan words <misa> 'mass' vs. <mesa> 'table' both turn invariably into [mesa] in most Quechua varieties and in the regional indigenous Spanish. The lowered allophones [e] and [o] of /i/ and /u/ are found mostly adjacent to uvular stops and fricatives. The following examples with uvular /q/ from Ayacucho are given here for illustrative purposes in five- and in three-vowel orthography: <qollqe> / <qullqi> 'silver, money' or <qellu> / <qillu> 'yellow', but with velar /k/ only <kullu> / (the same) 'tree-trunk' or <kiru> / (the same) 'tooth'. Some sound shifts related to stops, as for instance in the change in some varieties of velar /k/ to a fricative /x/ may lead to problems of the best choice of representation: Ayacucho <huk> sounds [huk], but Cuzco <huk> [hux].

Differences in phonemics, grammar and lexicon also may cause difficulties in understanding, even for related varieties of Quechua. In the Cuzco region (Quechua II C), there is a three-fold distinction for stops – simple, aspirated and glottalised, as can be seen from the minimal pairs <tanta> 'gathering, meeting', <thanta> 'old, used, worn' and /t'anta/ 'bread'. But the Ayacucho variety (also Quechua II C) has <tanta> as a cognate for Cuzco <t'anta> 'bread', an articulation leading to misunderstanding with <tanta> 'gathering, meeting' by a Cuzco speaker. Some more examples of stops in Cuzco are <qella> 'lazy' and <q'ellu> 'yellow', whereas in Ayacucho the corresponding words <qella> and <qellu> are articulated both with the same initial stop /q/. And, in the Quechua II B varieties, even the velar vs. uvular distinction (/k/ vs. /q/) was lost, as both stops merged into present-day /k/. In the Ancash-Huaylas variety (Quechua I), there is a negative suffix <-tsu> that corresponds to <-chu> in Quechua II C from both Ayacucho and Cuzco, but in the latter varieties, <-chu> is also used as a polar question marker, a function that is expressed in the Ancash-Huaylas variety by a different suffix.

Besides possible misunderstandings, another complication lies in the necessity to reduce elaborate and varied spoken language to writing and to grammar teaching. Many local subtleties are lost or ignored in order to press the language into the simple grammatical rules that are expected in prescriptive school grammars. The

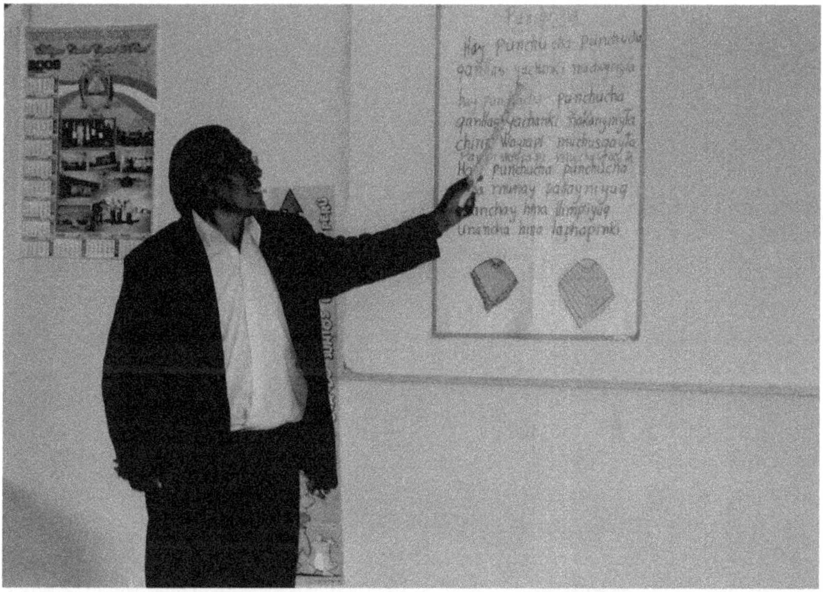

|27| School in Qullana, a Quechua community near Puno.
The unit is on the use of ponchos, the traditional garment in Highland Peru.

|28| School in Pacor, a Quechua community near Cuzco.

whole situation may be made even worse, if not only the school books do not fit the local variety, but also the teacher is a speaker of a different variety, as it will not be possible in every case to recruit fully fluent speakers of the respective variety as local teachers.

Reflecting the situation

Even though Quechua has the status of official language, only Spanish is used in most political, administrative and technical contexts. For these semantic domains and for all others relevant in higher education, no Quechua terminology has been systematically elaborated. Language planning efforts aimed at filling the gaps, substituting loan words from Spanish and creating an indigenous lexicon for neologisms have been undertaken, but have met with problems of acceptance. There is no sole representation or one single voice, although the *Academia de la Lengua Quechua* in Cuzco insists that it is the ultimate judge for standardisation.

The indigenous languages are used as a learning tool predominantly in the basic levels of education. A survey of indigenous students in primary and secondary schools in bilingual areas and in urban Ecuador (Otto 1993) revealed the preference for stories and legends written in Quechua and for the treatment of topics like social reciprocity, regional history and agricultural technology in indigenous languages. But, on the other hand, the same students are aware of the usefulness of Spanish as the primary language of communication. Thus, for the children the world is not divided into native Andean and Hispanic topics, but rather they see the world in a holistic manner.

The school system is regulated by rules that have to be applied to achieve planned results. The resistance that many parents express to bilingual intercultural education, among other things, stems from a deep distrust, if the use of indigenous languages in school and topics already known within the family and community will promote understanding. On the contrary, school is seen primarily as the opportunity to learn new skills associated above all with the Spanish language. Parents are frustrated in two ways: first, because the content of the education system lies outside the world of their experience, and the system arouses expectations of economic and social improvement. On the other hand, in bilingual intercultural education, innovative ideas are brought up, as for example, social equality, that cannot be fulfilled within the prescriptive official education system, and therefore often lead to situations of overt rejection.

Such reactions demonstrate the possibility of an acceptance of the values of the majority society by the indigenous people, and also mirror existing prejudice against the indigenous way of life. Language shift may be favoured for practical reasons, regardless of language loyalty or indigenous identity, pushing indigenous language to the back of one's mind as an aspect of that identity. A frequent occasion is temporary or permanent transregional, or even transnational, migration to another region or to a city. Nevertheless, in specific situations the same people may opt for language loyalty. And, although Spanish is the unrivalled tool for interaction with the national majority, quite often the insufficient command of the Spanish language – phonetic and grammatical deviations and different communicational styles /conventions – still stigmatises indigenous citizens, in particular in urban Hispanic contexts.

As another aspect of indigenous language reality, new registers of use of an indigenous language may intrude even into the intellectual domain of the national society, as in the case of some Peruvian *chansonniers* singing in Quechua, or of the regional educated class, as in the case of some illustrated children's books in Quechua, or combining Quechua with Spanish. This partial acceptance of aspects of indigenous language in the national context may further language loyalty, but at the cost of possible folklorisation.

Although far more favourable conditions can be identified for Quechua than for those languages of the peoples of Siberia and the Russian Far East discussed in this volume – a great number of speakers, the status of national language and long-established bilingual intercultural curricula, – these conditions do not by necessity lead to a stable bilingual situation or to a generally high degree of language loyalty.

Therefore, in education as in real life, all actors select intentionally from different, sometimes competing, cultural and social patterns, and transform these patterns to create a set of identities that is considered socially as well as individually appropriate. Favouring or obstructing experiences within the family, the community and school leave their marks on the language loyalty of each individual and on the way of transferring language skills to the next generations. Indigenous languages in this way will keep their relevance as markers of multiple ethnic, social, local or national identities – whether transferred as spoken languages or adapted, although in a fragmentary manner, to the need to serve as emblematic markers.

Notes

1 Some paragraphs of this paper are revised English versions taken from Valiente (2011).
2 In the Spanish original: "Muchos maestros rechazan también la aplicación de un currículo incomprensible en significado y función, y vuelven a utilizar el currículo de siempre" (Valiente 2011: 106).
3 In this article, angle brackets are used instead of italic typeface for graphemic representations of phonemes and words.
4 Orthographic peculiarities of the national language may also cause considerable confusion in teaching, as for instance in English-based orthography <oo> for /u:/ or <ee> for /i:/, whereas the corresponding short vowels are written <u> and <i>, or Spanish-based <qu> for /k/, if there are aspirated or glottalised stops as in /kh/ and /k'/ to be written with an additional letter.

Another example is palatalisation in Russian, which forms a central component of Cyrillic writing, either by special letters for palatalised vowels, as in <я>, <ю> and <ë>, or pairs of letters differentiating the status of palatalisation as in <ь> vs. <ъ> or <е> vs. <э>.

References

Adelaar, Willem F. H. 2006. Threatened Languages in Hispanic South America. In *Language Diversity Endangered,* M. Brenzinger (ed.), 9–28. Berlin: Mouton de Gruyter.

Adelaar, Willem F. H., with Pieter Muysken 2007. *The Languages of the Andes.* Cambridge: Cambridge University Press.

Apala, Pedro 2011. La educación intercultural bilingüe en Bolivia: avances y retrocesos. In *Desafíos de la educación intracultural, intercultural y plurilingüe en Bolivia en el marco del estado plurinacional*, G. C. Machaca Benito (ed.), 41–66. Cochabamba: FUNPROEIB Andes.

Cerrón-Palomino, Rodolfo 2003. *Lingüística quechua* (second edition). Cuzco: Centro de Estudios Rurales Andinos 'Bartolomé de las Casas'.

Gleich, Utta von, and Teresa Valiente Catter 2005. Interkulturelle zweisprachige Erziehung im vielsprachigen und plurikulturellen Ecuador. In *Ecuador. Welt der Vielfalt*, R. Sevilla and A. Acosta (eds.), 137–156. Bad Honnef: Horlemann Verlag.

Otto, Monika 1993. La educación bilingüe intercultural y el interés de la juventud indígena: Una encuesta entre alumnos de cuatro escuelas primarias del Proyecto EBI y cuatro colegios en diversas regiones andinas del Ecuador. *Pueblos Indígenas y Educación*, 27–28: 67–110. Quito: Abya Yala.

Valiente Catter, Teresa 2011. Educación intercultural bilingüe: visión de una propuesta y realidad de su práctica en la región andina. *Pueblos Indígenas y Educación*, 60: 101–129. Quito: Abya Yala.

14 EPILOGUE

Nikolai Vakhtin

> "Anyone who thinks we are close to final answers, or that we know how to find them, must surely be mistaken."
>
> *Wallace Chafe. Discourse, Consciousness and Time. 1994.*

1.

In 1992, more than twenty years ago, Kenneth Hale, Michael Krauss and several other linguists began a world-wide crusade to save what they labelled 'endangered languages' (Hale et al. 1992). Especially graphic was the message of Michael Krauss who wrote that "at the rate things are going the coming century will see either the death or the doom of 90 % of mankind's languages".

Krauss asked:

> "What are we linguists doing to prepare for this or to prevent this catastrophic destruction of the linguistic world? It behooves us as scientists and as human beings to work responsibly both for the future of our science and for the future of our languages, not so much for reward according to the fashion of the day, but for the sake of posterity. If we do not act, we should be cursed by future generations for Neronically fiddling while Rome burned" (Hale et al. 1992).

Two years later, Krauss's dire predictions were repeated in a report written for UNESCO (Krauss 1994). A draft of this report was circulated among his colleagues, and provoked a serious discussion. The community of linguists, followed by the media, the NGOs, and – last but not least – the funding agencies, turned their attention to the problem of language endangerment.

As often happens, the problem was known much earlier, but had no serious effect on the activities of the international community of linguists. The ground-breaking paper by Morris Swadesh was published as early as 1948 (Swadesh 1948), but passed more or less unnoticed, as usually happens with publications that are ahead of their time. John Gumperz used the phrase 'language shift' as a commonly accepted term already in 1968 (Gumperz 1968). The first comprehensive collection of papers on the topic appeared in 1977 (Dressler and Wodak-Leodolter 1977); it contained all the necessary ideas and formulas to prove that the authors were fully aware of the catastrophic situation ("the drama of dying languages that is taking place around the world," the editors wrote in the Introduction). However, for some reason the problem became everybody's concern and attracted broad attention only 15 years later, after the above-mentioned publication appeared in *Language*.

This was a great change of direction for modern linguistics: an increasing number of human and financial resources were now redirected from desk work to field work, from theorising to monitoring, documenting and revitalising endangered languages. We should be grateful to those linguists who convinced us that language shift was dramatic and dangerous, that we the linguists have no right to ignore it, even though there may have been some exaggerations in early interpretations of language shift. There can't be too much water in the bucket if the house is on fire.

Today, meticulous statistical analysis presented, for example, in Simons and Lewis (2012) demonstrates that, on the one hand, the largest number, fully two-thirds, of the languages of the world are at least safely maintained in everyday oral use in their communities or are sometimes at an even stronger level of development and recognition, but, on the other, 29 % of the world's languages are in some stage of loss or shift (ibid.: 17). This is much better than Michael Krauss's 90 % of the early 1990s, but, come to think of it, 29 % is also bad enough. It is these 29 % that the present book is about.

The geographic scope of the book comprises a vast and diverse area, mostly Asiatic Russia (Eastern and Western Siberia, the Arctic, the Far East) but with comparisons with European (Frisian and Kildin Saami), Chinese and South American cases. Most contributions rely on the first-hand field experience of the authors which is of course a very strong advantage of the whole collection.

This first-hand experience allows the editors of the present book to ask a difficult question: there are numerous attempts worldwide to maintain and (or) revitalise minority languages. At first sight it seems that most individual programmes and activities are appropriate and certainly quite useful. Why are the proclaimed goals – reversing language shift worldwide, preserving linguistic diversity – far from being accomplished?

It is quite clear that there can be, theoretically, two types of answers to this question. The first type – let's label it 'external reasons' – blames the imperfection of the outside world: in order to preserve minority languages (and minority cultures), one must change social, political, economic and legal conditions in certain countries or regions. According to this approach, the responsibility for language shift and loss rests with the environment: as soon as we *change the environment* (adopt governmental programmes of language revitalisation, allocate sufficient funds, change the legislation, support NGOs that do the work, etc., etc.) the situation will change for the better.

The second type of answer – let's call it 'internal reasons' – recognises the necessity of all measures mentioned above but doesn't expect external social, political, legal or financial changes to directly affect the situation of endangered languages. The only way those changes can work is if they influence the *motivation of the communities* to maintain their ethnic languages.

In a recent book on language revitalisation, the authors list separately internal and external obstacles on the road to language revival (Grenoble and Whaley 2006: 176 ff.); interestingly, potential *internal* problems (unrealistic goals lead to disappointment and lack of motivation; conflicts in the community, especially if the revitalisation programme develops successfully; lack of trained teachers; the 'short wind' of many local enthusiasts) are more numerous and are described in more detail than the *external* ones (language and educational policy of the state; funding; professional expertise).

The present book doesn't aim at a consolidated answer to the question: different authors naturally have different opinions about it. The editors seem to be more on the side of the 'internal' type of solution: they write in the *Introduction*: "Most vital for the success of any activity to sustain linguistic and cultural diversity is the motivation of the local people to share these concerns". Erich Kasten further supports this position in his contribution; some other authors share this approach as well. I, too, feel that this approach is worth supporting: more than 10 years ago, I suggested, in my book on language shift (Vakhtin 2001), a rather pointed formula to explain why people shift from their ethnic language to a majority language: "people don't speak their language because they don't want to", meaning insufficient motivation to use the ethnic language due to its low prestige.

Yes, low prestige and low motivation. The editors write in the Introduction: "The particular cultural heritage of one's people or ethnic group often no longer has sufficient status in the given native community". True, so what can we do to help the cultural heritage of these peoples acquire a higher status? and who is supposed to do it? The present volume aims to answer these difficult questions.

There are at least four actors in play: the minority ethnic group itself, ethnic activists, researchers, mostly linguists, and 'the outer world': government, local administration, local industries and business, etc. Whose behaviour is crucial for language preservation? I assume that language shift is highly probable unless *the first of* these actors, the group itself, is motivated to continue to use it. As far as Russian minorities are concerned, specifically, Northern (Siberian) minorities, "... strange as it may seem, inside ethnic minorities themselves, the attitude to this phenomenon [loss of ethnic languages – NV] is mostly neutral and indifferent" (Burykin n.d.).

Some authors of the present book also list 'external reasons' for language loss, and, consequently, suggest 'external action' as a way to stop or slow the process. Alexandra Lavrillier lists insufficient representation of indigenous minority *intelligentsia* in governmental institutions, insufficient governmental support, the lack of a system of NGOs that could "counteract this lack of financial support", and, very importantly, the lack of interaction between speaking communities in villages and the indigenous *intelligentsia* which has some power to act and to access funding. All this is true, of course. However, I am not sure that direct external measures, such as suggested by Tjeerd de Graaf and Hidetoshi Shiraishi ("The Ainu case can be ... used as a model for possible (legal) measures to be taken regarding minority languages and cultures such as Nivkh ...") can be productive unless the indigenous minorities themselves actively join the movement.

Another answer suggested by the editors of the present book to the question "why the proclaimed goals are far from being accomplished" is lack of coordination ("What might be missing is a coordinated strategy that places more emphasis on some very basic considerations for future orientations and relevant efforts"). This suggestion contradicts an approach that I like very much, namely, the one expressed in Ash, Fermino, Hale (2001):

> "There is reason for optimism because local language communities all over the world are taking it upon themselves to act on behalf of their imperiled linguistic traditions in full understanding of, and in spite of, the realistic perception that the cards are stacked against them. There is, in effect, an international movement in which local communities work in defiance of the forces pitted against their embattled languages. It has something of the character of a modern miracle, if you think about it – while they share the goal of promoting a local language, these groups are essentially independent of one another, coming together sometimes to compare notes, but operating in effective separation.
>
> Two factors in our optimism are the very existence of the movement itself and what is sometimes decried as a flaw in the movement: the feature of independence, the fact that local language projects operate separately from one another. But this is a strength, in fact, a true reason for optimism" (Ash, Fermino, Hale 2001: 20).

In other words, language revitalisation programmes are strong precisely because they are not coordinated: thousands of groups on all continents work independently, moving towards the same goal. It is very good of course that these groups can exchange experience, exchange types of teaching materials, sometimes employ the assistance of the same professionals – linguists, language teachers, computers or media specialists – but each programme, if it wishes to be successful, should form as a grass root initiative; its specific shape will depend on specific local conditions.

2.

The issues discussed in this book are extremely complicated. Perhaps the most complicated side of the problem is the relations between the local community and the researcher. In the Russian North, it isn't a rare situation when almost the only person who advocates language maintenance is the researcher: a Russian or sometimes a foreign linguist or anthropologist. The members of the community are often rather indifferent to the task and agree to make moves towards language (cultural) revitalisation (or sometimes, still worse, to *imitate* such moves) only so long as they gain from it, directly, by payments, or indirectly, by various kinds of 'symbolic capital'. As soon as the money flow runs dry, their enthusiasm also dries out, and all 'language revival' activities stop. Should we the researchers agree to such a role? Should we insist on language revival against the apparent resistance of the community?

A second aspect of the problem is connected with the above. Insistent appeals "to preserve heritage languages and cultures" can be interpreted (and sometimes are interpreted) as suppression of an alternative view, as a threat to diversity: if the dominant culture asserts the absolute value of all languages and cultures, why should minority cultures accept this assertion?

This is an old argument. In 1992, in the same issue of *Language* where the endangered language discussion was launched, there appeared a small note by Peter Ladefoged under the telling title *Another view of endangered languages* (1992). There were people, he wrote, who didn't consider their heritage language of value: for them, to shift to the dominant language was a highly desirable means of vertical social mobility, a conscious and voluntary choice. He gave several examples:

> "[The Toda] have accepted that, in their view, the cost of doing this [i. e. becoming part of modern India] is giving up the use of their language in their daily life. Surely, this is a view to which they are entitled, and it would not be the action of a responsible linguist to persuade them to do otherwise" [Ladefoged 1992: 810].

And another one:

> "Last summer I was working on Dahalo, a rapidly dying Cushitic language, spoken by a few hundred people in a rural district of Kenya. I asked one of our consultants whether his teenaged sons spoke Dahalo. 'No,' he said. 'They can still hear it, but they cannot speak it. They speak only Swahili.' He was smiling when he said it, and did not seem to regret it. He was proud that his sons had been to school, and knew things that he did not. Who am I to say that he was wrong? " (ibid: 811).

One year later, Nancy Dorian published 'a response' to Ladefoged in the same journal (Dorian 1993). She wrote (my apologies for the long quotation):

> "I would answer Ladefoged's rhetorical question about the smiling Dahalo speaker, 'Who am I to say that he was wrong?'..., by noting that the Gaelic-speaking East Sutherland fisherfolk have in one sense already been proven 'wrong', in that some of the youngest members of their own kin circles have begun to berate them for choosing not to transmit the ancestral language and so allowing it to die.
>
> Third-generation pursuit of an ancestral language is a phenomenon with a fairly obvious social basis. The generation who do not transmit an ethnic language are usually actively in search of a social betterment that they believe they can only achieve by abandoning, among other identifying behaviours, a stigmatising language. The first generation secure as to social position is often also the first generation to yearn after the lost language, which by their time is no longer regarded as particularly stigmatising. Some of these descendants see an ethnolinguistic heritage which eluded them and react to their loss, sadly or even resentfully. <...>

In other populations, rising consciousness of cultural loss resulting from a colonial past or other historically disfavouring circumstances produces similar results among modern-day descendants. <...> Reporting only on the abandonment phase of a language within a social group can obscure a longer-term dynamic, however, by overlooking reacquisition efforts on the part of members of a later generation within some social settings" (Dorian 1993: 576–577).

The editors and the authors of the present volume are, in this argument, more 'on the Dorian side'. In the Introduction, we read the following:

"... it is important for the credibility of the given joint effort that everybody lives up to the same standards that are proclaimed and set for the proper motivational foundation in such projects <...> *The entire native community should be convinced that it, in the first place, would benefit most in the long run from the expected outcome*" [my emphasis].

This is a rather strong claim; in order to counterbalance it, let me quote a similarly strong one from Ladefoged:

"So now let me challenge directly the assumption of these papers [in *Language*, 1992, vol. 68. – NV] that different languages, and even different cultures, always ought to be preserved. *It is paternalistic of linguists to assume that they know what is best for the community*" (Ladefoged 1992: 810; my emphasis).

Once again, in this controversy I am rather with the editors of the present book, not with their opponents. And of course I don't mean to say that the contributors 'impose' language revitalisation programmes on the communities, or are acting in a 'paternalistic' way. On the contrary, they work with and for those community members who expressed the explicit wish to maintain and to transmit their traditional knowledge to future generations. Still, this is a very complicated issue: as Alexandra Lavrillier writes in her contribution, applied anthropology often "transplants onto traditional societies some alien/foreign resources, techniques and knowledge (together with the development)". The authors of this book, as well as applied anthropology in general, have gone a long way from the paternalistic approach professed, for example, by Russian linguists in the early 20th century (see Elena Liarskaya's contribution to the volume). But we still find ourselves in a 'logical loop': if our language revitalisation project is a success – aren't we 'transplanting' alien values into the society we are supposed to be studying, thus decreasing the level of cultural diversity? Our struggle to preserve linguistic and cultural diversity at all costs can sometimes lead, paradoxically, to *unification* of approaches, to shrinking of diversity.

To which the editors of the volume could say:

"I do not really share your reservation about addressing values when we converse and interact with native people, as we do among ourselves. Why can't we share our concerns and opinions with them that many of us see the loss of cultural and lin-

> guistic diversity, globally, as a problem for the persistence of humankind? And why can't we address the proven fact that people who feel cut off and alienated from their particular cultural past often face certain behavioural problems, most prominent in many native communities who are currently experiencing such transitions? And why is it wrong to say that communities in the first place might benefit in the long run, if those who wish it are being assisted to maintain at least fragments of their traditional knowledge within their new modern-oriented lives? To address opinions and values does not automatically mean that we impose these on others – and here the circle closes, if we connect here to our proclaimed key issue of the free will and motivation of the given people to decide themselves if they want to get involved in this process" (Erich Kasten's letter to the author, 06.11.2012).

Of course my opponent is right. This only further proves that the present book addresses an extremely complicated problem, and I will not pretend that I know the answer to the dilemma described above. On the one hand, the mainstream conceptual framework of language revitalisation emphasises the absolute value of linguistic diversity and expects linguists, anthropologists and other field researchers to work hard for the sake of language and culture maintenance. On the other, to enforce one's set of values on other cultures, to persuade the indigenous communities that linguists and anthropologists 'know better' what is good for them sounds impossibly paternalistic. Thirdly, members of the local language community are often responsible and educated people, equal partners in the dialogue, who can of course "decide themselves if they want to get involved in this process".

We should, however, bear in mind what Dean Worth once wrote (on an entirely different topic), namely, that there are concepts that "can provide the necessary conceptual framework ... but they can also, and all too often, turn into a conceptual prison from which it is difficult to escape" (Worth 1985: 233).

3.

An epilogue is supposed not only to present a conclusion for the completed work but also to suggest directions for its continuation. The composition of the present collection, in my opinion, clearly calls for such a continuation.

In the 1920s and early 1930s in Russia (provisionally called at the time 'the Soviet Union') a very intensive and broad discussion took place: hundreds of articles in periodicals ardently discussed the very issues that constitute the core of the present collection. One can find there some most interesting discussions of the role of stick and carrot, that is, external pressure and internal motivation for developing indigenous languages. There are interesting arguments on the perennial problem of different dialects that have to be united, for the sake of formal education, under the single umbrella of a 'literary language'. A lot was written about the problem of the norm in general and the orthographic norm in particular: Cyrillic or Roman? Roman or

Arabic? Is it better for the school children to study one orthography for both their indigenous language and Russian, or is it easier for them to keep the two systems apart when they read and write?

The general context has changed greatly over the last 80 to 90 years, of course, as has the technology used at schools; but it is a pity that this abundant Russian experience lies unclaimed by the modern English-speaking (-reading) academic community. There aren't many publications in English describing this period and summarising the discussions that took place in it. Stephan Dudeck refers in his contribution to the famous book by Yuri Slezkine (1992), to a much less impressive publication by Dennis and Alice Bartels (1995), to Marjorie Mandelstam Balzer's 1999 book, and to two papers by Eve Toulouze (1999 and 2011). Perhaps one could add several more, but the list wouldn't be very long anyway. Part of Elena Liarskaya's contribution and a page in Dudeck's paper in the present volume that deal with the history of language policy and language planning in Russia is clearly not enough in this context.

For many academics today, especially younger ones, it is hard to believe that there could be anything from the 1920s worth reading today – with the exception of classical anthropological or linguistic works, of course. For many, 'real science' is only what has been published in the 2000s; even publications from the 1990s and 1980s are sometimes considered 'too old' to be interesting. This may be true in some fields; but language revitalisation belongs to a different category. Social environment, demographic circumstances, political systems and technologies can change dramatically; but the challenges of language planning; state paternalism vs. state indifference; variations of language attitudes, relations between minority and dominant languages and cultures, relations between vernacular varieties and the literary language are much less variable. So when I read that "In the 1950s six major 'Yi' dialects were identified, e.g. the Northern, Southern, Western, Eastern, Central and South-Eastern Dialects. Most of these are mutually unintelligible" or that "... determining the standard variety within each officially designated ethnic minority group was the most difficult and controversial aspect of language policy" (Olivia Kraef, *this volume*), I have a strong *déjà vu* feeling: these were exactly the problems Russian educators met with in the 1920s and 1930s, and they managed to find answers to some of them. In the great march for the noble cause of language maintenance and revitalisation, a lot could be learned from earlier experience, not only Russian.

To which the editors could say:

> "Should one blame young, and often western, scholars, for opting to study in the first place the exciting dynamics and processes that were taking place in native communities at that time, instead of sitting in archives in Russian cities and studying the documents of the 1920s – while missing first hand experience of what was going on around them in the communities in this crucial transition period?" (Erich Kasten's letter to the author, 06.11.2012)

And again, my opponent is absolutely right. Still, it would be useful to compile a reader, in English, on early 20th century Russian language policy – something similar to what Professor Patrick Seriot and his school are doing in Lausanne (in French). Such a book would be, in my opinion, of great help for those who are struggling today with very similar circumstances: at least, they would not have to reinvent some wheels.

4.

By way of conclusion, let me remind the reader of a story told by Leanne Hinton in her excellent article *Sleeping languages* (Hinton 2001: 416). In Indiana and Oklahoma, she writes, there is an indigenous group called Miami. The last speaker of the language died in 1962. Luckily, the language had been documented by linguists: information about the language had been collected for almost two centuries. In the 1990s, linguist David Costa published a good description of Miami morphology. Daryl Baldwin, a member of the Miami (Myaamia) community and a talented linguist, graduated in 1999 from the University of Montana with an M.A. with emphasis on Native American linguistics. He learned to speak Miami using Costa's book and some archival materials, and later he taught his wife and children to speak it. For the children, Miami is now their first language. Two more families are reported to have joined the project: the Miami-speaking community has thus literally 'risen from the dead'.

Many aspects of language revival are of course beyond the control of linguists. But, as this optimistic story teaches us, linguists, especially indigenous ones, are able to accomplish a lot. So let's continue our work, bearing in mind the words once said by Michael Krauss: "not so much for reward according to the fashion of the day, but for the sake of posterity".

References

Ash, Anna, Fermino, Jessie Little Doe and Ken Hale 2001. Diversity in Local Language Maintenance and Restoration: A reason for Optimism. In *The Green Book of Language Revitalization in Practice*. L. Hinton and K. Hale (eds.), 19–35. San Diego et al.: Academic Press.

Burykin A. A. n.d. *Yazyk men'shinstva kak "tainyi yazyk" v otechestvennom sotsio-kul'turnom kontekste.* [Minority language as secret language in the local socio-cultural context.] http://abvgd.russian-russisch.info/articles/10.html

Dorian, Nancy C. 1993. A Response to Ladefoged's Other View on Endangered Languages. *Language* 69 (3): 575–579.

Dressler, Wolfgang and Ruth Wodak-Leodolter (eds.) 1977. *Language Death*. International Journal of the Sociology of Language, 12. The Hague: Mouton.

Grenoble, Lenore A. and Lindsay J. Whaley 2006. *Saving Languages: An Introduction to Language Revitalisation*. Cambridge: CUP.

Gumperz, John 1968. The Speech Community. In *International Encyclopedia of the Social Sciences*, 381–386. Macmillan.

Hale, Ken, Michael Krauss, Lucille J. Watahomigie, Akira Y. Yamamoto, Colette Craig, La Verne Masayesva Jeanne and Nora C. England 1992. Endangered Languages. *Language* 68 (1): 1–42.

Hinton, Leanne 2001. Sleeping Languages. In *The Green Book of Language Revitalization in Practice*. Ed. by L. Hinton and K. Hale (eds.), 413–417. San Diego et al.: Academic Press.

Krauss, Michael 1994. *The Indigenous Languages of the North: A report to UNESCO on their present state*. ms.

Ladefoged, Peter 1992. Another View of Endangered Languages. *Language* 68 (4): 809–811.

Simons, Gary F. and M. Paul Lewis 2012. *The World's Languages in Crisis: A 20-Year Update*. Paper presented at the 26th Linguistic Symposium: Language Death, Endangerment, Documentation, and Revitalization. University of Wisconsin, Milwaukee, 20–22 October 2011; last revised: 21 April 2012.

Swadesh, Morris 1948. Sociologic Notes on Obsolescent Languages. *International Journal of American Linguistics* 14: 226–235.

Vakhtin, Nikolai 2001. *Yazyki narodov severa v 20 veke: Ocherki yazykovogo sdviga* [Languages of the Peoples of the North: Essays on Language Shift]. St. Petersburg: Dmitrii Bulanin.

Worth, Dean S. 1985. Vernacular and Slavonic in Kievan Rus'. In *The formation of the Slavonic literary languages*. Proceedings of a conference held in memory of Robert Auty and Anne Pennington at Oxford 6–11 July 1981. G. Stone and D. Worth (eds.), 233–241. UCLA Slavic Studies. Vol. 11. Columbus, Ohio: Slavica.

APPENDIX

Illustrations

Cover photo:
Koryak language class in Lesnaya (Kamchatka). *Source*: Erich Kasten.

1 Areas in Europe where Frisian is spoken. *Source:* Dürr/Kasten, on the basis of P. Tiersma, *Frisian Reference Grammar*, 1985, (p. 18).
2 Bilingual Frisian-Dutch signposts of placenames. *Source:* Province Fryslân-Friesland, (p. 21).
3 Trilingual school in Friesland. *Source:* Mercator European Research Centre on Multilingualism and Language Learning, Ljouwert/Leeuwarden, (p. 24).
4 Building of the Fryske Academy. *Source:* Mercator European Research Centre on Multilingualism and Language Learning, Ljouwert/Leeuwarden, (p. 24).
5 The collection of wax cylinders in the Pushkinsky Dom. *Source:* Victor Denisov, (p. 36).
6 Edison-Home-Phonograph (about 1905) with a collection of wax cylinders from the Berliner Phonogramm-Archiv. *Source:* Martin Franken 2002. Staatliche Museen zu Berlin-Preußischer Kulturbesitz. Ethnologisches Museum, (p. 36).
7 The Pushkinsky Dom. *Source:* Victor Denisov, (p. 37).
8 Catalogue of the sound collections for the project 'Voices from Tundra and Taiga', (p. 38).
9 Nivkh seminar in Nekrasovka (Sakhalin). *Source:* Hidetoshi Shiraishi, (p. 61).
10 Distribution of indigenous groups in Kamchatka. *Source*: Dürr/Kasten, (p. 66).
11 From 'Historical-ethnographical teaching materials for the Itelmen language', Khaloimova et al. (1997), new edition 2012, p. 101, (p. 79).
12 Sharing traditional knowledge with the grandson in Even language at a fishing camp near Anavgai. *Source:* Erich Kasten, (p. 80).
13 Integrated school class on Koryak language and local history with DVD learning tools in Lesnaya. *Source:* Erich Kasten, (p. 80).
14 Alayii in front of her tundra dwelling. *Source:* Cecilia Odé, (p. 101).
15 School children in Andriushkino. *Source:* Cecilia Odé, (p. 101).
16 During the nomadic school process, parents and children access a set of ethnographic multimedia documentation in the nomadic realm. *Source:* Alexandra Lavrillier, (p. 117).
17 Sample of language talking manual made in Power Point programme by the children of the French-Evenk nomadic school. *Source:* French Evenk nomadic school, (p. 117).
18 Map of field research area. *Source*: Max-Planck-Institut für ethnologische Forschung, Halle/Saale, (p. 139).
19 Yuri Vella, the founder of the school. *Source:* Stephan Dudeck, (p. 141).
20 Schoolboy in the classroom. *Source:* Stephan Dudeck, (p. 141).
21 *Jadej wada. Novoe slovo (bukvar' na nenetskom yazyke)* [New word. ABC book in Nenets language]. Moskva/Leningrad: Uchpedgiz (1934). *Source:* National Library of Russia, St. Petersburg, (p. 163).
22 Laborovaia village. *Source:* Department of Education, Aksarka, (p. 187).
23 Children in the winter tundra. *Source:* Roza Laptander, (p. 187).
24 Map of Kola peninsula. *Source:* Map by Joshua Wilbur, borrowed from M. Rießler and J. Wilbur 2007: 40, (p. 197).
25 Training course on *Archives, Technology and Tools for Kola Saami* (19–22. October 2011) at the computer lab of the vocational school PU-26 in Lovozero. In the foreground participants

Svetlana Danilova (left) and Mariia Medvedeva (right) with the teacher Jeremy Bradley, in the background participants Viktor Danilov and Elisabeth Scheller. *Source:* Michael Rießler, (p. 197).
26 Map showing the main varieties of Quechua in Ecuador, Peru, and Bolivia. *Source:* M. Dürr, on the basis of Paul Heggarty, *Quechua Languages and 'Dialects'* (http://www.arch.cam.ac.uk/~pah1003/quechua/Eng/Main/i_DIALS.HTM), (p. 253).
27 School in Qullana, a Quechua community near Puno. The unit is on the use of ponchos, the traditional garment in Highland Peru. *Source:* Teresa Valiente Catter, (p. 255).
28 School in Pacor, a Quechua community near Cuzco. *Source:* Teresa Valiente Catter, (p. 255).
29 Seminar at the Foundation for Siberian Cultures, October 2011, Fürstenberg/Havel. *Source:* Ulrich Kasten, (p. 274).
30 Seminar at the Foundation for Siberian Cultures, January 2012, Fürstenberg/Havel. *Source:* Ulrich Kasten, (p. 274).
31 Erich Kasten and Nikolai Vakhtin, 2005, in front of the Humboldt University in Berlin. *Source:* Kapitolina Fedorova, (p. 274).

Notes on the contributors

Victor Denisov studied English and Foreign Literature at the Udmurt State University, Izhevsk and got his Ph.D. in General Linguistics and Finno-Ugric Languages at the Leningrad State University. He worked at the Department of Phonetics and Lexicology of the English language, Udmurt State University and St. Petersburg Technological Institute. Since 2006 he has been coordinator of projects on the reconstruction of sound materials of endangered languages in the Russian Federation, supported by the British Library. Dr. Denisov is a member of the M.A. Castrén Society (Finland) and researcher at the Udmurt Institute for History, Language and Literature.
vicnicden@gmail.com

Tjeerd de Graaf has specialized in the phonetic aspects of ethnolinguistics. After a fieldwork trip with a Japanese expedition to Sakhalin in 1990, he has contributed to various research projects on endangered languages and sound archives related to ethnic minorities in Russia. Since his retirement in 2003 he spent a semester at the University of St. Petersburg as visiting professor, and worked as guest researcher at the Slavic Research Centre of Hokkaido University (Japan). He is a board member of the Foundation for Endangered Languages and research fellow at the Frisian Academy, which coordinates research on European minority languages.
tdegraaf@fryske-akademy.nl
http://www.mercator-research.eu/research-projects/endangered-languages/

Stephan Dudeck is a social anthropologist based currently at the Arctic Centre of the University of Lapland in Rovaniemi, Finland. He got his Ph.D. from the University of Leipzig in 2011, and has been working in the Russian North since the early 1990s, with field experience also in post-Soviet Central Asia. His main interests are

in the analysis of cultural intimacy, practices of hiding and exhibiting, taiga reindeer herding, and the impacts of extractive industries in the Russian North. He has produced several photo exhibitions and ethnographical documentaries on Khanty reindeer herders. Currently he works in the ORHELIA project on the relations between states and their northernmost residents with a focus on the European Nentsy.
stephan.dudeck@ulapland.fi
http://stephandudeck.wordpress.com/; http://arcticanthropology.org/

Michael Dürr is an anthropological linguist specializing in Mesoamerica and in the North Pacific Rim. He works as a librarian in Berlin and also teaches anthropology and Mayan languages at the Free University of Berlin. Since the 1990s, he has been supporting projects for the preservation of endangered languages in Kamchatka, and has dealt with multimedia materials for language learning. Recently, he took over the design of the 'World of Languages', a new combination of edutainment and library that will be part of the future Humboldt Forum in Berlin.
mduerr@zedat.fu-berlin.de
http://www.lai.fu-berlin.de/homepages/duerr/index.html

Erich Kasten studied social and cultural anthropology and taught at the Free University of Berlin. He has conducted extensive field research in the Canadian Pacific Northwest and in Kamchatka. He was the first coordinator of the Siberia research group at the Max Planck Institute for Social Anthropology in Halle and continued his research as a UNESCO expert in Kamchatka. He has been the curator of various international museum exhibitions and is, since 2010, the director of the Foundation for Siberian Cultures in Fürstenberg/Havel.
kasten@kulturstiftung-sibirien.de
http://www.kulturstiftung-sibirien.de/kasten_E.html

Olivia Kraef is a lecturer and Ph.D. candidate with the Seminar of East Asian Studies (Institute of Sinology/Chinese Studies) at the Free University of Berlin. Kraef began conducting research on the Nuosu-Yi of Liangshan, Sichuan Province, in early 2002 as part of her Master's thesis on gender and intellectual migration. Recent publications and her doctoral dissertation focus on Nuosu-Yi and Yi music, ethnic minority (cultural) policy, and cultural change in Liangshan.
olivia.kraef@gmx.de

Roza Laptander, researcher, works at the Arctic Centre, University of Lapland in Rovaniemi, Finland. She was born in Western Siberia in a Nenets reindeer herders' family and got her Ph.D. from the St. Petersburg Institute of Northern Peoples. Her field of research is socio-cultural change among Uralic peoples in the last two centuries and the analysis of Nenets life histories. She works on language documentation, Nenets traditional knowledge and oral history, mostly on the Yamal peninsula.
roza_laptander@yahoo.com

Alexandra Lavrillier is Associate Professor in Anthropology / Social and Cultural Anthropology at the European Center for the Arctic – OVSQ / University of Versailles. Her research interests cover comparative studies of nomadism, hunting, reindeer herding, landscape management, representations of the natural environment, lifestyles and adaptations brought on by postsocialism, the market economy and climate change, as well as shamanism among Evenk, Even and Yakut peoples. She has published extensively on ritual, the use of space and landscape, orienteering and linguistics.
alexandra.lavrillier@uvsq.fr

Elena Liarskaya is a researcher at the European University at St. Petersburg. Her main geographical areas of interest are Siberia and the Russian Arctic, especially Yamal Peninsula. She completed her Ph.D. in anthropology in 2004 at the Russian Academy of Sciences on the issue of Northern boarding schools for children of reindeer herders on Yamal. From 2006 to 2010 she was a postdoctoral research fellow at the Siberian Studies Centre of the Max Planck Institute for Social Anthropology. Her research focusses on the anthropology of education and gender, family planning, and the transformation of indigenous Siberian communities.
rica@eu.spb.ru

Cor van der Meer has a degree in sociology and research methodology from the University of Groningen. He works as project manager for the Fryske Akademy and is a member of the management team. He is manager of the Mercator Research Centre on Multilingualism and Language Learning, an NGO which is dedicated to researching, acquiring, circulating and applying knowledge which serves linguistic diversity in Europe. Van der Meer is an expert in the fields of multilingualism, regional and minority languages and language learning with an interest in early language learning and language vitality.
cvdmeer@fryske-akademy.nl

Cecilia Odé studied Slavic Linguistics and Phonetics at Amsterdam University. After her Ph.D. (Leiden 1989) on Russian intonation, she worked on Russian and Indonesian prosody and studied the Mpur language (West Papuan). She developed websites on Russian intonation (www.fon.hum.uva.nl/tori) and on Endangered Languages (www.endangeredlanguages.nl). At present she works at the University of Amsterdam on Tundra Yukagir as a linguistic fieldworker with experience in the study of exotic prosodic phenomena. She is a photographer, videocineast, and writes impressions of her fieldwork.
c.ode@uva.nl
http://www.uva.nl/profiel/c.ode/

Michael Rießler holds a Ph.D. in general linguistics from the University of Leipzig and an M.A. in Scandinavian studies from Humboldt University Berlin. Currently

he is affiliated with the University of Freiburg where he leads a project aiming at linguistic documentation and description of Kola Saami. Among the topics he has written on besides documentary linguistics are language contact and language sociology. He is also working with applied research on Kola Saami language revitalisation in Russia, Norway and Finland.
michael.riessler@skandinavistik.uni-freiburg.de
http://www.skandinavistik.uni-freiburg.de/institut/mitarbeiter/riessler/

Hidetoshi Shiraishi studied phonology and field linguistics at the International Christian University (B.A.) in Tokyo and at Chiba University (M.A.). He took part in several ethnological field work expeditions to Eastern Siberia and prepared a number of book publications on the language and culture of the Nivkh people on Sakhalin. In 2006, he defended his Ph.D. thesis Topics in Nivkh Phonology at the University of Groningen under the supervision of Tjeerd de Graaf. Currently, he teaches linguistics at the Sapporo Gakuin University in Japan and continues his work on Sakhalin.
toshi_shiraishi@hotmail.com
http://ext-web.edu.sgu.ac.jp/hidetos/

Nikolai Vakhtin is University Professor of Arctic Social Sciences at the European University, St. Petersburg. He graduated from St. Petersburg State University with a doctoral degree in linguistics. He published several books, including 'Native Peoples of the Russian Far North' (Minority Rights Group, 1992); 'Languages of the Peoples of the North in the 20th Century: Essays on Language Shift' (in Russian, 2001). He recently co-edited the collection Russian Cultural Anthropology after the Collapse of Communism (Routledge, 2012). He teaches courses on Arctic studies, sociolinguistics and linguistics.
nvakhtin@gmail.com

Teresa Valiente-Catter is an anthropologist with a doctorate from the Free University of Berlin. She has worked mainly in the Andes as a GIZ (*Gesellschaft für internationale Zusammenarbeit*) and EU project advisor and as an external consultant in intercultural bilingual education, basic education for young people and adults, and for teacher training. She is Associate Professor at the Free University of Berlin and at the University of Applied Sciences, FH Bielefeld.
tvalientecatter@yahoo.de

|29| Alexandra Lavrillier, Erich Kasten, Cecilia Odé, Michael Dürr, Teresa Valiente Catter (from left), during the first seminar, October 2011, Fürstenberg/Havel.

|30| Stephan Dudeck, Victor Denisov, Olivia Kraef, Tjeerd de Graaf (from left), during the second seminar, January 2012, Fürstenberg/Havel.

|31| Erich Kasten and Nikolai Vakhtin, 2005, in front of the Humboldt University, Berlin.

Index

aboriginal, peoples 13, 49, 57; inhabitants 58, decision makers 110
aborigines 52, 169, 183–185, 188
access, open 43; to the internet 25, 26, 70, 143, 144, 225, 227, 228, 232; to collections 46, 47; to archives 116, 117, 120; to traditional knowledge 67; to oral tradition 85; to education 152; to language technology 207–212
acculturation 219
acoustic, database 12, 35–37, 41, 61, 212
adaptation, difficulties 123; maladaptation 132; to school 142, 190, 192; to indigenous knowledge 252; to the modern world 9; to technology 70; to settled lifestyle 107; to the taiga 142
Adelaar, W.F.H. 249, 251, 258
administration, Soviet 130, 134; rayon 137, 146, 147; local 124, 216, 223; village 68, 136; school 108; multimedia link 70
advocacy 106, 145
Afanasyeva, N.E. 199, 201, 203, 206, 213–215
Afûk 23–25
agriculture 52, 224, 256
Aiello, L.C. 106, 125, 126
Aikio, P. 146
Ainu 13, 49–64, 84, 261
alcoholism 133, 186
Aleut 90
alienation, alienated 135, 265
Alkhalalalai 68, 69
allochtonous, population 111, 120, 125; institution 118; teachers 121
allophones, allophonic 61, 254
alphabet, cyrillic 11, 93, 94, 97, 106, 201–206, 214, 221 ; latin 57, 58, 109, 198, 199, 205, 250
Altai 108
Amazonia 249, 251
Amur 57, 111–115, 120, 124, 166
Anavgai 66, 73, 80
ancestors 9, 72, 88
ancestral, land 129; village 69; language 263
Anderson, J.R. 140, 148
Andes 249–251, 256
Andriushkino 14, 89–104
anthropological, projects 212; poetry 233; analysis 60; methodology 65; linguist 67; knowledge 121; expertise 125
anthropologists, applied 149
anthropology, applied 14, 83, 84, 105, 111, 119, 125, 264; cooperative 107
archaeology 55
Arkhangel'sk 182
artifacts 75
artist 65, 73–75, 79, 81, 84, 95, 109, 226, 229, 239
artistic, expressions 72, 79; events 120; work 73; pursuits 226; groups 228; elites 234
arts 73, 74, 76; fine 196, 213, 230; performing 13; decorative 74, 75
Asia, central 270; eastern 13, 49; northeast 50
Asian, languages 90; countries 136; community 227; context 240
assimilation 51, 52, 56, 136, 226
audio, materials 239; recordings 61, 94; books 25, 243; library 38; heritage 46;
audio-visual, data 70; documentation 73; recordings 74; illustrations 60, 100; teaching materials 71; courseware 95
Austerlitz, R. 57
authorities, Russian state 82, 112, 129; governmental 95, 120; regional 29; municipal 20; town 118; public 21; local 21, 82, 95, 102, 111–115, 120, 212, 125, 146; ethnic 224
autonomy, political and cultural 219, 223, 224, 228; religious 224
Ayacucho 253
Balzer, M.M. 130, 131, 266
Bartels, D. and A. 130, 266
Bashkir 45
Basque county 29
Bateson, G. 106
bear, songs 40; feast 148
behaviour, ecological 77
Beijing 220, 224, 229–234, 237, 238, 242, 243
Benedict, R. 10
bicultural, education 129
bilingual, education 16, 22, 28, 29, 191, 222–226, 242, 249ff.; schools 22, 29; curricula 251, 252, 257; teaching 250; didactics 28; speakers 20, 198; conversation 19; situation 24, 257; signposts 21; areas 224; province 20; 256; dictionary 26; newspaper 59; documents 21
bilingualism 20, 225, 249, 250
bilinguals 193, 204
Bimo (religious practitioner) 221, 222, 225, 226, 229, 231, 233, 238, 242
Bloch, A. 132

Bogoraz (Bogoras), V. 40, 77, 130
Bolivia 249, 251–254
boreal, forest 129, 131; steppe 131
boundaries, ethnic 138; administrative 253; spatial 66
Breton, school 123
Buddhism 219
bureaucracy 144, 152, 153
bureaucrats 137, 188
Burykin, A. A. 38, 40, 41, 60, 261
Cajamarca 253
calendars 117
census 45, 56–58, 109, 126, 131, 132, 182
ceremonies 52, 68, 69
Chawchuven (Koryak) 66, 78
childhood 96, 122, 174, 184, 186, 188, 189
children, from nomadic families 15, 108, 168, 114, 173, 177, 188, 191, 192; of reindeer herders 130, 134, 140, 141, 152, 181, 190; from the taiga 131; from the tundra 181, 185; of tundra dwellers 173, 174; preschool 132; boarding school 118, 148, 167, 189, 191
China 8, 15, 32, 86, 109, 219–244
christianity 249
christians 130, 160, 169
Chukchi 89, 91, 93, 97, 137, 150, 151, 166
Chukotka 161, 163
Chuvash 45
circumpolar 69, 110
citizens 21, 43, 165, 169, 184, 213, 257
citizenship 53
civilisation 15, 57, 150, 192
clan, system 220
classroom, multilingual 28; language 95, 102; presence 234; environment 236; lessons 241; situation 243
climate, change 107
clothing 74, 75, 133–136
Cochabamba 251, 253
collaboration, definition 107; with authorities 20; with university 75; with institution 76; with organisations 201; between institutions 120; with teachers 74; with nomads 112, 119, 126; students and teachers 55; indigenous villagers 122; parents and teachers 191
collaborative, research 65; process 82; project 84, 107, 119, 202, 209; anthropology 119
collaborator 201, 203, 209, 214
collection, text 199; oral and written literature 38; textbook, 102; ethnographic 83; sound 38; audio recordings 36, 94; wax cylinders 36, 39–42; digital 25; data 28
collectivisation 132
colonialism 106
colonist, past 264
colonisation 56
colony 56
commercial, mass media 8; contacts 20; counterparts 25
commercialised, social relations 81
commodity 9, 81
communication, systems 119; modes of 121, 122; styles 257; technology 46, 207; digital 196; internet and telephone 192, 209; of traditional knowledge 168; primary language of 256; problems 92; lack of 120
communism 8, 165, 273
communist 178, 198, 220, 230
competence, language 10, 70–72, 74; speech 11, 67; media 144, 145; education 147
competition 121, 122, 144, 171
computer, technology 207; fonts 207; literacy 208, 209; terminology 24; introducing to the taiga 119, 123, 145, 151
computerisation 208
Comrie, B. 56
concept, school 152; education 181; ethnopedagogics 149; native language 149; of culture 133; of Taiga school 139ff.; of superscription 238; top-down 86, 240; indigenous 107, 251; pedagogical 8, 12, 13ff; educational 140, 142, 152
conceptual, framework 265; prison 265
conflict 121, 122, 131, 134, 136, 142, 152, 201, 206, 252, 261
confucian, principles 223; ideals 239
consonants 203, 204
corpus (corpora) 25, 26, 200, 202, 207, 209–213, 222
cossacks 131
courseware 91, 95, 100, 102, 103
crafts, teaching 76, 170; learning/curriculum 54, 93, 148, 149, 151; learning tools 67, 75, 76
creativity 204
credibility 8, 10, 264
creolisation 28
cultbase 167, 170–174
curriculum 14, 29, 54, 66, 71, 72, 74, 78, 85; for Andriushkino 102ff.; for taiga school 129ff.; bilingual and intercultural 251ff.

curricular (extra-) 22, 165, 234
Cuzco 253–256
czarist 58
dance 52, 54, 93, 110; ensembles 72–74, 79, 81
database 12, 35, 37, 38, 40, 41, 60, 76, 209, 212, 213
decontextualisation 238
deities 50, 223; stories of 54
demographics, changing 143
demography, nomadic communities 111; table 132
depopulation 132
depression 89, 112
development, school 113, 122, 159, 160, 164, 170, 176, 181; children 118; knowledge 118, 252, projects 33, 125, 107; language 30, 43, 131, 162, 169, 200, 238, 240; responsibility 146; education 149, 176, 177, 188; personality 162, 163; sustainable 191; literacy 198; orthography 201; media 227; internet 239; learning content 252; learning tools 12, 13, 22, 35, 44, 49; curriculum 16, 102; anthropology 105, 106
diacritics 11, 204–206, 211, 214, 221
diaereses 203–206
dialects, Frisian 25; Russian 37, 38, 60; Germanic 37; (Amur/Sakhalin) Nivkh 57; (Magadan) Even 73; Koryak 75, 78; Even 85; Tundra Yukagir 94; Evenk 109, 110, 117, 120; Kildin (Kola) Saami 196, 199, 201; (Sichuan) Yi 225, 240; Shynra Yi 225–227, 233, 236, 237, 240, 243; Quechua 252, 253; cognate forms of 199, 254
diaspora 197, 229, 230, 238
dictionaries 11, 18, 26, 38, 59, 62, 78, 94, 98, 102, 199–203, 206–208, 211–214
didactic, bilingual 28; guides 200; materials 201; challenge 204
digital, infrastructure 15, 195ff.; collection 25; archive 237; data 212; discs 42; copies 46; techniques 46; cameras 117; teaching programmes 117; communication 196; dictionaries 202, 212; corpora 202, 211; writing devices 205; age 207; literacy 208; world 213; social networks 213
digitization 42
diglossic, situation 20
diphthong 94
discrimination 51–53
diversity, cultural and linguistic 7, 10, 13, 15, 28, 30–32, 35, 83, 84, 103, 145, 209, 260–265, 272; language 30f., 249; minority 223; information 227
Dolgan 89
dominance/dominant, language 18–20, 62, 89, 152, 182, 241, 250, 263, 266; state control 223; political and cultural 241
Dudinka 151
ecology, change 193; classes 78; tours 71
economy, traditional forms of 149; of the community 151; of the population 169
ecosystems 149
ecotourism 55
Ecuador 249ff.
Edison, phonograph 36
education, language of 43ff., 53, 59, 66, 85, 93ff., 95, 164, 191, 195, 196, 204, 213, 219; bicultural 129; intercultural 249ff.; bilingual 22, 191, 222, 224–226, 242, 249ff.; trilingual 23, 28, 29, 191; multilingual 204; system 14, 15, 29, 181ff., 225, 250, 256; rural 150, 250; primary 22, 23, 59, 84, 151, 181, 191, 250; secondary 23, 29, 190, 192; basic/higher levels of 20, 143, 234, 250, 256; vocational 23; Act 22, 23, 44; law 43, 165, 251; policy 26, 110, 143, 191, 261; formal 130, 136, 140, 265; informal 31; mass 14; school 19, 43, 134, 140, 142, 152, 159, 166, 169, 172, 176, 198; general 21, 22; ethnocultural 44; compulsury 51; language teaching 99, 100; level/quality of 115, 118, 122, 134, 144, 175; history of 130, 167; state 130, 147, 149, 152, 193, 224, 233; Soviet 132, 133, 161; boarding school 134, 135, 166, 183, 188; radio 137, 148; in the North 159, 160ff.; content 150,160; problems in 178; for tundra children 181ff., 188; and tundra school 189 ff.; family and tribal 191; traditional 193; academic 196; modernisation 181, 191
educational, programmes 55, 149, 249; process 11,14, 44, 118, 124, 251; practice 251; models 14, 30, 192; ideas 14, 129, 137, 148, 193; institutions 16, 20, 42, 44; methods 24, 45, 47, 142; principles 160; research 26, 202; efforts 55; experiences 73; agencies 106; system 129 ff.; reforms 136, 147, 177; concepts 140, 152; parents' function 142; other initiatives 147ff.; bureaucracy 152, 153
educator, parent 115, 124
Edufrysk 23–25
elder, generation 71
elderly, people 59, 167
elders 11, 51, 66–68, 71–73, 75, 77, 78, 90, 168

electronic, learning tools 68, 69, 75; technologies 117; games 124; dictionaries 207, 208, 211
elites, ethnic 86, 224, 234, 240; intellectual 240; Nuosu 224; political-cultural 229; ruling 223
emigrants, Frisian 25, 26
emotional, support 148; hype 241
emotionality 232
empire, Soviet 187; European 36; Russian 37; and local power 239
environment, school 152, 174, 222; urban 225; sociocultural 233; university 234; language 43, 67, 235; classroom 236; social 67, 152, 266; multilingual 14; natural 50, 66, 67, 69, 79, 108, 149, 172; cultural 74; socio-economic 79; taiga or tundra 109; nomadic 113; local 150; native 159; parents' 164; change 193
environmental, changes 107; knowledge 153
epics 54, poetry theatre 118
Esso 66, 72–74
Estonia 42, 195, 199, 212
Estonian, language 41, 208, 213
Estonians 195
ethics, environmental 77; religious 175
ethical 125, issues 14; reasons 46; questions 119, 125; instructions 221
ethically, correct/right 119
ethnicity 56, 65, 150, 152, 162, 195
ethnography, Russian 36; with participant observation 106
ethnolinguistic, heritage 263
ethnolinguistics 8
ethnomusicologist 113
ethnophonemic 253, 254
Evenks 11, 14, 84, 85, 89, 105–126, 137, 149–152, 188
Evens 11, 13, 65, 66, 70ff., 77, 78, 80, 84, 85, 89, 91, 93, 97, 99, 101, 107, 109, 111
extracurricular, language activity 234
facebook 9, 207
families, language 17, 39, 41, 90, 220, 249; songs 75, 77; nomadic 110, 115, 117, 119, 122, 188, 191, 192; herding 129, 138, 140, 144, 148; migrating 183; tundra 175; histories 172; mixed 185
feasts, bear 148; ritual 75, 81; regional 90
festivals 68, 68, 74, 75, 83, 120, 230, 232
films 11, 116, 126, 171, 194, 228
Finland 29, 42, 195ff.
fishermen 58, 89, 90, 130, 138, 189, 190
folklore 36, 38–40, 41ff., 60, 74, 149, 175, 186, 250 folklorisation 157
folkloristic, ornament 133, 152; elements 8; group 59; analysis 60
folktales 54
fonts 202, 206–214, 224
Forsyth, J. 91, 131
Franckesche Stiftungen 68, 72
fricatives, sound 205, 254
Frisian 12, 17–32, 50, 260
gender, shift 132, 133
genealogies 226
generation, younger 11, 62, 67, 70, 71, 113, 133, 147, 187, 222, 238, 241; older 45, 66, 68, 71, 75, 91, 92, 100,170, 222; middle 70; parents' 78, 84, 198; present 113; key 113; lost 114
Genetz, A. 198, 199
German(ic), languages 18, 31, 199; dialects 37
Germany, languages in 12, 17; tours in 72, 74, 79, 81; exhibitions in 69, 75
Gilyak 38, 56
global, context 250; scale 7; lifstyles 8; collaboration 39
globalisation 30, 124
globalised, world 213
glottalised, sound 254, 257
Goffman, E. 134
Golovnev, A. 183
governance 28, 120
government, provincial 19, 25, 27; regional 25, 146; local 18, 22, 120, 228, 125; Yakut 122; Russian 83, 125, 191; Japanese 49, 51–53, 59, 62; Hokkaido 53; Dutch (national, central) 20–22, 32; Soviet 166, 178; Yamal 189ff.; prefecture 231; language of 18; levels of 31
governmental, organisations 106; institutions 26, 108, 110, 120, 125, 261; authorities 95, 120; non-governmental institutions 253; support 10, 261; programmes 260
grammar, presentation 71; standards for 71; differences in 254; training 74; teaching 254; learner's 94, 102; school 254; lessons 67; Saami 199; Chinese 225; Frisian 18, 24, 25; Ainu 53; Itelmen 69
grammatical, deviations 257; rules 254
grapheme 11, 254, graphemic representation 257
grassroots, perspective 74; level 83; movements 7
Grenoble, L. 126, 151, 261
Harrell, S. 220, 222, 227, 228, 242
herders 89, 97, 102; reindeer 14, 91, 92, 100, 105–125, 129–153, 169, 174, 175, 181, 183, 185, 186, 189, 190, 193

heritage, cultural 35, 39, 41, 43, 46, 47, 67, 72, 73, 75, 77, 79, 81, 261; intangible 231; language 263; Ainu 54
hermeneutics, Chinese 231
heterogeneity, linguistic 219; ethnic 241
hierarchy, vernacular 150; cultural 231; of schools 152; of lifestyles 152; of use of languages 89; of ethnic cultures 241
histories, life 72; family 172
Hokkaido 13, 49–57, 59
humankind 10, 83, 84, 265
hunters 58, 89–91, 107, 112, 130, 133, 140, 169, 189, 190
husbandry, reindeer 135, 151, 167, 175
identity (identities), regional 31, 120; local 67, 223; collective 95, 240; indigenous 256, 136; ethnic 53, 55, 149, 150, 226, 230, 232; Udmurt 45; Itelmen 71; Tundra Yukagir 95; Nuosu 229; language 253; crisis 229; reaffirmation 231; assertion 233; set of 257; layered 9; safeguarding 20; revitilised 70; loss of 148
idioms 196
illiteracy 58, 167, 222; computer 208, 209
immersion, programmes 28
Indigirka 90
individualism 144
inferiority, complexes 114
information, technology 9, 11, 30, 44, 46, 207
infrastructure, digital 15, 195–213
innovations, linguistic 120; pedagogical 250; education 44
innovative, methods 74, 192; ideas 256; learning facility 25; principles 44; projects 144; ways of transmitting 75; skills 252
instruction, methods 53; language/medium of 22, 23, 25, 29, 59, 152, 163, 177, 222, 226; ethical 221; canonisation of 223; textbook-centred 54; direct 54; differentiated 102
intelligentsia 109, 174, 177; urban minority 107; indigenous 46, 109–111, 118, 120, 129, 133, 134, 137, 148, 261; Evenk 115; native 7, 145; northern minority 161; Yi 226
interaction, social 111; intergenerational 124
interactive, materials 70, 94
intercultural, education 16, 249–258;
interfaces, documentary linguistics 209; user-friendly 212
internet 9, 25, 26, 37–39, 60–62, 76, 79, 85, 145–147, 188, 189, 192, 196, 199, 206–209, 213; access to 25, 70, 143, 144; in China 219–244
Inuit 108
Irkutsk 109
Islam 219
Itelmen, language and culture 60, 65–73, 77–79, 84, 100; stories 11
Itelmens 11, 13, 65
Izhevsk 44, 46
Japan 8, 13, 49–62
jealousies 10, 122
Jews 37
Jochelson, V. 77
joiking 195
Kamchadal, vernacular 68, 70; texts 77
Kamchadals 70
Kamchatka 65–86, 175
Kamchatkan, languages 90
kamuy 50, 54
Kazym, river 131; uprising 131, 170
keyboards 207, 211, 214
Khabarovsk 82
Khanty 12, 35, 39–41, 72, 129–153, 166–168, 170–177, 182, 185, 194
Khruschev, N. S. 165, 178
Kildin, Saami 15, 195–214, 260
kindergarten 62, 91, 93, 99–101, 116, 151
kinship 95, 143, 144, 149
Klokov, K. 151
knowledge, ecological 9, 13, 67, 74, 76, 103, 149
Kola, peninsula 15, 196, 197; Saami 197, 199, 201, 209, 212
Kolyma, Yukagir 90, 97; river 90, 91
Komi 41, 45, 147, 153, 177, 182, 211
Koryak, villages 113; peoples 13; language and culture 60, 70–86, 113
Koryaks 11, 65, 66
Kovran 65, 66, 68
Krauss, M. 259, 260, 267
kultbaza 178
Kurilov, G. N. 93, 94
Kutkiniaku, (raven) stories 75–77
Laborovaia 186ff.
Ladefoged, P. 163, 164
Lecomte, H. 113, 126
Leeuwarden 23, 27, 28
legends 9, 50, 103, 256
legislation, minority language and culture 43; education 44; Ainu language and culture 52; Russian 150; change 260
legitimacy 226
legitimisation 147, 150

Lesnaya 66, 75, 78, 80, 269
lessons, classroom 241; school 11, 170; language 101; grammar 67; Frisian 22; Dutch 22; Yi 234, 235; Tundra Yukagir 93, 95–98; Evenk 114, 118
letters 11, 202–211, 214, 258
Lévi-Strauss, C. 106
lexical, description 199, 210; resources 212; data 213; level 20
lexicographer 213
lexicographic, work 26, 212; data base 212
lexicography 27, 209
lexicology 201
lexicon 109, 253, 254, 256
Liangshan 220ff.
lifestyle, hierarchy 152; global 8; modern 133; traditional 14, 51; forefathers 137; 152, 164; indigenous 133, 190; taiga 123, 140; nomadic 107, 108, 112, 114, 118, 119, 122, 130; reindeer herding 112, 137, 140, 142, 150, 169; settled 107, 116; village 124; local 130; rural/urban 114, 140, 142; Ainu 54; Russian 58; change 51, 135, 140, 143, 149; decisions 135; different 136; healthy 164
Linux 211
literacy 57, 160, 162, 163, 168, 169, 177, 183, 198, 222, 224, 225, 243; computer 208, 209, 211, 214
Lovozero 196, 197, 202
macron 203–206
Magadan, (Even) dialect 73
mainstream, culture 8; society 9, 129, 142; literature 132; education 142, 144; ethno-pedagogics 149ff.; documentary linguistics 210; language revitalisation 228, 265
Manchu 109
Manchuria 109
Mandarin 230, 242
Mansi 41, 129, 130
marginalisation 136
mathematics (math) 75, 76, 116, 123, 124, 250, 252
media 226ff.; print 75, 76; written 199; new 8, 13, 49; multimedia 25, 45, 55, 116–118, 120, 125, 143–145, 208, 209, 211, 212; mass 8, 110, 166, 183, 196; public 134; international 147; history 199; competence 144ff.; specialists 262; policies 21; covered by 83
Mennonites 37
mestizo 252
metadata 212
methodology 73, 75, 78, 97, 100, 102; linguistic 209; educational programmes 249; anthropological 65; language education 66; participatory 106
microblogging 232, 243
microblogs 228, 232, 233, 243
microsoft 208
minorities, northern 161, 162, 166, 167, 177, 183, 261; ethnic 13, 49, 53, 56, 59, 118, 178, 261, 266;
minority, context 15, 219ff.
missionary, schools 130, 168 ff.; efforts 249
monolingual 18, 58
Mordvinian, collection 41
morphology 200, 253, 267, Tundra Yukagir 97
morphophonology 200, 203
morphosyntactic 210
motivation 8ff., 59, 67, 68, 71, 73, 75, 79, 81, 82, 95, 97, 134, 137, 142–144, 232, 260, 261, 265
movement, revitalisation 132, 219; neo-traditionalist 137; national 162; political 183; language revival 220, 226, 230, 240; grassroots 7; ethnic 54
multicultural 55
multiethnic 55
multilingual, community 13, 89ff.; education 204; environment 14
multilingualism 12, 17ff., 182
multimedia 25, 45, 55, 116–118, 120, 125, 143–145, 208, 209, 211, 212
Murmansk 197, 201, 202
museums 27, 54, 110, 122, 185, 195; exhibitions 55, 79; local 134, 170; living 137
music 27, 40, 54, 90, 93, 113, 124, 227–236, 241
Nanai 109
Negidal 109
Nenets 11, 14, 15, 84, 89, 129ff., 159ff., 181ff.
Nerkagi, A. 15, 181, 186ff.
Nervander, J. 195, 213
Netherlands 17ff., 37, 38, 60, 61
network(s), schools 28, 29, 160, 162; social 11, 207–209, 213, 234; media 229; translocal 230; Mercator European 30ff.
networking 227, 228, 237
Nganasan 11
Nivkh 49ff., 84, 90, 262
Nizhnevartovsk 138, 143
Nogliki 58
Norway 195, 196, 202, 203
Nuosu 219ff.

Nymylan (Koryak) 66, 75, 78, 81
Obdorsk 167, 170, 173, 177
obshchina 118
Okhotsk 72; sea 72
orality 221
ornamentation, ethnic 8, 150
Oroch 109
Orok 38, 56, 109
orthodox, mission 168; camp 186
orthodoxy, Russian 160
orthography 71, 77, 94, 110, 117, 198ff., 253, 254, 257, 266
Osherenko, G. 183
Ossora 66, 75
Palana 66, 69, 73, 74, 76
palatalisation 203–205, 258
paternalism, state 165, 266
pedagogical, aims 164; goals 249; reasons 253; programme 116, 120; literature 166, 178; manuals 125; concepts 8, 12, 13ff.; knowledge 200; activitity 44, 117; process 123; institutions 125; team 114; innovation 250; results 112; dilemma 254; grassroots perspective 74
pedagogics 164, 169, 191
pedagogue 111, 112, 115, 116, 123
pedagogy 71, 143, 208; ethno- 145, 147ff.
perestroika 132, 134, 136, 147
Peru 249ff.
Petersburg, St. 12, 35–39, 41–43, 46, 47, 50, 51, 60, 175
Petropavlovsk-Kamchatsky 66, 70, 72
phonemes 61, 94, 253, 257
phonemic, system 254; scripts 204; transcription 199; ethnophonemic spelling 253, 254; vowels 254; differences 11
phonemics 253, 254
phonetic, form 224; script 235; spelling 225; deviations 257; analysis 39; database 60
phonetically 98
phonetics 60
phonogram, archives 36–41, 46
phonological, distinctions 204; misinterpreted 205; analysis 210; transcription 212
phonology 25, 61, 200, 203
Pika, A. 137
poems 26, 94, 230, 232, 233, 243
poet 137, 139
poetics 228ff.
poetry 11, 25, 97, 118, 221, 226, 233, 239, 241
polylingualism 20
preschool 23, 54 132, 186, 196
prestige 19, 68, 133, 140, 148, 167, 168, 175, 261
pride 9, 46, 73, 95, 229; ethnic 9, 53, 224, 232ff.
primer 203
psychological, aims 164; development 118; dynamism 118; identity 187; sense 28; health 192; problems 9, 114; trauma 114; danger 123
Puno 251, 255
Pushkinsky Dom 36–39, 41, 42, 46
Quechua 16, 249ff.
Quito 251, 253
radio, education 137, 148; school 22, 27
Raipon 111, 113, 126
reciprocity 256
religion 221, 225, 227
repression 39, 56
residential, school 131, 134, 139
resistance 54, 131, 134, 144, 147, 153, 256, 263
responsibility 20, 55, 81, 82, 146, 229, 233, 243, 260
revitalisation, (native) language 13, 25, 45, 49ff., 59, 62, 67, 78, 96, 105, 110, 111, 113, 125, 132, 198, 201, 203, 206, 208–210, 214, 219, 230, 260–266; traditional feasts 81
revival, language 18, 56, 209, 219, 226, 228ff., 234, 240, 261, 263, 267; ethnic 241; of traditions 110
revivalism, cultural 134
ritual, practices 74, 107, 116; festival 75; feast 75; fire 102
rituals 81, 93, 221
Robbek, V. A. 150
russification 57, 132, 159, 164–169, 172, 173, 178
Saami 15, 55, 112, 146, 195ff., 260
sacred, contexts 221, site 131
Sakha 89–91, 94, 97, 102, 108, 110, 137, 146, 150, 151, 183, 188
Sakhalin 13, 38, 49ff.
Salekhard 181, 186, 188
samurai 51
Sapporo 53, 61
satellite, phones 119, 144; internet access 143
script 97, 221–226, 229, 230, 234–239, 242–244
scripts, phonemic 204; XSLT- 212; traditional 221
scriptures 221, 229, 231
Sekalan 113, 119, 124, 126
Selkups 149, 182

shaman 40, 72
shamanism 107, 148
Shirokogoroff, S.M. 40
Shternberg, L. 40, 130
Skolt (Saami) 196
Slezkine, Yu. 130, 162, 266
socialisation 72, 133, 134, 140, 146, 148, 149, 153, 166, 189–192
societies, traditional 106, 238, 264; modern 207; mainstream 129; Siberian 106, 108; changing
society, computerised 207
software 70, 117, 209
solidarity 144, 149
songs 26, 40, 60, 61, 67, 69, 72, 74, 75, 77, 90, 94, 95, 113, 116, 221, 226, 229, 230, 236–238, 243
songwriter 230
Spanish 249ff.
speakers, number of 7, 131, 132; term/typology 10, 90; native 65, 68, 108, 254; first-language 19; Frisian 17ff.; Ainu 53ff.; Nivkh 57ff.; Itelmen 78; Tundra Yukagir 89ff.; Evenk 108 ff. Russian 185; Kildin 197ff.; Nuosu/Yi 220ff.; Quechua 249 ff.; good 90; fluent 90, 91; active 11; passive 197; last 267
speech, patterns 71; variants 65, 73; examples 117; sounds 39, 61; technology 208; competence 11, 67; contests 54, 59; spontaneus 60; active 74; conversational 99; community 209; fragmentary 19
spellcheckers 208
spirit, of competition 122; ethnic 234
spirits, evil 102;
spiritual, relationship 50; meaning 223
spiritualisation 232
standard, dialect 239, written language 11, 18, 106, 109, 253; literary 11; variety 266; Frisian 19; Itelmen language 66, 68; Evenk language 109, 110, 114
standardisation, of learning materials 73, 240; of script 225; Kildin Saami 198ff.
standardised, language 73, 196; teaching/learning materials 7, 11, 65, 68, 71, 73, 78, 98, 241, 252; varieties/variants 68, 253
Steinitz, W. 39 ff.
stereotype 54, 130
storytellers 54, 59, 77; telling 124
subdialects 224
suffix 109, 120, 254
suicide 112, 133, 186
superscription 219ff.
Surgut 129, 138, 143
sustainable, efforts 241; resource use 76; development 191, 198; digital linguistic infrastructure 209; fieldwork 107
switching, code 28; language 219; to Spanish 250; between variants 173
syllabary 221, 222, 226, 242
syllabic 225
symbol, of indigenous culture 153; negative 169
symbolic, power 224; capital 262; recognition 21; relationship 140; language 197
symbolism, national 195
symbols, letter 204
syntactic, rules 200; descriptions 210; morpho-syntactic 210
Taimyr 151, 182
Tatar 45, 182
Tatarstan 183
technology, language 15, 202–212, 256; information 9, 11, 30, 44; electronic 117; multimedia 120; modern 13; new 119, 126, 145, 188; communication 46, 147, 207; at schools 266; current 111, 116; nomadic 118
telephone 227, 151, 188, 189, 192
television 19, 22, 27, 58, 225–229, 231, 236, 243
textbooks 54, 67–69, 71, 73, 94, 102, 109, 162, 198–203, 206, 214, 222, 224, 226, 251
thesauri 208
Tibetan, Buddhism 219; script 242
Tibetans 221
Tibeto-Burman, languages 220
Tiersma, P.M. 18
Tiuitiakha 129ff.
Tiumen 182, 186
tongue, mother 15, 20, 31, 43–45, 58, 67, 71, 78, 149, 151, 152, 219ff.
Toulouze, E. 130, 148, 183, 266
traditionalism, neo- 137
traditions, oral 9, 38, 54, 60, 71, 75–77, 85
transcription 71, 73, 85, 94, 199, 210, 212, 223
translation, machine 208, 210; method 93
transliteration 73, 76, 242
transmission, language 11, 30, 113, 226, 227, 230; information 242; cultural 124, 134; indigenous knowledge 136, 153; songs 221; traditional script 226; intergenerational 113
triglyphs 204
trilingual, education 23, 28, 29, 191; schools 24, 26, 29, 92

Tungus 60; speaking people 72; -Manchu 109
Tungusic, languages 38, 60
Udegei 109
Udihe 109
Udmurt 12, 13, 35, 39, 41ff.
Udmurtia 41ff.
Uilta 38, 56, 60, 109
Ulcha 109
Unesco 46, 62, 69, 72, 94, 113, 122, 144, 231, 259
Unicode 202, 205, 206, 209, 211, 212, 214
Uralic, languages 12, 35ff., 41, 42, 194, 204
uvular, stops 254
Uygur 242
variants, language 9, 25, 66–69, 71, 76, 220, 222, 230, 224; script 222, 242; speech 65, 73; orthography 199, 203; alphabet 203, 204; native culture 173, 174; keyboard 211; allophonic 61, 254
variation, language 68, 71, 73, 76, 77, 213, 266; orthography 253; oral traditions 77, 85; by storytellers 77
varieties, vernacular 266; language 16, 68, 213, 221, 224, 225, 242, 249, 266, 270; Quechua 252–256; dialectical 11
Vepsian 41
vernacular 76, 108, 150, 266; Kamchadal 68, 70
video, library 38, 60; recording 60, 62, 72; materials 68–70, 236, 241; format 72; presentations 77; data 212
virtual platforms 15, 219ff.; revival 228ff.; communities 25
vocabulary 26, 67, 68, 70, 108, 199, 200, 213, 233, 240, 241
vocational, education 23; school 197
voiceless, sound 205
voicelessness, consonants 204
vowel 94, 203–206, 254, 257, 258
Vries, de M. G. 50, 51
Vyrdylina, A. G. 89, 92, 93, 97, 99, 102, 103
wax cylinders 36, 39, 40, 77
web 69, -based 208; surfer 213; page 223; domain 238; show on the 70, 79
website 15, 29, 31, 33, 46, 89, 144, 145, 228, 234–237
Wikipedia 207, 213
Windows 208, 211, 212
Witsen, N. 50, 51
worldviews 9, 26, 66, 72, 148
Yakut 45, 89, 107, 108, 122, 177; language 60, 89, 91–93, 97–101, 110, 113, 120; schools 123
Yakutia 38, 60, 90, 107, 112, 113, 120, 122, 123, 137, 146, 149, 150
Yakutsk 89–93, 111
Yamal 14, 15, 133–137, 159ff., 181ff.
Yi 15, 219ff.
Yiddish 37
youtube 9
Yugra 129, 130, 132, 136, 137
Yukagir(s) 38, 60, 96, 99, 113; Tundra 14, 89ff.
Zyrians, Komi- 177, 211